The Communicator's Commentary

Psalms 1-72

THE COMMUNICATOR'S COMMENTARY SERIES
OLD TESTAMENT

Lloyd J. Ogilvie

General Editor

The Communicator's Commentary

Psalms 1-72

Donald M. Williams

WORD BOOKS, PUBLISHER • WACO, TEXAS

THE COMMUNICATOR'S COMMENTARY SERIES, OLD TESTAMENT, Volume 13: *Psalms 1–72.* Copyright © 1986 by Word, Inc. All rights reserved. No portion of this book may be reproduced in any form whatsoever, except for brief quotations in reviews, without written permission from the publisher.

Library of Congress Cataloging in Publication Data
Main entry under title:

The Communicator's commentary.

  Bibliography: p.
  Contents: OT13. Psalms/by Donald Williams.
  1. Bible. O.T.—Commentaries. I. Ogilvie, Lloyd
John. II. Williams, Donald.
BS1151.2.C66 1986   221.7'7   86–11138
ISBN 0–8499–0419–6 (v. OT13)

Printed in the United States of America

67898 FG 987654321

To
my parents
Martha and Don Williams
from whom I
first heard
the Psalms

Contents

Editor's Preface

God has called all of His people to be communicators. Everyone who is in Christ is called into ministry. As ministers of "the manifold grace of God," all of us—clergy and laity—are commissioned with the challenge to communicate our faith to individuals and groups, classes and congregations.

The Bible, God's Word, is the objective basis of the truth of His love and power that we seek to communicate. In response to the urgent, expressed needs of pastors, teachers, Bible study leaders, church school teachers, small group enablers, and individual Christians, the Communicator's Commentary is offered as a penetrating search of the Scriptures of the Old and New Testament to enable vital personal and practical communication of the abundant life.

Many current commentaries and Bible study guides provide only some aspects of a communicator's needs. Some offer in-depth scholarship but no application to daily life. Others are so popular in approach that biblical roots are left unexplained. Few offer impelling illustrations that open windows for the reader to see the exciting application for today's struggles. And most of all, seldom have the expositors given the valuable outlines of passages so needed to help the preacher or teacher in his or her busy life to prepare for communicating the Word to congregations or classes.

This Communicator's Commentary series brings all of these elements together. The authors are scholar-preachers and teachers outstanding in their ability to make the Scriptures come alive for individuals and groups. They are noted for bringing together excellence in biblical scholarship, knowledge of the original Hebrew and Greek, sensitivity to people's needs, vivid illustrative material from biblical, classical, and contemporary sources, and lucid communication by the use of clear outlines of thought. Each has been selected to contribute to this series because of his Spirit-empowered ability to help people live in the skins of biblical characters and provide a "you-are-there" intensity to the drama of events of the Bible which have so much to say about our relationships and responsibilities today.

The design for the Communicator's Commentary gives the reader an overall outline of each book of the Bible. Following the introduction, which reveals the author's approach and salient background on the book, each chapter of the commentary provides the Scripture to be exposited. The New King James Bible has been chosen for the Communicator's Commentary because it combines with integrity the beauty of language, underlying Hebrew and Greek textual basis, and thought-flow of the 1611 King James Version, while replacing obsolete verb forms and other archaisms with their everyday contemporary counterparts for greater readability. Reverence for God is preserved in the capitalization of all pronouns referring to the Father, Son, or Holy Spirit. Readers who are more comfortable with another translation can readily find the parallel passage by means of the chapter and verse reference at the end of each passage being exposited. The paragraphs of exposition combine fresh insights to the Scripture, application, rich illustrative material, and innovative ways of utilizing the vibrant truth for his or her own life and for the challenge of communicating it with vigor and vitality.

It has been gratifying to me as Editor of this series to receive enthusiastic progress reports from each contributor. As they worked, all were gripped with new truths from the Scripture—God-given insights into passages, previously not written in the literature of biblical explanation. A prime objective of this series is for each user to find the same awareness: that God speaks with newness through the Scriptures when we approach them with a ready mind and a willingness to communicate what He has given; that God delights to give communicators of His Word "I-never-saw-that-in-that-verse-before" intellectual insights so that our listeners and readers can have "I-never-realized-all-that-was-in-that-verse" spiritual experiences.

The thrust of the commentary series unequivocally affirms that God speaks through the Scriptures today to engender faith, enable adventuresome living of the abundant life, and establish the basis of obedient discipleship. The Bible, the unique Word of God, is unlimited as a resource for Christians in communicating our hope to others. It is our weapon in the battle for truth, the guide for ministry, and the irresistible force for introducing others to God.

A biblically rooted communication of the Gospel holds in unity and oneness what divergent movements have wrought asunder. This commentary series courageously presents personal faith, caring for individuals, and social responsibility as essential, inseparable dimensions of biblical Christianity. It seeks to present the quadrilateral Gospel in its fullness which calls us to unreserved commitment to Christ, unrestricted self-esteem in His grace, unqualified love for others in personal evangelism, and undying efforts to work for justice and righteousness in a sick and suffering world.

A growing renaissance in the church today is being led by clergy and laity who are biblically rooted, Christ-centered, and Holy Spirit-empowered. They have dared to listen to people's most urgent questions and deepest needs and then to God as He speaks through the Bible. Biblical preaching is the secret of growing churches. Bible study classes and small groups are equipping the laity for ministry in the world. Dynamic Christians are finding that daily study of God's Word allows the Spirit to do in them what He wishes to communicate through them to others. These days are the most exciting time since Pentecost. The Communicator's Commentary is offered to be a primary resource of new life for this renaissance.

It has been very encouraging to receive the enthusiastic responses of pastors and teachers to the twelve New Testament volumes of the Communicator's Commentary series. The letters from communicators on the firing line in pulpits, classes, study groups, and Bible fellowship clusters across the nation, as well as the reviews of scholars and publication analysts, have indicated that we have been on target in meeting a need for a distinctly different kind of commentary on the Scriptures, a commentary that is primarily aimed at helping interpreters of the Bible to equip the laity for ministry.

This positive response has led the publisher to press on with an additional twenty-one volumes covering the books of the Old Testament. These new volumes rest upon the same goals and guidelines that undergird the New Testament volumes. Scholar-preachers with facility in Hebrew as well as vivid contemporary exposition have been selected as authors. The purpose throughout is to aid the preacher and teacher in the challenge and adventure of Old Testament exposition in communication. In each volume you will meet Yahweh, the "I AM" Lord who is Creator, Sustainer, and Redeemer in the unfolding drama of His call and care of Israel. He is the Lord who acts, intervenes, judges, and presses His people into the immense challenges and privileges of being a chosen people, a holy nation. And in the descriptive exposition of each passage, the implications of the ultimate revelation of Yahweh in Jesus Christ, His Son, our Lord, are carefully spelled out to maintain unity and oneness in the preaching and teaching of the Gospel.

One of the most rewarding adventures in Old Testament exposition is in teaching and preaching from the Psalms. Athanasius said, "Most Scripture speaks to us, while the Psalms speak for us." In the Psalms we enter into the experience of the psalmist as he pours out his heart to God or allows his heart to be filled with a fresh word from God. There is no human thought or emotion unexpressed in the Psalms. And there is no need we face today that is left untouched by the prayers of the psalmist and the answers he receives from the Lord. It is remarkable how our concerns today were expressed by the psalmists so long ago. They praised the Lord in words we long to emulate in our own prayers. And yet they are no less authentic in the unbridled flow of their thoughts and feelings about the hurts, injustices, and problems of life. We discover how to pray in the difficulties and delights of life.

Alexander Maclaren said, "If the rest of Scripture may be called the speech of the Spirit of God to man, this book (the Psalms) is the answer of the Spirit of God in man." The more we read and study the Psalms, the more our language takes on the dimension of depth. Our prayers become more real, authentic, and bold. And as a result, our inner self is invaded by the Lord Himself. We come to Him as we are, and we learn to know Him as He is.

Preaching and teaching through the Psalms is to rediscover the prayer book of the Lord Jesus Christ. We sense His presence as we underline verses that are prophetic of His life and death and as we see the forthcoming drama of the Atonement.

Every age has turned to the Psalms for courage, comfort, and challenge. The early church used the Psalms as the first Christian hymnbook. The Reformation was spurred on by the reading and singing of the Psalms. We join Luther's voice as we read Psalm 46 and sing "A Mighty Fortress Is Our God!" We agree with Calvin when he said, "The Psalms open up to us familiar access to God." In Scotland, the metrical paraphrases of the Psalms became the hymnbook of John Knox. And many of our great hymns today in modern hymnbooks are based on the Psalms.

John Donne said that the Psalms are, "Like manna which tasted to every man like that he loved best." And we would add—what each person needs most. The Psalms speak to our condition. Our concerns are perfectly matched by any encounter with God who confronts and comforts us.

Alexander Whyte, the famous Scottish preacher of another generation (1836–1921), once exclaimed to his theological students, "Ah, I envy you . . . with your ministry before you, and especially that you have ahead a lifetime of explaining the Psalms to your people!"

This volume, the first of two on the Psalms by Dr. Donald Williams, will assist you immeasurably in the opportunity Dr. Whyte described so wistfully. Dr. Williams has written what I believe is one of the most dynamic commentaries on the Psalms in our time. It is a magnificent combination of penetrating scholarship, in-depth application, and illuminating illustration.

You will appreciate Dr. Williams's exacting mind and close attention to the text of each psalm. His scholarly expertise in dealing with exegetical issues will be of great assistance. The virtual line-by-line analysis leaves no gem in the treasure chest of the Psalms unexamined.

Based on this exegetical foundation, Dr. Williams moves to address the practical issues facing the communicator of Scripture. His breadth of pastoral experience enriches each chapter, as he relates the biblical text to the church today, to our cultural milieu, to our time of history, and to our personal life of faith. The application and illustration could not be broader in scope, truer to life, nor more timely in relevance. The worship of God, the power of God, the kingdom of God—these themes emerge time and again with rich illustration. The most personal of the Psalms are dealt with in an intimate way that allows us to encounter God in a refreshing, renewing way in our own lives.

Don Williams's academic preparation and pastoral experience has uniquely prepared him to write this commentary on the Psalms. He is a graduate of Princeton University, Princeton Seminary, and received his Ph.D. from Columbia University. Through the years since his formal training, he has become recognized as a biblical scholar of distinction.

For ten years Don served as pastor to students at the First Presbyterian Church of Hollywood. I first met him in 1972 when I was called to be Senior Pastor of the church and was able to observe at first hand Don's outstanding teaching and preaching as well as innovative leadership with college students and youth on the streets of Hollywood. Hundreds of young adults, many from the ranks of those disaffected from church and society during the turbulent period of the sixties and early seventies, were brought to Christ. A significant number of these have become leaders, clergypeople, and vital laity in the church throughout the nation. The life, mission, and evangelism of the Hollywood Church itself were deeply impacted by the sound biblical leadership of Don's imaginative vision for the church.

In the years after his work in Hollywood, Don developed a national ministry of teaching, speaking, and writing. He taught at Claremont McKenna College and Fuller Theological Seminary. He spoke at colleges, churches, retreats, and conferences throughout the country. During this period, he wrote several books, including *The Apostle Paul and Women in the Church* and *The Bond That Breaks: Will Homosexuality Split the Church?* In these years of broadly based ministry, Don developed a profound understanding of the church, while God placed within his heart a fervent commitment to the renewal of the local congregation.

During the past four years, Dr. Williams has been Pastor of the Mt. Soledad Presbyterian Church in La Jolla, California. Under his leadership, this church has discovered the presence and power of our Sovereign Lord. His preaching of the Word of God has brought many into the Kingdom. The worship life of the church has been distinguished by praise, joy, and freedom. Through the church's healing ministry, the power of God has been experienced in abundance, with bodies healed, oppressed persons set free, and hearts made whole.

The Mt. Soledad church has become a laboratory for renewal of the institutional church, a place where new forms of program and ministry have been developed and empowered by the Holy Spirit. Throughout this commentary, you will see the authentic evidences of the renewal which marks Don's ministry. This work was written in the midst of his ongoing responsibilities as a pastor, teacher, and leader in the ministry of healing. That makes it all the more vital and applicable for other communicators who seek to preach and teach in a way that brings lasting renewal to individuals and the church.

This commentary covers the first seventy-two psalms. The second volume on the remaining seventy-eight will be published subsequently. We anticipate that it will provide the same excellence of scholarship so magnificently displayed in this volume.

I commend this commentary to you in the hope that it will enrich your own personal devotional life and be an invaluable guide and inspiration as you communicate God's Word through the Psalms.

LLOYD JOHN OGILVIE

Author's Preface

This commentary does not presuppose that the reader has a knowledge of Hebrew. Thus references to the original language are transliterated into English and supplied in parentheses. Usually the words cited are from *A Hebrew and English Lexicon of the Old Testament* by Brown, Driver, and Briggs (Oxford: The Clarendon Press, 1953). The vowels of the verbs are pointed according to the basic entry in the lexicon for easy reference. Adjectives and nouns cited are normally offered in the singular for the same reason, although they may be plural in the passage.

For modern scholarly studies in the Psalms the reader is referred to F. Delitzsch, *Psalms,* Volume V of the classic Keil & Delitzsch, *Commentary on the Old Testament in Ten Volumes* (Grand Rapids: Eerdmans, 1982); Artur Weiser, *The Psalms* (Philadelphia: Westminster, 1962); A. A. Anderson, *The Book of Psalms,* Vols. 1 and 2 (Grand Rapids: Eerdmans, 1981); Peter C. Craigie, *Word Biblical Commentary,* Vol. 19, Psalms 1–50 (Waco: Word, 1983); and Leslie C. Allen, *Word Biblical Commentary,* Vol. 21, Psalms 101–150 (Waco: Word, 1983). Along with the New King James Version of the Bible, the Masoretic text has been referred to throughout this study.

Special thanks are due to Lloyd Ogilvie for his invitation to participate in this project and to my wife, Kathryn, for her patience and encouragement.

Introduction

The Psalms for the Church Today

In 1968 I made my first visit to Calvary Chapel, built on the edge of a bean field in Costa Mesa, California. The small church building was bursting at the seams with a new generation, "Jesus Freaks," the media would later dub them. As Lonie Frisbee, a young, long-haired evangelist, led his congregation in worship, he had them open their Bibles to the Book of Psalms and sing through several passages, accompanied by a rock band called "The Love Song."

These young people were in the vanguard of an evangelistic movement in the Counter Culture that would sweep three million converts into the church over the next several years. Leaving behind a life of rebellion, drugs, sexual promiscuity, and futile spiritual questing, they instinctively turned to the Bible, and more especially for worship, to the Psalter. With their recent experience of the Vietnam War, they could identify deeply with the groanings of the psalmist and know his solace and healing.

The era of the Jesus Movement has now passed, but in common with the Reformation of the sixteenth century, it gave an important gift to the larger church—the recovery of the use of the psalms in worship and private devotions. Several aspects of the Psalter are especially relevant to the church today in her teaching and preaching.

1. Renewal in worship. The Psalms model praise and devotion as they flow from the hearts of people who know the living God. They meditate upon God's majesty and respond to His intervention by giving Him glory. They ring with shouts and singing. They summon every living being and every human instrument into a choir of praise to the merciful and mighty God (Ps. 150). The renewal of the church begins in a renewal of worship. The psalms will lead us into a deeper in-

17

timacy with our Creator and Redeemer and show us how to praise Him properly.

2. Renewal in our own self-awareness. As God reveals Himself, He reveals us; as we become intimate with God, we become intimate with ourselves (see Calvin's *Institutes,* I). The full range of human emotions is displayed in these living prayers, without the hypocrisy and pretense so often characteristic of the modern church. Thus the psalms of lament teach us to accept ourselves before God, "warts and all" (Cromwell), as the Lord accepts us.

3. The display of the absolute mercy of God and the walk of faith which finds its fulfillment in the coming of Jesus Christ. In this sense the Psalms are "evangelical" and "gospel-centered." No wonder Luther loved them. There he found the gift of God's righteousness shining as brightly as in Romans (see, e.g., Ps. 51). The psalms also have a prophetic dimension which points to the coming Messiah-King, thus they are knit into the fabric of the New Testament. As the evangelical awakening continues in the church, the psalms will nourish its mission and call.

4. A realistic response to the suffering and warfare in this world. The cry of lament heard throughout these prayers has great relevance to our own troubled era and also to the individual believer who must engage in a continual warfare against Satan's deception. At one level, the Psalter is a bloody book for a bloody world. But not only do the psalms reflect crisis, they also witness to God's healing power. Here again, we are at a renewal point in the church. The good news for our brokenness is that the living, loving God not only forgives sins but also heals the whole person: spirit, soul, and body. The teaching of the psalms will nurture our faith and facilitate the release of God's healing power in the church today.

5. The reflection of the community of God's people, worshiping the Lord, witnessing to His mighty deeds, and working together, upbuilding the whole body of believers. Our fractured church desperately needs its community rebuilt. The psalms will renew us together, if we allow them not merely to be great devotional literature but the mighty word of God in our midst, forming a people for God Himself.

Title

The Jews called the Psalms *sēper tᵉhillīm,* "book of praises" or simply "praises." Our word "psalms" transliterates the Greek of the New Testament, *biblos psalmōn,* which corresponds to the Hebrew. A few manuscripts in the Septuagint have the word *psalterion,* "stringed instrument" or "collection of songs." From this comes the word *Psalter.*

Authorship and Date

The Hebrew Masoretic text ascribes seventy-three psalms to David, Israel's archetypal king. Just as the law was centered in Moses and wisdom in Solomon, so worship was centered in David. He himself was a musician and poet, filled with the Spirit of God. He enjoyed intimacy with God as "a man after God's own heart." As king, he also brought the ark of the covenant, symbolizing God's presence, to Jerusalem, focusing worship there (2 Sam. 6:12). The psalm titles ascribe thirteen psalms to specific events in David's life. Much modern scholarship disputes these ascriptions, arguing against any direct Davidic influence on the Psalter. However, it must be remembered that oral tradition is intensely conservative in nature. The poetic form of the psalms themselves aided memory in making faithful transmission possible. Assuming the center of some of the Psalter to have been in the worship in the temple in Jerusalem, faithful transmission through liturgical usage is highly probable. Also, if many psalms found their origin in the enthronement ceremony of the king, as modern scholars suppose, then they are at least pre-exilic. Since these introductions are so disputed we will mention them only where internal evidence in the psalm itself supports their assertions.

The psalms of David are customarily identified in several collections: 3–41; 51–70; 138–145, plus a smaller group, 108–110; and those which stand alone. Beyond the Davidic psalms, those ascribed to the Levite musician Asaph of David's time (1 Chron. 15:17–19; 16:4–5) make up the block 73–83, plus Psalm 50. The psalms of the sons of Korah, Levites descended through Kohath (1 Chron. 6:22), are found in 42–49 and 84–88 (excepting 43 and 86). These families were guilds of temple singers known to us from Chronicles.

Psalms grouped by subject matter include the songs of ascent (120–134) and the Hallel ("praise") collection (113–118, 146–150). Other psalms are ascribed to Solomon (72, 127), Moses (90), Ethan the Ezrahite (89), and the musical director (more than fifty times). Thirty-four are anonymous.

What conclusions can then be drawn about the issues of authorship and date? In general, scholarship today tends to be conservative in dating the psalms. The radical position that almost all come from the post-exilic Maccabean period has been abandoned, and it is generally agreed that the Psalter was probably substantially complete by the fourth century B.C. In the title over the seventy-three psalms ascribed to David, the Hebrew preposition l^e which precedes the name, can mean "by David," or "for David," or "concerning David." Unless there is compelling evidence to the contrary, we will tend to assume Davidic authorship for those psalms traditionally ascribed to him.

It should be remembered that the Psalter is Israel's prayerbook and hymnal, with songs and prayers spanning generations of God's people. Often we have no indication of the original incident or setting which led to their creation. Rather than being a problem for us, however, this very liberation from the specific gives these prayers universal application in all times and places.

Structure

The final editors of the Psalter divided the book into five smaller books, probably on the analogy of the Five Books of Moses (the Pentateuch). These divisions are: 1–41; 42–72; 73–89; 90–106; 107–150. Each division closes with a doxology. With Psalm 42 the so-called Elohistic Psalter begins, running through Psalm 83. The designation refers to the change of the name used for God from "Yahweh" to "Elohim" by an editor.

Form

The psalms are poetic in form. They arise out of oral speech and are best known for their use of "Hebrew parallelism," in which two or three parallel phrases are employed to give variations on the same theme. The second member may repeat the content of the first in different words (synonymous parallelism):

> Blessed is the man
> Who walks not in the counsel of the ungodly,
> Nor stands in the path of sinners.
>
> Ps. 1:1

The second member may also contrast sharply with the first (antithetic parallelism):

> For the Lord knows the way of the righteous,
> But the way of the ungodly shall perish.
>
> Ps. 1:6

Or the second member may take the thought further (synthetic parallelism):

> But his delight is in the law of the Lord,
> And in His law he meditates day and night.
>
> Ps. 1:2

In regarding the psalms as poetry, scholars have also sought to analyze in them some sort of metrical regularity, but with no resulting consensus.

Of more importance to us are the categories for the individual psalms. Designations from the temple liturgy, such as royal cult songs, hymns, accession songs, and national laments, have been used. While the possible cultic context of many psalms is not to be denied (they were [and are] employed in public worship [cf. Ps. 100]), too much has been made of this approach.

Klaus Westermann (in *Praise and Lament in the Psalms*) challenges the whole cultic thesis and simply groups the psalms into two major categories: psalms of praise and psalms of lament, thus encompassing the whole of human existence from birth to death. For Westermann the life setting of the psalm is neither cultic nor literary: God's intervention is the determining factor. When God acts, praise must be sung to Him. Thus the psalms of praise fall into two categories: descriptive, "Yahweh is," and declarative, "Yahweh has done." In praise God is the subject. Praise is also a public act and has a forensic element. Therefore, the individual psalmists had to "go public" in their praise.

The psalms of lament can be subdivided as either laments of the people or laments of the individual. These psalms carry no specific requests but petition for supplication in time of need, and there is always a distinctive cry for salvation that takes its character from the lament. The psalms of petition are the largest group in the Psalter.

Psalm Terms

The word *psalm* occurs fifty-seven times. It probably denotes a poetic composition sung to the accompaniment of stringed instruments. A *maschil* is a special type of psalm. Commentators, however, disagree over its meaning. Some suggest a "didactic poem," others propose a "meditation," or a "skillful psalm."

The word *Selah* is found seventy-one times in the Psalter. Its interpretation is uncertain. Either it marks a pause during which something was sung or played or, according to Jewish tradition, it means "forever." Other suggestions are that it may offer directions to sing more loudly or to fall prostrate before God. As we exposit the psalms we will disregard its presence in the text.

Conclusions

In the study that follows, occasional attention will be given to the possible cultic setting of a particular psalm. Nevertheless we accept Brevard Childs' assertions in his *Introduction to the Old Testament As Scripture* that the canonization of the psalms determines their authority. Thus their use in the continuing worship of God's people is their proper setting.

Our primary concern in this commentary then is not to establish the psalms' origin and historical setting, but to see what they mean and how they build the life of the church today. The psalms are to evoke praise—our praise! The psalms are to express lament—our lament!

We believers in Jesus Christ are, in this age, God's Israel (Gal. 6:16). Since the Old Testament is written for us as well as the Israelites (1 Cor. 10:11), it was proper for the risen Christ to explain to His disciples that everything in the law of Moses and the prophets and the psalms is fulfilled in Him (Luke 24:44). Therefore, we are to teach and admonish one another with "psalms and hymns and spiritual songs, singing with grace in [our] hearts to the Lord" (Col. 3:16).

If the canon of the psalms continues to bring God's word to His people and to evoke their response, and if its proper setting continues to be the worshiping community of believers rather than the academic lecture hall, then one final point can be made. In the words of Dietrich Bonhoeffer, Christ is the secret of the psalms.

How can this be? Since Christ is the head of the church, His body, and since the church is formed by the canon of Scripture, as the living church prays the psalms, her Lord prays them with her and through her. This explains the bitter imprecatory psalms and the psalms of the Passion. They are not Israel's psalms, nor are they the church's psalms. Bonhoeffer writes, "Someone else is praying, not me. . . . The One who is here protesting His innocence, who is invoking God's judgment, who has come to such infinite depths of suffering, is none other than Jesus Christ Himself. He it is who is praying here, and not only here but in the whole Psalter" (*Life Together,* p. 31).

If indeed Christ is the mediator of revelation, and if Christ is the goal of redemptive history, and if Christ is the true humanity in whom we are made new, and if Christ is the High Priest who always intercedes for us, then Bonhoeffer is exactly right. But this is not simply a theological point to be made and debated. It is an experience to be received as we enter into the presence of the living God and raise our psalms of praise. Here, in worship, the authentication is given. Luther perceived a profound truth when he began his lecture on Psalm 1: "The first psalm speaks literally concerning Christ. . . ."

CHAPTER ONE

Which Way Are You Going?

Psalm 1

For the Bible, life is a journey offering two roads. Regardless of how offensive this idea may be to the modern mind, it is "either / or," rather than "both / and." There are two perceptions of reality: the supernatural and the natural. There are two conflicting kingdoms: the kingdom of God and the kingdom of Satan. There are two entry points: the wide gate leading to destruction and the narrow gate leading to life (Matt. 7:13–14). As Francis Schaeffer stresses, unlike Hegel's dialectic (thesis, antithesis, synthesis), Biblical thought is antithetical: thesis / antithesis. There is no reconciliation of opposites (synthesis).

Thus Psalm 1 is structured antithetically: verses 1–3 treat the righteous; verses 4–5 treat the ungodly; verse 6 treats both together. The righteous person is like a tree planted (v. 3); the ungodly person is like chaff driven (v. 4); the way of the righteous is known to the Lord, while the way of the ungodly shall perish (v. 6). As with the structure of the psalm, the parallelism in the language itself (see *Introduction*) gives grammatical expression to this "either / or" perception of reality.

Psalm 1 stands as the great vestibule leading us into the whole Psalter. It pronounces a blessing upon us as we enter: "Blessed is the man." Clearly this psalm is linked to the wisdom literature in Proverbs with its stress on meditating on the law of the Lord (v. 2; see Prov. 2:1 ff.) and the warning of the two ways (v. 6; see Prov. 2:8–13). Yet, as the introduction to the Psalter it leads us beyond legislation and wise sayings. The prayers and songs of Israel too are *Torah*—"law," "instruction," "revelation." The unknown author of Psalm 1 calls us to this word, given both to the Lord and from the Lord—expressed in praise, prophecy, lament, hope: the shouts, the songs, and the cries of God's people. The thought moves from the way of the righteous (vv. 1–3) to the way of the ungodly (vv. 4–5) and concludes with their final disposition (v. 6).

25

The Way of the Righteous

1 Blessed *is* the man
Who walks not in the counsel of the ungodly,
   Nor stands in the path of sinners,
   Nor sits in the seat of the scornful;
2 But his delight *is* in the law of the LORD,
   And in His law he meditates day and night.
3 He shall be like a tree
   Planted by the rivers of water,
   That brings forth its fruit in its season,
   Whose leaf also shall not wither;
   And whatever he does shall prosper.

Ps. 1:1–3

In verses 1–3, we find a meditation on the way of the righteous in the form of a blessing. In the first great antithesis, the blessed man doesn't do certain things (v. 1), does do certain things (v. 2), and reaps the benefits of what he does do (v. 3).

In verse 1 the word *"blessed"* is a call to happiness, an invitation with a promise, like Jesus' Beatitudes. The *negative* part of the blessing is expounded first: The blessed person is one who does not *"walk,"* *"stand,"* or *"sit"* with the *"ungodly,"* the *"sinners,"* or the *"scornful."* First, then, he *"walks not in the counsel of the ungodly."* His world-view, his ethical life, and his moral decisions are no longer dictated by the godless. Next, he no longer *"stands in the path of sinners."* His identity, his standing, his lifestyle are no longer determined by those in rebellion against God. Finally, he no longer *"sits in the seat of the scornful."* He neither learns nor judges from the perspective of those bearing the acid authority of cynicism and pride.

While these three clauses may simply be viewed as variations on the same theme, they may also form a mini-exposition of progressing depravity: Heeding the wisdom of the ungodly (walking) leads to identification with sinners (standing), which results in being settled, established in the authority of their judgments (seated). The warning is not to start the downward spiral—to avoid the counsel of the ungodly.

In our media-centered world today we get to the heart of this warning only when we recognize that the Christian is engaged in a battle of world-views, that it is our whole perception of reality that is at issue. We have been so indoctrinated by the modern scientific world-view with its anti-supernatural bias that we are practically closed to the presence and power of God in our day-by-day existence. We look upon the experiences of Jesus and His disciples in healing the sick, cleansing the lepers, and raising the dead as a unique historical moment rather than as a continuing ministry for the church. We isolate certain gifts of the Spirit as belonging to the apostolic age and create our own canon within the canon, dictating what God may and may not do. Carl Becker sums up our modern, secular world-view as follows: "What is man that the electron should be mindful of him! Man is but a foundling in the cosmos, abandoned by the forces that created him. Unparented, unassisted and undirected by omniscient or benevolent authority, he must fend for himself, and with the aid of his own limited intelligence find his way about in an indifferent universe" (*The Heavenly City of the Eighteenth-Century Philosophers,* p. 15). This is the counsel of the ungodly and we are all tainted by it.

By contrast, the blessed man has been redeemed from the whole structure of this fallen world with its egocentricity, its lies, its moral failure, and, ultimately, its satanic seduction—he indeed is on his way to happiness.

The negative expression in verse 1 prepares us for the positive in verse 2. Here the blessed person has an *"attitude"* of *"delight"* in *"the law of the Lord,"* which leads him to an *action* as *"in His law he meditates day and night."* We need not enter the contemporary debate as to whether attitudes determine actions or actions determine attitudes. The fact is, the right attitude, delight, will lead to the right action, meditation. If we delight in a person, we want to be with him or her. If we delight in a song, we want to sing it. If we delight in a book, we want to read it. If we delight in God's law, we will want to meditate upon it.

What is God's answer to Satan's seduction, His response to the world's illusions? Revelation! Torah! The word of God is the way to blessedness. We are to delight in that word as did Bunyan's Pilgrim who rushed away from the City of Destruction holding his Bible and crying, "Life, life, eternal life!"

Our attitude toward the word, our delight and pleasure in it, however, must lead to action—our meditation upon it: *"And in His law he meditates day and night."*

Biblical meditation, unlike many recent popular techniques, is not content-less but content-full. It is not accomplished by eliminating thought but by redirecting thought to the Word of God. The Hebrew word for "meditate" (*hāgâh*) means "to utter sounds, to speak." It often appears in synonymous parallelism with *zākar,* "to remember, call to

27

mind," and *śiaḥ*, "to consider, ponder." For example, Psalm 143:5 reads: "I remember the days of old; / I meditate on all Your works; / I muse on the work of Your hands." To meditate, then, is to recall all that God has said and done. Meditation includes audible recitation, and it is to be done continually, *"day and night."* So God says to Joshua, "This Book of the Law shall not depart from your mouth, but you shall meditate in it day and night, that you may observe to do according to all that is written in it" (1:8). Jesus also calls us to the same lifestyle determined by the word of God: "If you abide [continue, dwell, remain] in My word, you are My disciples indeed. And you shall know the truth, and the truth shall make you free" (John 8:31–32). Walking in the counsel of God is the call to Bible study, to Scripture memorization, to a daily time of personal devotion in the word of God.

Maintaining a disciplined devotional life has been one of my major struggles. If you share this battle, you might try to attach your devotional time to an area of discipline you've already learned to control in your life. Get to work a few minutes early and spend this time with God. Go to the library and read the Bible before you turn to your textbooks. Even better, find a place where you can withdraw for prayer and study and work toward setting a time that is yours and God's alone. Remember, either our attitudes and actions are being molded by God or by the ungodly. In computer jargon, "Garbage in, garbage out." There is no neutral ground.

Verse 3 uses a simile to describe the blessed person as a tree, *"planted by the rivers of water."* These rivers are like irrigation ditches: as the believer meditates, he will be continually watered by the word. The results of this nourishment are twofold. First, we will bear fruit in season. Second, we will be evergreen.

The fulfillment of our fruitfulness lies in Jesus' promise that we will bear fruit as we abide in Him (John 15:1 ff.). The fruit comes by His grace. It also comes *"in its season,"* that is, in His time, not ours. This is a lesson I continually have to relearn. In a former church a period of fruitlessness led to a personal crisis. Should I leave the ministry? I resolved that God had called me there and He, not circumstances, would have to call me elsewhere. A few months later, as I remained faithful to that call, a time of tremendous blessing came as the "Jesus Movement" broke in upon us, and we saw untold numbers reached for Christ.

The further promise that we will be evergreen means that we will not wither, even in barren times. Since the word of God stands forever (Isa. 40:8), we too will stand forever in that word.

This section of the psalm concludes with a promise: *"And whatever he does shall prosper."* The blessed person delights in God's Torah, meditates upon God's Torah, and *prospers*. Guided and guarded by God's word, we will live in fullness and blessing as a firm, fruitful tree, rooted deeply against the winds of change.

The Way of the Ungodly

4 The ungodly *are* not so,
   But *are* like the chaff which the wind drives away.
5 Therefore the ungodly shall not stand in the judgment,
   Nor sinners in the congregation of the righteous.

                                                    Ps. 1:4–5

The ungodly, already identified with "sinners" and the "scornful" in verse 1, are the opposite of the righteous. Rather than being a sturdy oak, they are *"like the chaff which the wind drives away."* The metaphor is that of threshing, in which kernels of wheat, having been thrown into the air, fall back to the ground as the wind blows away the worthless chaff. To be severed from the word of God is to have no root, no nourishment, no fruit, no life, or as in Jesus' parable, it is to be like the house built upon the sand, demolished by the storms of life (Matt. 7:24–27).

The results of this ephemerality in verse 5 are twofold: the ungodly have no real future and they have no real present. First, they *"shall not stand in the judgment."* It does not matter whether the psalmist is thinking here of the final Day of Judgment or a less ultimate trial. In Israel every court action rehearses the final Day when all of our secrets will be revealed and God's absolute justice will triumph. Unprepared for any judgment, the ungodly are unprepared for the final judgment. Second, sinners do not presently stand *"in the congregation of the righteous."* They are excluded when God's people are called together. Psalm 24:3–4 asks, "Who may ascend into the hill of the Lord? Or who may stand in His holy place?" and answers, "He who has clean hands and a pure heart." The judgment of personal isolation *now* points to the eternal isolation to come.

The ungodly experience bitter hopelessness before the future judgment and alienation from believers in the present. The deepest joys

of security and community are missing as they live in the death of
their own egos, separated from God and God's people.

THE ASSURANCE OF THE RIGHTEOUS

6 For the LORD knows the way of the righteous,
But the way of the ungodly shall perish.

Ps. 1:6

The assurance of the righteous is that the Lord knows their way.
The verb *yāda'* means "to know, to have intimate relationship with."
Here the psalmist uses a verb form that indicates that the Lord "keeps
on knowing" the way of the righteous. His eye is upon them, His ear
is open to them, and in Christ His Spirit abides within them forever
(John 14:17). Their security, temporal and eternal, is not in the way
itself but in the Lord who communes with them on the way. Luther
said, "The way I do not know, but well do I know my guide." Thus
the eternal God will keep the righteous for eternity in union with Himself.

The ungodly are not so. Captive to their sin, governed by this world,
they have taken a way that leads to death. They will not stand in the
judgment but will perish. The root meaning of the Hebrew verb used
here is "to wander off." Like an animal who has wandered far from
the safety of the flock, those who stray from the watchful eye of the
Lord will surely suffer the ultimate disaster.

Psalm 1, then, is a call to meditation upon the revelation of God.
The deep prayers of the Psalter are not a formless exercise of mindless
mysticism but a response to Torah, revelation, and in that response
they too become revelation. We are blessed and delivered from the
vanity of this world as we delight in God's word and respond in prayer.
As we study through the psalms so we must pray through them. It is
here that the blessing becomes ours.

The very call to blessing, however, precipitates a crisis. Who can
avoid the counsel of the ungodly in our secular society? Who can meditate on the word of God day and night? Who can be fruitful and evergreen? Certainly we cannot fulfill this high calling. But take heart—
One can and does. This very calling is consummated by the Lord Jesus
Christ. It is He who lives in perfect communion with the Father (John
5:19–20). It is He who delights in the word of God, and it is He who
prospers in all His ways. In Christ we become the blessed person of

Psalm 1. He is the God-man who fulfills the divine demand and incorpo-
rates us into the divine life (1 John 1:3). It is He who gives us His
own righteousness. As we live in communion with Him, we will be
that tree planted and our way will be known to the Lord. As we live
in communion with Him, His psalms become our psalms and the road
to happiness, to blessing, is ours.

CHAPTER TWO

What's This World Coming To?

Psalm 2

Psalm 1 deals with the word; Psalm 2 deals with the world. Psalm
1 contrasts the righteous with the ungodly; Psalm 2 contrasts the nations
with their divine ruler. Psalm 1 deals with personal life; Psalm 2, with
historical life. Psalm 1 deals with the particular; Psalm 2, with the universal.

In a certain sense, Psalm 2 also serves, along with Psalm 1, as a vestibule into the Psalter. It alerts us to the fact that here we are not only
dealing with our interior devotional life and personal destiny but also
with the whole purpose of God in history and the destiny of the nations.
In the sense that Psalm 1 gives us God's word as the conceptual frame-
work for our meditation, Psalm 2 gives us the movement of that word
in history and its interpretive key: "Yet I have set My King / On My
holy hill of Zion" (v. 6).

The Bible, as the written word of God, reveals both God's plan for
the world and its center, the living Word of God, Jesus Christ (John
1:1–2, 14). Thus the psalms and the whole of the Bible must be interpreted christocentrically. As Luther puts it, in the Bible we have the
words of God which are to be understood by the *Word* of God, Jesus
Christ. All meditation on Scripture, therefore, and all movement in history must take us to Christ.

Some commentators identify Psalm 2 as a coronation psalm written for the Davidic kings' enthronement ceremony. In this view, the transition from one ruling king to another provides the occasion for vassal states to revolt (vv. 1–3). The new king's coronation then restores order (vv. 7–12). Older expositors, however, as well as the New Testament itself, see this royal psalm as prophetic and messianic. It is all the nations of the earth who are in revolt against God's kingdom, not merely local vassal states (vv. 2, 8, 10), and the King himself (v. 6) is the Anointed (v. 2), the begotten Son of God (vv. 7, 12). Moreover, the rebellion takes place not in an interim period before a new king is crowned, but during the reign of a king who exercises divine sovereignty (v. 2). F. F. Bruce asserts, "It is inconceivable that such notions were entertained in any directly personal way concerning the line of monarchs who followed in Judah. We have here, therefore, either the most blatant flattery the world has ever heard, or else the expression of a great ideal" ("Messiah," in *The New Bible Dictionary*, p. 814), and, I would add, a great prophetic promise.

In the synagogue at Pisidian Antioch, Paul applied "You are My Son, today I have begotten You" (v. 7) to Jesus and His resurrection (Acts 13:33). Hebrews 1:5 connects the same verse to Jesus, to show that as the Son of God He is above the angels. The Book of Revelation also sees Psalm 2 fulfilled eschatologically in the final triumph of Christ's kingdom (Rev. 2:26–27).

It seems clear that we may take this psalm as both messianic and prophetic. In calling it "messianic," however, we do not deny that ancient Israel would have applied it to the Davidic monarchy. The promise given to David was for an eternal throne, and God's relationship to his heirs was to be as a father to a son (2 Sam. 7:12–16). The universal aspect of the psalm, however, points beyond any Davidic king to the fulfillment of David's kingdom in the coming of the Messiah. For the New Testament, the fulfillment of that kingdom points beyond Jesus' ministry in Palestine to His ultimate reign throughout the universe. Thus there are three levels to the prophetic passages in the Old Testament. The first is God's word to His people in the immediate situation; the second is the future aspect of that word fulfilled in the first coming of Christ; the third is the final aspect of that word fulfilled in the second coming of Christ. We are only true to the whole of Scripture when we account for all three levels.

The author of Psalm 2 is unknown, although traditionally it has been held to be David. The movement of thought is from rebellion (vv. 1–

3), to God's response with His Messiah (vv. 4–9), and final resolution (vv. 10–12).

The Nations' Rebellion

> 1 Why do the nations rage,
>   And the people plot a vain thing?
> 2 The kings of the earth set themselves,
>   And the rulers take counsel together,
>   Against the Lord and against His Anointed, *saying,*
> 3 "Let us break Their bonds in pieces
>   And cast away Their cords from us."
>
> *Ps. 2:1–3*

"Why do the nations rage, / And the people plot a vain thing?" Throughout the Psalter we will be pummeled by honest questions. If God is the sovereign Lord of history, why this rebellion? If God is a God of order, why all this chaos? Here the nations seethe in revolt; literally, they *"rage"* or "throng tumultuously," and *"plot"* or "imagine," or "growl" vanity.

The question of why they rage is not immediately answered but is instead intensified by a parallel statement in verse 2 as the subject changes from the nations to their leaders. Rather than squelching this upheaval, the rulers *"take counsel together"* and join in an alliance *"against the Lord and against His Anointed,"* here meaning "King" (see v. 6 and 1 Sam 16:1–13). The Hebrew word is *māsîah*, from which we get our word "messiah."

The point of the nations' rage and the rulers' counsel becomes clear in verse 3. It is open revolt: *"Let us break Their bonds in pieces, / And cast away Their cords from us."* The question, *"Why do the nations rage . . . ?"* now receives its answer. They no longer want to be submissive to God, His King, or His kingdom. They see submission to God as bondage and His sovereignty as restrictive, His will as demeaning. The nations want autonomy; they want freedom. Responding to the serpent's whisper to Eve in the garden, they want to be like God (Gen. 3:5). They want to be their own God.

The Messiah's Reign

> 4 He who sits in the heavens shall laugh;
>   The Lord shall hold them in derision.

5 Then He shall speak to them in His wrath,
   And distress them in His deep displeasure:
6 "Yet I have set My King
   On My holy hill of Zion."
7 "I will declare the decree:
   The LORD has said to Me, 'You *are* My Son,
   Today I have begotten You.
8 Ask of Me, and I will give *You*
   The nations *for* Your inheritance,
   And the ends of the earth *for* Your possession.
9 You shall break them with a rod of iron;
   You shall dash them to pieces like a potter's vessel.' "

Ps. 2:4–9

God's response to the nations' rebellion is twofold. In verse 4 He derides them for their foolishness, and in verses 5–6 He directs them to His King on Zion.

To begin with, then, God sits and laughs at the nations. Being seated is a sign of His authority: He is the eternal Creator and the transcendent Lord of all things. News from earth doesn't dismay Him or make Him nervous. He doesn't read the daily paper to keep current. "Behold, the nations are as a drop in a bucket. . . . All nations before Him are as nothing, and they are counted by Him less than nothing and worthless. . . . It is He who sits above the circle of the earth, and its inhabitants are like grasshoppers. . . . He brings the princes to nothing; He makes the judges of the earth useless" (Isa. 40:15, 17, 22, 23).

The presumption of the nations and their leaders causes God to laugh. How can those who are temporal fight the Eternal? How can the creation fight the Creator? God's laughter, as we face the terror of our history, keeps things in perspective. It reminds us of the answer to the question "Who is in charge?" Ultimately, neither ecological disaster nor nuclear nightmare are in charge; God is!

God's laugh, however, is not the laugh of the aloof but the laugh of One who is offended at our absurd rebellion against His authority. Responding in wrath (v. 5), He now exercises His power by intervening in our history through His King whom He has installed on Zion: *"Yet I have set My King, / On My holy hill of Zion"* (v. 6).

But God's wrath in His King is, in Karl Barth's phrase, His "next to last word." It is for the sake of our repentance (v. 11) and His mercy (v. 13). The "last word" is always the word of the gospel. Here is our theological, historical, and interpretive center.

In verse 7 the King witnesses to God's decree concerning Himself, revealing His *identity*. In verses 8–9 the King declares His *destiny* over the rebellious nations. Yahweh decrees two things about His King: First, the King is His Son, and, second, the King is begotten by Him.

In the Old Testament the title *son* indicates intimate relationship and subordination. As Son, the King's rule is divinely authored and legitimized. As Son, the King represents God, His Father, and mediates His authority and will in His reign. At this point in the progress of revelation *"You are My Son"* neither asserts nor denies the pre-existence of the Messiah-King. It does assert, however, the present relationship of unity and subordination. Hebrews 1 later reveals that the full meaning of this verse includes pre-existence. Ultimately the Son is Son by nature as well as by decree and obedience.

The decree then continues, *"Today I have begotten You"* (v. 7). While the Hebrew verb "beget" means "to bear" or "to generate," the original intention of the time-element, *"today,"* excludes all physical concepts of begetting, contrasting God's King with Egyptian theories of kingship. It is also eschatological: Today God's King is enthroned on Mt. Zion (v. 6) to rule the nations (v. 8). Paul rightly proclaims that this promise of enthronement is now fulfilled in the resurrection of God's Son from the dead. Easter inaugurates the new age—the age of salvation (Acts 13:13). It is through His resurrection that Jesus, in conquering death, receives all authority and rules all things (Matt. 28:18–20). While He is eternally God's Son, He is declared Son of God in power by His resurrection from the dead (Rom. 1:4). In this sense, the Son is "begotten" by the Father to be the second Adam, the "Firstborn from the dead," the progenitor of a whole race of new men and new women sharing His resurrection life (see 1 Cor. 15:22–23).

The Anointed King on Mt. Zion then is the Son of God mediating God's presence and bearing God's kingdom. That this kingdom or rule is effective is seen in verses 8–9. First, there is the *what* of His kingdom in verse 8. God promises to give Him the nations and the continents. His destiny is to rule this whole planet: *"I will give You / The nations for Your inheritance, / And the ends of the earth for Your possession."*

Second, there is the *how* of His kingdom in verse 9. The nations will be broken with a rod of iron and shattered like a clay pot. His rule ultimately will be one of power and judgment, and He *will* rule.

We are to take heed! While Christ comes now in this age of grace to rule in our hearts by His love, it will not always be so. Another day will dawn and, in the imagery of the Book of Revelation, the conquering Lord will come on a white charger with the armies of heaven: "Now out of His mouth goes a sharp sword, that with it He should strike the nations. And He Himself will rule them with a rod of iron. He Himself treads the winepress of the fierceness and wrath of Almighty God" (Rev. 19:15). Here Psalm 2:9 is fulfilled.

THE CONCLUDING CALL

10 Now therefore, be wise, O kings;
   Be instructed, you judges of the earth.
11 Serve the LORD with fear,
   And rejoice with trembling.
12 Kiss the Son, lest He be angry,
   And you perish *in* the way,
   When His wrath is kindled but a little.
   Blessed *are* all those who put their trust in Him.

                                                      Ps. 2:10–12

The sober description of judgment in verses 8–9 leads to a call in verses 10–12. The end has not yet come. It's as if the offer to the Messiah-King, "Ask of Me, and I will give You / The nations for Your inheritance" has yet to be accepted. There is still time for the rulers of the nations to be wise and to receive divine instruction before they are broken with a rod of iron. The kings and judges need to come to their only King and Judge. Stop the rebellion! Submit to the King! How they may answer the call is addressed in verses 11–12. The thesis is simple: Worship the Lord! *"Serve the Lord with fear"* (v. 11a). *"Serve"* includes the surrender of the will and the submission of the heart. It means to come under the King's rule and obey Him, as a slave surrenders to his master. In the Old Testament "serve" is often used in parallel with the verb "worship." The NASB renders verse 11a, "Worship the Lord with reverence," and Psalm 100:2 summons us to worship: "Serve the Lord with gladness; / Come before His presence with singing." That worship means submission is seen in Psalm 95:6: "Oh come, let us worship and bow down; / Let us kneel before the Lord our Maker." The *"fear"* in service comes from a sense of awe and even terror before the numinous majesty, power, and holiness of God (see Exod. 20:18–21).

Worship also includes joy: *"And rejoice with trembling"* (v. 11b). This joy comes from the very presence of God: "In Your presence is fullness of joy" (Ps. 16:11). It is not sentimental, however; it includes the *"fear"* of the previous phrase now manifest by *"trembling."*

An attitude of submission to the Lord and joy and awe in His presence leads then to an *act* of submission in verse 12: *"Kiss the Son, lest He be angry, / And you perish in the way, / When His wrath is kindled but a little."* Kissing the Son is the act of worship itself. It is the concrete sign of surrender. Thus, the Greek word for worship, *proskuneō,* means "come toward to kiss."

To surrender to Christ, to rejoice in His presence, and to kiss Him in an act of submission, means that the rebellion is over. Apart from this, there is only His anger, wrath, and our perishing. If He does not ride into our hearts on a donkey, He will ride down our hearts on a white charger.

Psalm 2's ending blessing echoes Psalm 1:1 and links the two psalms together: *"Blessed are all those who put their trust* [literally, "seek refuge"] *in Him."* To make the Son the object of our faith and to flee to Him is to be blessed. This is the way to happiness.

Two final points are in order. This psalm is evangelistic. It is addressed to the nations. It beats with a missionary heart. It is the nations who are in revolt against Christ (v. 2). It is the nations, however, who are promised to Him (v. 8) and it is the nations who are called to Him (v. 10). Psalm 2 directs the nations to the Son, warns them of judgment to come, and promises them blessing if they will worship Him. Thus the Psalter is for those who make this submission. It is for the nations, the Gentiles who submit to God's Son and King. In the psalms they will learn how to *"serve the Lord with fear, rejoice with trembling,"* and *"kiss the Son."* As in the whole Bible, the indicative mood of the verb ("I have set My King on My holy hill of Zion") is followed by the imperative ("Serve the Lord. . . . Kiss the Son"). As J. I. Packer points out, there is no real evangelism without both. We must tell people what God has done, and we must also tell them what they must do in response.

Finally, while we cannot accept responsibility for the rebellion of the nations, we can accept responsibility for our own rebellion, our illusions of freedom, our quest for material security, our chafing against the Lord's sovereign will.

Psalm 2 really structures an evangelistic invitation. It defines the problem: our revolt. It offers the solution: God's Son. It then warns of judgment to come and calls us to surrender to Him in worship. The road back to the Father's house is already marked and the door is open. It is Christ who stands at the door. We must come and greet Him . . . "kiss the Son."

CHAPTER THREE

Morning Devotions: Fear or Faith?

Psalm 3

Children often face the terror of the night. As a boy I remember being afraid of going into the upstairs of our house where there was a large playroom, for fear that some monster or enemy was there to grab me. I would sing loudly, turn on all the lights, and check each room to dissipate my anxiety. Then there was a period when I could only sleep with a night light on and when nightmares came with horrible frequency. After such dreams it was hard to start a new day because of the emotional hangovers.

As adults, we too must contend with the terror of the night and the terror of the day. Every morning when we awake, the choice stands before us: fear or faith? Our enemies, however, become more real than children's fantasies. All of us, like the psalmist, face adversaries who challenge us, and the older we grow, the more numerous they become. We can identify with the complaint of this psalm: "Lord, how they have increased who trouble me!" (v. 1). This trouble may come from people who attack us, from supernatural spiritual opposition, or from our own emotional wounds.

Psalm 3 is a psalm of lament or complaint. For those who find its origins in the worship at the Jerusalem temple, the designation "royal protective psalm" may be useful. Its individual and situational aspects, however, cannot be denied. Enemies are multiplying (v. 1). Since God has checked them in the past (v. 7), the psalmist is unafraid as he faces opposition in the future (v. 6).

The traditional authorship and occasion are given in the subtitle "A Psalm of David when he fled from Absalom his son." There are valid arguments for this setting. The first is the increase in enemies. Absalom led a growing revolt against his father (2 Sam. 15:6). The second is the fact of the revolt itself: "Many are they who rise up against me" (v. 1; see 2 Sam. 15:12). The third is the justification for revolt by denying God's continuing presence with David (v. 2; cf. 2 Sam. 16:8). The fourth is the large number of opponents surrounding David in

military formation: "I will not be afraid of ten thousands of people /
Who have set themselves against me all around" (v. 6; see 2 Sam.
17:11, 24). The fifth is the call to God to go into battle with the reminder
of His past victories (v. 7).

Moreover, God is addressed in military images which come from a
soldier's heart. He is David's shield (v. 3), and the one who rises up
in battle (v. 7). David also cries to the Lord (v. 4) facing Zion where
he has left the ark of the covenant in his flight from Jerusalem (2 Sam.
15:24–29). There is even the distinct possibility that he offers this prayer
on the morning of the battle with Absalom (v. 5; cf. 2 Sam 17:27–29).

Setting this psalm in the context of David's heartbreak over his son's
civil war lends historical color and concreteness to its interpretation.
At the same time, the psalm could easily have been used before any
battle by the king or those in command. Moreover, it is now a psalm
for Israel and the church, universalized beyond that fateful day with
Absalom. As God's people, we all have our enemies and battles to fight.
So, while we accept the traditional ascription as probable and refer
this psalm to David himself, this is our psalm too.

Psalm 3 consists of two major sections. Verses 1–2 describe David's
dilemma. Verses 3–8 relate God's response. This includes both who
He is and what He will do.

HUMAN ADVERSITY

1 LORD, how they have increased who trouble me!
   Many *are* they who rise up against me.
2 Many *are* they who say of me,
   "*There is* no help for him in God."   Selah

   Ps. 3:1–2

Whenever adversity strikes we have a choice: we can turn from God
or we can turn to God. We can use suffering to justify unbelief, or
we can use suffering as a spur to belief. David leads our way; he turns
to the Lord in direct address.

First, David complains of the *increase* of his adversaries. The growing
opposition becomes overwhelming. Absalom's revolt has caught on, and
the nation follows him.

The price for leadership is loneliness. Harry Truman used to say,
"If you can't stand the heat, get out of the kitchen." We may not

lead nations, but if we take a bold stand for Christ our enemies will increase. Our families, our circle of friends, our business associates, our "public" will feel the effect.

Over a decade ago I was invited to teach in the religion department of a secular college. I was to be the "evangelical voice." My presence, however, was a threat to the "liberal" scholarly religious establishment. I was accused of brainwashing my students and using the lecture hall as an evangelistic platform. Ultimately, my role and my professional ability were vindicated, but only after a time of severe attack. Such opposition, however, does not simply come from the world. While I was serving a former parish, an adult Bible class saw my evangelistic ministry as a threat to the kind of church they wanted. Some, I found out later, began to circulate petitions asking the elders to remove me. Jesus promises, "In the world you will have tribulation" (John 16:33). So it always is for God's people—from the world or worldly Christians.

Along with the increase of his adversaries David experiences *assault* on his faith. In verse 1 he adds that many *"rise up against me,"* and say, *"There is no help* [yĕšû‘âh, salvation] *for him in God."* Thus the success of the opposition rallies others and justifies the charge: God has abandoned him. If the Lord has rejected David then the people are free to do so also.

The "bottom line" of our adversity lies not simply in the strength of our opponents but also in the charge "there is no help for him in *God.*" Here is the threat of practical atheism. It bears so many nuances. First of all, from God's side, practical atheism charges that God is impersonal, at best a "first cause." He is aloof; He doesn't care. Or God is so holy, He must be angry with us. Or, God is unable to help; He is weak and impotent. Second, from our side, practical atheism laments, "there is no help for *him* in God." We are too evil, too faithless, too unworthy—God certainly wouldn't help us! The consequences for us are clear. The first attack is that God has abandoned us; the second attack is that we aren't worth His attention anyway. The third attack is in the conclusion that we should give up our faith in Him and turn elsewhere for help.

Thus the skepticism of others and our own self-doubt do battle against the faith in our hearts. As the evil in the world explodes upon us, and as our own frailty and compromises become more and more evident, the lie "there is no help for him in God" sounds like the truth. If we are going to fight against this lie we must remember its origin. Jesus says of Satan, "He was a murderer from the beginning, and does not stand in the truth, because there is no truth in him. When he speaks a lie, he speaks from his own resources [or nature], for he is a liar and the father of it [or the father of lies]" (John 8:44). Our human attack against God, therefore, is ultimately satanic in its origin. Thus Paul exhorts the Ephesians to take "the shield of faith with which you will be able to quench all the fiery darts of the wicked one" (Eph. 6:16). This is exactly what David does in verse 3. We must turn from the lie to the living God.

THE DIVINE ANSWER

3 But You, O LORD, *are* a shield for me,
    My glory and the One who lifts up my head.
4 I cried to the LORD with my voice,
    And He heard me from His holy hill.   Selah
5 I lay down and slept;
    I awoke, for the LORD sustained me.
6 I will not be afraid of ten thousands of people
    Who have set *themselves* against me all around.
7 Arise, O LORD;
    Save me, O my God!
    For You have struck all my enemies on the cheekbone;
    You have broken the teeth of the ungodly.
8 Salvation *belongs* to the LORD.
    Your blessing *is* upon Your people.   Selah
                                        Ps. 3:3–8

David now moves from the character of his adversaries to the character of God: *"But You, O Lord"* (v. 3). As his eyes turn to the greatness of God, his fear is met by faith. He discovers what Corrie ten Boom witnessed in the Nazi concentration camp at Ravensbrook. When she and her sister were condemned to death for hiding Jews from the Gestapo, she said that in the depths of despair God was deeper still.

As David the warrior turns to the Lord, his mind is filled with military metaphors. First, God is his *"shield."* He protects him from his enemies' attack. Spiritual battles must be fought spiritually. David needs a physical shield to take the insurgent army's arrows, but he knows that armament alone guarantees nothing. Faith grows as David focuses on the protective power of God, a power that is also personal: *"You . . . are a shield for me."* The God who rules the stars guards the heart of David. He is that intimate, that close, that real.

Second, God is also David's provision, his victory, his glory. The word *"glory"* (*kābôd*) literally means "heavy." Troops going to battle went out light, and when they were victorious, they came back heavy, bringing the spoils with them. Thus they brought "glory" and they received "glory" for their triumph. In this battle the spoils, the "glory," is God's, not David's.

Third, God lifts David's head. The lowered head signifies shame and humility. Before his rebellion Absalom had been rejected by David and then restored to favor. This restoration is recorded in 2 Samuel 14:33: "He [Absalom] came to the king and bowed himself on his face to the ground before the king." What David did next lifted him up: "Then the king kissed Absalom."

Later David's head was lowered in shame by Absalom's revolt, but the God who protects and provides will go on to lift his head in triumph. David's dignity will be restored when the Lord wins the battle for him. God will do the same for us. In our battles He protects, He provides, and He lifts us up. As Peter writes, "But may the God of all grace, who called us to His eternal glory by Christ Jesus, after you have suffered a while, perfect, establish, strengthen, and settle you. To Him be the glory and the dominion forever and ever. Amen" (1 Pet. 5:10–11).

The sequence of action from verse 3 to verse 4 shows us a secret of effective prayer. We begin by worshiping the Lord and calling to mind His character. As we describe Him and remember what He has done, our faith grows. The vitality of our prayers will reflect our conception of God. Dr. Louis Evans, Jr., said of the great Christian educator Henrietta Mears that when she prayed she reached up to heaven and shook the throne of God. She prayed mighty prayers because she had a mighty God.

Thus David calls upon the Lord: *"I cried to the Lord with my voice, / And He heard me from His holy hill."* David's prayer is *audible.* He "cries out." If your mind wanders in prayer, try praying out loud. It is an excellent discipline; it will help keep you focused on the Lord. David's prayer is also *productive;* he "gets through"—God hears. There is a confidence that comes in prayer itself, not simply in answers to prayer. When we pray in faith and are open to the Holy Spirit we receive the assurance that God hears, that we are in communion with Him. Then, David's prayer is *directed* toward Mt. Zion, God's *"holy hill,"* where the presence of God is symbolized by the ark of the covenant. We now pray directed toward a person, the Lord Jesus Christ, rather than toward a place. His risen body is our temple. He is our mediator, and we have access to the Father in His name (see John 2:13–22).

Next, the consequences of David's cry to the Lord are sketched in verses 5–6. First, he is sustained in sleep: *"I lay down and slept; / I awoke.
. . ."* Sleep is the sign of God's peace. David is able to sleep because God is awake (Ps. 121:3–4), and he has given his burdens to Him. Now through the night David is kept by God: "He gives His beloved sleep" (Ps. 127:2). Then he awakens, *"for the Lord sustained me."* Thus this psalm is composed in David's morning devotions.

Second, David is now serene before his enemies: *"I will not be afraid of ten thousands of people, / Who have set themselves against me."* Here is the fundamental answer to prayer as David's faith triumphs over his fears. As is often said, God never promises to change our circumstances; God always promises to change us.

With the assurance of who God is and peace in his heart, David is ready for battle. He calls upon the Lord to fight and is confident of the outcome.

The call *"Arise, O Lord; / Save me, O my God"* is David's summons to God to go to war. It is Yahweh who fights Israel's battles. He is the "Commander of the army" (Josh. 5:14). Moreover, David, reminding God of His past victories, expects Him to inflict mortal head wounds: *"For You have struck all my enemies on the cheekbone."* In our battle against Satan, we also must remember that it is Christ, "the Seed of the woman" (Gen. 3:15), who mortally bruises the head of the serpent.

There are times in fighting spiritual enemies when we should exercise our authority in Christ and, calling on His name, rebuke the Evil One and his control. David calls out with a boldness bordering on presumption: *"Arise, O Lord; / Save me, O my God!"* But when we recognize that we have been given divine authority over even unclean spirits (Matt. 10:1; 28:18–20), we realize that not to command "Arise, O Lord" indexes our faithlessness and disobedience. When Paul was troubled in Philippi by a slave girl possessed with a spirit of divination, he addressed the spirit with holy boldness, "I command you in the name of Jesus Christ to come out of her" (Acts 16:18), and she was released that very hour. As Luther puts it in "A Mighty Fortress Is Our God":

> And tho' this world with devils filled
> Doth threaten to undo us;
> We will not fear for God hath willed
> His truth to triumph through us.

With the Lord going into battle, and the outcome secure, David now expresses his confidence: *"Salvation belongs to the Lord"* (v. 8). It is God who delivers the godly from their enemies and brings victory. But God's action is not only negative, in removing enemies; it is also positive, in giving blessing. Thus David concludes: *"Your blessing is upon Your people."* *"Blessing"* comes from God's bringing happiness and prosperity to the recipients of His power. David pronounces this blessing upon Israel as the result of God's grace to him.

Saving David from his enemies, then, is not an end in itself; it is for the sake of blessing the nation. So Christ saves us from sin, Satan, and death in order that we may be the means of blessing His body, the church, and the world for which He died.

Summarizing the movement of Psalm 3, we see the crisis of adversaries; the cry to the Lord; and the confidence that God hears, God answers, God fights the battle, God defeats our enemies, and God blesses His people. As we have already noted, David probably composed this psalm on the day of battle. This word of God to us is important because we too have our battles against Satan and all his minions. David shows us here who fights these battles for us, and how we are to fight. It is in prayer that we conquer when fear is met with faith. There is a moment when we break through to assurance and we know that God has heard. Then we are ready to command His deliverance and victory, confident that we are praying in His will. His salvation and blessing become not just ours, but His gift to all who walk with Him.

CHAPTER FOUR

Evening Devotions:
Security in Stress

Psalm 4

What is at stake in the Bible is not the philosophical question of the existence of God but the personal question of the character of God. The glory of the Bible is that it reveals the God who enters into relationships with His people. Martin Buber, the Jewish rabbi and theologian, describes Biblical faith as "dialogical." Here God is in constant communication with His people, and they with Him. From verse 1, where David calls upon God to hear him, to the final verse in which he expresses his profound confidence in his security in God, we feel the living relationship between the Lord and His servant. This very dynamic at times creates abrupt transitions, and changes in subject matter or mood. But this is not an artificial literary composition; rather it is personal communion in prayer.

While commentators often call Psalm 4 a lament, its major point is confidence in the character of God. God gives righteousness, relieves distress (v. 1), sets apart the godly (v. 3), hears prayer (v. 3), is trustworthy (v. 5), gives gladness (v. 7), peace (v. 8), and safety (v. 8). The title of Psalm 4 indicates that it was incorporated into Israel's public worship at an early date. While we may assume Davidic authorship, the specific circumstances for its composition, revealing the divine complaint against the sons of men (v. 2) and against the many who say "Who will show us any good?" (v. 6) are now lost. Traditionally, commentators have connected this psalm with Absalom's revolt, also the background for Psalm 3. From verse 4 we may surmise that this prayer was written at the end of the day: "Meditate within your heart on your bed, and be still" and verse 8, "I will both lie down in peace, and sleep." Thus as Psalm 3 is a devotional for the morning hour, Psalm 4 serves the same function for the evening hour.

The movement of thought in this psalm is from confidence that God hears and answers (vv. 1–3), to our calling to trust in the Lord (vv. 4–

5), a confession of faith in Him (vv. 6–8), and gladness in His presence that allows us to sleep in safety.

CONFIDENCE: THE LORD HEARS THE HOLY

1 Hear me when I call, O God of my righteousness!
   You have relieved me in my distress;
   Have mercy on me, and hear my prayer.
2 How long, O you sons of men,
   Will you turn my glory to shame?
   How long will you love worthlessness
   And seek falsehood?   Selah
3 But know that the LORD has set apart for Himself
      him who is godly;
   The LORD will hear when I call to Him.

Ps. 4:1–3

The emphasis by repetition in verses 1–3 is on God's hearing prayer: *"Hear me when I call. . . . Have mercy on me, and hear my prayer." "The Lord will hear when I call to Him."* Whatever the causes of the distress in verse 1, the answer lies in God's spoken word and in bold, believing prayer.

When David begins in verse 1 with a call upon God to hear Him, it's as if he has picked up the phone and said hello. At the same time, he identifies the One to whom he calls: *"O God of my righteousness!"*

"Righteousness" (*ṣedeq*) in the Old Testament is a rich and varied term. God is righteous because of His consistent and absolute action. He is His own standard of righteousness, and there is no greater measure. Righteousness implies relationship: God is righteous in that He keeps His covenant with His people, upholds His moral law, and fulfills His promises. Thus as "righteous," God is both our just judge and our savior.

David addresses God as *"my righteousness"* because it is God who has made His Covenant with him; it is God who has established his kingdom; it is God who has promised him a throne forever (2 Sam. 7:15–16). In a word, God is righteous and He has given His righteousness to David.

David's address, *"O God of my righteousness,"* also points to the final gift of righteousness given in Jesus Christ. It is Christ who is righteous because He has fulfilled the law in perfect obedience to the Father

46

(Matt. 5:17; Rom. 10:3–4). It is Christ who dies on the cross, not for His own sins (for He had none), but for our sins. When we receive Christ, we receive also His righteousness. Paul writes, "For He [God] made Him [Christ] who knew no sin to be sin for us, that we might become the righteousness of God in Him" (2 Cor. 5:21). God hears us when we call because we are clothed in the righteousness of Christ. Indeed, we all may say God is the "God of my righteousness."

David immediately reminds God of His past action: *"You have relieved me in my distress."* The root meaning of *"distress"* here is "to be bound, tied up, restricted," much like an army besieged on all sides by the enemy. God's "relief" is "to make room" by removing the restriction.

Since God has given relief before, David can expect relief again. His memory serves a twofold function. David holds God accountable from the past for His future action and, at the same time, he builds his own faith to expect help again. Here we see that power in prayer comes in part from our memories. Satan wants to make us forget the answers to prayer which we have already received. When I prepare to preach an evangelistic message, he whispers, "But what if no one responds?" Then I have to reply, "God saves people; I don't. And since He has answered my prayers and used me before, He will do so again." As we pray, we need to remember the track record of God's mighty works. Memory, however, is not presumption. So David cries, *"Have mercy on me, and hear my prayer."* Once again, he throws himself before the Lord.

Most commentators take verse 2 as the substance of David's complaint: *"How long, O you sons of men, / Will you turn my glory to shame?"* The context may be his son Absalom's revolt, especially since the term *"sons of men"* is technical, referring to the leaders of God's people. The *"shame"* (the Hebrew word may also mean *"worthlessness,"* and *"falsehood"*) would refer to their attack upon David which is at the same time an attack upon the God who made him king.

Another possibility is that verse 2 is a prophetic word from God given through David. If this is so, we have here a clear example of the dialogical nature of Scripture. David speaks. God answers. Perhaps David is tested indirectly by the Lord: Is he a part of the *"sons of men"* who turn God's glory into *"shame,"* who love *"worthlessness,"* and who seek *"falsehood"*? If so, why should he expect God to hear his prayer? Then, too, has not the whole chain of sin, going back to David's adultery with Bathsheba, led to the civil war which is an attack upon God's glory, creating such a sham in Israel?

The question "How long . . . / Will you turn my glory to shame? / How long will you love worthlessness / And seek falsehood?" still stands. The glory of His name embarrasses us and we in turn embarrass Him. *Christian*, literally, "little Christ," has become an empty word in our society's love of "the passing show," our care about image rather than substance. Our passion is the designer label rather than the design of the Lord. We live in the age of magazines called *People, Money,* and *Self.* Our "hype"-generation seems to want to be deceived by extravagant claims. Coffee, a stimulant, is sold to calm our nerves. Cancer-causing cigarettes are brand-named "Life." God is still asking, "How long. . . . How long?"

In verse 3 David responds to the question: *"But know that the Lord has set apart for Himself him who is godly."* Greater than the civil war, greater than David's sin, greater than the pursuit of worthlessness and falsehood, is God's call, God's claim upon his life. God has set him apart. He is *"godly"* (ḥāsîd, "kind, pious"). If God is his justification, his righteousness (v. 1), then God is also his sanctification (v. 3). David prays because God has set him apart. This defines his godliness, and this is the basis for his assurance: *"The Lord will hear when I call to Him."*

In verses 1–3, then, David addresses God in confidence. God is his righteousness, God has delivered him, God has set him apart. Whatever the denial of God, nothing can keep David from boldly coming to Him. In so doing, he is simply holding God to His own character, and calling upon the God who has already claimed him for Himself.

CALLING: THE GODLY TRUST THE LORD

> 4 Be angry, and do not sin.
>   Meditate within your heart on your bed, and be still.
>   Selah
> 5 Offer the sacrifices of righteousness,
>   And put your trust in the LORD.

> Ps. 4:4–5

David's confidence in God now leads to a series of exhortations: *"Be angry . . . do not sin. Meditate . . . be still. Offer the sacrifices . . . put your trust in the Lord."* All of this activity prepares us for the sleep mentioned in verse 8.

The first imperative, *"Be angry, and do not sin,"* seems strange until we remember that anger unexpressed yields many a restless night. We see too that God Himself is angry at the nations' idolatry and Israel's sin. Since anger is a divine attribute, it is not to be despised. God's anger, however, is moral. It is a consequence of His holiness when He encounters our unholiness. When we in turn express our anger against sin we identify with God's holiness. We also identify with God's mercy, knowing that Christ as the lamb of God has borne away sin. On a psychological level we release that anger to the Lord, which prepares us for restful sleep (cf. 8). Paul echoes David, " 'Be angry, and do not sin': do not let the sun go down on your wrath" (Eph. 4:26).

When our anger has been expressed and released, we are ready for the next imperative: *"Meditate within your heart on your bed, and be still."* As we turn from all of the injustice and rebellion of our world, our hearts are open to the Lord, His truth, His word, His will.

The phrase *"meditate within your heart"* employs the Hebrew verb (ʾāmar) which means "to consider, to reflect." We are to think carefully in our hearts in order to reach clear conviction. The verb is parallel to "meditate" (hāgâh) in Psalm 1:2. As we reflect, our minds actively consider the day now behind us, our plans for the future, our problems, our needs, and God's word in relation to all of this.

David continues, *"and be still."* After our minds have been active in meditation, we must stop and be silent. In the silence, God will speak to us. When, after a time of reflection, I am silent before the Lord, I find I am receptive to what God wants to say to me. I receive a phrase from Scripture, a directive or an impression from the Lord. Too often our prayer is one-way. We tell God what we want, we think over our problems, and then we complain that the Lord never speaks to us. Anthony Campolo says it's as if we called someone on the phone, talked a blue streak, and then hung up complaining of their silence, before they ever had a chance to say anything in return.

A friend of mine had terrible feelings of rejection from his angry father. As he sat before the Lord in prayerful silence, God spoke in an almost audible voice, "He's not angry, he's afraid." This word transformed their relationship. As we are *"still"* before the Lord, insight, direction, and healing will be ours.

Next David calls us to worship: *"Offer the sacrifices of righteousness."* The Hebrew verb used here for *"offer"* is the basic word for ritual sacrifice. In its noun form it means animal sacrifice. The literal execution of this command for "righteous sacrifice" would be to offer the proper slaughtered animal. Since this would be impossible while lying upon his bed, however, David is probably referring to the "sacrifices of joy" before the Lord (Ps. 27:6). The word of God leads to the worship of God. After we have praised Him, offering "the sacrifice of praise to God, that is, the fruit of our lips, giving thanks to His name" (Heb. 13:15), then we are ready to find our security in Him. Thus the final exhortation *"And put your trust in the Lord,"* or, literally, "upon" the Lord, is fulfilled. This is not merely an intellectual act. It is throwing ourselves upon God—all that we are, much as John leaned upon Jesus' breast (John 13:23).

In sum, our confidence is that God hears the ungodly, and our calling is to trust the Lord who hears. The road to trust is to express and clear our anger, engage our minds before the Lord, listen to Him in silence, respond in praise, and surrender afresh to His love and faithfulness. Here, indeed, are our evening devotions.

CONFESSION: SAFE IN THE LORD ALONE

6 *There are* many who say,
  "Who will show us *any* good?"
  LORD, lift up the light of Your countenance upon us.
7 You have put gladness in my heart,
  More than in the season that their grain and wine
    increased.
8 I will both lie down in peace, and sleep;
  For You alone, O LORD, make me dwell in safety.

Ps. 4:6–8

David's prayer is not ended with his call to trust in the Lord. The objection of the many now comes into his mind: *"Who will show us any good?"* It is great to withdraw into private spirituality, but what about all of the evil in the world? What of starvation, oppression of human rights, the arms race, the nuclear nightmare? What of the evil of the human heart with all of its manipulation and hidden agendas?

The cry to "show good," however, is not to be met here by promises of material prosperity, technological breakthroughs, or human compassion. The cry is met by a call: *"Lord, lift up the light of Your countenance upon us."* The ultimate good is no relative human advance. It is the goodness of God—His presence, the light of His countenance.

God's face is light. "God is light and in Him is no darkness at all"

(1 John 1:5). Jesus, the Son of God, declares, "I am the light of the world. He who follows Me shall not walk in darkness, but have the light of life" (John 8:12). Light communicates holiness, purity, and majesty, and light reveals. God is light both in His character as holy and in His person as revealer. The absence of goodness in this world, the darkness of sin and ignorance, is met in the light of God's countenance. As light, God dispels both our sin and our ignorance. Our good and the world's good are found in Him.

David continues in verse 7: *"You have put gladness in my heart."* The gladness is that God who is self-revealing fills our dark and empty hearts. It is grace: *"You have put."* God is always the initiator and provider. This is no scheme for self-help. God is light; the light shines and the gladness comes. As C. S. Lewis points out, we will never know joy by seeking it. Joy or gladness comes as a side-effect of the presence of the living God. When Lewis became a Christian, he was in his words "surprised by joy."

The joy of God's presence, David continues, is more than that of the harvest when *"grain and wine increased."* It is more because we are dealing with the Creator rather than the creation. It is more because we are dealing with a person rather than with things, with the Eternal Presence rather than with passing material gain. It is *God's* gladness that has invaded David's heart.

The consequences of this presence are sleep and serenity. David concludes: *"I will both lie down in peace, and sleep."* The stress is on *"peace"* (šālôm). Literally, he writes, "In peace—together I will lie down and sleep." Out of the assurance that God hears his prayer, and out of the worship and devotion of his heart, now peace and wholeness are David's as he surrenders to sleep, a sleep that comes from the security of Yahweh: *"For You alone, O Lord, make me dwell in safety."* It is only the Lord who can guard him through the night and fill him with His presence.

The phrase "dwell [lie down] in safety" is found repeatedly in the Old Testament (Isa. 14:30; Hos. 2:18; Deut. 12:10; Jer. 23:6). This security in the Lord is the substance of our confidence.

This psalm is a rewarding exercise for the evening. By following its guidelines and directive for devotion, it becomes a perfect prescription for peace. Out of a heart of trust in the Lord will result the serenity and joy of His effective presence. "The Lord will hear when I call. . . . put your trust in the Lord. . . . For You alone, O Lord, make me dwell in safety."

CHAPTER FIVE

Prayer for Protection

Psalm 5

We live in an age of flattery. Manipulation and deception are all-encompassing. Technicians, trained in the social sciences, mold people's values, tastes, and behaviors. With the wedding of psychology to mass communications, we are all subject to the exploitation of our fears for economic and political gain. It was Hitler who fused technology and propaganda to become the last twentieth-century European to command world history. His field general, Rommel, always traveled with a camera crew that sent daily newsreels back to the Third Reich. Hitler built an empire by deceiving untold millions. He made flattery an art, promising Germany a one-thousand-year empire. In our time, when a national hamburger chain claims in a glowing TV commercial "we do it all for you," we fail to resist. In fact, they don't do it all for *us*. They do it all for themselves, their management, their stockholders. Psalm 5 warns us against this deception, the violent abuse of words, the costumes that veil the heart's intentions (v. 9). This psalm is incredibly timely.

In a prayer of deep personal devotion, the psalmist moves between the polarities of God's absolute holiness and man's unmitigated sin. The psalm begins with an individual cry to the Lord (vv. 1–3) and ends with a comprehensive invitation to the faithful (vv. 11–12). What the psalmist experiences in his own worship, he then calls upon all the righteous to share.

Moreover, the descriptions of evil are profound. The broad canvas of the boastful, the workers of iniquity, those who speak falsehood, the bloodthirsty and deceitful in verses 5–6 finds its focus in verse 9 in those who have no faithfulness in their mouths. They are the psalmist's enemies—and ours as well.

Psalm 5 is often called a prayer of personal lament. While traditionally attributed to David, and certainly standing in this tradition, the mention of the temple (v. 7) which was built by his son Solomon seems to demand a later date. The reference to "morning" in verse 3 indicates that this psalm was written at the beginning of the day. The psalm begins with a cry to the Lord as King (vv. 1–3) and is followed by a contrast of the wicked and the righteous and a call for judgment of the wicked (vv. 4–10). The righteous, however, trust and rejoice in the Lord who blesses and protects them (vv. 11–12).

PERSONAL CALL: HEAR ME

1 Give ear to my words, O LORD,
    Consider my meditation.
2 Give heed to the voice of my cry,
    My King and my God,
    For to You I will pray.
3 My voice You shall hear in the morning, O LORD;
    In the morning I will direct *it* to You,
    And I will look up.

Ps. 5:1–3

The psalmist opens with a very personal cry. God is not merely to be felt, He is to be addressed. Our words directed to Him reopen the dialogue. We speak; God hears. His ear is inclined to us. We do not speak into space, we speak into the ear of the Lord.

The next phrase, *"Consider my meditation,"* can be more literally translated "Consider my groaning." If it is the latter, already the psalmist expresses his troubles in the opening address. His words to the Lord come in anguish.

Having mentioned God's ear, in verse 2 he now mentions his own voice. Here the anthropomorphic language keeps the prayer personal. He is not praying to "the Great Someone in the great somewhere." He lifts his voice to the ear of the living God, Yahweh, who is King in Israel (cf. 1 Sam. 8:7) and the source of all good things, including help in adversity. Note the boldness with which the psalmist addresses God as *"my King."* Here is both personal submission and confidence. Because our God reigns, we can come to Him when in trouble. He both hears and has the power to *act* since He is King.

As the psalmist continues, the new thought is the time notation *"in the morning."* Here is another psalm (cf. Ps. 3) for the beginning of the day. It is proper and important to begin the day asking the Lord to hear us and to protect us. God's guidance and care are extended as we present our agendas to Him. How presumptuous it is of us to expect to face our enemies without the Lord reigning over us and in us. As verse 3 concludes, the psalmist's gaze goes from earth to heaven, and his perspective is regained.

During the Second World War a U.S. arms plant was producing defective bomb sights. Sabotage was suspected. It was discovered, however, that the defects came because the employees were working so carefully on a small part that their eyes went out of focus. The remedy was for them to break periodically and look away at a distance to rest their eyes. Then their work became flawless. As we rest our souls, looking up to our King and God, whose ear is open to us, we have clear vision to face the battles of the day.

COMPREHENSIVE JUDGMENT: WHOM YOU DON'T HEAR

4 For You *are* not a God who takes pleasure in
    wickedness,
  Nor shall evil dwell with You.
5 The boastful shall not stand in Your sight;
  You hate all workers of iniquity.
6 You shall destroy those who speak falsehood;
  The LORD abhors the bloodthirsty and deceitful man.

Ps. 5:4–6

Next, the psalmist defines God over against the evil of this world. As he does this he also inventories his own heart, and implicitly distinguishes himself from the sinners who are not heard by the Lord.

There is a bold intimacy expressed in verse 4: *"For You are not a God who takes pleasure in wickedness."* It is solidly Biblical for God's people to remind Him of who He is and who He isn't. When the Lord threatens judgment upon Israel, Moses recalls His past dealings by praying, "Pardon the iniquity of this people . . . according to the greatness of Your mercy, just as You have forgiven this people, from Egypt even until now" (Num. 14:19). Certainly God doesn't have amnesia, and in His holiness He has every right to judge sin. When we recall His mercy in prayer, however, we establish in our hearts the basis upon which we seek and expect God's favor.

Nevertheless, by stressing God's holiness here, the psalmist calls upon the Lord to stand with him against his enemies. One by one those whom God opposes are listed in verses 4–6. First, God does not take *"pleasure"* in or delight in *"wickedness."* The noun here means "criminal acts." God opposes lawbreakers. He stands on the side of justice. Second, God does not allow evil in His presence: *"Nor shall evil dwell with You."* The Hebrew word used here for *"evil"* denotes a broad concept including "distress, injury, misery, calamity." It is anything other than God's holiness and perfection, and it is excluded from Him by definition. Third, neither will the boastful stand before God's gaze. "God resists the proud, / But gives grace to the humble" (1 Pet. 5:5, Prov. 3:34). Dwight L. Moody used to say, "In heaven there will be no self-made men." Fourth, God hates *"all workers of iniquity."* The hatred of God is not an irrational outburst, but God's moral response to our immorality, or, here, to those who do evil. The phrase *"workers of iniquity"* appears often in the individual psalms of lament. As a rule it means groups of people who scheme together, boast together, and use words as their evil weapons (see Ps. 64:2–4). This thought is picked up in verse 9. Fifth, God destroys liars (v. 6). In the context of verse 5, these are the workers of iniquity. The Hebrew verb for *"destroy"* is commonly used for destroying enemies in battle and the destruction of heathen cults. The Lord takes up arms in judgment against *"those who speak falsehood."* The ultimate source of the lie is Satan himself; in destroying liars, God rolls back his evil kingdom. Sixth, *"the Lord abhors the bloodthirsty and deceitful man."* The verb *"abhor"* refers to both ritual and ethical rejection. The *"bloodthirsty"* may be murderers or those who cause the death of the innocent by false testimony and lies.

Throughout this catalog of evil we have the strong ethical sense of God's holiness and judgment against human sin. God says no to wickedness, boasting, workers of iniquity, liars, and those who kill by deceit. Their prayers are not heard; their destruction is certain. The rejection of those who speak falsehood and deceive points to the exposition of the liars (v. 9) who are the psalmist's enemies and the subject of his lament. We too need to take moral inventory as we come before the holy God. What separates us from sinners, however, is not our righteousness but His mercy. God hears us, not because we are good, but because we have received the goodness of His Son.

PERSONAL PROMISE: MY WORSHIP AND OBEDIENCE

7 But as for me, I will come into Your house in the
   multitude of Your mercy;

In fear of You I will worship toward Your holy temple.
8 Lead me, O Lord, in Your righteousness because of
    my enemies;
Make Your way straight before my face.

Ps. 5:7–8

The psalmist now distinguishes himself from the unrighteous: *"But as for me."* The distinction lies, not in his righteousness, but in God's mercy. He prays, *"I will come into Your house in the multitude of Your mercy."* Entrance into God's house, God's temple, God's presence is based on divine grace, "abundant mercy" (*ḥesed*). His "covenant love," expressed in providing sacrifices for sins, is the grounds of our fellowship with Him. According to Hebrews, this is beautifully fulfilled in Christ who as our high priest enters into God's presence for us: "Not with the blood of goats and calves, but with His own blood He entered the Most Holy Place once for all, having obtained eternal redemption" (Heb. 9:12).

At the same time, God's mercy is no grounds for presumption: *"In fear of You I will worship toward Your holy temple"* (v. 7b). This *"fear"* is reverence before the holiness of God and wonder before His luminous power and awesome works. John experienced this fear when he saw a vision of the risen Christ and "fell at His feet as dead" (Rev. 1:17). The verb translated *"worship"* literally means "to bow down" in reverence and submission. It is an act of surrender.

Mercy, then, results in worship and worship results in obedience. So the psalmist prays: *"Lead me, O Lord, in Your righteousness because of my enemies."* When we are surrounded by liars and deceivers, it is only the Lord's guidance in His perfect will that keeps us from being seduced. Verse 8 concludes with a parallel request: *"Make Your way straight before my face."* Again God's righteousness is revealed in the straight way He makes before us. According to Romans 12:1–2, when we offer our bodies to the Lord as living sacrifices in worship, we then know the will of God, that which is good (moral), acceptable (agreeable), and perfect (growing us into maturity).

COMPREHENSIVE JUDGMENT:
DESCRIPTION AND DESTINY OF THE UNRIGHTEOUS

9 For *there is* no faithfulness in their mouth;
    Their inward part *is* destruction;

> Their throat *is* an open tomb;
> They flatter with their tongue.
> 10 Pronounce them guilty, O God!
> Let them fall by their own counsels;
> Cast them out in the multitude of their transgressions,
> For they have rebelled against You.
>
> *Ps. 5:9–10*

Now the general indictment of verses 4–6 becomes specific. Verse 9 describes the enemies and verse 10 gives their ultimate destiny. It is as if the psalmist becomes a prosecuting attorney whose central charge against the guilty is lying.

The *"mouth,"* the *"inward part,"* the *"throat,"* and the *"tongue"* are all named as vehicles of deception. The absence of *"faithfulness"* or steadfastness is covered up by flattery. The interior destruction and death, the depths of depravity, represented by the jolting metaphor of the throat as *"an open tomb,"* are all disguised by smooth words. We are reminded of Jesus' attack on the Pharisees and His description of them as "whitewashed tombs . . . full of dead men's bones" (Matt. 23:27).

Verse 9 brings us to the central issue of this psalm. No wonder the psalmist groans and cries for help; no wonder he addresses God as the One who destroys those who speak falsehood and who abhors deceitful men; no wonder he prays for the Lord to reveal His way and guide him in it. His enemies come with murderous hearts and words that are not to be trusted; they manipulate the truth for their own gain. Behind the disguise of life lies death. Only the light of God can protect the psalmist in the midst of such illusion and confusion.

Verbal violence is as much an epidemic for us as it was for ancient Israel, and we, too, fail to see the depths behind the cunning. Programed hype, the slick sale, the unkept promise, the false hope, the seduction—all these and more mask not simply political lies or useless products, but death itself. With our minds filled with verbal and visual nonsense, we find ourselves distracted from the real questions of life—our meaning and destiny. "The Devil's shining light / It can be most blinding" (Bob Dylan).

Thus the call in verse 10 for judgment is in order: *"Pronounce them guilty, O God!"* It is God alone who can see the heart, who is righteous in declaring His judgments. The prosecutor asks a sentence of ultimate irony: that the guilty *"fall by their own counsels."* Those who deceive will thus become the prisoners of their own deception as they begin to believe their own lies and their own counsels cannot hold them up. This same passive wrath of God is described in Romans 1. God gives us up to our own sin as a sign of His "no" against us.

The further call is for God to drive away the deceivers. Since they have rebelled against Him, He now should reject them, sunk *"in the multitude of their transgressions"* (v. 10).

This verse describes the downward spiral of judgment. First comes the sentence: "Guilty." The execution follows—the passive wrath of "stewing in their own juice" until the active wrath of final expulsion. This is the awful destiny of those who cover the tomb of their hearts by flattery.

COMPREHENSIVE INVITATION:
CALL AND CONFIDENCE OF THE RIGHTEOUS

11 But let all those rejoice who put their trust in You;
Let them ever shout for joy, because You defend them;
Let those also who love Your name
Be joyful in You.
12 For You, O LORD, will bless the righteous;
With favor You will surround him as *with* a shield.

Ps. 5:11–12

This psalm ends on a note of holy hilarity. In contrast to the liars, there are the joyful. True joy, a spontaneous expression of the heart, comes from those who, in verse 11, *"put their trust in [the Lord]."* To trust in God means to trust in the One who is faithful and true. In Him there is no deception, only security and stability. Those who trust in the Lord are to shout for joy because they are defended (literally, "covered") by the living God. It is He who protects them from their enemies' deception. This should lead to perpetual, expansive, vocal delight: *"Let them ever shout for joy."*

True joy comes from God's faithfulness and God's protection, all summed up in God's name. That name reveals the character of God, the nature of God and personhood of God. To call upon His name in prayer is to actualize His presence, and to be in His presence is joy itself. Here love is fulfilled before the beloved.

Finally, verse 12 gives the grounds for loving the name of God: *"For*

You, O Lord, will bless the righteous." All of God's bounty is for the righteous, for those who receive His mercy and respond in worship and obedience (vv. 7, 8). Like a *"shield"* of protection, the *"favor"* of the Lord will *"surround"* those who trust in Him. Blessing and *"favor"* are for those who love the name of the Lord.

Psalm 5, then, is a prayer for protection from deception. It is only before the one true God, in submission to Him and in worship, that we will find the truth and be defended from the deception of Satan and his apostles of death. It is God who by His Spirit crushes the lies about us, establishing us steadfastly in Himself. Since God is reality, He makes us real. This is the favor which surrounds us "as with a shield."

CHAPTER SIX

Prayer for Healing

Psalm 6

Health care is a major issue in our culture today. With an estimated 10 percent of the gross national product going to the medical field, it seems obvious we are a nation preoccupied with getting well. While the church pioneered the establishment of mission hospitals, the issue of God's healing has been largely abandoned by Christians, being deferred to doctors and psychiatrists. "Faith healers" have operated in the Pentecostal tradition, but they have been viewed with extreme skepticism by the mainline churches. The suspicion of theatrics, emotional manipulation, and the use of mob psychology have left most Christians disenfranchised from God's healing power administered through prayer.

For ancient Israel, however, God's activity in our physical lives was not remote. There are at least two reasons for this. First, human nature was viewed holistically. The mind-body dualism of Plato was unknown

59

to the Hebrews, who saw our moral, spiritual, emotional, and physical parts as all interrelated. Second, the Bible makes an absolute connection between the fall of man, the disordering of a good creation, and divine judgment. It was common in Jewish theology to see illness as a result of sin (John 9:2). For example, during the exodus, God unleashed boils upon Egypt as a part of the plagues (Exod. 9:9). Moreover, Satan also employs illness and demonic attack to destroy God's people (Job 2:7; Mark 1:21–28). This means, however, that when God lifts His judgment and defeats Satan, healing is a part of His salvation. Again, during the exodus, God promised Israel, "I will put none of the diseases on you which I have brought on the Egyptians. For I am the Lord who heals you" (Exod. 15:26). Moreover, when Jesus came as God's Messiah, announcing the kingdom of God, creation began to be restored to its original order and goodness. Thus Jesus rolled back Satan's domain by healing disease and delivering those who are demon-possessed. When illness strikes, it seems proper for God's people to cry out to Him for His healing touch. This is exactly what the writer of this psalm does.

An individual prayer for healing, Psalm 6 is called a "lament" by commentators and is traditionally ascribed to David. The petitions here relate to both internal illness (v. 2) and external enemies (vv. 7–8, 10). The reference to "all night" may mean that this is a morning psalm similar to Psalms 3 and 5. This prayer reflects severe pain, deep depression, and, at the same time, faith and relief in the presence of God. It moves from a call for healing (vv. 1–5), to complaint (vv. 6–7), to resolution (vv. 8–10).

A CALL TO GOD

1 O LORD, do not rebuke me in Your anger,
  Nor chasten me in Your hot displeasure.
2 Have mercy on me, O LORD, for I *am* weak;
  O LORD, heal me, for my bones are troubled.
3 My soul also is greatly troubled;
  But You, O LORD—how long?
4 Return, O LORD, deliver me!
  Oh, save me for Your mercies' sake!
5 For in death *there is* no remembrance of You;
  In the grave who will give You thanks?

Ps. 6:1–5

Verse 1 begins with a surprising cry: *"O Lord, do not rebuke me in Your anger."* Why does David need to deflect God's wrath as he prays? One possibility, of course, is that he sees his illness as a sign of God's judgment against his sin. Or, David may simply be affirming that while as a sinner he deserves punishment, he will ask for mercy (see v. 2). A further possibility is that he fears that in asking for healing he may be fighting the will of God which is revealed in the suffering he now experiences. If this is true, the intention of verse 1 would be: "O Lord, don't be angry with me as I pray for healing—as I ask for a change in Your will toward me."

Whatever the cause of David's plea, his focus is on God's wrath as he begins his prayer. He employs two basic Hebrew words for divine judgment: *"anger"* and *"hot displeasure."* The former word comes from a root meaning both "anger" and "nose"; there is a clear connection between anger and the "blast of breath" or snorting of Psalm 18:15. The latter word is derived from the verb "to be hot"; God's anger burns.

The wrath of God is a consequence of His covenant with Israel. God's saving relationship with His people demands their obedient response; thus His anger is kindled when the covenant is broken. In Psalm 6, however, His wrath is remedial rather than punitive.

When David asks that God not *"rebuke"* him, it is in the sense of "correct" him in His anger or *"chasten"* ("discipline") him in His displeasure. Rather, he prays in verse 2 that the Lord's grace may come upon him: *"Have mercy on me, O Lord."* As the parallel phrase suggests, this mercy will specifically manifest itself in healing: *"O Lord, heal me."*

The basis for this prayer is twofold. The first is God's mercy, which triumphs over His wrath. The second is David's condition: *"I am weak . . . my bones are troubled."*

Already debilitated through physical illness, David finds that his *"soul"* (*nepeš*) or his *"self"* is also *"troubled."* The Hebrew verb is strong, meaning "terrified." David is sick in his whole person: his bones are terrified; his soul is terrified. Every aspect of his being is gripped by illness and fear. Later, we will see that his mind is on death and that he groans and cries all night as illness consumes him.

In reading this description we think of cancer patients today. When tumors begin to grow, especially in the colon, weight loss sets in and dull and intense pain is always present. Initial anger gives way to depression, and guilt may also be present because of the demands made on loved ones and their grief at impending death. I experienced all of this with the loss of my father-in-law who died at fifty-two years of age. Cancer has also struck other close relatives and church members. The question can easily come: "What have I done to deserve this?" Now we can identify with the opening of this psalm: *"O Lord, do not rebuke me in Your anger."*

In the midst of pain, however, David's heart is lifted to the Lord. As we have seen, he considers God's wrath, but calls upon God's mercy. Then he simply cries out, *"But You, O Lord—how long?"* (v. 3). This haunting question stands unanswered at this point. Here we are given permission to question God, permission to cry out in our pain. If our prayers are not honest they are not prayers.

Now David calls upon the Lord to come again to Him: *"Return, O Lord, deliver me! / Oh, save me."* Notice the sequence. David, in his pain, has felt the absence of God. Now, however, he calls upon the Lord to return as his first request. Next, he prays for release from the sickness of body and soul, along with a parallel call: *"Oh, save me for Your mercies' sake."* Salvation here embraces the whole person and is grounded in Yahweh's "mercy," His covenant love. Thus when Jesus comes healing the sick, he can say, "Your faith has saved you," or "Your faith has made you well" (Mark 5:34). Salvation, as we have seen, is not merely release from sin but includes the restoration of the fallen creation, which means physical healing as well.

Next, David appeals for healing not only because of God's mercy and his need, but because of the finality of death. God is to be remembered for His mighty works and worshiped as the proper response to that memory. Death, however, blots out the memory and the worship. So David reminds the Lord: *"For in death there is no remembrance of You; / In the grave who will give You thanks?"* (v. 5).

This verse witnesses to the progressive nature of Biblical revelation. Its truth lies in its affirmation of the importance of this life and the denial of reincarnation or mere "soul survival" as offering meaning beyond the grave. Its limitation, however, lies in David's ignorance of the resurrection and the reality of the re-creation of all things in Christ. Only as the full course of revelation unfolds does this truth become clear. Biblical hope is not in mere immortality but in resurrection, grounded not in a doctrine of an indestructible soul, but in the event of Easter. So Paul writes, "But now Christ is risen from the dead, and has become the firstfruits of those who have fallen asleep. For since by man came death, by Man also came the resurrection of the dead.

For as in Adam all die, even so in Christ all shall be made alive" (1 Cor. 15:20–22). It is in Christ that the memory and praise of God transcends death. It is only in Christ that we shall "never die" (John 11:26).

Here in David's call for healing we have both the terror of sickness and confidence in God's mercy to save. In our mortality we know the terror, but in our faith we can know God's power to restore us. Prayer is the power point, bringing the healing of God's Spirit to the wounds of our lives.

COMPLAINTS OF ILLNESS

6 I am weary with my groaning;
   All night I make my bed swim;
   I drench my couch with my tears.
7 My eye wastes away because of grief;
   It grows old because of all my enemies.

Ps. 6:6–7

In these two verses David elaborates on his emotional state and introduces a new thought. Not only does he experience pain; he has enemies as well.

To begin with, David expresses the toll pain takes. He is weary with his groaning. Here is a mini-exposition on the thought in verse 2: "I am weak." Next, his nights are sleepless: *"All night I make my bed swim; / I drench my couch with my tears."* Literally, he causes his bed to float in his tears. Thus sleepless weeping is added to the groans. The downward spiral is only intensified by losing the restoration that rest can bring.

"My eye wastes away because of grief; / It grows old" (v. 7). The loss of vision, related to the sickness and the crying, represents weakness and illness (cf. Matt. 6:22–23) and is caused by *"grief,"* also translated "vexation" or "anger." This deep emotional distress has come from the sense of God's absence, the consuming illness, and the enemies who use David's debilitation to attack him. It is ironic that when we are down, others often exploit our situation like sharks going for blood.

Verses 6–7 portray the emotional anatomy of all illness—groaning, crying, sleepless nights, outside attacks. What else can David do but call upon the Lord?

63

Newfound Confidence

8 Depart from me, all you workers of iniquity;
　For the Lord has heard the voice of my weeping.
9 The Lord has heard my supplication;
　The Lord will receive my prayer.
10 Let all my enemies be ashamed and greatly troubled;
　Let them turn back *and* be ashamed suddenly.

Ps. 6:8–10

Now the mood changes, and David rallies. The very prayer itself has done its work. David has opened himself up to the Lord, expressing his fears of God's wrath and silence and asking "How long?" In cataloging his symptoms—weakness, troubled bones, troubled soul, fear of death, groaning, weeping, sleeplessness, dimmed eyesight—and in addressing his enemies, he has released his anger and despair. At the same time, he has confessed his faith in the living God. The Lord is merciful, the Lord heals, the Lord returns, the Lord remembers His covenant love.

Out of this comes a new strength, and in verse 8 David commands: *"Depart from me, all you workers of iniquity."* God has answered David's prayer! The phrase *"workers of iniquity"* appears in many individual psalms of lament (see Ps. 5:5). Here they are those who harm a sick man for their own advantage. David can order them away because *"the Lord has heard the voice of [his] weeping."* With the Lord's ear open to him and His love upon him, David now has strength against those abusing him.

Not only has God heard David's weeping, He has also heard his *"supplication."* The noun used here means "request for favor or grace." The cry for healing and salvation has been accepted by the Lord—God has heard and He *will* hear: *"The Lord will receive my prayer."*

With new strength, with health on its way, with release from grief and depression, David ends this psalm by cursing his enemies: *"Let all my enemies be ashamed and greatly troubled"* (v. 10). The request that his enemies be *"ashamed"* is motivated not so much by revenge as by the desire that by his recovery their falsehood will be seen. In attacking David they have attacked the living God. In seeing David's sickness as God's judgment, they have failed to see God's mercy and His covenant love. Thus instead of David's bones and soul being troubled, his enemies will be troubled. Again he prays, *"let them turn back and be ashamed suddenly."* As they *"turn back"* or "repent" from their falsehood and their evil and see God's salvation for David, shame will come upon them dramatically. Thus God will be glorified in David's healing and delivery. Indeed, God will be known as Yahweh "your healer" (Exod. 15:26, NASB).

There is much we can learn from Psalm 6 about praying for the sick. First of all, the chain of sin, sickness, and judgment can be broken. While it is true that we reap what we sow (Gal. 6:7), God is fully able and desirous of breaking that chain. Beyond His judgment is His mercy. When He comes to us in His Son, He is full of "grace and truth" (John 1:14). Thus as we pray for healing, like David, we are to focus on the mercy and the love of God.

Next, most illness is complex, and the physical ailment often comes from spiritual and emotional pain. When bodies and spirits are troubled (as in vv. 2–3) healing must include both the physical and the spiritual. It is important to pray for relief from pain. But unless there is also prayer for "inner healing," only the symptoms may be alleviated.

Furthermore, correct diagnosis for healing is important. We must lay out all our symptoms before the Lord in honesty and open ourselves totally to the healing power and the love of God.

We must also rebuke any external enemies with faith and boldness. Christ has come to give us authority over our enemies, who are His enemies. He silences the demons, and in His name we can order away all evil powers: "Depart from me, all you workers of iniquity" (v. 8).

Finally, as we pray we are to trust the healing hand of God upon us. David confesses, "The Lord has heard my supplication; / the Lord will receive my prayer" (v. 9). We may not see an immediate change as we pray. Keep on praying! Keep on trusting! As Francis McNutt teaches, often healing is progressive as more of God's power through prayer is focused on our sickness.

Today God is restoring His healing ministry to the church. Jesus' simple promise that those who believe "will lay hands on the sick, and they will recover" (Mark 16:18) is more and more the experience of Christians who take God at His word and step out in faith. In our own church we are increasingly seeing people healed and improved through prayer. Why? Because we are praying for more people, knowing that Christ has come to save us, restoring His creation—soul and body. Thus He makes all things new (Rev. 21:5).

CHAPTER SEVEN

Prayer for Justice

Psalm 7

"Treaties are made to be broken." In the realm of politics, this cynical saying is the rule rather than the exception. There is nothing more common than for a new government to invalidate the order and arrangements of the past. Since nations are self-serving, their own interests, rather than justice or morality, determine which commitments they will keep. In our century Hitler littered the European landscape with broken and renounced treaties as he devoured a continent. International law was meaningless. As Herman Goering put it, "The law and the will of the Führer are one."

While this self-serving morality dominates international relationships, it is also true today in business. A friend told me that there isn't a contract that cannot be broken. When there is no longer any sense of justice, moral responsibility, or accountability, the societal order and individual relationships collapse.

Psalm 7 addresses the issue of injustice. Using a mixture of images from the court of law and the battlefield, the psalmist responds to the unjust attack of his enemies by inviting God's intervention and resolution. Above our lives in this world stands the eternal God. He is the righteous judge. When we bring our case to Him, He answers.

The psalmist speaks of "those who persecute," of "enemies," and of the "wicked." They want to rip him up "like a lion," they "rage," they do "wickedness," they bring forth "iniquity," conceive "trouble," and bear "falsehood." Moreover, these enemies claim that the psalmist has "iniquity in [his] hands," that he has "repaid evil" to him who was at peace with him and that he has "plundered [his] enemy without cause." Thus it is before God that he brings his case and asks for vindication.

Commentators identify this psalm as a psalm of individual lament. Tradition, which we follow, ascribes it to David. The psalm moves from a cry for deliverance (vv. 1–2) to a confession of righteousness (vv. 3–5), a call for judgment and salvation (vv. 6–10), a confession of

God's justice and a curse on the wicked (vv. 11–16), and ends with a commitment to worship (v. 17).

CALL FOR DELIVERANCE

1 O LORD my God, in You I put my trust;
   Save me from all those who persecute me;
   And deliver me,
2 Lest they tear me like a lion,
   Rending *me* in pieces, while *there is* none to deliver.

Ps. 7:1–2

Verse 1 begins then with a confession and a call which both reveals the character of God and David's relationship with Him: *"O Lord my God."* The possessive pronoun *"my"* reveals that Yahweh is personal to David. For this reason, he calls Him by name and claims intimacy with Him. *"In You I put my trust"* literally means "In You I took refuge." As he might flee for security to a fortress or a cave, David flees to the Lord.

Because God is trustworthy, David can pray, *"Save . . . and deliver."* The call for salvation is the call for liberation or rescue. The verb translated *"save"* means "to give width and breadth, to give space." The Lord is called into battle here to give David breathing room, to establish his space against those who persecute him or, literally, "pursue" him. The parallel phrase, calling upon God to *"deliver"* him, employs a verb that can be used for taking prey out of the mouth of an animal. David uses this very verb when he recalls that as a shepherd he rescued a lamb from the lion's mouth: "I . . . delivered the lamb from its mouth; and when it arose against me, I caught it by its beard, and struck and killed it" (1 Sam. 17:35). Verse 2 employs this same image for David's deliverance from his enemies: *"Lest they tear me like a lion, / Rending me in pieces, while there is none to deliver."*

David's call for deliverance is based upon God's faithfulness, love, and power to rescue. David relies upon the character of God to face his enemies.

CONFESSION OF DAVID'S RIGHTEOUSNESS

3 O LORD my God, if I have done this:
   If there is iniquity in my hands,

4 If I have repaid evil to him who was at peace with
   me,
  Or have plundered my enemy without cause,
5 Let the enemy pursue me and overtake *me;*
  Yes, let him trample my life to the earth,
  And lay my honor in the dust.   Selah

Ps. 7:3–5

But why should God deliver David? If he has sinned, should not his sins find him out? How can a just God not allow His judgment to come upon David? There are, of course, several answers to this question. Beyond the justice of God is the mercy of God. David himself has experienced God's forgiveness. Here, however, David knows that his enemies lie and that he has not acted unjustly. Thus in good conscience he calls upon God, not for mercy for his sin, but for his vindication.

Verses 3–5 are an oath, structured in a familiar formula: "If I have done this, then let this happen to me." Using the same personal address as in verse 1, *"O Lord my God,"* he is ready to stand naked before the God who searches all things.

The content of the charge against him is now revealed. The general complaint—that *"there is iniquity in [his] hands"*—is detailed in the specific accusations that he has repaid evil to his friends and plundered his enemies without cause. The purpose of this charge is evidently to sow seeds of suspicion among those who trust him. Questions fill the air: "Is he really honoring his treaty?" "Will he keep our covenant?" In today's terms, "Will he fulfill the contract?" "When the chips are down will he turn his back on us?"

Not only is David accused with undercutting his allies; second, he has *"plundered"* (or, better, "delivered") his enemies *"without cause."* The Hebrew here is literally translated "I have even delivered him who was my foe carelessly." This means that David was treacherous toward his allies by double-dealing with their enemies. He changed alliances and rescued those with whom he should have been at war. Thus the balance of power has secretly been changed.

David now responds to the charges in verse 5 with battle imagery. If he is guilty as charged, he calls upon God to execute judgment against him by sending an enemy army who will chase him, run him down, and roll over him. His curse concludes by calling upon the enemy to *"lay [his] honor in the dust."* David's *"honor"* (*kābôd,* "glory") is all the fame and accomplishment of his life which evoke praise (see 1 Sam. 18:7).

Having asserted his innocence and having prayed for deliverance, he is ready for judgment. Opening himself up to God's retribution, David now calls upon God to act directly.

CALL FOR JUDGMENT

6 Arise, O LORD, in Your anger;
  Lift Yourself up because of the rage of my enemies;
  Rise up for me *to* the judgment You have
      commanded!
7 So the congregation of the peoples shall surround You;
  For their sakes, therefore, return on high.
8 The LORD shall judge the peoples;
  Judge me, O LORD, according to my righteousness,
  And according to my integrity within me.

Ps. 7:6–8

Wisely, David does not take judgment into his own hands. After all, only God can judge absolutely, for only God sees the heart, and only God is totally righteous: " 'Vengeance is Mine, I will repay,' says the Lord" (Rom. 12:19). David pictures God rising from His throne: *"Arise, O Lord, in Your anger."* In like manner, Psalm 76:8–9 relates, "The earth feared and was still, when God arose to judgment." Later Isaiah prophesies, "They shall go into the holes of the rocks . . . from the terror of the Lord and the glory of His majesty, when He arises to shake the earth" (2:19).

In the next phrase, David calls for God to meet with His own anger the anger of David's enemies: *"Lift Yourself up because of the rage of my enemies."* God's wrath is His moral response to our immorality. The KJV conclusion *"And awake for me"* is probably better here than the NKJV in indicating a call for God to rouse Himself to action. All the verbs in the verse are thus a strong plea for God to move: *"Arise . . . lift Yourself up . . . awake."*

The object of David's call is given at the end of verse 6: he desires *"the judgment You [God] have commanded."* It is God who is just and God, therefore, who is the judge of all things and who commands judgment.

As God opens His court, the peoples are gathered: *"So the congregation of the peoples shall surround You"* (v. 7). The plural suggests more than simply Israel. (A significant parallel occurs in Matthew 25:32, where

Jesus gathers the nations for judgment.) The text continues: *"For their sakes, therefore, return on high."* A more literal rendering translates this phrase "And over it [the congregation of the peoples] return on high." Thus David summons the Lord to sit in judgment upon all peoples, a thought that is restated in verse 8, *"The Lord shall judge the peoples."* Here David is careful to include himself: *"Judge me, O Lord, according to my righteousness, / And according to my integrity within me."*

This universal call to judgment is not fearful for David. He has already asserted his innocence and called down judgment upon himself if he is guilty. The standard here is his own conscience, his own motivation— *"my righteousness . . . my integrity within me."*

We may well marvel that David can present himself before God so freely, invoke His judgment, and be so certain of his innocence. In observing this, however, we must remember the context. David is not pleading that he has led a totally righteous life or calling upon God to bring in the final judgment. He is only asking for a limited judgment against the lies concerning his supposed injustices toward his friends and enemies.

The thought at the beginning of verse 8, *"The Lord shall judge the peoples,"* reminds us of a deeper truth: all of God's judgments in this life are dress rehearsals for the final judgment. God Himself is the goal of history. Indeed, we will all finally stand before Him. He will try the secrets of our hearts and reward or punish us according to our deeds. But the good news now is that Christ "became for us wisdom from God—and righteousness . . ." (1 Cor. 1:30). Our judge has become our Savior and we stand in Him.

CALL FOR SALVATION

> 9 Oh, let the wickedness of the wicked come to an end,
>   But establish the just;
>   For the righteous God tests the hearts and minds.
> 10 My defense *is* of God,
>   Who saves the upright in heart.
>
> *Ps. 7:9–10*

Having invited God's judgment, David now cries out for resolution. He invokes the Lord to deal with both the wicked and the righteous. God does not merely pronounce His sentence—He executes it as well. When David prays, *"Oh, let the wickedness of the wicked come to an* end" (v. 9), he knows it is God, not he, who will terminate the lies and attacks. David cannot commit his case to the Lord and then execute his own judgment. Just so, we too, having put our lives in the Lord's hands, must wait upon Him.

At the same time, David expects his own vindication. He continues: *"But establish the just"* (ṣaddȋq, "the righteous"). David has righteousness because God is righteous and, therefore, he is confident before the righteous God: *"For the righteous God tests the hearts and minds* [literally, the "hearts and kidneys," considered by the Hebrews to be the organs of thinking and feeling and thus the whole person]" (v. 9).

This prayer is only fully answered in Christ. When David prays *"But establish the just"* before the God who is just, we find so much sin in our lives that we cannot join him here. Take heart! This prayer is Christ's (Bonhoeffer). He is the spotless Lamb (1 Pet. 1:19). In Him we are righteous. In Him we are established. For God "made Him who knew no sin to be sin for us, that we might become the righteousness of God in Him" (2 Cor. 5:21).

David concludes: *"My defense* ["shield"] *is of* ["upon"] *God"* (v. 10). God, as his defense, either holds his shield or is his shield, protecting him from his enemies. Next, David confesses that this God *"saves the upright in heart."* As he has prayed in verse 1, "Save me," he knows that it is God's nature to save the one whose heart is "straight" or "upright." Our God protects us like a shield and delivers us like a warrior. As Jesus teaches us to pray, "Lead us not into temptation, but deliver us from evil" (Matt. 6:13, KJV).

I remember walking down Forty-second Street in New York one wintry night years ago. Pornographic stores were everywhere and it was tempting to go inside to escape the cold. Suddenly I saw a little lady standing in the snow with a sign. It read: "If we walk in the light as He is in the light, we have fellowship with one another, and the blood of Jesus Christ His Son cleanses us from all sin" (1 John 1:7). She was my angel. As I read her sign the Holy Spirit filled my heart. The moral battle was over. With joy and praise I went my way. The Lord had protected me and delivered me. *"My defense is of God, / Who saves the upright in heart."*

CONFESSION OF GOD'S RIGHTEOUSNESS

11 God *is* a just judge,
And God is angry *with the wicked* every day.

12 If he does not turn back,
   He will sharpen His sword;
   He bends His bow and makes it ready.
13 He also prepares for Himself instruments of death;
   He makes His arrows into fiery shafts.

Ps. 7:11–13

Having asserted his own righteousness, David once again confesses the righteousness of God. God is a *"just judge"* who is *"angry with the wicked every day."* The word translated here as *"angry"* has the connotation of "curse," meaning that God punishes the wicked continually, *"every day."*

David seals the idea of God's judgment with an image of God as an avenging warrior, but begins it with a qualifier: *"If he does not turn back."* Judgment is reserved for an unrepentant spirit. God always remains just. Like the father of the prodigal son, He welcomes us home if we return. But if we continue in sin, God prepares for battle in order to execute His sentence. Like a soldier getting ready for combat, *"He will sharpen His sword; He bends His bow and makes it ready. He also prepares for Himself instruments of death; He makes His arrows into fiery shafts."* Armed with a sharp sword, ready bow, and flaming arrows, God is ready to carry out His judgment. Indeed, it is a fearful thing for unrepentant sinners to fall into the hands of the living God.

This is not merely a primitive, Old Testament picture of God. The New Testament also warns of severe judgment to come (see 2 Cor. 5:10–11). No wonder the call to repent is a loving call. Without it we have no hope.

CONDEMNATION OF UNRIGHTEOUSNESS

14 Behold, *the wicked* brings forth iniquity;
   Yes, he conceives trouble and brings forth falsehood.
15 He made a pit and dug it out,
   And has fallen into the ditch *which* he made.
16 His trouble shall return upon his own head,
   And his violent dealing shall come down on his own
      crown.

Ps. 7:14–16

The issue of the psalm now becomes clear. In a rough image David sees his enemy pregnant with iniquity in verse 14: *"Behold, the wicked brings forth* [KJV, conceives] *iniquity."* The Hebrew word here is closely associated with "deception," "vanity," and "deceit" in the Old Testament. Thus iniquity *"conceives trouble"* ("mischief") and then bears *"falsehood."* Here we see how the lies saying David is treacherous toward his friends have caused him to express his anguish in this psalm.

Judgment, however, is certain. And the God who executes judgment will allow David's enemy to fall by his own weight. *"He made a pit and dug it out, / And has fallen into the ditch which he made"* (v. 15). The very pit that he dug for David will, much like an animal trap, instead trap him, and his *"violent dealing"* ("hate"), coming from false accusation, *"shall come down on his own crown."* God executes His judgment now by letting sin run its course. This is His passive wrath (see Rom. 1:18 ff.) whereby He gives us over to our sin and we are destroyed by it. As Paul reminds us in Galatians 6:7, "God is not mocked; for whatever a man sows, that he will also reap." However difficult it is to see at times, there is a judgment of peoples and nations *in history.* Hitler proclaimed his Thousand-Year Reich, but within a few fleeting years, Germany lay in ruins and he had his own personal holocaust in Berlin as the Russians advanced on the city. Caesar called himself a god, but today his Colosseum stands gutted and a simple cross planted in the foundations reminds us that "Jesus is Lord." Indeed, the unrighteous will be condemned.

CALL TO WORSHIP

17 I will praise the LORD according to His righteousness,
And will sing praise to the name of the LORD Most
High.

Ps. 7:17

Confident that his prayer is answered, David now concludes his psalm. God will save him from those who persecute him. He will rise up in judgment and test all hearts and minds, destroying the wicked. In declaring, *"I will praise the Lord according to His righteousness,"* David affirms all that he has said earlier in the psalm. God *is* righteous; He restores His kingdom; He rules; He is trustworthy; He vindicates David, whose praise now comes from a full heart: *"And [I] will sing praise to the name of the Lord Most High."* *"The Lord Most High"* is a phrase found in Genesis 14:18 and elsewhere meaning that God is above all other gods; thus in defeating David's enemies He also defeats their gods.

Certain of God's rescue and His justice toward his enemies, David goes out from his lament with song. Just so, God is our resolution in distress, and before Him we sing our praises—our proper response to the One who hears and answers.

CHAPTER EIGHT

Praise the Creator!

Psalm 8

This psalm contains one of the best-known verses in all of the Bible: "What is man that You are mindful of him . . . ?" Ringing down the generations, this haunting question pursues us. As our knowledge of the universe has grown, the query has become more pressing. Carl Sagan notes, "As long as there have been humans we have searched for our place in the cosmos. Where are we? Who are we? We find that we live on an insignificant planet of a humdrum star lost in a galaxy tucked away in some forgotten corner of a universe in which there are far more galaxies than people." Is this the only answer modern science can give? If so, then we are doomed to a sense of helplessness and hopelessness as we stand, in Sagan's words, on the "shores of the cosmic ocean."

If science as science is reduced to using the words "insignificant," "humdrum," and "forgotten" when looking at our world, then we need another source to answer the question "What is man . . . ?" In Psalm 8, rather than being imprisoned by reason, we are liberated by revelation as the glory of humankind is seen in light of the glory of God. It is only after praise to the living God, "O Lord, our Lord, / How excellent is Your name in all the earth," that the question about human beings can be properly raised. Now each of us finds that he or she is a being before God (Helmut Thielicke). This is the revelation of the Bible.

Psalm 8 is a psalm or hymn of praise. In it, our place in the cosmos

is established. Traditionally, the psalm is ascribed to David. It contains
an individual meditation, "O Lord," and it also embraces the community
of God's people, "our Lord." This psalm reflects upon the opening of
the Old Testament (vv. 6–8), and it is echoed in the New Testament,
where it finds its fulfillment in Christ (see 1 Cor. 15:27; Eph. 1:22;
Heb. 2:6–8). The thought moves from the glory of God (vv. 1–2) to
the glory of humankind (vv. 3–8). The final verse (9) repeats the refrain
of verse 1.

The Glory of God

> 1 O Lord, our Lord,
>   How excellent *is* Your name in all the earth,
>   Who have set Your glory above the heavens!
> 2 Out of the mouth of babes and nursing infants
>   You have ordained strength,
>   Because of Your enemies,
>   That You may silence the enemy and the avenger.
>
> *Ps. 8:1–2*

David begins his psalm by addressing God by His personal name:
"O Lord" ("Yahweh"). God is known because He has chosen to make
Himself known: He revealed His name to Moses, "I am who I am,"
and called him into a relationship with Himself (Exod. 3:14). Knowing
His name actualizes communion with Him. In a sense, we get God's
attention when we call Him by name.

I remember years ago trying to explain a personal relationship with
Christ to a fellow student in New York. We had both been undergradu-
ates at Princeton, where my friend had played varsity basketball. Now
in theological seminary, he had a concept of God but no real personal
walk with Him. I shared how I had come to Christ and the difference
He had made in my life. As we talked, my friend began to get the
picture. Then suddenly his eyes lit up. "You mean I can play one-on-
one with Him?" he asked. This metaphor from basketball, where two
athletes by themselves play offense and defense against each other illumined the point. "Yes," I said, "it's one-on-one." "O Lord," David prays,
one-on-one. Yahweh is also Israel's Lord, so David immediately adds,
"our Lord."

Next, David gives value to God's name: "How excellent is Your name *in all the earth."* The adjective *"excellent"* here means, at its root, "to be broad, large, powerful." Thus to call God *"excellent"* is to call Him incomparable in His omnipotence. In the context of Psalm 8 the excellent name of God is revealed in the majesty of both earth and heaven. God's name is *"excellent"* in all the earth; He is the one universal God throughout this planet. David continues, "[You] *have set Your glory* ["majesty"] *above the heavens."* It is Yahweh's lordship over all things that reveals His glory. Similar thoughts appear in Psalm 104:1–2: "O Lord my God, You are very great: / You are clothed with honor and majesty, / Who cover Yourself with light as with a garment, / Who stretch out the heavens like a curtain."

The glory of God is witnessed to by the whole of creation, earth and heaven. David continues, *"Out of the mouth of babes and infants / You have ordained strength."* Children as well as adults praise Yahweh because of His greatness. Through their worship of Him God has ordained His *"strength"* or "stronghold," *"Because of Your enemies, / That You may silence the enemy and the avenger,"* David adds. That newborn babes are praising God even in their weakness and foolishness stops the enemy. In like manner, Paul tells the Corinthians that the preaching of Christ crucified is foolishness: "But God has chosen the foolish things of the world to put to shame the wise, and God has chosen the weak things of the world to put to shame the things which are mighty . . . that no flesh should glory in His presence" (1 Cor. 1:27–29). When God's people, weak and strong alike, begin to praise His name, the realm of Satan and his demons is rolled back.

THE GLORY OF MAN

3 When I consider Your heavens, the work of Your
    fingers,
  The moon and the stars, which You have ordained,
4 What is man that You are mindful of him,
  And the son of man that You visit him?
5 For You have made him a little lower than the angels,
  And You have crowned him with glory and honor.
6 You have made him to have dominion over the works
    of Your hands;
  You have put all *things* under his feet,
7 All sheep and oxen—
  Even the beasts of the field,

8 The birds of the air,
   And the fish of the sea
   That pass through the paths of the seas.

Ps. 8:3–8

Recognizing the vastness of creation and the majesty of God "above the heavens," we are now pressed by the question of our own identity and destiny. David meditates before the Lord: *"When I consider* ["see"] *Your heavens, the work of Your fingers, / The moon and the stars, which You have ordained . . ."* Perhaps this psalm was written at night with the heavens stretched out before David so that he literally "sees" them and the moon and the stars that are fixed in them.

Today, we can marvel at the heavens with more data than was available to David's unaided eye. For example, we know that in one second a beam of light travels 186,000 miles, which is about seven times around the earth. It takes eight minutes for that beam to go from the sun to the earth. In a year the same beam travels almost six trillion miles. Scientists call this a "light-year." Eight billion light-years from earth is halfway to the edge of the known universe. Within the universe there are a hundred billion galaxies, each with a hundred billion stars, on the average. In all the galaxies, there are perhaps as many planets as stars, ten billion trillion. These statistics take us beyond human comprehension. No wonder David asks, "What is man . . . ?"

It is important to see, however, that for David, beyond the vastness of the universe is the vastness of God. The moon and stars are merely *"the work of Your fingers."* God has molded the universe as a potter might form a jar on his turning wheel. No wonder the name of Yahweh is "excellent . . . in all the earth." No wonder His glory is "above the heavens." The whole universe sits on His potter's wheel; the whole universe stands on His workbench.

Before the majesty of both the Creator and the creation David asks: *"What is man that You are mindful of him, / And the son of man* [a synonym for "man"] *that You visit him?"* The adjective *"mindful"* here derives from the verb "remember" (*zākar*). Will God keep us in His mind? *"Visit"* here means "to attend to, to observe." Will God keep His eye on us? Before such overwhelming physical odds, such seemingly endless space and time, will God think of us and see us?

The twofold answer to these questions is given in verse 5, where David asserts humankind's place in creation: *"For you have made him a little lower than the angels."* Possibly a better meaning is, "a little

77

lower than God" (*ĕlōhîm*). David is quite probably reflecting here on Genesis 1:26, "Then God (*ĕlōhîm*) said, 'Let Us make man in Our image, according to Our likeness.'" Little lower than God, we are made to represent Him in this world, reflecting His character, and living in a relationship with Him.

But there is something more. God has *"crowned [us] with glory and honor."* The content of this "crown" is given in verse 6, *"You have made him to have dominion* ["rulership"] *over the works of Your hands."* Consider again Genesis 1:26, "let them [male and female] have dominion over the fish of the sea, over the birds of the air, and over the cattle, over all the earth and over every creeping thing that creeps on the earth." This is our vocation. Our glory and honor are to be to the world as God's *"glory and honor"* are to the universe. When we look out at the vast universe we seem so small, but when we look at this world we are great in God's purpose for us here. The next parallel phrase states, *"You have put all things under his feet,"* a symbol of sovereign reign. Verses 7–8 then elaborate on our reign, again reflecting Genesis 1.

Our greatness is thus in being made little less than God and being placed in this world to exercise His sovereignty over the planet. Both in nature and vocation, we are given divine glory.

How do we then respond? First, we only know our greatness in relationship to God. This knowledge does not come through "general revelation" in creation itself, but through "special revelation." The God who makes Himself known makes us know ourselves in Him. Calvin, in his *Institutes,* asserts that there is no proper knowledge of humankind apart from the knowledge of God. When God reveals Himself, He reveals us at the same time. Thus the God who reveals His excellent name, His glory above the heavens and the vastness of creation, also reveals that we are made little lower than He and given dominion over the earth.

Second, we do not presently see the order of creation as we look at this world. Humankind, made to be a little lower than God, by declaring itself to be its own god, has become a devil. This world that was created to be ruled by us has been raped by us instead. Thus Psalm 8 points beyond itself to the redemption given in Christ.

As the second Adam, the head of a new redeemed race, Jesus has defeated sin, Satan, and death. He will reign, as Paul writes, "Till He has put all enemies under His feet," and even death itself will finally be destroyed (1 Cor. 15:25). Again, Paul tells the Ephesians that Christ now reigns, having "put all things under His feet" (1:22). And Hebrews 2:6–9 sees Psalm 8:4–6 in the process of being fulfilled in Christ to whom all things have been made subject.

The final answer to the question "What is man . . . ?" is given in Christ, the head of a new humanity. It is Christ who has restored this fallen creation, Christ who will return and consummate all things in Himself. As God comes to this earth in His Son, the greatness of God and the grandeur of the cosmos are met in the grace of the Lord Jesus Christ.

The Glory of God

9 O Lord, our Lord,
  How excellent *is* Your name in all the earth!

Ps. 8:9

Like a final chorus, verse 9 repeats verse 1: *"O Lord, our Lord, / How excellent is Your name in all the earth!"* Our place in God's order evokes this final note of praise. As we discover our divine destiny, we will participate in making God's name excellent in all the earth. In Christ, this now is our certainty. It is Christ who bears the divine name: "Yahweh" equals "Lord." As Paul tells the Philippians, "At the name of Jesus every knee should bow, of those in heaven, and of those on earth, and of those under the earth, and . . . every tongue should confess that Jesus Christ is Lord, to the glory of God the Father" (2:10–11).

CHAPTER NINE

Justice Now!

Psalm 9

A crucial area of Biblical studies is eschatology. What does the Bible teach about the future? For some, the Bible is a mathematical puzzle to be decoded. For others, the Bible is mythology to be discarded. For still others, the Bible speaks with a realism to be embraced.

As has often been noted, Biblical eschatology does not begin with Daniel or Ezekiel. Rather, the whole Bible is eschatological because the whole Bible is teleological; that is, from Genesis to Revelation the Bible reveals the God who pursues His purpose through history to its final consummation. Biblical man lives in the tension between promise and fulfillment, the kingdom that has come and that is coming. Thus there is always a tension between "futuristic eschatology" and "realized eschatology." This is true in the Old Testament as well as in the New. This tension reaches its ultimate point, however, in the New as the final goal or end breaks in upon us in the Incarnation. Now God Himself is here!

The Old Testament witnesses to futuristic eschatology in its prophetic and Messianic hope, as well as to realized eschatology in its experience of God's acting directly in the lives of individuals and in Israel's unique history. The "End" breaks in when God bares His arm in judgment and redemption. Every experience of the ultimate points beyond itself to that final judgment when God Himself will come "once for all" (see Heb. 9:26–28).

Psalm 9 is a witness to realized eschatology. God has acted in the psalmist's past: "I will tell of all Your marvelous works" (v. 1); "You have rebuked the nations, You have destroyed the wicked" (v. 5). God will act again: "He has prepared His throne for judgment. / He shall judge the world in righteousness" (vv. 7–8). But this is no distant hope for the final Day of Judgment. This is an immediate expectation: "Arise, O Lord . . . Let the nations be judged in Your sight" (v. 19). In other words, God is the living God, active now in history and human life. He is not locked into some past dispensation where He once chose to do miracles, but no longer does. He is not excluded from His universe by a closed system of cause and effect. He is the present, living God. At any moment He may move upon us or upon our enemies. The prayer, "Arise, O Lord" is not an idle, "spiritual" hope. When God arises, the nations will be judged and the cry "Put them in fear, O Lord" (v. 20) will be answered. Since God has not changed, this psalm is for us just as much as it was for ancient Israel.

Psalm 9 is usually identified as a psalm of praise. Its traditional authorship, held here, is given to David. This is supported by its royal substance. David's enemies are opposing nations (vv. 6, 15, 17). Moreover, his witness to God's mercy will be told in Jerusalem (v. 14).

Since this psalm is structured following a slightly broken acrostic pattern (each succeeding verse begins with the next letter of the Hebrew alphabet, starting with *aleph,* the first letter, in verse 1) which is completed in Psalm 10, many scholars speculate on an organic interrelationship between the two prayers. Their earlier unity has now been lost through editing and liturgical usage. Psalm 9 covers the first eleven letters of the Hebrew alphabet except *daleth,* the fourth letter.

Psalm 9 is written in crisis. David's enemies hate him and have pushed him to the "gates of death" (v. 13). In his hour of peril, he turns to the Lord. As he begins his prayer, however, he reveals neither terror nor fear. He refuses to rush into God's presence with panic demands. Rather, he begins in praise and worship. We too would do well to start with the Lord when we are in crisis, when we usually demand "justice now." The movement of thought goes from worship (vv. 1–2) to God's judgment, including both vindication and security (vv. 3–10), a call to worship and witness (vv. 11–12), a call for mercy (vv. 13–14), and the judgment of the nations (vv. 15–16), ending with resolution (vv. 17–20).

CONTEXT: PERSONAL WORSHIP

1 I will praise *You,* O LORD, with my whole heart;
   I will tell of all Your marvelous works.
2 I will be glad and rejoice in You;
   I will sing praise to Your name, O Most High.
                                             Ps. 9:1–2

Psalm 9 begins with David's declaration of intent: *"I will praise You, O Lord, with my whole heart."* His thanksgiving is total and comes with all his heart. Since the heart is considered by the Hebrews to be the seat of thought, David worships with full consciousness, engaging his mind and his memory. This is no rote prayer or mumbled hymn. He invests himself totally in his worship. Both the majesty of God and the urgency of the hour call forth his best. What then does it mean to praise God?

In his classic *Praise and Lament in the Psalms,* Klaus Westermann suggests the following aspects of praise (pp. 27–28). In praise the one being praised is elevated; we are directed toward the one whom we praise. Praise is expressed in freedom and spontaneity. Praise has a forum, occurs in a group, and is public. Praise is essentially joyful. Genuine praise occurs where the one being praised is the object as here: *"I will praise You, O Lord."*

David now becomes specific: *"I will tell of* ["recount"] *all Your marvelous works." "Marvelous works"* comes from a verb meaning "to be surpassing, extraordinary, wonderful." In the Exodus the plagues are God's wonderful works. As God promises Moses, "So I will stretch out My hand and strike Egypt with all My wonders which I will do in its midst" (Exod. 3:20). David, then, is praising God for His miraculous, direct intervention.

I have often seen tears of joy and shouts of praise when a person really comes to Christ. The miracle of the new birth leads to public witness. The old-fashioned "testimony meeting" was a time of telling of the marvelous works of God.

More recently, I have experienced the same praise for the miracles of God's healing. Francis MacNutt, a leader in the renewal movement, held a healing conference at our church. For months afterward I heard our people witness with joy to the healing they received. For example, Charles is in his sixties and his left wrist has been broken several times. The normal five bones there were shattered into ten and his wrist was swollen to twice its normal size. He was in chronic pain. The doctors at the Veterans' Hospital in La Jolla where he was being treated offered surgery as a distant hope, but they promised no real improvement. As Charles was being prayed for during a meeting for physical healing at the conference, the pain left instantaneously for the first time in years. Then, over a ten-day period, his wrist returned to its normal size and the bones fully healed. The doctors have no explanation for this miracle. As Charles told me of his healing, tears streamed down his cheeks.

Recalling God's works opens up David's heart. He continues: *"I will*

be glad and rejoice in You; / I will sing praise to Your name." The memory
of God's miracles brings David to God **Himself**. The mighty acts of
God reveal the character of God. We do not worship the works however;
we worship the Worker. The language here—*"glad," "rejoice," "sing
praise"*—recalls Psalm 4:11. The verbs **express** holy hilarity. To be *"glad"*
is "to take pleasure in, to exult." To *"rejoice"* is a synonym also meaning
"to exult." Doubling the verbs makes **the praise** more emphatic: *"I
will* be glad *and* rejoice *in You."*

Such joy naturally leads to singing: *"I will sing praise to Your name,
O Most High."* As king, David wrote **psalms to** lead Israel in worship.
In a similar psalm of thanksgiving **when the** ark was placed in the
tabernacle, David begins:

> Oh, give thanks to the Lord!
> Call upon His name;
> Make known His deeds
>   among the peoples!
> Sing to Him, sing psalms to Him;
> Talk of all His wondrous works!
> *1 Chron. 16:8–9*

With ancient Israel, we share a singing **faith.** Whenever the Church
is being revived there is a fresh outburst of song.

The title used here for God, *"O Most High,"* appears often in the
psalms (e.g., 21:7; 46:4; 50:14). It expresses God's transcendence over
all other powers and created beings. Thus Satan's fall results from his
attempt to scale the hierarchy of heaven, saying, "I will be like the
Most High" (Isa. 14:14). David, however, adopts the opposite stance.
He sings to the God who is above all gods in the universe.

CONTENT: JUDGMENT AND VINDICATION

> 3 When my enemies turn back,
>   They shall fall and perish at Your presence.
> 4 For You have maintained my right and my cause;
>   You sat on the throne judging in righteousness.
> 5 You have rebuked the nations,
>   You have destroyed the wicked;
>   You have blotted out their name forever and ever.
> *Ps. 9:3–5*

David turns now from the context of worship to the content of judgment. Strengthened by praise, with faith renewed, he is confident that God will deliver him from his enemies. First, they will be routed; they will *"turn back"* in retreat. Second, this will lead to their stumbling or falling, the sign of their collapse. Third, they will *"perish."* This, however, is no human victory. Yahweh the Warrior-King goes into battle for David and for Israel. Thus David's enemies perish *"at [His] presence."*

It is the presence of God that guarantees Israel's life. As God promises Moses, "My Presence will go with you, and I will give you rest" (Exod. 33:14). Here too, the divine presence means the defeat of all David's enemies because sin and Satan cannot stand before the numinous presence and power of the Lord.

David continues *"For You have maintained my right and my cause."* His enemies perish in God's presence not because of racial privilege or tribal loyalty, but because of David's *"right"* (mišpoṭ), David's moral integrity. His *"right"* is upheld by the God who is "right," the Holy One of Israel. Thus when God defeats David's enemies He exercises His judgment against their injustice and vindicates him. As David confesses: *"You sat on the throne judging in righteousness."* The justice of David is determined and upheld by the justice of God.

This leads to a vivid description of the end of the evil nations. *"You have rebuked the nations."* Here God is viewed as a fierce warrior who "cries out" (this is the root meaning of *gāʿar*, the verb used here) in anger to drive away His enemies. The nations vanish before His judgment. He has *"destroyed the wicked."* Their name is gone, *"blotted out,"* and with their name goes their posterity. Where is the fame today of the nations who hounded Israel? Phoenicia, Babylon, Assyria, Persia, Greece, Rome?

Thus as our enemies are destroyed, as the power of sin and Satan over us is broken, our faith in the living God is vindicated. Now Jesus is our righteousness; in His name we are saved and healed, and our enemies perish in the presence of God's powerful Holy Spirit.

Content: Judgment and Refuge

6 O enemy, destructions are finished forever!
    And you have destroyed cities;
    Even their memory has perished.

7 But the LORD shall endure forever;
  He has prepared His throne for judgment.
8 He shall judge the world in righteousness,
  And He shall administer judgment for the peoples
    in uprightness.
9 The LORD also will be a refuge for the oppressed,
  A refuge in times of trouble.
10 And those who know Your name will put their trust
    in You;
  For You, LORD, have not forsaken those who seek You.
                                              Ps. 9:6–10

David's power and faith are renewed and he turns from direct prayer to addressing his enemy. He can say with authority: *"O enemy, destructions are finished forever!"* It is possible that here David utters a prophetic word that actually comes from the Lord.

Having pronounced judgment, David also remembers the greatness of his adversary: *"And you have destroyed* [literally, "uprooted"] *cities; / Even their memory has perished."* But by the power of God, the destroyer is now destroyed. He who took away the memory of other peoples will no longer be remembered.

Next, David contrasts the temporal passing of his enemy with the eternal power of Yahweh: *"But the Lord shall endure forever."* The Hebrew verb translated *"endure"* (yāšab) literally means "to sit, to remain." *"He shall judge the world in righteousness"* (ṣedeq; cf. v. 4). God the eternal sitting judge is the absolute by which our lives are measured and to which our lives are accountable: *"He shall administer judgment for the peoples in uprightness"* (v. 8).

In verse 9 David's thought turns from his enemies to his friends. *"The Lord also will be a refuge for the oppressed."* *"Refuge"* here means "secure height, stronghold." As God is the avenging Warrior-King-Judge to His enemies, so He is a secure fortress for the oppressed. They find their protection in Him *"in times of trouble,"* or "destitution." In the metaphor here, when invading armies ravage the land, the oppressed flee to the Lord, their stronghold.

Verse 10 provides the positive meaning of the *"refuge"* metaphor: *"And those who know Your name will put their trust in You."* Those who *"know"* (yāda‘, "have intimate communion with") God's name are God's people. He calls them by name and they call Him by name. Their relationship is secured, for to know Yahweh is also to trust Him. The verb for *"trust"* means "to feel secure, be unconcerned." The oppressed feel secure in God as their refuge because He is trustworthy.

"Refuge" is given further meaning as David returns to prayer: *"For You, Lord, have not forsaken those who seek You."* God is trustworthy because He does not leave or abandon us. When we *"seek"* or "inquire" of Him, He is there; He answers. Jesus promises, "Ask, and it will be given to you; seek, and you will find; knock, and it will be opened to you. . . . If you then, being evil, know how to give good gifts to your children, how much more will your Father who is in heaven give good things to those who ask Him!" (Matt. 7:7, 11).

This section gives us the assurance of the destruction of our enemy by the God who reigns forever in eternity. At the same time, this God is our fortress when we flee to Him. The God of judgment is the God of mercy. Sinai becomes Calvary when the heart of God is fully known.

EXHORTATION: CALL TO CORPORATE WORSHIP

11 Sing praises to the LORD, who dwells in Zion!
   Declare His deeds among the people.
12 When He avenges blood, He remembers them;
   He does not forget the cry of the humble.

Ps. 9:11–12

David, God's songster, now calls the people to worship. Having meditated on the judgment of God and the mercy of God, he is ready again for praise: *"Sing praises to the Lord, who dwells in Zion!"* When God's security is known, as in verses 9–10, music is the order of the day. The Lord *lives* on Mount Zion (see Ps. 2:6). There is His ark. There will be His house or temple. It is the God of Israel who is to be praised.

As we have seen in verses 1–2, worship includes witness. So David continues: *"Declare His deeds among the people."* The mighty acts of God evoke praise. It is the living God who is worshiped. Paul writes to the Ephesians: "Now to Him who is able to do exceedingly abundantly above all that we ask or think, according to the power that works in us, to Him be glory in the church . . ." (3:20, 21).

The specific deeds that David witnesses to are now given. God is to be praised *"when He avenges blood."* God judges evil, repays injustice, executes the murderer, and defeats the enemy.

David continues, saying that when God executes His judgment, *"He remembers them [His people]; / He does not forget the cry of the humble."*

The *"humble"* are the "poor, afflicted, weak, pious" (see Ps. 10:8–9). Proverbs 3:34 reads, "Surely He scorns the scornful, / But gives grace to the humble."

God is to be worshiped as He executes His judgment and redemption promised in verses 3–10. Here is realized eschatology. Here is the God who acts. This call to worship is based on the assumption that things will be different *now* because God is carrying out His sentence; He is saving His people.

SUPPLICATION: CALL FOR MERCY

> 13 Have mercy on me, O LORD!
>   Consider my trouble from those who hate me,
>   You who lift me up from the gates of death,
> 14 That I may tell of all Your praise
>   In the gates of the daughter of Zion.
>   I will rejoice in Your salvation.
>
>   Ps. 9:13–14

As David calls upon God to work, he promises Him worship. What he cries out for is grace: *"Have mercy on me, O Lord!"* Here David becomes personal and intimate. As he asks for *"mercy"* or *"grace"* he reveals the depths of the crisis. Those who *"hate"* him have driven him to the edge. God now is the one who lifts him *"up from the gates of death."* *"Death"* here is seen as a walled city, and David has reached its very entrance (cf. Matt. 16:18). It is appropriate for him to call to Yahweh because ultimately only He can save him (and us) from death. At the same time, it is too often the case that only in a major crisis will we really turn to the Lord. C. S. Lewis notes that God is so gracious that He will even take us when we use Him as our last resort. When the dying thief called out to Jesus to remember him when He came into His kingdom, Jesus replied with divine mercy, "Assuredly, I say to you, today you will be with Me in Paradise" (Luke 23:43).

After David experiences God's mercy, he promises worship and witness, to *"tell of all Your praise / In the gates of the daughter of Zion."* Having been delivered from the gates of death, he will praise God in the gates of Jerusalem. The *"daughter of Zion"* refers to the people of Jerusalem. In Jewish culture, cities were often regarded as mothers of their people, and their inhabitants as sons and daughters (cf. Isa. 4:4).

Here then in his capitol city David will recount praises and *"rejoice in [God's] salvation."* His praises are his expressions of thanks for Yahweh's "marvelous works." These saving acts can be summed up in a word: *"salvation"* (yĕšûʿôt—the plural form in the Hebrew adds intensity to the meaning of the word).

The point of God's mercy here is not merely for our own self-satisfaction; it is for His glory, expressed by our worship. When God delivers us from our enemies, He also delivers us from ourselves so that we may be free to praise Him. This praise is public, and it is to be offered in our congregation as a witness of God's love and power. As our *"daughters of Zion"* hear us praise Him, their faith in turn will be strengthened.

CONDEMNATION: JUDGMENT EXECUTED

15 The nations have sunk down in the pit *which* they
    made;
    In the net which they hid, their own foot is caught.
16 The LORD is known *by* the judgment He executes;
    The wicked is snared in the work of his own hands.
                Meditation.   Selah
Ps. 9:15–16

"The nations" now receive God's *"judgment,"* expressed in His passive wrath as He lets sin run its course and destroy them (cf. Rom. 1:18 ff.). The *"nations"* (gôyim) here are pictured as hunters who have set traps for David. They, however, have fallen into the very pit that they dug to catch the wild animal Israel (cf. Ps. 7:15). Thus Paul warns Timothy that those who reject sound teaching have been snared by the devil, *"having been taken captive by him to do his will"* (2 Tim. 2:26). Part of God's judgment on our rebellion is to turn us over to Satan. In His sovereignty, He even uses the devil as an instrument of His righteous will. Thus God's judgment is seen here in the nations' being caught in their own trap.

Now David writes: *"The Lord is known by the judgment He executes; / The wicked is snared in the work of his own hands."* If we rightly see the internal judgments of history upon oppression, segregation, the exploitation of the poor, and the destruction of our environment we will see them as the judgments of God. Although God does not intervene dramatically, this is a part of His realized eschatology. These judgments also anticipate active, direct judgments and the final judgment which will be absolute and from which no one will escape.

RESOLUTION: THE WICKED AND THE NEEDY

17 The wicked shall be turned into hell,
   And all the nations that forget God.
18 For the needy shall not always be forgotten;
   The expectation of the poor shall *not* perish forever.

Ps. 9:17–18

These two verses contrast the disposition of the *"wicked"* with the *"needy"* and the *"poor."* The *"wicked"* ("hostile enemies of God," see vv. 5–6) shall *"be turned into hell"* or Sheol, the silent abode of the dead (cf. Ps. 88:3–12). They are a part of *"all the nations that forget God."* Here to *"forget"* means to forsake. Next, the needy, although apparently forgotten, will not always be so. Yahweh is a refuge "in times of trouble" and He does "not forget the cry of the humble." *"The expectation of the poor shall not perish forever."* Their hope will be realized. As Psalm 1:6 puts it, "For the Lord knows the way of the righteous, / But the way of the ungodly shall perish."

What David suggests here is that for the present moment the wicked appear to prosper, while the needy and the poor have only their hope to sustain them. Nevertheless, help is on the way. God's eschatological intervention still lies in the future. While the poor will experience His saving grace, the wicked will experience the bitter fruit of their own sin—death.

I remember in the mid-sixties in Hollywood being burdened for the poor and needy. They were a lost generation getting stoned on drugs, selling their bodies, searching for "love and peace, brother," roaming the Sunset Strip and Hollywood Boulevard. Then, in the midst of their despair and their diminishing hope for change, God moved. His Spirit began to be poured out and many thousands came to Christ. The longing for a new life was found in God, not in drugs. "Peace and love, brother" was Jesus' gift to them, as the so-called Jesus Movement was born. Indeed, it was a fulfillment of verse 18: the needy were not forgotten and the expectation of the poor did not perish.

CALL FOR JUDGMENT

19 Arise, O LORD,
  Do not let man prevail;
  Let the nations be judged in Your sight.
20 Put them in fear, O LORD,
  That the nations may know themselves *to be but* men.
  Selah

Ps. 9:19–20

The final two verses form David's call for a fully realized eschatology. David summons God to *"arise,"* to stand up from His throne; to enter into battle and overcome a fallen humanity—the wicked; and to bring His judgment and the vindication of His name to the nations (see Isa. 2:19, 21; Ps. 76:9). When they are confronted by Him, by His presence, justice will be done.

The result of God's intervention will be that the nations will be put in *"fear"* of Yahweh. They will *"know themselves to be but men,"* not the gods they presumed to be. They will cry out with Isaiah, "Woe is me . . ." (Isa. 6:5). They will fall down like Peter and say, "Depart from me, for I am a sinful man, O Lord!" (Luke 5:8). They will receive justice and the righteous will shine like the sun (Matt. 13:43).

CHAPTER TEN

Is God Absent?

Psalm 10

We often suppose that unbelief is a modern problem. While atheism as an ideology is a product of the nineteenth century and is seen most clearly in Marxism, pragmatic atheism is as old as the garden. The serpent's suggestion that we can be "like God" has always been alluring

(Gen. 3:5). The vague notion that God is "somewhere," out of reach, frees us to live as if He does not exist.

This is the context of Psalm 10. God seems distant. The wicked prosper. Prayers go "unanswered." There is no justice. Where is God, anyway?

As we noted in the introduction to Psalm 9, Psalm 10 continues the broken acrostic pattern that began in Psalm 9. This has led scholars to speculate on an earlier organic interrelationship between the two. Their unity is now lost, and thus we are treating them as separate prayers. This psalm picks up the Hebrew alphabet with the twelfth letter, *lamedh,* and continues with some breaks to the last, *taw.* As in Psalm 9, we assume David's authorship. Commentators describe this psalm as a communal lament. It begins with a complaint about God's absence and the wicked's pride (vv. 1–4), which is then elaborated upon as the wicked prosper at the expense of the poor (vv. 5–11). Next, God is called into battle (v. 12), and judgment and justice will be the result (vv. 14–18).

QUESTION AND CONFIRMATION: GOD SEEMS ALOOF

1 Why do You stand afar off, O LORD?
  Why do You hide in times of trouble?
2 The wicked in *his* pride persecutes the poor;
  Let them be caught in the plots which they have
    devised.
3 For the wicked boasts of his heart's desire;
  He blesses the greedy *and* renounces the LORD.
4 The wicked in his proud countenance does not seek
    God;
  God *is* in none of his thoughts.

Ps. 10:1–4

David begins with a bold question, or is it an implied accusation? *"Why do You stand afar off, O Lord?"* God, of course, may be distant for several reasons. On the one hand, our sin may make Him *seem* distant when the real distance is our own doing. The same goes for doubt. Even Jesus could do no mighty work in Nazareth because of the people's unbelief (Mark 6:5). On the other hand, God, for His own reasons, may choose not to act. As we have seen in Psalm 9, He may be exercising His passive wrath by letting sin run its course. Often, the matter is one of timing, and the eternal God is not accountable to our schedule.

David's complaint about God's distance is elaborated upon in the parallel half-verse: *"Why do You hide in times of trouble?"* The noun translated *"trouble"* means "death, destitution." In Jeremiah 14:1 the same word connotes a time of drought. Much as in our own age, the "trouble" here, however, is moral. So David continues: *"The wicked in his pride persecutes the poor."* The verb for *"persecutes"* means "hotly pursues." The wicked person is violently and actively engaged in crushing those who are helpless, those whose only refuge is the Lord.

David then offers an oath or curse: *"Let them be caught in the plots which they have devised."* This picks up the common theme that God exercises His judgment through the moral order of life itself. Thus the evil people, in planning the doom of others, really plan their own doom (see Ps. 5:10; 7:14–16; 9:15).

It is true that our sins will find us out. In a recent move against the Mafia's control of the Fulton Fish Market in New York City, the case was broken open when investigators discovered that the mob boss had transferred $168,000 from a high interest fund to a low interest bank account so that he could get free bonus TVs. Why would a man who was squeezing millions in cash payoffs from the fish market bother with free TVs? The answer is greed—and his greed trapped him.

David continues his complaint by pointing out that the wicked man even *"boasts of his heart's* ["soul's"] *desire"* and *"blesses the greedy."* It is greed which motivates his pursuit of the poor. In standing with the greedy he also *"renounces the Lord."*

David's statement in verse 4, *"The wicked in his proud countenance does not seek God,"* is another way of saying that pride separates us from God. We cannot seek God at the same time we seek ourselves. We cannot serve two masters. This is why, as Bonhoeffer says, "When Jesus calls a man, He bids him come and die." Only with the death of the ego will we truly seek God. For the wicked, however, not only is God not the object of his search, God doesn't even enter his mind. Thus David says, *"God is in none of his thoughts."* A literal translation renders this phrase, "God is not there in the whole of his devices."

In these opening verses has David painted a portrait of the wicked man. He is controlled by his passions. Greed is the motive of his heart. In renouncing God he enthrones his own ego. Thus he is free to persecute the poor and press them for his own gain. The passions of man are set free in an empty universe. The result? Pure chaos. What was true a thousand years before Christ is true today. Time changes, human nature remains the same.

ELABORATION: THE WICKED PROSPER, THE POOR ARE OPPRESSED

5 His ways are always prospering;
Your judgments *are* far above, out of his sight;
As *for* all his enemies, he sneers at them.
6 He has said in his heart,
"I shall not be moved;
I shall never be in adversity."
7 His mouth is full of cursing and deceit and oppression;
Under his tongue *is* trouble and iniquity.
8 He sits in the lurking places of the villages;
In the secret places he murders the innocent;
His eyes are secretly fixed on the helpless.
9 He lies in wait secretly, as a lion in his den;
He lies in wait to catch the poor;
He catches the poor when he draws him into his net.
10 So he crouches, he lies low,
That the helpless may fall by his strength.
11 He has said in his heart,
"God has forgotten;
He hides His face;
He will never see."

Ps. 10:5–11

Verses 5–11 elaborate on the theme of the wicked man. The first part tells us what he thinks and says. The second part tells us what he does.

David begins this section with a general thesis concerning the wicked man: *"His ways are always prospering."* The verb for *"prospering"* means literally "to be strong, firm, stable." The wicked are on top, they are in charge, they are steadfast.

Next David observes the wicked man's attitude toward God: *"Your judgments are far above, out of his sight."* Having failed to see the avenging hand of God, the wicked man feels free to go his own way. "Out of sight, out of mind." It is as if the more he sins, the less he knows of God. The more distant God becomes to his experience, the more his heart is hardened. He fails to see that this itself is a part of God's judgment (cf. Pharaoh's hardened heart in Exodus).

Not only is God absent from the wicked person's experience, his enemies are too weak to dent his ego. Thus David writes, *"As for all his enemies, he sneers at them."* The verb for *"sneers"* literally means "puff, blow, snort." The picture is that of a charging bull, panting in anger.

Secure against both God and his enemies, the wicked man inwardly boasts in arrogance, saying in his heart, *"I shall not be moved; / I shall never be in adversity"* (v. 6). In other words, he believes, "Nothing can touch me." Indeed, he holds himself to be the captain of his fate. Here is functional atheism, the ego eclipsing God. Contrast the claim *"I shall not be moved"* (v. 5) with Isaiah 40:6–7: "All flesh is grass. . . . the grass withers . . . surely the people are grass." Jesus warns that the rich man who builds bigger barns for a more prosperous life forgets one thing—his own mortality. And God says to him, "You fool! This night your soul will be required of you" (Luke 12:20).

Next, the wicked person exposes his heart through his mouth. To begin with, he is *"full of cursing and deceit and oppression"* (v. 7). Whenever he opens his mouth, out they come. The word for *"cursing"* here when used in legal and covenantal settings means "oath." In the mouth of the wicked person, however, it is an oath gone bad. *"Deceit"* (or "treachery") is crafty speech, hiding the truth for evil ends. The word for *"oppression"* comes from a root meaning "to tread under foot, overcome." The wicked person uses his mouth to intimidate, to mislead, and to force submission.

There is more, however: *"Under his tongue is trouble and iniquity."* The phrase *"under his tongue"* represents things that the wicked person relishes. He keeps them under his tongue as a baseball player does with his chewing tobacco. The word used for *"trouble"* here means "toil" or "labor." The same word in Jeremiah 20:18 is parallel to sorrow: "Why did I come forth from the womb to see labor and sorrow, / That my days should be consumed with shame?" *"Iniquity"* in the Old Testament is paralleled with "violence," "lying," and "vanity." Here the context is "oppression," namely, "the wicked in his pride persecutes the poor" (v. 2). When Paul appeals to the Old Testament in Romans 3:10 to prove that "there is none righteous, no, not one," he quotes from verse 7 of this psalm's comprehensive picture of evil.

Next, in a series of brief poetic pictures, David turns from what the wicked person thinks and says to what he does. *"He sits in the lurking places of the villages; / In the secret places he murders the innocent"* (v. 8). The wicked man has deception on his tongue, and now he finds a blind from which to deceive his prey. He murders the *"innocent"* ("clean, free from guilt") in a dark alley. He seeks out the powerless as his target and turns his radar on them: *"His eyes are secretly fixed on the helpless."*

In verse 9 the metaphor changes. *"He lies in wait secretly, as a lion in his den; / He lies in wait to catch the poor."* The ambush (*"lurking places"*) in the village now becomes the lion's den or covert. The emphasis continues to be on secrecy and deception, as the "innocent" and "helpless" of verse 8 are the "poor" of verse 9.

Sustaining the theme of the hunt, David switches image to that of a trapper at the end of verse 9: *"He catches the poor when he draws him into his net."* The poor man is snatched like a bird.

Verse 10 summarizes the various metaphors: *"So he crouches, he lies low, / That the helpless may fall by his strength."* The murderer jumps out in the alley, the lion leaps, and the trapper springs his net. The result is the same: the helpless falls, overpowered by the wicked person.

Why this evil? Why do dictators rise with a Machiavellian contempt for human life? Why do major industries market sex and violence to pre-adolescent children through toys and music? Why do international corporations exploit cheap labor and natural resources in the Third World, leaving land and people stripped bare? David concludes: "[The wicked] *has said in his heart, / 'God has forgotten; / He hides His face; / He will never see.' "* The denial of deity leads to the denial of humanity. To lose the knowledge of who God is is to lose the knowledge of who we are.

The expression "to say in his heart" is to adopt a mental attitude and conviction. *"God has forgotten"* signifies, in other words, that God is not omniscient. He has a memory lapse. He does not keep records and I am not accountable to Him. Second, *"He hides His face"*; that is, God is not omnipresent. He cannot see what we do, and, therefore, we can do as we please. Third, *"He will never see"*; that is, the future is ours, not His. As the sovereignty of God is reduced, the supposed freedom of humankind is increased. The drama of Eden becomes a tired rerun.

CALL TO BATTLE

12 Arise, O Lord!
   O God, lift up Your hand!
   Do not forget the humble.

13 Why do the wicked renounce God?
   He has said in his heart,
   "You will not require *an account*."

Ps. 10:12–13

Having exhausted his description of the mind and behavior of the wicked, the psalmist now abruptly calls upon Yahweh to intervene. It is as if he is both disgusted and overwhelmed by evil. If God does not act, human cruelty will triumph, and the innocent poor will be ground into dust.

"Arise, O Lord!" as we have seen in Psalm 9:19, is a call to battle, a summons to God to take the field against the wicked man. The parallel *"O God, lift up Your hand!"* expresses the same thought. This gesture symbolizes taking arms against an opponent (see 2 Sam. 18:28; 20:21).

The call to battle is immediately followed by an exhortation to Yahweh: *"Do not forget the humble."* The charge that "God has forgotten" will be answered when God avenges those who have been abused. The word for *"humble"* is the same word translated as "poor" in verse 2.

Then follows the question: *"Why do the wicked renounce God?"* The same thought has already appeared in statement form (v. 3). The answer follows at once: *"He has said in his heart, / 'You will not require an account.' "* The verb for *"require"* is used in legal contexts for interrogation or investigation. The wicked person has renounced God because he decries God's justice, God's judgment, and his accountability to Him. Paul describes the "enemies of the cross of Christ" as those "whose end is destruction, whose god is their belly, and whose glory is in their shame—who set their mind on earthly things" (Phil. 3:18, 19). This is the "earthly mindset" of practical atheism. The shock awaiting the wicked man will come when Yahweh arises against him.

CONSEQUENCES: DELIVERANCE AND JUDGMENT

14 But You have seen, for You observe trouble and grief,
   To repay *it* by Your hand.
   The helpless commits himself to You;
   You are the helper of the fatherless.
15 Break the arm of the wicked and the evil *man;*
   Seek out his wickedness *until* You find none.

Ps. 10:14–15

In contrast to the wicked, David trusts the living God, even in times of silence. While the wicked claim God's ignorance and absence, he knows otherwise. God has seen the boasting, the greed, the murderous spirit, and the oppression and grief of the poor. *"Grief"* (v. 14) includes "vexation and anger." The poor are vexed by the injustice they receive. They grieve at their oppression and loss.

God, however, is on the side of the innocent poor. David knows that He will bring justice. The wicked will be intercepted by the power of God.

Notice the whole value system in this psalm. The wicked man pursues the poor, the innocent, the helpless, the humble, the orphan, while Yahweh saves the poor and the innocent. God is on the side of the defenseless, the broken, the alienated of this world. He stands with the "outsider," the "underdog." It is the little children whom Jesus blesses, and we must become like them to enter the kingdom (Mark 10:14–15).

David now turns from the promise of mercy for the fatherless to judgment upon oppressors. He prays: *"Break the arm of the wicked and evil man."* The metaphor of breaking the arm of the wicked means rendering him powerless. If his arms are broken, he cannot continue his attack on the poor. David says: *"Seek out his wickedness,"* that is, "Avenge his wicked behavior." As in verse 13, the verb for *"seek"* is used in a legal sense, "require an account." When the Lord arises (cf. v. 12) He will repay the wicked with judgment and help the fatherless. God's apparent distance and silence will be broken, and the question of verse 1, "Why do You stand afar off, O Lord?" will be answered.

CONFESSION: GOD AS RULER AND JUDGE

16 The LORD *is* King forever and ever;
   The nations have perished out of His land.
17 LORD, You have heard the desire of the humble;
   You will prepare their heart;
   You will cause Your ear to hear,
18 To do justice to the fatherless and the oppressed,
   That the man of the earth may oppress no more.
                                          Ps. 10:16–18

The psalm ends with a ringing confession: *"The Lord is King forever and ever."* Yahweh reigns! His sovereignty is for all eternity. He alone is King. Moses sang the same refrain after Pharaoh's defeat at the Red Sea: "The Lord shall reign forever and ever" (Exod. 15:18).

The consequence of God's reign, *"The nations have perished out of His land"* (v. 16b), refers in its immediate context to the expulsion of the Gentiles (*gôyim*) from Palestine. Ultimately, however, this will be fulfilled in the judgment of unbelievers and the gathering of the redeemed into God's eternal kingdom.

In verse 17 David turns from confession to adoration: *"Lord, You have heard the desire of the humble."* The same word used for *"humble"* here is translated "poor" in verse 9. God knows their need for deliverance, their longing for salvation.

David continues: *"You will prepare their heart."* Here *"prepare"* means "to establish, make firm, secure." God both hears and acts. He will take away the fear; He will make firm the hearts of the poor. They will know peace. Moreover *"You will cause Your ear to hear."* God will incline His ear to their prayers.

The result is that God will *"do justice to the fatherless and the oppressed, / That the man of the earth may oppress no more."* *"Justice"* is "judgment" toward the orphans and the humble poor. God's judgment for them, however, is mercy. The oppressor is destroyed. The oppressed are delivered. When God reigns, peace reigns and His land is restored.

Is God absent? At times He seems so, especially in the midst of the wicked's persecuting the poor. As David considers this, however, he does not speculate on how his faith can grow when his prayers are unanswered, nor on what the poor are learning under persecution. Neither does he offer theological possibilities about God's self-limitation in this world. Rather, in simple faith, David sees the oppression, hears the egotism of the wicked, and then cries out, "Arise, O Lord!" David expects God to *do* something. "Break the arm of the wicked," is his prayer.

Do we expect God to answer our prayers? Do we experience Him as the living God? Paul prays that we may know "what is the exceeding greatness of His power toward us who believe . . ." (Eph. 1:19). May God deliver us from our practical atheism. He is not absent; He is present. "Arise, O Lord!"

CHAPTER ELEVEN

When the Foundations Crumble

Psalm 11

The twentieth century has seen the collapse of order in the West. With the Reformation, the order of the Bible replaced the order of the church. Then, with the Enlightenment, the order of reason replaced the order of the Bible. Today, however, reason as an absolute has fallen under the attack of the irrational, of relativism ("process philosophy"), and of the naked will to power. Indeed, it seems that traditional foundations have all but crumbled and left humankind standing alone in an empty universe.

Long ago, the psalmist experienced a similar destruction. The threat of irrational assassination shook the foundations of his moral and political order. As a result, he was tempted to flee, to find his own security (v. 1) in a world stalked by evil men who "shoot secretly at the upright in heart" (v. 2). Then, as now, terrorism ripped apart the structure of life. The righteous were under siege.

The theme of this psalm, however, is that God will defend the righteous. Commentators call Psalm 11 an individual psalm of confidence or trust. It is a meditation rather than a prayer and traditionally its author is held to be David. The thought moves from the attack of the wicked (vv. 1–3), to the Lord's response (vv. 4–6), to a final confession of faith (v. 7).

THE WICKED DESTROY THE FOUNDATIONS

1 In the LORD I put my trust;
　How can you say to my soul,
　"Flee *as* a bird to your mountain"?
2 For look! The wicked bend *their* bow,
　They make ready their arrow on the string,
　That they may shoot secretly at the upright in heart.
3 If the foundations are destroyed,
　What can the righteous do?

Ps. 11:1–3

99

The psalm begins: *"In the Lord I put my trust"* (or "took refuge"). His trust in Yahweh inhibits David's temptation to escape calamity, but still an inward voice suggests, *"Flee as a bird to your mountain."* This longing for flight may come from David's own fear, an outside advisor, or satanic suggestion. He is faced with the alternative that confronts us all in crises: make God your refuge or try to create your own. The ultimate issue is whether we will trust Him or trust ourselves. Who will be the effective God of our lives?

"For look! The wicked bend their bow" is the basis for the temptation. The terror, however, is not in the attack itself but in the enemies' plan to *"shoot secretly at the upright in heart."* The *"upright"* person is "straightforward" or "just," and is the object of an assassin. An ambush is being set. Known enemies can be dealt with; it is the unknown who are so intimidating.

Verse 3 reveals the heart of David's fear: *"If the foundations are destroyed, / What can the righteous* [those who follow God's law] *do?"* The implied answer is, "Not much."

A regime of terror bases its power upon fear of the violent unknown. When informers are everywhere and people vanish, trust vanishes with them as it becomes obvious that the reign of law has ended. In a police state one never knows when the secret police will knock at the door. Much of our world today faces exactly that intimidation. The great enemy of such terror is the Christian, the person who can say with David, *"In the Lord I put my trust."* It is the believer who finds a security and order outside himself or his circumstances. Irrational evil cannot control him or break him down. Apart from the security of faith, however, even the strongest person will finally cave in to those who *"shoot secretly."* In this terrorist-filled world it is the Christian who is the counter-revolutionary.

THE LORD DESTROYS THE WICKED

4 The LORD *is* in His holy temple,
  The LORD's throne *is* in heaven;
    His eyes behold,
  His eyelids test the sons of men.
5 The LORD tests the righteous,
  But the wicked and the one who loves violence His
    soul hates.

> 6 Upon the wicked He will rain coals;
> Fire and brimstone and a burning wind;
> *Shall be* the portion of their cup.
>
> Ps. 11:4–6

With verse 4, David turns his thoughts to the God whom he trusts. God dwells, not merely in Jerusalem locked into tribal space and relative time, but in heaven itself, where He reigns (see Solomon's prayer at the temple dedication, 1 Kings 8:27). In other words, when the foundations crumble we need another foundation, and we have it in the eternal, living God. From His throne of judgment *"His eyes behold, / His eyelids test the sons of men."* God sees us. God knows us. He knows David. He knows his attackers. He knows the terrorist and his victims, and all are interrogated. God's *"eyelids test* ["examine"] *the sons of men."* He squints in scrutiny as He tests. The righteous are included in the test but it is the wicked who fail. They are the ones who "love violence." In His inner self, *"His soul"* (*nepeš*), God *"hates"* them. The *"coals,"* *"fire,"* *"brimstone,"* and *"burning wind"* of verse 6 all symbolize the anger or wrath of God executed against the wicked. Like Sodom and Gomorrah, they will be consumed by God's judgment (Gen. 19:24). Our own history has seen signs of the divine fire, and there is a warning for us here as a nation. God hates the violent. If we engage in terror, we too will feel the fire of His wrath. Thus David concludes: *"This shall be the portion of their cup."* The *"cup"* here is the cup of destiny (cf. Mark 14:36).

The Lord Upholds the Righteous

> 7 For the LORD *is* righteous,
> He loves righteousness;
> His countenance beholds the upright.
>
> Ps. 11:7

This verse closes David's meditation on the character of God. It is because *"the Lord is righteous"* that the wicked are judged (v. 5). Because He is righteous, *"He loves righteousness."* (The word translated "righteousness" is a plural form, signifying "full, complete righteousness"). Thus *"His countenance* ["face"] *beholds the upright."* He looks upon them; He welcomes them into His presence and they stand before Him for eternity. As Jesus says in His parable of the wheat and the tares after the tares are cast into the furnace of fire, "then the righteous will shine forth as the sun in the kingdom of their Father" (Matt. 13:43).

What do we do when the foundations are destroyed? Psalm 11 answers this question by giving us another foundation: Trust in the Lord. Make Him our security, our refuge. Know that He inhabits eternity and reigns over the chaos of this world. His throne is in heaven. His moral order and kingdom transcend this world and cannot be overthrown. He is the just judge who tries all hearts and hates men of violence. These will know His wrath, but the righteous will know His presence for all eternity. God's character is righteous, and it will be made known!

A postscript is in order here. Throughout Psalm 11 there is a stress on the righteous and righteousness. In our age of relativism, our pulpits tend to be silent on this theme. We are in danger of being so accommodated to the world that the call to righteousness falls on deaf ears, or worse yet, is never even spoken.

Revival always comes with a deep conviction of sin and a consequent call to righteousness. Whole cities were brought to a standstill by Charles Finney as he proclaimed God's call to righteous relationships and righteous living. Hundreds of thousands responded and came to Christ. To know the Lord, to know His love and to see His face, we must be righteous. This is both Christ's gift and His call to us (2 Cor. 5:21). Nothing less satisfies the character of God.

CHAPTER TWELVE

I Can't Stand Hypocrites

Psalm 12

A common charge against the church today is that it is "filled with hypocrites—actors." The average Christian plays his or her part well, dressing properly, following the order of service, greeting people warmly, on cue, and punctuating conversation with comforting phrases—"praise the Lord," "God is good." Some years ago, Keith Miller dropped a bomb by writing *The Taste of New Wine*. This best-seller exposed the false fronts Christians erect to keep themselves emotionally aloof from each other. Miller attacked "performance Christianity" with a candor unique for the time and launched "relational Christianity," an attempt to build a faith that moved beyond the conceptual and integrated theology and psychology. This was all done in the name of honesty and had as its goal the renewal of the church. The need for such a movement was clear and has had a lasting impact on today's Christians.

Psalm 12 deals with hypocrites. The problem here, however, is deeper than relational insecurity and dishonesty. Underneath these sins lies moral deception. Those who speak idly "with flattering lips and a double heart" (v. 2) mask their attack on the poor and the needy (v. 5). Their "vileness" is exalted and the wicked run riot (v. 8). Therefore, the psalmist calls to the Lord for help, asking Him to "cut off all flattering lips, / And the tongue that speaks proud things" (v. 3).

These lying, deceitful, egotistical people then deceive the faithful and oppose God. They especially use false promises and manipulation to oppress the poor. The answer to the psalmist's cry is given by God Himself (v. 5). He will "arise" on their behalf.

Commentators identify this psalm as either a community lament or an individual lament. Tradition, which we follow here, ascribes authorship to David. The thought moves from a cry for help and a call for judgment against the hypocrites (vv. 1–4) to God's response (v. 5) and David's affirmation (vv. 6–7). The final verse adds a postscript on the wicked (v. 8).

CALL FOR HELP

1 Help, LORD, for the godly man ceases!
  For the faithful disappear from among the sons of
    men.
2 They speak idly everyone with his neighbor;
  With flattering lips *and* a double heart they speak.
3 May the LORD cut off all flattering lips,
  And the tongue that speaks proud things,
4 Who have said,
  "With our tongue we will prevail;
  Our lips *are* our own;
  Who *is* lord over us?"

Ps. 12:1–4

Verse 1 begins with a cry for Yahweh to act: *"Help, Lord, for the godly man ceases!"* The verb for *"help"* means "save, deliver." The reason for his request is that the *"godly"* are a vanishing breed. These "covenant people" who honor right relationships are being snuffed out by the wicked. It seems to David that the faithful have left the earth entirely, as he notes in verse 1b, where *"the sons of men"* refers to humankind in general. Verse 2 documents the loss of the godly. *"They speak idly* ["vanity"] *everyone with his neighbor."* The substance, the truth, is gone, as everyone "speaks idly" [in "vanity"] with his neighbor. This "vanity" comes from *"flattering* ["smooth"] *lips"* masking a *"double heart"*; literally, "heart and heart."

For David right relationships are faithful or truthful relationships built on the covenant. Now, however, his world is filled with deceivers who talk smoothly and never let people know their real selves. They have a *"double heart."* *"Heart"* here includes both mind and volition. It is the self thinking and willing or desiring.

Our world is like David's. We live in an age of unprecedented manipulation through mass communications. The female body is used to sell every imaginable product. We are assured that we will be sexy, sociable, and successful by purchasing things to enhance our odor or our ardor. Likewise, the church has become concerned about its image in the community rather than with the substance of its life. In a senior homiletics class in theological seminary we spent a large amount of time examining bulletin covers from church services so that our future parishes would be properly advertised to those who attend. Vanity and flattering lips are not remote even from our pulpits as research into people's "felt needs" tells us how to preach motivationally to them. Then, too, liturgy can be used as "theater," a substitute for life. I heard Professor Ed Dowey of Princeton remark, "The less a minister has to say the more he wears and does."

Verses 3 and 4 tell us the kind of help David requests from the Lord: *"May the Lord cut off* ["kill," see Ps. 37:38] *all flattering lips, / And the tongue that speaks proud things."* Bluntly, David wants Him to come in judgment and destroy the flatterers. The context reveals that this is not as harsh as it appears.

The flatterers speak *"proud things."* The word here translated *"proud"* has the basic meaning "great." The intent is to say that the flatterers speak "too great things" or "presumptuous or haughty things" (cf. Jer. 45:5). The great or haughty things reveal the true heart of the flatterers.

The real evil of these people is now exposed. Their boast *"With our tongue we will prevail; / Our lips are our own; / Who is lord over us?"* is a claim to autonomy. This is in stark contrast to God's word to Moses, "Who has made man's mouth? Or who makes the mute, the deaf, the seeing, or the blind? Have not I, the Lord? Now therefore, go, and I will be with your mouth and teach you what you shall say" (Exod. 4:11–12). The flatterers, however, assert their own power. They speak *"proud things"* climaxing in the question *"Who is lord over us?"* And, of course, the answer is no one. No wonder they deserve God's judgment. Paul writes, "And even as they did not like to retain God in their knowledge, God gave them over to a debased mind . . . being filled with all unrighteousness, . . . covetousness, maliciousness; full of envy, . . . strife, deceit, evil-mindedness; they are . . . proud, boasters, inventors of evil things . . . who, knowing the righteous judgment of God, that those who practice such things are deserving of death, not only do the same but also approve of those who practice them" (Rom. 1:28–32).

The church today is often guilty of flattery and vanity. As in David's time, the purpose is to mask moral corruption. Long ago Billy Graham warned pastors that there were two things that would ruin their ministries: sex and money. A pastor friend of mine in a prestigious church was with his elders in a meeting when a woman stormed in accusing him of seducing her. It turned out that there were four other women in his parish who had been the objects of his lust. The result was that he was quickly removed. His situation there as a powerful "father figure" for the church and as an advocate of moral relativism and psychological fulfillment set him up for the kill. Unfortunately, this is not a rarity in the modern church. Like David we cry, *"Help, Lord, for the godly man ceases!"*

GOD'S RESPONSE

5 "For the oppression of the poor, for the sighing of
   the needy,
  Now I will arise," says the LORD;
  "I will set *him* in the safety for which he yearns."
                              Ps. 12:5

Many commentators speak of this verse as a prophetic oracle and envision it as being spoken in the temple to the psalmist. This view, however, is unnecessary. In fact, God speaks to His people directly. He personally called Abraham, wrestled with Jacob, and addressed Moses out of the burning bush. In the New Testament He speaks through prophecy, words of wisdom, words of knowledge, and interpretation of tongues to His church through all of its members (see 1 Cor. 12–14). That the Lord carried on a direct dialogue with David is amply illustrated in Scripture (see 1 Sam. 23:1 ff.). Thus here we read: " *'For the oppression of the poor, for the sighing of the needy, / Now I will arise,' says the Lord."* The Hebrew noun for *"oppression"* means "violence, devastation." The poor are being wiped out by these hypocrites who are defrauding them. In turn, they sigh or groan under their injustice. God, however, rises up in judgment from His throne to go into battle on their behalf (cf. Ps. 76:7–9; Job 31:14).

In responding to David's cry for help, Yahweh promises, *"I will set him in the safety for which he yearns."* The noun for *"safety"* here also means "welfare, prosperity," indicating that the poor will be rescued from their calamity and find the fullness of life for which they long.

We must always remember that God has a special place in His heart for the poor. He hears their cries (see Exod. 2:23–25) and promises to anoint His Messiah to bring good news to them (Isa. 61:1). This is fulfilled by Jesus who comes to preach to the poor, heal them, and deliver them from the oppression of Satan (see Luke 4:16–21).

Likewise, the poor in God's church who are deceived by unrighteous pastors and who are robbed for human religious glory and gain will be delivered from their oppressors. The Lord will arise from His throne and give them the *"safety"* for which they yearn. As God restores His church today the sham of religiosity is being revealed for what it is, and the glory of God is being manifested through the power of His Spirit.

DAVID'S RESPONSE TO GOD

6 The words of the LORD *are* pure words,
    Like silver tried in a furnace of earth,
    Purified seven times.
7 You shall keep them, O LORD,
    You shall preserve them from this generation forever.

                        Ps. 12:6–7

Having heard God, David now responds. First David reflects on God's trustworthiness: *"The words of the Lord are pure words, / Like silver tried in a furnace of earth."* The Hebrew for *"words"* here means "utterance or speech" and can also mean "promise or command." God has promised to act. This is a *"pure"* promise, with no mixture of hypocrisy or smooth flattery in it. Neither is it vain or empty. David then uses a vivid simile to express his thought—God's words are *"like silver tried in a furnace."* They are *"purified seven times."* The number *"seven"* is the number of perfection. For example, God created the world in seven days and it was "good," "complete" (*ṭôb;* see Gen. 1:31–2:2).

Since God's words are so pure, David can pray with assurance in verse 7: *"You shall keep them, O Lord, / You shall preserve them from this generation forever."* The question is to what does "them" refer? It may designate the poor or it may designate God's words. If David means that God will keep the poor, then the verb *"keep"* (*šāmar*) means "preserve" or "protect." However, if the verb refers to God's words, then it means "to watch over," "to observe and do." In the immediate context it seems better to take *"them"* as referring to God's words. God promises Jeremiah, "I am ready to perform [*šāmar*] My word" (Jer. 1:12). Moreover, God preserves His words *"from this generation forever,"* that is, from now on to eternity. "The word of our God stands forever" (Isa. 40:8).

Here God's words are *"pure"*—trustworthy, true, and lasting; they are eternal. When we learn, study, and obey them we are building solidly and the results will endure the testing fire (1 Cor. 3:13). "Heaven and earth will pass away, but My words will by no means pass away" (Mark 13:31).

DAVID'S POSTSCRIPT

8 The wicked prowl on every side,
   When vileness is exalted among the sons of men.

Ps. 12:8

David concludes with the observation that *"the wicked"* are set loose and surround the righteous *"on every side, / When vileness is exalted among the sons of men."* The noun for *"vileness"* means "worthlessness, insignificance." It is, again, the consequence of vanity and flattering lips. When this is the atmosphere of the times, the wicked will *"prowl"*; they will be on the hunt.

In desperation, then, David cries out for God's intervention: When the truth of God is surrendered, only human emptiness will be left. As Mother Teresa puts it, "All our words will be useless unless they come from within—words which do not give the light of Christ increase the darkness."

Do we have David's longing to see God judge our hypocrisy? Do we long to see Him bring us to repentance and purify our hearts? Do we long to see His words exalted rather than our worthless thoughts? Here is the narrow road to genuine revival and renewal in the church.

CHAPTER THIRTEEN

Praying in the Silence

Psalm 13

A dear friend of mine recently died of cancer. She spent her final months at home lovingly cared for by her family and friends. They fed her, gave her shots, exercised her; they were there day and night. While she deeply appreciated the love, she also felt guilty that she had absorbed her family's time and energy. Often I reminded her that if the roles had been reversed she would have done exactly the same thing. In her confinement she often felt God to be distant. Why were our prayers for healing not answered? Where was God in the midst of the pain? She lived with the question that forms the haunting refrain in verses 1–2, "How long . . . ?" So too, as the psalmist senses God's absence, he reveals inner sorrow and outer trouble (v. 2). Death seems near (v. 3). The enemy prevails (v. 4). Psalm 13 then deals with a question we all face: How do you pray in the silence?

Commentators call this psalm an individual lament. With tradition, we accept David as the author. The thought of the psalm moves from question (vv. 1–2) to petition (vv. 3–4) to resolution (vv. 5–6).

THE CRITICAL QUESTION

1 How long, O LORD? Will You forget me forever? How
   long will You hide Your face from me?
2 How long shall I take counsel in my soul,
   Having sorrow in my heart daily?
   How long will my enemy be exalted over me?

                                                      Ps. 13:1–2

Verse 1 asks the critical questions which face every sufferer. David doesn't even offer specifics in the first cry. It is *God's* absence, not the absence of answers that troubles him. Here David voices the agony of every sensitive heart. We, however, have our specifics. We look at a body weakened by cancer, a baby born with Down's syndrome, a person trapped by mental illness, and we ask, *"How long, O Lord?"* When David complains that God hides His face, the meaning of the phrase is that He "withdraws His favor."

David's questions, like ours, become specific in verse 2. Here he contends with continual sorrow and a victorious enemy. In all these calamities, it is as if God has turned from him—at least this is what he supposes. The irony here is that if God were really far, his prayer would be futile. But at any rate David *feels* that God is absent. And when God seems absent, Satan seems near. So the counsels of his soul are with sorrow rather than joy.

THE CRUCIAL PETITION

3 Consider *and* hear me, O LORD my God;
   Enlighten my eyes, Lest I sleep the *sleep of* death;
4 Lest my enemy say,
   "I have prevailed against him";
   Lest those who trouble me rejoice when I am moved.

                                                      Ps. 13:3–4

David now expresses his central concern. *"Consider and hear me, O Lord my God."* The verb for *"consider"* literally means "look," in contrast to God's averted face in verse 1. The request he asks God to hear is: *"Enlighten my eyes."* Otherwise, he says, they will close in death and his enemies will triumph. His eyes are "enlightened," or made to "shine" when God looks upon David once again, lifting up "the light of [His] countenance" upon him (Ps. 89:15). In the words of Psalm 36:9, "In Your light we see light." Thus David is "enlightened" when his *relationship* with God is restored. As John puts it, "God is light and in Him is no darkness at all. . . . If we walk in the light as He is in the light, we have fellowship with one another" (1 John 1:5, 7).

At the same time, the restoration of the relationship will bring the truth of God to David again. Thus his prayer, *"enlighten my eyes,"* is also a prayer for that truth. When Jesus declares Himself to be the "light of the world" (John 8:12), He exposes our darkness, our bondage to sin and to Satan. How will we know victory over these enemies? By letting His word reveal them and then knowing that they have been defeated by Him.

The alternative to this enlightenment, both relationally and conceptually, is death and defeat. So David asks God to light up his eyes: *"Lest I sleep the sleep of death; / Lest my enemy say, / 'I have prevailed against him'; / Lest those who trouble me rejoice when I am moved"* (vv. 3–4). The ultimate answer to the disaster of death and the triumph of the wicked is simply God's presence, His face turned toward David and David's face turned toward Him. Likewise, Paul speaks of the power of seeing God's glory: "But we all, with unveiled face, beholding as in a mirror the glory of the Lord, are being tranformed into the same image from glory to glory, just as by the Spirit of the Lord" (2 Cor. 3:18).

THE CONFIDENT RESOLUTION

> 5 But I have trusted in Your mercy;
>   My heart shall rejoice in Your salvation.
> 6 I will sing to the LORD,
>   Because He has dealt bountifully with me.
>
>   *Ps. 13:5–6*

David now moves with the assurance that his prayers will be answered. *"But I have trusted in Your mercy / My heart shall rejoice in Your salvation."* Since he has known God's mercy (*hesed*) in the past, he is certain that he will receive God's salvation and rejoice in it once again. The God who comes with truth also comes with power. Once David prays for enlightenment, God reminds him of His mercy and rekindles his hope for *"salvation"* (*yĕšûʿâh*) or *"deliverance."*

David ends this psalm in triumph. *"I will sing to the Lord, / Because He has dealt bountifully with me."* David's thought has moved from God's silence to God's illumination, to God's salvation—and worship is the proper response. God has answered His prayer with His presence.

As we have noted, we too find God distant at times. Our own emptiness or our overwhelming enemies may bring this despair upon us. What shall we do? Pray!—even if all we can cry out to God is "How long?" When we do this, however haltingly, the answer comes.

My friend who died of cancer was sustained throughout her painful illness by prayer. Finally, during her last week she had a dream. In it Jesus came to her and told her that she would go to be with Him "before supper." She died in the Thursday morning of Easter week when the church celebrates Jesus' final Passover supper with His disciples. Her death was the release from suffering for which we had prayed. Indeed, for her, death was the ultimate healing.

God does open our eyes to Himself. Once again we get in touch with His mercy from the past and have the assurance of His salvation for the future, bringing forth our songs of praise.

CHAPTER FOURTEEN

This World's Ship of Fools

Psalms 14 and 53

"The fool has said in his heart, 'There is no God,' " is perhaps one of the best-known verses in the Bible. Vast numbers of people today would say exactly the opposite, "The fool has said in his heart, 'There is a God.' " Atheism in the modern world has become both a religion and an ideology. The Marxist state is established upon an avowed denial of any supernatural being or beings. While in the West religion still has its formal place, there are also vast numbers of atheists. The Bishop of Paris said recently that in France it takes tremendous courage for a young person to go through confirmation and confess his or her faith in Jesus Christ. This is certainly also true in parts of the United States, especially in educated circles. Why so?

The denial of God in the East and the West is based on several points. Apart from a general unbelief due to willful sin, atheism found its entry into the modern age through the Enlightenment. With the discovery of the so-called laws of nature, it became "foolish" to think that the God of creation would violate His own created order, which seemed to move in perfection. Would the God who made both natural law and moral law Himself become a "lawbreaker"? The Jewish philosopher Spinoza argued this way: "The universal laws of nature are decrees of God following from the necessity and perfection of the Divine nature. Hence, any event happening in nature which contravenes nature's universal laws, would necessarily also contravene the Divine decree, nature and understanding; or if any one asserted that God acts in contravention to the laws of nature, he, *ipso facto,* would be compelled to assert that God acted against His own nature—an evident absurdity." Thus Spinoza concluded, "One might easily show from the same premises that the power and efficiency of nature are in themselves the Divine power and efficiency, and that the Divine power is the very essence of God" (*A Theologico-Political Treatise,* chap. vi). The conclusion this argument drives us to is that nature is God, that there is no longer a transcendent deity who both orders His creation and directly breaks into it at any time He pleases. The deistic clock of the universe, wound up and abandoned, is now running.

Once the scientific method held sway, the power of reason to control all reality was applied, little by little, to the whole of human life. To know the truth, we no longer needed divine revelation or the authority of the church. We only needed ourselves. The modern era has shifted from humility before God to "humility" before humankind. Thus we came to be in awe of ourselves. Through reason we would conquer superstition and discover the laws behind the apparent chaos of human life. For Marx, economics unlocked history. For Darwin, evolution unlocked nature. For Freud, our biological drives and the unconscious unlocked the human psyche.

Not surprisingly, the Bible was subjected to the same rational, scientific method. This was not all bad, to be sure. A better original text was assured to the translators. The historical setting of the Biblical books and the meanings of their words became clearer. With the denial of the supernatural, however, and with the application of social Darwinism to Biblical history, practical, if not theoretical "fools" held court. They said in their hearts, "There is no God." The suffering and mass destruction of the world wars seemed to document their thesis. God was viewed as absent, and these wars were never held to be the judgment of God upon modern egotism.

Today, in our chaotic, existential age, "post-modern" man continues to deny God, not because of the order of the world but because of its absurdity. Physics now sees an indeterminate universe. There seem to be no absolutes. How can God exist in such chaos? What we have, however, are two realities. The first is a relative order to life, while at the same time the second is a break or an unpredictability in that order. Doesn't this open the door again to the living God who upholds the universe by the word of His power and yet exercises His dynamic will in its midst? Could it be that the arguments against God both from reason and from chaos fall short of the mark? Are they not both, in their own time and place, given by intellectual fools who say in their hearts "There is no God"? Isn't the problem our point of departure? If we start with ourselves, like Descartes, will we not always end up in unbelief? Must we not start with God, His glory, His power, His revelation? Must we not listen to Him speak to us again?

Psalms 14 and 53 are separate editions of the same meditation or individual lament. The existence of both in the Psalter is similar to the presence of many similar sayings of Jesus in the Gospels. The two psalms may reflect a common oral tradition. Psalm 14 employs the Hebrew name "Yahweh." Psalm 53 uses "Elohim." Clearly both psalms assumed an independent life in the worship of Israel. The reference to "captivity" in 14:7 and 53:6 need not be a technical term for the post-exilic period and thus does not prohibit the traditional ascription of this psalm to David. The thought moves from the denial of God (v. 1) to the depravity of man (vv. 2–3), the consequences of sin (vv. 4–6), and the longing for salvation (v. 7).

ATHEISM AND ITS CONSEQUENCES

1 The fool has said in his heart,
"*There is* no God."
They are corrupt,

They have done abominable works,
There is none who does good.

Ps. 14:1

1 The fool has said in his heart,
    "There is no God."
They are corrupt,
    and have done abominable iniquity;
    There is none who does good.

Ps. 53:1

The first verse identifies the fool and the consequences of his foolishness: *"The fool has said in his heart, 'There is no God.'"* The *"fool"* is the man who has no perception of ethical and spiritual claims. Whether or not he is a theoretical atheist in the modern sense of the word is irrelevant. In Psalm 74:22 the "foolish man" reproaches God daily. He believes just enough to be angry. Since "the fear of the Lord is the beginning of wisdom" (Prov. 9:10) the fool, in denying God, denies wisdom itself. This is foolish indeed.

The surrender of the knowledge of God or even the formal belief in God, opens the door to all kinds of human corruption. To deny God means, ultimately, to deny any transcendent basis for morality. With order and accountability lost, all the darkness of the human spirit is unleashed. The irony of the twentieth century is that the period of the greatest technical advance has been also the period of the greatest mass destruction. The judgments offered in verse 1 as a consequence of saying *"There is no God"* are demonstrated in our own history.

The first result of denying God, David says, is: *"They are corrupt."* By *"corrupt"* he means moral corruption. The same thought appears in Genesis 6:12 prior to the flood: "So God looked upon the earth, and indeed it was corrupt; for all flesh had corrupted their way on the earth." Next, this corruption is seen in *"abominable works."* The acts of these fools include ritual and ethical violations of God's law.

The concluding thought universalizes the problem: *"There is none who does good."* This thought, and the sequence of denying God and then denying our humanity lies behind Paul's indictment of the race in Romans 1:18–3:20. Once we no longer know who God is, we no longer know who we are. We destroy ourselves and each other as good vanishes from the earth. If it were not for God's grace and providence, we would all self-destruct.

Universal Depravity

2 The Lord looks down from heaven upon the children
   of men,
   To see if there are any who understand, who seek
   God.
3 They have all turned aside,
   They have together become corrupt;
   There is none who does good,
   No, not one.

Ps. 14:2–3

2 God looks down from heaven upon the children of
   men,
   To see if there are *any* who understand, who seek
   God.
3 Every one of them has turned aside;
   They have together become corrupt;
   There is none who does good,
   No, not one.

Ps. 53:2–3

God may be absent from the human heart, but He is not absent
from heaven. However much we may dim our gaze heavenward, God
does not dim His gaze earthward. David stresses God's transcendence
as he continues: *"The Lord looks down from heaven."* Human pride, however monumental, shrinks before the holiness and glory of God who
is exalted upon high. As Isaiah puts it, "In the year that King Uzziah
died, I saw the Lord sitting on a throne, high and lifted up . . ." (Isa.
6:1).

As God looks down He sees *"the children of men."* This phrase could
describe not only Israel, but all humankind as well. The Lord is looking
"to see if there are any who understand, who seek God." If we understand
properly, if we know the truth, then we will seek the source of that
truth, God Himself. For His part, God looks for those looking for Him.
Jesus said, "So I say to you, ask, and it will be given to you; seek,
and you will find; knock, and it will be opened to you" (Luke 11:9).

The view from heaven is grim: *"They have all turned aside, / They
have together become corrupt; / There is none who does good, / No, not
one."* These absolute clauses center upon the total rebellion of the race:
"all . . . together . . . none . . . no, not one." Paul picks these verses

up in Romans 3:12. They serve as his final argument for the whole world's standing under the wrath of God and every mouth's being stopped before His judgment.

The indictment begins with all humanity's having *"turned aside,"* or having turned its back not only on the Lord's way but on the Lord Himself. Next, *"they have together become corrupt."* The verb for *"corrupt"* means "tainted" morally. The consequences follow: *"There is none who does good."* Anticipating our objection, David adds: *"No, not one."*

As we have seen, when we surrender our knowledge of God, we also surrender our knowledge of ourselves and of life itself. Corruption is the result. The deepest Biblical revelation about this is the truth that when we rebel against God's kingdom there is only one alternative, Satan's kingdom, the dominion of darkness (Col. 1:13). As the human race turns from God and His ways there is a false sense of freedom; where they imagine liberation there is only bondage. Our denial of God in no way affects His reality. Moreover, He will not be negated forever.

SIN AND ITS CONSEQUENCES

4 Have all the workers of iniquity no knowledge,
   Who eat up my people *as* they eat bread,
   And do not call on the LORD?
5 There they are in great fear,
   For God *is* with the generation of the righteous.
6 You shame the counsel of the poor,
   But the LORD *is* his refuge.

Ps. 14:4–6

4 Have the workers of iniquity no knowledge,
   Who eat up my people *as* they eat bread,
   And do not call upon God?
5 There they are in great fear
   Where no fear was,
   For God has scattered the bones of him who encamps
      against you;
   You have put *them* to shame,
   Because God has despised them.

Ps. 53:4–5

The answer to verse 4's opening rhetorical question is clearly "Yes." The *"workers of iniquity"*—those who do "abominable works" (v. 1) and those who do no good (v. 3)—lack knowledge. As fools they have denied the existence of God, and thus do not seek Him. Living a life of low visibility they believe that they can devour God's people *"as . . . bread"* and deny God by not calling on His name. In other words, the two great commandments—to love God and to love their neighbor— are absent from their consciousness and from their lives (see Luke 10:27).

In Psalm 14:5 the consequence of this sin is clear. Those who work iniquity *"are in great fear, / For God is with the generation of the righteous."* Even though they deny God, they live with underlying anxiety. Either this anxiety or fear is unconscious, or they know well that God is with the righteous after all, and that evil workers cannot escape Him.

It may be that those who violently deny God the most are in some ways psychologically closer to Him than they would admit. They know that He is with *"the generation of the righteous"* and not far from them. It is interesting to note that Joseph Stalin studied for the priesthood and Hugh Hefner's father was a Methodist minister.

In Psalm 14:6 David continues: *"You shame the counsel of the poor."* *"Counsel"* refers to "wisdom" or "advice." While the atheists undercut the poor person's thought God still protects him: *"The Lord is his refuge."*

Psalm 53:5 diverges from Psalm 14:5 in some respects. It affirms that the workers of iniquity are in great fear, but the reason is not simply God's presence with the righteous. Rather, the reason for the fear is God's judgment: *"For God has scattered the bones of him who encamps against you; / You have put them to shame, / Because God has despised them."* Employing warfare imagery here, David pronounces defeat upon the enemies of God's people. They experience the shame of conquest, which is a consequence of God's despising them.

In Psalm 14:4–6 the denial of God and the violence of life lived in His absence result in confrontation with Him. God lives with the righteous and provides refuge for the poor. Wherever ideological atheism has sought to extinguish the church, there has been an encounter with the God of the cross. Jesus stands with His martyred church. Indeed, the blood of the saints is the seed of that church. In communist countries today the church suffers but also prospers in her trials. Thus revival has spread in China and the underground church grows in the USSR.

In Psalm 53:4–5 God brings judgment upon His atheistic enemies. Today Hitler's Germany lies in ruins. After he scattered the bones of

Christians, his own bones were scattered. God will triumph over blasphemers and vindicate His name.

LONGING FOR SALVATION

7 Oh, that the salvation of Israel *would come* out of
    Zion!
  When the LORD brings back the captivity of His
    people,
  Let Jacob rejoice *and* Israel be glad.

Ps. 14:7

6 Oh, that the salvation of Israel would come out of
    Zion!
  When God brings back the captivity of His people,
  Let Jacob rejoice *and* Israel be glad.

Ps. 53:6

With a cry, David concludes his meditation on those who deny God and live lives of moral chaos. *"Oh, that the salvation of Israel would come out of Zion!"* Is this a messianic longing? It is certainly that in Psalm 2:6: "Yet I have set My King / On My holy hill of Zion." David's call for salvation is now fulfilled for us in Jesus Christ. As the Lord enters Jerusalem, Matthew quotes Zechariah 9:9: "Tell the daughter of Zion, 'Behold, your King is coming to you'" (Matt. 21:5). Thus the salvation of Israel comes from Zion to the ends of the earth.

Finally, David promises that the Lord will bring His people back from captivity. The noun for *"captivity"* may simply mean "restore fortunes." It is also prophetic, however, referring to the future return of Israel from Babylon, and the ultimate deliverance of God's people from captivity to Satan and death.

The historical and spiritual deliverance will result in worship. Thus the psalm concludes with the response to salvation: *"Let Jacob rejoice and Israel be glad."* The reference to *"Jacob"* as a name for Israel may especially allude to Jacob's deliverance from his self-willed life which was death (see Gen. 32:22–32). These parallel clauses call upon all of God's people to praise Him for His salvation which vindicates the Lord God and exposes the true foolishness of the man who says in his heart, "There is no God." The mighty salvation of the Lord will shut the mouths of unbelievers. The ship of fools will sink. In that day God will be God!

CHAPTER FIFTEEN

Prescription for Life

Psalm 15

In a famous debate between theologians Paul Tillich and Karl Barth, Tillich claimed that our theology should be an "answering theology." This means that the world asks the questions which theology then answers. For Tillich the issue was one of relevance. Psychologists teach us that we should address "felt needs." Barth, however, replied No, and he went on to say that the world doesn't know the right questions to ask. God must reveal the questions as well as the answers. Here in Psalm 15 God reveals the right questions and the right answers. This psalm begins with life's critical issue: who may "abide" in God's tent and "dwell" in His holy hill?

Psalm 15 is a didactic wisdom poem establishing guidelines for living that will usher us into God's presence. It covers our walk, our works, and our words (v. 2). While the psalm could be interpreted legalistically, this would be wrong. The psalmist is concerned with our attitude, not just our action. As C. S. Lewis points out in *The Great Divorce,* throughout our lives we are either growing closer to God or further from Him. This psalm is a directive into His presence.

Commentators describe this psalm as an entrance liturgy or a torah liturgy. Traditionally its authorship is attributed to David. The reference to God's tabernacle or "tent" supports this view (v. 1). The wisdom style of the psalm may simply indicate that David employed a variety of known styles in his compositions. The movement of thought is from our question (v. 1) to God's answer (vv. 2–5).

LIFE'S QUESTION

1 Lord, who may abide in Your tabernacle?
Who may dwell in Your holy hill?

Ps. 15:1

Verse 1 begins with a direct address to the Lord, asking the eschatological question: Who may live in the presence of God? Who can stand before Him? Who can know Him now and forever? Who can go to heaven?

David does not just ask the superficial question of who may enter the tabernacle or visit God's holy hill. With his use of the words "abide" and "dwell" he raises the issue of permanence. Jesus also calls us to dwell or abide with Him (John 15). In both cases it is a question about knowing God intimately and remaining with Him eternally.

The questions of verse 1 include both the destination, God's presence, and the qualifications, who can go there?

GOD'S ANSWER

2 He who walks uprightly,
    And works righteousness,
    And speaks the truth in his heart;
3 He *who* does not backbite with his tongue,
    Nor does evil to his neighbor,
    Nor does he take up a reproach against his friend;
4 In whose eyes a vile person is despised,
    But he honors those who fear the LORD;
    He *who* swears to his own hurt and does not change;
5 He *who* does not put out his money at usury,
    Nor does he take a bribe against the innocent.
    He who does these *things* shall never be moved.

Ps. 15:2–5

The answer as to who may dwell with God is given in verse 2, and the rest of the psalm is devoted to its exposition. The first response is general. The remaining verses make this generalization specific.

The one who dwells in God's presence is the one who (1) *"walks uprightly,"* (2) *"works righteousness,"* and (3) *"speaks the truth."* To *"walk uprightly"* is to live in God's path according to God's rules. To work *"righteousness"* is to do those things which are consistent with the character of God and a godly walk. To *"speak the truth"* is to speak the things which are in conformity with our walk and work. This truth, David says, is to be in our *"heart,"* not just on our lips. It is to come from the center of our being.

All of life is to be sanctified. It is to be "whole" *and* "holy." The person integrated in submission to God throughout his entire character and behavior is the person who dwells with God now and who will dwell with Him forever (see 1 Thess. 5:23). It is through Jesus Christ that this is possible for us. He is the Righteous One and we are righteous in Him (2 Cor. 5:21).

While all of this is true, how does it become functional? For most of my Christian life the call to holiness or sanctification provoked my deep frustration. There were so many areas, especially attitudes, that were unredeemed in my life. I was left with a mixture of guilt and faith: I simply had to trust my justification in Christ and find peace for my troubled conscience (Rom. 5:1). Recently, however, I have come to see exciting new dimensions of God's work in my life. First, I have come to know that God wants to fill me with His Holy Spirit as a verifiable empowering experience (Acts 1:8). Second, I have come to know that the Lord wants to heal me inside and deliver me from those areas and attitudes of sin which Satan has taken over in my life and which are dominated by the flesh. He wants to release me from past hurts and memories. Through the power of the Holy Spirit and prayer, I have experienced, and will experience, significant healing so that verse 2 will not just accuse me and mock me. "Therefore if the Son makes you free, you shall be free indeed" (John 8:36).

In verse 3 David becomes specific as to what this person who dwells with God is to do. He is to resist gossip or slander: *"He . . . does not backbite with his tongue,"* that is, he *"speaks the truth."* He is to refrain from acting badly, from doing *"evil to his neighbor."* Thus he *"works righteousness."* Third, he does not *"take up a reproach against his friend"* (literally, "neighbor, the one near"). That is, he does not pass on slander or lies about those close to him. Again, he *"speaks the truth."*

Verse 3, then, gives specific directions about fulfilling the command to love our neighbor as ourselves (Lev. 19:18). All of these imperatives are lived out by Jesus as He *is* the truth, speaks the truth, and does the truth (John 8:31–32; 14:6, 10). As we yield to His Spirit He will do this in us.

Next, the one who dwells in God's presence despises God's enemies, *"a vile person"* ("reprobate"), and honors God's friends, *"those who fear the Lord"* (v. 4). God's character now becomes his standard of judgment. Thus in Christ we come to understand that all of us are first God's enemies, and that only by His mercy do some of us become His friends. We see the judgment of God against all sinners and know that that judgment prepares us for His mercy toward those who believe. Nevertheless, we can still identify with God's rejection of those who reject Him, knowing that in this age of grace, God's wrath, His "no," prepares us for His "yes" in Christ (Karl Barth, on Rom. 1–3).

Furthermore, the righteous person makes oaths which may result in his own harm or financial loss. He is the one who *"swears to his own hurt."* However, he stays steadfast in those oaths; he *"does not change."*

Finally, the righteous person refuses immoral gain in financial affairs: *"He . . . does not put out his money at usury, / Nor does he take a bribe against the innocent"* (v. 5). Usury was prohibited for Israel because those who normally borrowed money were in financial difficulty. Loans in this case were to be secured by a pledge and repaid interest-free. In loans to foreigners, however, interest was acceptable (Deut. 23:19–20). Loans in Israel represented a stable economy for a tribal culture where, ideally, capital was not amassed and where all the land was the Lord's. In practice, this did not take place. Thus the prophets warned the rich and powerful against exploiting the poor (see Amos 4:1 ff.). The banning of bribes especially has its context in judicial matters where corrupting justice is prohibited.

Verse 5 ends with a postscript. The one who lives righteously *"shall never be moved."* He is the one who dwells in God's presence.

In summary, David's concern here is with the totality of life determined by the character of God. This includes right speech with our neighbor and integrity in legal and financial matters. Oaths are to stand. Money is to honor God. The innocent are to be protected. We see these standards fulfilled in Christ, and then fulfilled in us who abide in Him and walk "not . . . according to the flesh but according to the Spirit" (Rom. 8:4). Jesus is the One in whom there is no sin (1 Pet. 2:22). He is the One who manifests the righteousness of God, first, for us and, second, in us (2 Pet. 2:24).

The world and a worldly church care nothing for righteousness. David's question about who can dwell in God's tabernacle on Mt. Zion, however, still stands and has pressing relevance for us today. This question and the answers which follow are a prescription for life—abundant now and eternal forever in Christ (John 10:10; 11:25).

CHAPTER SIXTEEN

Resurrection Promise

Psalm 16

On the day of Pentecost, Peter, filled with the Holy Spirit, preached Jesus as raised from the dead. His documentation for this was twofold. First, the Old Testament prophesied it, and second, he and the other apostles witnessed it (Acts 2:25–32). A central text appealed to by Peter that day is found in Psalm 16:8–11. It includes, "My flesh also will rest in hope. / For You will not leave my soul in Sheol, / Nor will You allow Your Holy One to see corruption" (vv. 9–10). After citing this passage, Peter went on to say that it could not apply to David, its author, since David was dead. Thus it is prophetic: "He [David], foreseeing this, spoke concerning the resurrection of the Christ, that His soul was not left in Hades, nor did His flesh see corruption. This Jesus God has raised up, of which we are all witnesses" (Acts 2:31–32). Similarly, Luke tells us that in Antioch Paul appealed to Psalm 16 as proof for Jesus' resurrection (Acts 13:35–37). Throughout the New Testament the claim is made that Easter rests on prophecy given in the Old Testament. As Paul tells the Corinthians, "Christ . . . rose again the third day according to the Scriptures . . ." (1 Cor. 15:3–4).

Many modern scholars, however, look at Psalm 16 not through the eyes of the apostles, but through the historical-critical method. Thus they assert that Psalm 16 has nothing to do with the Messiah and His resurrection but is rather a "psalm of confidence" centered in temporal deliverance from the threat of death (v. 10). If this is so then the "path of life" and the Lord's presence in the conclusion in verse 11 are just as temporal. Nothing here applies beyond the grave.

Before studying this text, then, a basic decision needs to be made. Shall we interpret Psalm 16 in the modern reconstructed context of its ancient setting, or shall we view it in light of the fulfillment of all of God's promises in Jesus and His resurrection (see 2 Cor. 1:20)? I prefer the latter choice, but deciding that Jesus stands at the center of this psalm does not force us to deny its original meaning. Old Testament prophecy often has several levels of fulfillment, with progressive revelation. The Holy Spirit certainly can inspire David to write in one setting and can then apply that revelation to Jesus in another. Moreover, as the Son of David (Rom. 1:3), sitting on his throne (2 Sam. 7:16), Jesus also inherits all the promises given to and through David. Moreover, David can speak prophetically beyond his own age and experience, under the inspiration of the Holy Spirit. Peter is right. David is dead and the fulfillment of the promise "Nor will You allow Your Holy One to see corruption" is given to His resurrected Son, the Lord Jesus Christ.

Psalm 16 then, in its ultimate intent, is an Easter psalm. It rings with hope. God will preserve the psalmist (v. 1). God is his goodness (v. 2). God is his inheritance (vv. 5–6). God is always before him (v. 8). God gives hope (v. 9). God is not the God of death (v. 10) but of life (v. 11). "In Your presence is fullness of joy; / At Your right hand are pleasures forevermore."

Traditionally, authorship of this psalm is ascribed to David. The specific setting in which it was written, and the proper translation, especially of verses 2–3, are disputed, but the overall theme of triumph is clear. The movement of thought is from a cry for preservation (v. 1) to a meditation on saints and sinners or idolaters (vv. 2–4), a confession of faith in the Lord (vv. 5–8), and a concluding statement of triumph (vv. 9–11).

CRY FOR PRESERVATION

1 Preserve me, O God, for in You I put my trust.

Ps. 16:1

Verse 1's cry for preservation is made in light of idolatry (v. 4) and the threat of death (v. 10). Whether these issues are pressing cannot be determined. They certainly are the general context in which David lived his life. Periodically, threats to his life and the temptation toward syncretism became crisis points. The word *"preserve"* here means to "keep," or to "watch over." It can be used of tending a flock (1 Sam. 17:20) or guarding captives (1 Kings 20:39). Here David prays that God will be his keeper and his guardian, even through death itself (see v. 10).

The basis for this prayer is trust, *"for in You I put my trust."* "Trust" here means "to seek refuge." God will keep David because he finds his shelter and security in Him.

This was also true of Jesus as a man during His earthly ministry. So Hebrews says of Him, ". . . in the days of His flesh, when He had offered up prayers and supplications with vehement cries and tears to Him who was able to save Him from death, . . . [He] was heard because of His godly fear" (Heb. 5:7). God preserved Him through life and death because He found His shelter in Him: "Father, 'into Your hands I commit My spirit'" (Luke 23:46).

SAINTS AND SINNERS

2 *O my soul,* you have said to the LORD,
  "You *are* my Lord,
  My goodness is nothing apart from You.
3 As for the saints who *are* on the earth,
  "They are the excellent ones, in whom is all my
    delight."
4 Their sorrows shall be multiplied who hasten *after*
    another *god;*
  Their drink offerings of blood I will not offer,
  Nor take up their names on my lips.
                                        Ps. 16:2–4

Having called upon God for preservation, David now addresses himself. This text is difficult to translate and understand. *"O my soul"* is absent from the Hebrew. It has been supplied because the verb ("[you] have said") is feminine, while David, assumed to be the speaker, is of course masculine. "Soul" *(nepeš),* however, is feminine and thus can be the subject agreeing with the feminine verb form. Meditating on his relationship to God, David recalls his confession: *"You are my Lord."* Thus he is submitted to the God whom he calls upon. Next, he adds: *"My goodness is nothing apart from You."* The word *"goodness" (ṭôb)* here means "completedness." As his Lord, God supplies all his needs and that supply is perfect and fulfilling.

In verse 3, David's mind turns to the saints on earth. *"Saints"* can refer to anything from pious Israelites to pagan gods. If the reference is to pagan gods, then verses 2–3 reveal a divided, syncretistic soul. It is probably better to see the word as designating the pious. Thus David reflects on God first and then His saints, whom he speaks of as *"the excellent ones."* The Hebrew word can refer to nobles, chieftains, or priests. David's delight is in them.

This verse embraces the true meaning of life: God and people. The two great commandments are fulfilled in loving the Lord and loving our neighbor. We are not created for "I-it" relationships but for "I-Thou" relationships (Martin Buber). When we love God as we should, we will love those around us as we should.

A friend of mine was a professional musician who was also involved in the drug traffic. Violence was his middle name. Three years ago he was almost killed in a motor bike accident north of Los Angeles. As he was recovering, he came to Christ and his heart began to change. The old hardness melted. A care for people surfaced. Now he is devoting his life to reaching his generation with the gospel. There is a tenderness behind his steel-blue eyes which touches people deeply. At the end of our evening service recently, I was praying for a woman in deep emotional pain. Suddenly I heard my friend's voice praying for her too. He had laid his hand gently on her shoulder as he asked Jesus to heal her. Now, with David, he can say of the saints, *"They are the excellent ones, in whom is all my delight."*

If verse 3 refers to the faithful, verse 4 refers to the faithless: *"Their sorrows shall be multiplied who hasten after another god."* Here idolaters will receive *"sorrows"* or *"pain."* The pain includes the disappointment of worshiping an impotent god and the sting of Yahweh's wrath against the "no-gods" and those devoted to them.

Over against the pagans and those Israelites who mix the worship of the true God with idols, stands David. Moreover, he refuses to offer *"drink offerings of blood"* or to name the names of false gods. The *"drink offerings of blood"* probably refer to sacrifices made with blood-stained hands. *"Names"* would refer to those of pagan deities. To name them is to know them and to come under their authority. David refuses to worship the idols or to confess their *"names."* His soul has said to the Lord, *"You are my Lord."*

ADDRESS AND CONFESSION

5 O Lord, *You are* the portion of my inheritance and
   my cup;
   You maintain my lot.
6 The lines have fallen to me in pleasant *places;*
   Yes, I have a good inheritance.
7 I will bless the Lord who has given me counsel;
   My heart also instructs me in the night seasons.

8 I have set the LORD always before me;
Because *He is* at my right hand I shall not be moved.

Ps. 16:5–8

David now speaks to the Lord and offers his personal confession. As he thinks of his God he sees Him as his inheritance, his wisdom, and his security. God is his goal, his guide, and his ground or anchor in life.

David addresses the Lord in verse 5. Behind his language lies God's promise of a land for His people. Now, David spiritualizes this concept. Since he already has the land, it is Yahweh, the giver of the land, who is his *"portion,"* his *"inheritance."* Yahweh is also his *"cup."* This may refer to the cup of blessing used in festal meals (see Ps. 23:5), or it may mean his "lot." This usage appears in Psalm 11:6, "Upon the wicked He will rain coals . . . [this] shall be the portion of their cup" (cf. Mark 14:36).

Not only is the Lord David's inheritance for the future, He also sustains his present inheritance in the land: *"You maintain my lot."* The *"lot"* is cast to divide property (see Josh. 18:6). Thus when David goes on to speak of his *"lines,"* he refers to boundary lines *"in pleasant places."*

He concludes that he has a good inheritance, knowing that ultimately the Lord Himself is his inheritance (v. 5). This also serves as a pointer to the truth that in the fullness of time Jesus comes as God's heir to establish our eternal inheritance. This is a part of our resurrection hope: "The Spirit Himself bears witness with our spirit that we are children of God, and if children, then heirs—heirs of God and joint heirs with Christ, if indeed we suffer with Him, that we may also be glorified together" (Rom. 8:16–17).

David continues: *"I will bless the Lord who has given me counsel; / My heart also instructs me in the night seasons"* (v. 7). Here David blesses God for the wisdom and guidance He gives him. The Lord gives him *"counsel"* or "advice" and his *"heart"* responds by giving him admonition as he meditates *"in the night seasons."* God speaks and David's heart speaks. They are in harmony together.

Verse 8 expresses David's security in having always set the Lord before him. God precedes him as the pillar of cloud and the pillar of fire preceded Israel (Exod. 13:21). He also steadies him by being at his *"right hand."* David adds *"I shall not be moved,"* or "shaken." No wonder Peter quoted this verse in his Pentecost sermon. There he says that Jesus, the eternal Son of God, always had Yahweh before His face. Not even death could shake Him because God was always at His right hand. What was temporarily true for David was eternally true for Jesus. Here again is the basis for resurrection faith.

THE TRIUMPHANT CONCLUSION

> 9 Therefore my heart is glad, and my glory rejoices;
>   My flesh also will rest in hope.
> 10 For You will not leave my soul in Sheol,
>   Nor will You allow Your Holy One to see corruption.
> 11 You will show me the path of life;
>   In Your presence *is* fullness of joy;
>   At Your right hand *are* pleasures forevermore.
>
> *Ps. 16:9–11*

Because God is David's inheritance, wisdom, and security, he now reaches a triumphant conclusion which transcends his own condition: *"Therefore my heart is glad, and my glory rejoices; / My flesh also will rest in hope."* David worships God, certain of His character. His *"heart,"* the center of his personality, is glad. His *"glory,"* which may refer poetically to his head (cf. Ps. 8:5; 1 Cor. 11:7), also rejoices. But the deepest conviction here is *"hope"* or, literally, "security." Thus God will guard and keep David *"in hope"* physically, in his *"flesh."* For him this may have meant the physical security of his inheritance in the land (v. 5); for us, however, in light of the resurrection, it is Jesus who is kept secure through death unto life eternal by His resurrection. The basis for this appears immediately: *"For You will not leave my soul in Sheol, / Nor will you allow Your Holy One to see corruption"* (v. 10). Here David speaks prophetically, beyond his own time and experience, of the Messiah to come who will conquer death.

The negative assertion in verse 10 means that God will not give the Messiah's soul to *"Sheol,"* the place of the dead. For the Old Testament Sheol is silent and endless. The Messiah, however, will not experience this. The parallel statement gives similar assurance beyond the grave: *"Nor will You allow Your Holy One to see corruption."* The fulfillment of these promises, as Peter notes, cannot be with David (see Acts 2:29). Thus they point prophetically to Jesus' resurrection. He alone was not left in Sheol. By the resurrection of His body, He alone did not see corruption.

The positive assertion in verse 11 follows logically: *"You will show me the path of life."* This *"path"* is a full life in this world. It also includes eternal life leading into the very presence of God. Here, David asserts, is *"fullness of joy"* (cf. Ps. 21:6). Indeed, joy is derived from the vision of God Himself. There, before Him, at His *"right hand"* (the place of His authority) are *"pleasures* [or, delights] *forevermore."* Once again, it is Jesus through His resurrection who takes this path of life into the presence of God. He alone fulfills this promise of triumph over the grave (Sheol) issuing in eternal life. Christ, the Lord, is preserved by God, given His inheritance, not moved or shaken, secured from death, and ushered into the presence of the Father where there is fullness of joy. This hope then becomes our hope in Him. We too share His Easter victory. In Him we rest in hope. In Him our souls are not abandoned to Sheol. In Him we do not see corruption and in Him we will know the very presence and pleasures of God.

The resurrection of Christ, based on Psalm 16, means for us that what God promises, He delivers. We are held by this hope until we see Jesus face to face and rest before Him.

CHAPTER SEVENTEEN

Vindication!

Psalm 17

Courts are frightening places. I remember several years ago when I received four traffic tickets for moving violations. As a result, under California law, I had to appear before the judge. I couldn't just pay the fines and walk away. So there I was at 9:00 A.M. on a week-day morning, sitting in a traffic court in downtown Los Angeles. As I looked around I saw a microcosm of the whole world. There were bankers and bums, professionals and pimps. When the judge entered, dressed in a black robe, his face solemn, we all rose in respect. The court was called into session, and I confess I was very nervous as the proceedings began. Almost everyone there pled, "Not guilty," although a few said,

"Guilty—with an explanation." I thought sarcastically, "What an incompetent police force. They have arrested a room full of innocent people!"

Being there that day was a good learning experience for me. I was able to imagine that this was a dress rehearsal for the Day of Judgment when we will all appear before God Himself and give an account of our lives. In Psalm 17, the author calls upon God to come and be the judge. Thus this psalm, like my day in court, at its ultimate level, prepares us for the final Day.

Psalm 17 has a more immediate context as the author goes to court against his enemies. God is the Judge before whom he presents his case, his "just cause" (v. 1). The psalmist asks God to vindicate him and to protect him from the deadly enemies who surround him (v. 9). He accuses them of having fat hearts and fat egos (v. 10). They are like lions in ambush (vv. 11–12).

Furthermore, the psalmist wants God to execute judgment against a specific enemy: "Deliver my life from the wicked with Your sword" (v. 13). These are the people of the world who live only for this life (v. 14).

Here, then, God is both judge and executioner. In this psalm God's judgment is no abstract idea or "spiritual" reality alone. The psalmist expects God's active intervention on his behalf. For him justice is an event executed by the Just One.

When I went to traffic court, I knew that I would get off easily. When we go before God, however, the stakes are ultimate and final, life or death. The author of Psalm 17 wants nothing less than vindication by God. There is an echo and a longing in each of our hearts for similar vindication. The good news is that God has given us exactly that in His Son! This psalm is an individual lament or prayer for protection. Tradition views David as its author. The thought moves from a petition for judgment (vv. 1–2) to divine interrogation (vv. 3–5), a call for intervention (vv. 6–9), complaint (vv. 10–12), and finally resolution (vv. 13–15).

PETITION FOR JUDGMENT

1 Hear a just cause, O LORD,
    Attend to my cry;
    Give ear to my prayer *which is* not from deceitful
    lips.

130

2 Let my vindication come from Your presence;
Let Your eyes look on the things that are upright.

Ps. 17:1–2

In verse 1 the word for *"just cause"* (*ṣedeq*) indicates that which is right or normal and applies to what is *"just"* in a court of law (cf. Ps. 35:27). When David comes to God, the Ruler-Judge, to present his petition for a hearing, as defendant, he claims not only that his cause is right but also that he is innocent. Confident that his lips are pure, he is bold in verse 2 to ask God to justify him. The word for *"vindication"* (*mišpoṭ*) in verse 2a means "right" or "rectitude." The parallel clause of verse 2b asserts that his claim is honorable and, therefore, that God can look at it.

Note that in these opening verses David makes a double assertion: "I am righteous and my cause is righteous." What is striking about this is that David can say these things with confident boldness to the living God. He knows that his God tries all hearts (Ps. 51:6) and nothing is hidden from Him. Yet, just so, David prays for God's presence (or face) and eyes to be upon him. We too share David's boldness, not because we have a clear conscience or a *"just cause,"* but because we have a Savior who cleanses us and who has made us His cause before the Father. As Paul writes in Ephesians 3:12, we have "boldness and access with confidence through faith in Him."

DIVINE INTERROGATION

3 You have tested my heart;
You have visited *me* in the night;
You have tried me and have found nothing;
I have purposed that my mouth shall not transgress.
4 Concerning the works of men,
By the word of Your lips,
I have kept away from the paths of the destroyer.
5 Uphold my steps in Your paths,
That my footsteps may not slip.

Ps. 17:3–5

David reminds God that He has examined him; in fact, He has done so in the darkness when evil things are hidden. But David's claim to righteousness stands; his record is clear. Moreover, he has resolved not to say anything against God's will. His heart and his lips, his thoughts and his words are justified before God's all-seeing eye.

David turns to his life in this world, affirming in verse 4 that he has lived by the word of God: *"Concerning the works of men, / By the word of Your lips, / I have kept away from the paths of the destroyer."* Since it is God's word that has guided him, David has not followed the ways of the *"destroyer"* or the "violent." It is, of course, the violent whom David is calling upon God to judge.

Nevertheless, David is not presumptuous, and in verse 3 he prays for God to keep him in His ways. Only God can keep him from slipping into the wicked ways from which he seeks vindication.

This is a crucial verse. Grace underlies what in verses 1–5 may appear to be excessive claims to moral perfection. David is serious about God's judging him, and the God he knows is not to be trifled with. But the God who reveals His ways to David also keeps him walking in those ways. As Augustine says, "You give what You command." It is all through grace "lest anyone should boast" (Eph. 2:9). Thus God interrogates the heart which He Himself holds. "Create in me a clean heart, O God, / And renew a steadfast spirit within me. . . . / And uphold Me with Your generous Spirit" (Ps. 51:10, 12).

Call for Intervention

> 6 I have called upon You, for You will hear me, O God;
>   Incline Your ear to me, *and* hear my speech.
> 7 Show Your marvelous lovingkindness by Your right
>   hand,
>   O You who save those who trust *in You*
>   From those who rise up *against them.*
> 8 Keep me as the apple of Your eye;
>   Hide me under the shadow of Your wings,
> 9 From the wicked who oppress me,
>   *From* my deadly enemies who surround me.
>
> *Ps. 17:6–9*

Having established his integrity before God, David petitions for His intervention. He prays because God hears (v. 6). Here the verb for *"hear"* also means "answer" (ʿānâh). David is pragmatic—he prays not as a religious formality or even as a pious act, but because his prayers are answered. God hears, speaks, and acts. He is the living, dynamic

God, intervening in David's life. This affirmation is followed by a request: *"Incline Your ear to me, and hear my speech."* God's face is toward him. God's eyes are upon him, and now God's ears are open to him. David has His full attention.

But what does David want? In a word, "salvation." *"Show Your marvelous lovingkindness by Your right hand, / O You who save those who trust in You / From those who rise up against them"* (v. 7). David wants God to intervene against his enemies, to act both as judge and executioner. As the ruler who is also the commander of His troops, God establishes what is right and then goes into battle for righteousness. He manifests His *"marvelous lovingkindness,"* His "covenant-love," through the right hand of His authority and power (cf. Deut. 15:6; Eph. 1:20–21).

Not only does David ask for deliverance, he also wants continuing protection. He asks God to see him with special favor, *"As the apple of Your eye"* (literally, "keep me as the pupil, the daughter of the eye"; cf. Deut. 32:10). He also wants to be secure under God's wings like a chick under a mother hen (cf. Matt. 23:37).

In God's care, David is safe *"from the wicked who oppress me, / From my deadly enemies who surround me"* (v. 9). He does not pray to be excused from the battle but to be kept in the battle. Likewise, Jesus says to the Father, "I do not pray that You should take them [the disciples] out of the world, but that You should keep them from the evil one" (John 17:15).

As God saves David *from* his enemies, He saves David *for* Himself. Noah was saved *from* the flood and *for* the Lord. In the Bible, salvation always has both these negative and positive dimensions. As he is saved, David will be *"under the shadow of* [God's] *wings"* (v. 8).

A CATALOG OF COMPLAINTS

> 10 They have closed up their fat *hearts;*
>   With their mouths they speak proudly.
> 11 They have now surrounded us in our steps;
>   They have set their eyes, crouching down to the earth,
> 12 As a lion is eager to tear his prey,
>   And like a young lion lurking in secret places.
>
> *Ps. 17:10–12*

Next, David offers his current complaints to God. The first clause of verse 10 reads literally, "they have closed up their fat." In Deuteronomy 32:15 "to be fat" is to rebel against God; and to be rebellious is to be proud, from the Garden of Eden to the present. A fat heart reveals a fat ego. Thus *"they speak proudly."*

David paints a graphic picture of his enemies in verse 11. Here they are all about him (see v. 9), and they are like a lion in ambush, with his eyes fixed, ready to lunge, *"eager to tear his prey"* (v. 12). David offers a fearful image of strength, deception, and cunning.

We too are faced with rebellious, prideful enemies who seek our doom. While they may not be pagan hordes storming our city gates, they are just as real, or, perhaps, even more real than David's foes. So Peter warns us of our ultimate enemy in a similar image: "Be sober, be vigilant; because your adversary the devil walks about like a roaring lion, seeking whom he may devour" (1 Pet. 5:8).

REQUEST FOR RESOLUTION

> 13 Arise, O Lord,
>   Confront him, cast him down;
>   Deliver my life from the wicked with Your sword,
> 14 With Your hand from men, O Lord,
>   From men of the world *who have* their portion in *this*
>   life,
>   And whose belly You fill with Your hidden treasure.
>   They are satisfied with children,
>   And leave the rest of their *possession* for their babes.
> 15 As for me, I will see Your face in righteousness;
>   I shall be satisfied when I awake in Your likeness.
>   *Ps. 17:13–15*

Now David calls for God to resolve his crisis and go into battle: *"Arise, O Lord."* It seems that here a specific enemy or enemy commander is in his mind (note the singular object *"him"* in v. 13). David wants God to meet this enemy face to face, *"confront him"* (the Hebrew reads literally, "confront his face"), and to destroy him, *"cast him down."* Thus God will be his Savior.

Furthermore, God is to save David from the men of this world whose portion is merely their belly and their progeny. They have *"their portion in this life,"* and are *"satisfied with children."* They know no future life, no heavenly hope. Paul writes of those "whose end is destruction, whose god is their belly . . . who set their mind on earthly things" (Phil. 3:19).

In verse 15, David contrasts in his own response to God's action. Rather than being determined by this world, David is determined by God. He longs to see God's face and to be in His likeness, to be righteous as God is righteous. He longs for creation to be restored as God's likeness is recovered in him (see Gen. 1:26–27). Although it is not explicitly stated here, what David ultimately longs for is the Messiah who will come and recreate us to be conformed to Himself: "But we all, with unveiled face, beholding as in a mirror the glory of the Lord, are being transformed into the same image from glory to glory, just as by the Spirit of the Lord" (2 Cor. 3:18).

In Psalm 17, then, David goes to God as his judge for action. He wants his case heard and he wants results. His willingness to go directly to the Lord reveals his honesty, his faith, and his certainty that God will hear and act on his behalf.

David believes that his case is just because he is just. He also knows that God will not merely hear and answer someday in heaven or test his patience on earth—he knows that the living God will do something now.

While David asks for deliverance, he also longs to be like God himself (v. 15). He knows that this will only come fully someday; this is his messianic hope.

In Christ we too can have David's boldness and David's confidence that God will act for us and against our enemies. We can also be certain that we will share in our Lord's likeness when we are glorified with Him (Rom. 8:29–30). This makes Psalm 17 our psalm. David's vindication is our vindication. Indeed, we will all stand before God on that final Day when all secrets are revealed, but we can know now with assurance that there is no condemnation for those who are in Christ Jesus (Rom. 8:1).

CHAPTER EIGHTEEN

Thy Kingdom Come!

Psalm 18

Jesus teaches us to pray for the coming of God's kingdom. When we follow His instruction, we ask that God's rule or reign may be manifest and extended throughout the earth. As His kingdom comes, the other kingdom, the kingdom of Satan, is rolled back and defeated. The roots of this world-view lie deep in the Old Testament and include Psalm 18.

This psalm is a song of thanksgiving for God's triumph through David and his seed (see v. 50); thus it is called a royal psalm. A parallel text appears in 2 Samuel 22, securing Davidic authorship deeply in the Old Testament tradition.

While Psalm 18 has a specific reference in David's military victory over his enemies (vv. 3, 14, 17–18, 37–42), its setting is in the larger context of all of God's saving work. God *is* salvation (vv. 1–3). His wrath against David's enemies is cosmic, embracing nature as well as history (vv. 7–15). Since David does God's will (vv. 20–24) with humility (vv. 25–27) and by divine grace (vv. 31–36), he knows victory in battle (vv. 37–42). This establishes his kingdom, which extends beyond Israel's borders (vv. 43–45). God also secures David's reign against rebellion, and David in return witnesses to the Gentiles (vv. 46–49). Thus David's· kingdom is really God's kingdom and lasts forever (v. 50).

This epic prayer embraces the whole scope of God's work in judgment and redemption. It witnesses to His kingdom, established through David by the defeat of his enemies. It also witnesses to the extension of that kingdom throughout the world and the duration of that kingdom to eternity.

Throughout this psalm the character and power of God are magnified. It is He who has done a mighty work, and it is He who is to be mightily worshiped. Thus the poetic language of Psalm 18 is expansive. Imagery abounds as points are made. Here is "salvation history" which is fulfilled and recapitulated in Christ.

The thought moves from a confession of God's saving power (vv.

1–3) to David's distress (vv. 4–6), divine vengeance (vv. 7–15), David's deliverance and reward (vv. 16–24), a contrast between the humble and the haughty (vv. 28–36), David's victory (vv. 37–42), David's kingdom (vv. 43–45), and finally to God's glory and David's confession (vv. 46–50).

GOD'S SAVING POWER

1 I will love You, O LORD, my strength.
2 The LORD is my rock and my fortress and my
    deliverer;
  My God, my strength, in whom I will trust;
  My shield and the horn of my salvation, my
  stronghold.
3 I will call upon the LORD, *who is worthy* to be praised;
  So shall I be saved from my enemies.

Ps. 18:1–3

David's simple statement of intimate devotion—*"I will love You, O Lord, my strength"*—identifies him immediately as a man after God's own heart. David loved God. Dietrich Bonhoeffer startled his students on the streets of Berlin in the early thirties when he turned to them and asked, "Do you love Jesus?" He was profoundly aware that it is out of a deep personal apprehension of love toward God that all else flows. There is no question more profound, no confession more central.

The assertion that God is David's *"strength"* (vv. 1, 2) is really the thesis of this psalm. God is his strength in avenging wrath, in certain deliverance, in securing his kingdom, and in ensuring his throne. In the verses that follow, the strength of God emerges fully.

Describing God as his Savior, David makes his confession of faith in verses 2–3. Note that he is not philosophically abstract about the divine attributes. David knows God's character because of the way He acts. Thus he says of God, He is "my rock, my fortress, my deliverer, my strength, my shield, the horn of my salvation ["horn" probably derived from animals' horns], my stronghold." All of these metaphors have a military context. God is the one who protects, secures, and gives victory in battle. He extends His kingdom against his enemies through David. Notice also the repeated first person possessive pronoun, *"my."* Yahweh is personal to David. He knows Him and counts on Him. Thus when David calls on this God, something happens; he is saved from his enemies. Likewise, Jesus promises that when we call upon His name, something will happen: "Until now you have asked nothing in My name. Ask, and you will receive, that your joy may be full" (John 16:24). Moreover, it is in Jesus' name that demons are cast out; it is in His name that the darkness is overcome (Acts 16:18).

Since God is his protection, David resolves to call upon Him, to praise Him, and to be *"saved"* or *"delivered"* from his enemies. We also call upon God and count on His answer because of His character revealed in what He says and does.

DAVID'S DISTRESS

> 4 The pangs of death surrounded me,
> And the floods of ungodliness made me afraid.
> 5 The sorrows of Sheol surrounded me;
> The snares of death confronted me.
> 6 In my distress I called upon the LORD,
> And cried out to my God;
> He heard my voice from His temple,
> And my cry came before Him, *even* to His ears.
>
> Ps. 18:4–6

David's primary concern in these verses is obviously with death. He experiences *"the pangs of death. . . . the sorrows of Sheol . . . and the snares of death."* The phrase *"the floods of ungodliness"* (v. 4) literally means "the floods of Belial." Belial may be a euphemism for "Sheol," the place of the dead, or it may be derived from the verb meaning "to swallow down." The noun form has the meaning "the swallower," "the abyss." The threat of death is a real one because of David's enemies already mentioned.

What do we do when death presses in upon us? Cower in fear? Escape into denial? Resign to the inevitable? David's response in distress is prayer. He cries out to the God who is his Savior. He knows *who* God is; He is Yahweh, his God. He knows *where* He is to be found—in His *"temple,"* namely, in heaven where he dwells (cf. Ps. 11:4). And he knows how to address Him: he cries *"to His ears"* (v. 6). Our God is not like the deaf idols; He hears our address. As Psalm 10:17 says, "Lord, You have heard the desire of the humble . . . You will cause Your ear to hear."

GOD'S VENGEANCE

7 Then the earth shook and trembled;
　The foundations of the hills also quaked and were
　　shaken,
　Because He was angry.
8 Smoke went up from His nostrils,
　And devouring fire from His mouth;
　Coals were kindled by it.
9 He bowed the heavens also, and came down
　With darkness under His feet.
10 And He rode upon a cherub, and flew;
　He flew upon the wings of the wind.
11 He made darkness His secret place;
　His canopy around Him *was* dark waters
　And thick clouds of the skies.
12 From the brightness before Him,
　His thick clouds passed with hailstones and coals of
　　fire.
13 The LORD thundered from heaven,
　And the Most High uttered His voice,
　Hailstones and coals of fire.
14 He sent out His arrows and scattered the foe,
　Lightnings in abundance, and He vanquished them.
15 Then the channels of the sea were seen,
　The foundations of the world were uncovered
　At Your rebuke, O LORD,
　At the blast of the breath of Your nostrils.

Ps. 18:7–15

God's answer to David's cry is dramatic and overwhelming. It includes "earthquake," "smoke," "devouring fire" (volcanic? forest fire? meteor shower?), "darkness" (eclipse?), "wind," "thick clouds" (thunderheads, storms), "hailstones and coals of fire," "thunder," and "lightnings." "Channels of the sea" (v. 15) that uncovered "the foundations of the world" resembled the parting of the waters in the Exodus (see Exod. 15:8). All of these "natural" forces are "supernatural" instruments in the hand of God. Nature rages "because He was angry," or, literally, "because it was wrath [burning] to Him" (v. 7). The smoke comes from God's nostrils and the fire from His mouth. He bows the heavens, spreading them apart, and comes down, riding upon "a cherub," one of the angelic beings who guard Eden (Gen. 3:24). At the same time, "darkness" veils

God; His secret place is in *"thick clouds."* From there He sends *"hail-stones"* and *"coals of fire,"* and addresses His enemies with the awesome thunder of His voice. He also shoots lightning bolts from the divine darkness like *"arrows"* against his foes.

Finally, the rivers flood and the springs of the earth break forth to carry everything away in judgment (v. 15; cf Gen. 7:10–11).

For the Bible, in distinction to modern man since the Enlightenment, nature is neither autonomous nor neutral; it is held in the hand of God. Through it He exercises His wrath on David's behalf in a mighty theophany, or manifestation of His presence (cf. Exod. 19:16–18). Elsewhere, drought or rains come to Israel according to God's word to Elijah (1 Kings 17:1 ff.), and in Mark 4:39 it is Jesus' word which controls the storm.

While we may find it hard to see God's judgment in nature today, this does not make it less true. Although in God's providence the rain falls on the just and the unjust, if He is sovereign over His creation, He can unleash its power at any moment as the direct expression of His will. This is exactly what David experiences.

David Delivered

16 He sent from above, He took me;
   He drew me out of many waters.
17 He delivered me from my strong enemy,
   From those who hated me,
   For they were too strong for me.
18 They confronted me in the day of my calamity,
   But the LORD was my support.
19 He also brought me out into a broad place;
   He delivered me because He delighted in me.

Ps. 18:16–19

While there is judgment for David's enemies, there is redemption for David. God reaches down and sends for him, summoning him into His presence as his sovereign King. He lifts him from *"many waters."* These are the waters of divine wrath (see v. 15). He also delivers David from his *"strong enemy . . . those who hated me."* Although David's foes are too strong for him, they are not too strong for God. Yahweh was there in David's day of calamity: *"the Lord was my support."* But God grants more than His presence; He grants His deliverance. The

Lord brings David *"into a broad place"* where he can no longer be constricted by his enemies or his fears. David concludes God's motive for His action was that *"He delivered me because He delighted in me"* (v. 19). The verb *"delighted"* here means "to be mindful of, to be attentive to, to keep, to protect, to have pleasure in." David is the apple of God's eye.

David has experienced here a twofold deliverance. He has been pulled from the waters of God's wrath and rescued from his enemies. In Christ we have the same deliverance. He takes God's wrath from us (Eph. 2:15; 1 Thess. 1:10) and rescues us from the power of the evil one who rules this age (1 John 5:18–19; 3:8). Moreover, Jesus comes to set us in the broad place of His peace (John 14:27) because He is delighted in us (cf. John 13:1).

For many years I believed that Jesus had taken God's wrath from me and delivered me from my sins, but I supposed that I still had to deal with my enemies. Certainly He would be there with me and I would know His presence, but the battle would still be mine. Recently, however God has shown me what David knew three thousand years ago. The Lord gives us both His presence and His *power*. When I call upon God He is ready to fill me with His Spirit. When I battle against Satan and his emissaries, when I deal with the powers of this world and my own flesh, I too have a power, the power of the Holy Spirit. And in that power the power of the evil one is broken (See Matt. 4:1 ff.).

DAVID REWARDED

20 The LORD rewarded me according to my righteousness;
   According to the cleanness of my hands
   He has recompensed me.
21 For I have kept the ways of the LORD,
   And have not wickedly departed from my God.
22 For all His judgments *were* before me,
   And I did not put away His statutes from me.
23 I was also blameless before Him,
   And I kept myself from my iniquity.
24 Therefore the LORD has recompensed me according
      to my righteousness,
   According to the cleanness of my hands in His sight.

                                          Ps. 18:20–24

David is delivered because of his righteousness. This righteousness consists of clean *"hands"* keeping Yahweh's *"ways"* or commandments and being *"blameless"* by rejecting *"iniquity."* The stress here is on obedience, external actions. For David, however, this does not preclude internal attitudes. As he writes in Psalm 24:4, those who come into God's presence must have both "clean hands and a pure heart."

The statement in verse 20, however, that Yahweh *"rewarded me according to my righteousness"* seems to assert that God's deliverance is based upon David's performance. Is this "works" theology? Is this a grounds for David's pride and boasting? One way to answer the question is to note that in the larger context David stresses God's mercy and grace (see vv. 28–30). The Lord is his salvation. David can only trust in Him (vv. 1–3). Thus David's *"righteousness"* (ṣedeq) is only in response to grace. Then, too, *"righteousness"* here is a word of the covenant. God's mercy creates the covenant, and righteousness defines right-relationships within that bond. Furthermore, the claim of a reward for righteousness is prophetic and eschatological. David, inspired by the Spirit, anticipates the coming of the Righteous One who alone can confess, *"I was . . . blameless before Him"* (v. 23). As Paul puts it, "For Christ is the end of the law for righteousness to everyone who believes" (Rom. 10:4). "End" (Gr., *telos*) can mean both goal and abolition. Righteousness then is consummated in Christ who in His sinlessness is our righteousness and who makes us righteous by faith alone (Rom. 1:16–17). While the assertions of innocence in the psalms are difficult for us to understand, David's righteousness, David's victory over his enemies, and David's kingdom all point to Christ. It is Christ who in the Spirit prays here through David, and it is Christ who is the fulfillment of David's prayer.

Within the covenant ultimately fulfilled in Christ, David receives the reward of God's deliverance, *"according to the cleanness of my hands."* The cleanness of his hands, symbolizing observed purity, is defined positively as keeping Yahweh's ways (v. 21) and negatively as keeping himself from iniquity (v. 23). And how does David know good and evil? They are defined as God's *"judgments . . . and . . . His statutes"* (v. 22). To have clean hands then, it is not enough to abstain from evil. Clean hands are for doing the will of God. John puts it, "But whoever has this world's goods, and sees his brother in need, and shuts up his heart from him, how does the love of God abide in him? My little children, let us not love in word or in tongue, but in deed and in truth" (1 John 3:17–18). The church is called to take its clean hands and get them dirty in the world's need. Here is righteousness, washing feet alongside Jesus (John 13:14).

THE HUMBLE AND THE HAUGHTY

25 With the merciful You will show Yourself merciful;
   With a blameless man You will show Yourself
      blameless;
26 With the pure You will show Yourself pure;
   And with the devious You will show Yourself shrewd.
27 For You will save the humble people,
   But will bring down haughty looks.

Ps. 18:25–27

Having meditated upon God's deliverance, David now addresses God directly, revealing the true source of his claim to righteousness (see vv. 20, 24). God is *"merciful"* (*ḥāsîd*) to the merciful, *"blameless"* (*tāmîm*) to the blameless, *"pure"* to the pure (vv. 25, 26). It is the *"merciful"* who receive mercy. The word for *"merciful"* also means "kind, pious." Mercy is a reflection of God's covenant love. This verse is echoed by Jesus in the Beatitudes: "Blessed are the merciful / For they shall obtain mercy" (Matt. 5:7). Moreover, to the *"blameless"* God will not impute blame. The word *"blameless"* here means "sound, innocent, perfect." Again, Jesus reflects this thought in the Beatitudes: "Blessed are the pure in heart, / For they shall see God" (Matt. 5:8). David promises that God will be *"pure"* to the pure. To those morally and spiritually separated to Yahweh, He will show Himself separated to them in the exclusive relationship of the covenant.

The *"merciful," "blameless,"* and *"pure"* are all among the *"humble"* who find their character in the character of God. With the devious, however, God will be *"shrewd"* and outwit them. Human pride will fall; God *"will bring down haughty looks"* (v. 27). From these verses we learn that David's previous claim to righteousness in no way contradicts his sense of humility. God saves the *"humble"* and judges the *"haughty."* The humble learn that all that they have is a gift by grace alone. It is only as little children that they enter God's kingdom, where they are molded into the divine character. The humble then show forth God's face.

God's Grace

28 For You will light my lamp;
   The LORD my God will enlighten my darkness.
29 For by You I can run against a troop,
   By my God I can leap over a wall.
30 *As for* God, His way *is* perfect;
   The word of the LORD is proven;
   He *is* a shield to all who trust in Him.
31 For who *is* God, except the LORD?
   And who *is* a rock, except our God?
32 *It is* God who arms me with strength,
   And makes my way perfect.
33 He makes my feet like the *feet of* deer,
   And sets me on my high places.
34 He teaches my hands to make war,
   So that my arms can bend a bow of bronze.
35 You have also given me the shield of Your salvation;
   Your right hand has held me up,
   Your gentleness has made me great.
36 You enlarged my path under me,
   So my feet did not slip.

Ps. 18:28–36

David now meditates upon the grace of God, which arms him for battle. It is Yahweh who illumines him, who lights his *"lamp"* in the *"darkness"* (v. 28). All that David knows and does comes from divine revelation. Applying this thought to the battle before him, he acknowledges it is God who strengthens him to *"run against a troop"* and to *"leap over a wall,"* that is, to scale the defenses of a besieged city (v. 29). God's way and God's word shield David and *"all who trust in Him"* (v. 30). Thus God is both his *"strength"* for battle and his protection in battle.

Moreover, God is David's *"rock,"* his refuge and fortress, because Yahweh alone is God (v. 31; cf. v. 2). The God who is David's strength gives him *"strength"* (v. 32). Furthermore, the Lord who is perfect makes his *"way perfect"* or *"blameless"* (see vv. 23, 25). He gives David speed and security like that of a deer in high places, and trains David *"to make war,"* bending a *"bow of bronze"* (vv. 33, 34). He also gives him the *"shield of [His] salvation"* or deliverance from enemy spears and arrows. The Lord does this because He Himself is "a man of war" (Exod. 15:3).

God then supports His king: His right hand has held David up (v. 35). The right hand is the hand of power and authority (see Ps. 20:6). Paradoxically, as mentioned earlier, it is God's *"gentleness"* or "humility" that makes David great and keeps him from falling. Where the living God is at work there is manifest an uncanny combination of authority and humility. We see this fully expressed in Jesus' ministry. God, out of His abundant grace, equips David for battle and assures him of victory. Moreover He offers the same to us today. Through His word He illumines our darkness and shows us where the real battle is to be fought against Satan and his hosts, "the rulers of the darkness of this age" (Eph. 6:12). Then He gives us the strength of His Spirit for the battle, to leap over walls, to pull down strongholds (2 Cor. 10:4). In the fight God arms us with spiritual weapons and teaches us how to use them (Eph. 6:13–18). He grants us His authority and humility and keeps us secure in Himself. His kingdom is at war with Satan's kingdom and we, like David, are soldiers in His army.

DAVID'S VICTORY

37 I have pursued my enemies and overtaken them;
   Neither did I turn back again till they were destroyed.
38 I have wounded them,
   So that they could not rise;
   They have fallen under my feet.
39 For You have armed me with strength for the battle;
   You have subdued under me those who rose up against
       me.
40 You have also given me the necks of my enemies,
   So that I destroyed those who hated me.
41 They cried out, but *there was* none to save;
   Even to the LORD, but He did not answer them.
42 Then I beat them as fine as the dust before the wind;
   I cast them out like dirt in the streets.

Ps. 18:37–42

Armed for battle, David graphically describes the fight. By God's work within him he advances the kingdom by becoming the aggressor. He routs his enemies, pursues them, overtakes them, and destroys them. The verb sequence describes total victory. While his foes turned their backs to David, he did not *"turn back again."*

Once David overtakes his enemies, he delivers a mortal wound (v. 38). The verb for *"wound"* is strong. It means "to smite through, to shatter." Thus they were not able to rise. The parallel line, *"They have fallen under my feet,"* means to fall in death rather than to surrender.

David's victory is really Yahweh's victory. So he continues, saying that it is God who has *"armed me with strength for the battle"* (cf. vv. 1, 32). It is God who has broken his enemies. He gave David their *"necks"* and he *"destroyed"* them. Thus their cry for mercy went unheeded by God and men, and David ground them into *"dust"* and threw them out *"like dirt in the streets."*

These gruesome lines realistically portray the battlefield in ancient Israel. In these lines we can hear the clash of arms, smell the smoke, and feel the pain. War is brutal and final. No quarter is given. David's foe does not surrender. He is slaughtered.

The point here is clear. David fights only as God gives him the strength and the victory. Thus David's triumph is by grace alone. Indeed, "the Lord is my rock and my fortress and my deliverer" (v. 2).

If this is true for David it must be true for us. We conquer only in Christ. He is the one who is at God's right hand interceding for us. Although in this world we experience tribulation, distress, persecution, famine, nakedness, peril, and sword, "Yet in all these things we are more than conquerors through Him who loved us" (Rom. 8:37). We are not, however, to be victims of these things. We are to take on the world, Satan's domain, and challenge its authority, as Jesus in His ministry confronted the devil and his demons and took authority over them. We too are called into a spiritual battle to fight against the powers of evil (Eph. 6:12–13), and in this, we can expect a victory like David's. As Paul tells the Romans, "the God of peace will crush Satan under your feet shortly" (Rom. 16:20).

DAVID'S KINGDOM

43 You have delivered me from the strivings of the
      people;
   You have made me the head of the nations;
   A people I have not known shall serve me.
44 As soon as they hear of me they obey me;
   The foreigners submit to me.
45 The foreigners fade away,
   And come frightened from their hideouts.

Ps. 18:43–45

David's victory in battle assures us that his kingdom, which represents the kingdom or rule of God, is established. He is delivered from the turbulence of the people and the threat of the nations. Now ruled by him, they are submitted to him: *"A people I have not known* [i.e., the Gentiles] *shall serve me."* Because of his triumph, nations now capitulate to him without a struggle and become his vassals: *"The foreigners submit to me."* No one wants to do battle with David. They fade away from combat and emerge from their bunkers, hands in the air.

This description of David's reign is, once again, prophetic and eschatological, foreshadowing Christ's kingdom. Jesus now rules His church and will one day rule the nations after Satan's power is destroyed. In the vision of Revelation, when the New Jerusalem appears, "the nations of those who are saved shall walk in its light, and the kings of the earth bring their glory and honor into it" (Rev. 21:24; cf. Isa. 61:5–6).

In this interim before the Lord's return, we battle, but we battle in His strength and victory. We also know the outcome of our war. Like David's enemies, our enemies will be *"as the dust before the wind"* and will *"come frightened from their hideouts."*

GOD'S GLORY

46 The LORD lives!
  Blessed *be* my Rock!
  Let the God of my salvation be exalted.
47 *It is* God who avenges me,
  And subdues the peoples under me;
48 He delivers me from my enemies.
  You also lift me up above those who rise against me;
  You have delivered me from the violent man.
49 Therefore I will give thanks to You, O LORD, among
    the Gentiles,
  And sing praises to Your name.

Ps. 18:46–49

With the confidence of victory and reign before him, David turns to worship. He makes his confession: *"The Lord lives!"* Next, he blesses God: *"Blessed be my Rock!"* God is his refuge and security. Then he calls for God to be lifted up in His saving work: *"Let the God of my salvation be exalted."* The work of God is for the worship of God; we are humbled before His power and exalted in His love in order that we may fall at His feet in adoration.

As David calls for God to be exalted in His salvation, he recapitulates in verses 47–48 the mighty works which he has seen. It is God who saves and delivers David. His victory in battle is only possible because of the outstretched hand of God. God will also deliver him from any future rebellion.

Remembering what God has done, David vows praise: *"Therefore I will give thanks to You, O Lord."* But his worship is also witness; it is given *"among the Gentiles."* They too behold the glory of Yahweh. Not only does David give thanks; he also will *"sing praises"* to God's name. In singing, joy is released. As Karl Barth reminds us, theology is only true when it can be sung. Singing makes it a glad theology. For David theology is doxology (Marcus Barth).

The goal of our salvation is that we worship, finally joining the mighty heavenly chorus in praise to the living God (see Rev. 5:13). As the church is renewed and prepared for the full manifestation of God's kingdom, it will become a worshiping church. Salvation will lead to celebration. No longer will we limp through a liturgy, but the desire to pour out our praises to the Lord in intimate devotion will flow from our hearts. As unbelievers (our "Gentiles") see us worship they will know that God is in our midst.

DAVID'S CONFESSION

50 Great deliverance He gives to His king,
    And shows mercy to His anointed,
    To David and his descendants forevermore.

Ps. 18:50

This psalm ends on a confessional note: *"Great deliverance He gives to His king."* Perhaps this is a response from worshipers in the temple or soldiers on the battlefield. With the whole of God's salvation so clearly exposited in this psalm, we too must join in saying that God delivers His king and gives *"mercy to His anointed, / To David and his descendants forevermore."*

From this text, then, we see in the psalm's conclusion the gospel story. Another David has come. He has defeated God's enemies and established His reign. Even the Gentiles now come to Him. As a result, a great chorus of praise ascends to the throne of God.

Psalm 18 reveals the God who controls nature and history, who establishes His King and His kingdom. He is not absent but present, not distant but near, not aloof but active, not powerless but powerful. In His Son, the kingdom has come and is coming. Light breaks through the darkness and the devils tremble. Yet we await the full dawn. In this hope we live, and we pray, "Thy kingdom come!"

CHAPTER NINETEEN

God Speaks

Psalm 19

Psalm 19 is virtually peerless in its poetic power and theological depth. It reveals the God who is continually communicating through His works (vv. 1–6) and through His word (vv. 7–14). Reflecting the foundational themes of Genesis 1–3, the psalmist moves in his thought from the general revelation given in heaven and earth, to the special revelation in God's law or Torah. Having begun with the vast reaches of the cosmos, he ends with his own heart (v. 14). It is God's intention in communicating through all the splendor of nature and through all the specifics of His word to reach *us*. God speaks, or "shouts," at us, with all the stops pulled out, in order that we might hear and respond. Behind the primeval explosion of creation and behind the smoke and fire of Sinai is the loving heart of God seeking our hearts. "God speaks" is the thesis of this psalm.

The unity of Psalm 19 has been debated because of the two clear sections, one dealing with creation (vv. 1–6), and one with Torah or revelation (vv. 7–14). In the first section God is called "El"; in the second He is called "Yahweh." Both parts, however, are united in exposing the general and special revelation given in the opening chapters of Genesis. In creation God is appropriately called "El." In redemption, through His covenant with Israel, He makes Himself known as "Yahweh." So we accept the unity of this psalm. Tradition, often challenged, holds the author to be David. The question may be left open here. The thought moves from the works of God (vv. 1–6) to the word of God (vv. 7–11) and ends with intercession (vv. 12–14).

MEDITATION: THE WORKS OF GOD

1 The heavens declare the glory of God;
   And the firmament shows His handiwork.
2 Day unto day utters speech,
   And night unto night reveals knowledge.
3 *There is* no speech nor language
   Where their voice is not heard.
4 Their line has gone out through all the earth,
   And their words to the end of the world.
   In them He has set a tabernacle for the sun,
5 Which *is* like a bridegroom coming out of his chamber,
   And rejoices like a strong man to run its race.
6 Its rising *is* from one end of heaven,
   And its circuit to the other end;
   And there is nothing hidden from its heat.

Ps. 19:1–6

This psalm begins with a meditation on the works of God *"The heavens declare the glory of God; / And the firmament shows His handiwork."* We can hardly read these lines without hearing "In the beginning God created the heavens. . . . Then God said, 'Let there be a firmament . . .'" (Gen. 1:1, 6). As we "listen" to the heavens we hear God's glory. They "continually declare" as they both worship the Creator with their praise, and witness His glory to us. The *"glory"* of God is His splendor. Not even the hardest of hearts can see a blazing sunset over the Pacific without some sense of awe. I live near the beach, and every evening as the sun goes down I see a stream of people head for the water's edge to watch the spectacle. As they stand in transfixed silence, they are a continual witness to the heavens declaring *"the glory of God."*

The parallel line, *"And the firmament shows His handiwork,"* adds the truth that the hand of God is seen in creation. Like an artist, God signs His work. The *"firmament"* is the vault of heaven above the waters (see Gen. 1:6–8).

The psalmist continues, turning to the two great divisions of time (see Gen. 1:5): *"Day unto day utters speech, / And night unto night reveals knowledge."* Creation reveals the Creator continually. His glory, His handiwork, is declared and shown day and night. The verb for *"utters"* literally means "to bubble up, pour forth." Day to day, creation effervesces with God's speech. The light of the day, the darkness of the night, the brightness of both the sun and the moon, all witness to the glory of God.

The affirmation of verses 1-2 is now reinforced by reverse expression in verse 3, as the NKJV renders the Hebrew: *"There is no speech nor language / Where their voice is not heard."* The literal translation, however, reads, "[There is] no speech and [there are] no words / Not heard [is] their voice." Thus verse 3's negation qualifies verses 1-2. The revelation booming at us from creation has been described poetically. We are not to listen for literal speech from it; we are not animists. There is, however, real communication. Thus Paul sees all of us accountable to God because of creation. He writes to the Romans, "For since the creation of the world His invisible attributes are clearly seen, being understood by the things that are made, even His eternal power and Godhead, so that they are without excuse" (Rom. 1:20). One of the realities being recovered in the church today is that God is not limited to words in His communication with us. He employs angels, visions, dreams, even impressions and mental pictures (see the whole book of Acts). Since God is *the* communicator we need to hear Him speaking to us far beyond the capabilities of our left brain, with its linear, logical limitations.

While God's speech in creation is not verbal, it is nevertheless real. The psalmist continues, *"Their line has gone out through all the earth, / And their words to the end of the world."* The word given here as *"line"* is difficult to translate. Some have suggested that it is a musical chord. Others propose that a *lamedh* has been dropped by the Hebrew transcribers and the word should be "voice." However this problem is solved, the point is clear. The parallel line uses *"words,"* and both clauses stress the comprehensive nature of revelation. It streams forth *"through all the earth"* and goes *"to the end of the world."* No place or person is without some knowledge of God. Missionaries like Don Richardson (*Eternity in Their Hearts*) have documented many tribal groups who have awaited the arrival of evangelists bringing a book telling of a Savior. By general revelation they have already known of the Creator and the fall. Thus God has prepared the way through His continual speech, and the door is wide open for evangelism.

The psalmist now turns to the marvel of the sun, describing it in poetic terms as a *"bridegroom"* and a *"strong man"* (v. 5). *"In them [the heavens] He has set a tabernacle for the sun, / Which is like a bride-*

groom coming out of his chamber." The "tabernacle" or tent represents the place where the sun goes when it sets. When a new day dawns, the sun is like a "bridegroom" adorned for his bride, as he emerges from his wedding chamber. He is radiant, glowing with light. Moreover, the sun "rejoices like a strong man to run its race." The picture here is either one of a warrior or an athlete plunging into a race with joy.

Verse 6 completes the thought: "Its rising is from one end of heaven, / And its circuit to the other end." Indeed, the heavens are filled with the sun. God communicates to us in the sun that "rejoices" before Him, crossing the heavens so that all the earth receives its splendor and the glory of the Creator. The psalmist concludes his thought: "And there is nothing hidden from its heat." For C. S. Lewis (Reflection on the Psalms) this is the key line of Psalm 19. It marks the transition from the works of God to the word of God and links them both together. As the sun rules the day, so God's Law rules us. Both the sun and the Law radiate the light of the God who is light. Nothing is hidden before the sun and before the God who made the sun.

The opening of Psalm 19, then, reveals the God who communicates His glory to us through His creation. His continual communication is a witness to His desire always to be known and worshiped by us. He is also the universal God claiming all people for Himself. There is a problem, however; sin has darkened our perception of Him. We have "errors," "secret faults," and "presumptuous sins" (vv. 12–13). Thus we need more than the witness of creation. We need the word of God so that we can understand the works of God. General revelation holds us accountable, but it also condemns us because in our sin we deny the Creator. But in the darkness, God speaks.

MEDITATION: THE WORD OF GOD

7 The law of the LORD is perfect, converting the soul;
   The testimony of the LORD is sure, making wise the
      simple;
8 The statutes of the LORD are right, rejoicing the heart;
   The commandment of the LORD is pure, enlightening
      the eyes;
9 The fear of the LORD is clean, enduring forever;
   The judgments of the LORD are true and righteous
      altogether.

10 More to be desired *are they* than gold,
Yea, than much fine gold;
Sweeter also than honey and the honeycomb.
11 Moreover by them Your servant is warned,
And in keeping them *there is* great reward.

Ps. 19:7–11

This psalm now turns to God's special revelation given in His word. Verses 7–11 show its value and use. The word of God is described as *"law," "testimony," "statutes," "commandment," "the fear of the Lord,"* and *"judgments."* Its value is declared as *"perfect," "sure," "right," "pure," "clean," "true,"* and *"righteous."* It is more desirable than *"gold"* or *"honey."* Its purpose is given as *"converting the soul," "making wise the simple," "rejoicing the heart," "enlightening the eyes,"* and *"enduring forever,"* and *"righteous altogether."* Through God's word we are warned and, as we obey, rewarded. Here we come to understand that as the sun is comprehensive for our world, the word is comprehensive for our lives. Before the word of God, "there is nothing hidden from its heat."

In verse 7 we read that *"the law of the Lord is perfect, converting the soul."* The word *"law,"* Torah, means "revelation," not just legislation. By being *"perfect"* (*tāmîm*) the law is "complete, sound, whole." This can be taken both ethically and theologically. As the Anglican Thirty-nine Articles put it, "God has given us everything in His word necessary for our salvation." The function of the law is to convert us. Through it we are "restored" or "returned" (*šûb*) to our Creator. Thus the legislation in the Torah reveals God's holiness and our sin. It drives us to despair so that we may be driven to Christ (Luther). The full revelation is given, however, when the work of the legislation is done. So Paul writes, "For Christ is the end of the law for righteousness to everyone who believes" (Rom. 10:4).

Next, the psalmist writes, *"The testimony of the Lord is sure, making wise the simple."* When God testifies about Himself, He tells the truth. The word *"sure"* here means "steadfast, faithful." We can throw our weight on God's testimony, and it will hold us up. The *"simple"* are those who are "open-minded or open to instruction." The instruction of wise fathers as they teach their children is carried in the meaning of this word. The purpose of Proverbs, for example, is "To give prudence to the simple, / To the young man knowledge and discretion" (Prov. 1:4). Again wisdom calls, "Whoever is simple, let him turn in here"

(Prov. 9:4). Psalm 119:130 picks up this theme: "The entrance of Your words gives light; / It gives understanding to the simple."

Now the psalmist asserts: *"The statutes of the Lord are right, rejoicing the heart"* (v. 8). The *"statutes"* are the "commandments or precepts" of the Lord. Because they are just and righteous, the *"heart"* (lit., mind) rejoices. Through them the seat of our intellectual faculties knows what to do and how to please the Lord. This brings joy and gratitude. In the Bible, the knowledge of God is for the worship of God.

A parallel thought follows: *"The commandment of the Lord is pure, enlightening the eyes."* The commandment is *"pure"* because it is given by the holy God. It is ritually clean and morally right. It is sanctified by Him, and, therefore, it brings enlightenment to the eyes. When we look at the commandments, our eyes transmit the light of God to our souls. In Christ, we become light and we are to live in that light. Paul exhorts the Ephesians, "For you were once darkness, but now you are light in the Lord. Walk as children of light" (Eph. 5:8).

In the context of modern relativism and our rebellious quest for "freedom," the thought that statutes bring joy and light seems foreign. While outside of Christ the law evokes guilt, when we are in Christ, with a regenerated, Spirit-filled heart, God's will becomes our joy. What Jesus desires for Himself will become our desire. As He tells the Jews, "I do not seek My own will but the will of the Father who sent Me" (John 5:30).

Next, the psalmist reflects that *"the fear of the Lord is clean, enduring forever."* Why is the revelation of God called *"the fear of the Lord"*? There are at least two answers to this question. First, when God reveals His will, it is awesome. The law comes from Sinai with thunder, smoke, and fire. God is Holy. To encounter His will is a numinous experience (see Exod. 20:18–21). Second, God's will is fearsome because of our sin. When God reveals Himself in His holiness we cry out with Isaiah, "Woe is me!" (Isa. 6:5).

"The fear [i.e., the word] *of the Lord is clean."* This means that it is sacramentally and morally pure and separate. We read in Psalm 12:6, "The words of the Lord are pure words, / Like silver tried in a furnace of earth, / Purified seven times." Because the *"fear of the Lord"* is uncorrupted by this world, it endures forever. As Jesus says, "Heaven and earth will pass away, but My words will by no means pass away" (Matt. 24:35).

The next line reads: *"The judgments of the Lord are true and righteous altogether."* It is through the Torah of God, the revelation of God, that

God establishes His justice and, therefore, His judgment. Thus the judgments are *"true,"* trustworthy, and *"righteous."* Here God reveals what is true and right. We are accountable to that revelation on the Day of Judgment. The good news is that God's truth and righteousness have been incarnated for us in Christ who is "the way [right], the truth, and the life" (John 14:6). As our Mediator He gives us His own truth and righteousness when we abandon our untruths and unrighteousness and flee to Him.

Having dealt with the value and use of God's revelation throughout verses 7–9, the psalmist now comes to his conclusion on both of these issues.

Verse 10 summarizes the value of God's words. *"More to be desired are they than gold, / Yea, than much fine gold."* So Torah is our true treasure. Jesus warns us, "Do not lay up for yourselves treasures on earth . . . but lay up for yourselves treasures in heaven" (Matt. 6:19–20). To hear His word and to do it is to build our house upon the rock. To seek, to study, and to obey God's word is to labor with that which lasts. No precious metal can compare.

God's word is not only our treasure, however; it is our delight, *"sweeter also than honey."* The word is a treasure to be claimed and a taste to be enjoyed. Israel loved honey. When God offered a land to His people, He promised that it would be flowing with "milk and honey." Our real, lasting treat then is the word of the Lord.

After drawing his conclusions on the value of Torah, the psalmist turns to the use of Torah: *"Moreover by them Your servant is warned, / And in keeping them there is great reward."* Notice that the author now identifies himself as being submitted to his master. He delights to do His will. When God warns us through His word, He admonishes and instructs us as His servants. Paul asserts the value of Scripture: "All Scripture is given by inspiration of God, and is profitable for doctrine, for *reproof,* for *correction,* for *instruction* in righteousness . . ." (2 Tim. 3:16). By the word itself then, *"Your servant is warned."*

Verse 11 continues with the thought that *"there is great reward"* in obeying God's Torah. The reward is threefold. It is, first, the reward of doing the Father's will. It is, second, the reward of living a fulfilled life—converted, wise, rejoicing, enlightened, enduring, true, and righteous. It is, third, the assurance of being ready to stand before Christ's judgment seat: "For we must all appear before the judgment seat of Christ, that each one may receive the things done in the body, according to what he has done, whether good or bad" (2 Cor. 5:10).

APPLICATION: INTERCESSION

12 Who can understand *his* errors?
    Cleanse me from secret *faults.*
13 Keep back Your servant also from presumptuous *sins;*
    Let them not have dominion over me.
    Then I shall be blameless,
    And I shall be innocent of great transgression.
14 Let the words of my mouth and the meditation of
       my heart
    Be acceptable in Your sight,
    O LORD, my strength and my Redeemer.
                                                    Ps. 19:12–14

Because of the darkness of sin and the deceit of the devil (John 8:34–44) the word of God is neither our natural instruction nor our natural delight. Thus the word must come in the power of God's Spirit to bring conviction of sin and cleansing from sin. After meditation on God's natural and special revelation, the constant broadcast of His will to our broken receivers, the psalmist turns to fallen humanity. He asks, *"Who can understand his errors?"* Apart from revelation, the answer is "no one." However, as Calvin says, the word of God is like a mirror. In God's law we see our true condition and crisis. Our rationalizations are exposed. Our repressions are surfaced. Verse 12 continues: *"Cleanse me from secret faults."* After God opens us up, He cleanses us (see 1 John 1:9). What joy to be forgiven!

The psalmist also prays for protection: *"Keep back Your servant also from presumptuous sins."* But it is not enough to be cleansed and protected; we need the power to live a new life. So the psalmist continues: *"Let them* [presumptuous sins] *not have dominion over me."* While John baptized in water for repentance, the promise is that Jesus will baptize us with the Holy Spirit, the power of God (Mark 1:8). It is in the power of the Holy Spirit that this prayer is answered for us. When He has dominion in our lives, we will be controlled by nothing else.

After we are convicted of our sin and cleansed and protected from our sin, and after the Holy Spirit has taken control of our lives, finally we can say *"Then I shall be blameless, / And I shall be innocent of great transgression."* *"Blameless"* here means "to be whole, complete." This now is our position in Christ (Rom. 8:1) and our possibility through the Holy Spirit. The final fulfillment of this promise will be when we are face to face with our Lord.

Psalm 19 concludes with one of the great short prayers of the Bible, still found throughout the worship life of the church today: *"Let the words of my mouth and the meditation of my heart / Be acceptable in Your sight, / O Lord, my strength and my Redeemer."*

Since the psalmist has received the knowledge of God given in creation and in His word, and has also received the cleansing and empowering of God, he can now pray for this to be reflected both in his words and in the thoughts that lie behind them. He asks that what he says and what he thinks may be acceptable to the Lord. How can this be accomplished?

It is the word of God which is acceptable to God. It is the word of God which is perfect, sure, right, clean, true, and righteous. Therefore, as this word convicts, cleanses, and instructs, the psalmist's thoughts and words will mirror the word of God. Molded and trained by that word, he will stand with assurance before the Lord. Jesus says, "If you abide in My word, you are My disciples indeed" (John 8:31), and He prays, "Sanctify them by Your truth. Your word is truth" (John 17:17).

Finally, the psalmist confesses who God is. He prays that his words may *"be acceptable in Your sight, O Lord, my strength and my Redeemer."* He will only live in the word of God by the power of God, and that power is the power to deliver, to redeem. Our God is the God of the Exodus and of Calvary. He sets us free from spiritual, social, and political bondage so that we may love Him and serve Him, and be acceptable to Him.

All of revelation, general and special, all of God's streams of communication to us, have but one goal. God wants us to know Him, to worship Him, to love Him, to obey Him. All of the heavenly "mass media" and all of the Biblical "special programing" are for us. By faith we must switch on the receiver.

A dear friend of mine had fallen away from Christ and had compromised his morals. In crisis we talked. As he struggled with returning to the Lord, he said, "I know the phone is there. All I have to do is pick it up." Will you pick it up? Will you keep listening? Do it! God speaks.

CHAPTER TWENTY

The Calm Before the Storm

Psalm 20

Living next to the Pacific Ocean has sensitized me to "the calm before the storm," that eerie moment of silence just before the winds and rains crash in upon us. The skies become leaden. The wind subsides momentarily. The smell of rain is in the air. It is as if nature pauses before its holocaust breaks loose. Similarly, life has its moments of calm. Battlefields lie quiet; then the bombardment begins. Anxious reporters freeze as news of the president's condition comes from the emergency room. Marital strain can grip a family in silence before the cracks appear.

Psalm 20 is such a pause. Israel is ready for battle; the "day of trouble" has come. The legions with their banners are ordered for war. But while pagans trust in chariots and horses, God's people trust in His name. In "the calm before the storm," the commanders go up to the temple with their troops where the king offers his sacrifice and Israel is blessed for battle. Only when spiritual preparation is completed can the opposing forces be joined.

Commentators hold this psalm to be a "royal psalm," a "liturgy" of preparation for battle. The first five verses form a prayer addressed to the king and ask God's protection and support in the coming battle. The affirmation, "The Lord saves His anointed" (v. 6) signals assurance that the Lord will "rescue" or "deliver" His king. Warfare and worship imagery dominate the poetry. Davidic authorship fits easily into the military context. The thought moves then from a combination petition-benediction (vv. 1–5) to a confession of faith (vv. 6), a conclusion of trust (vv. 7–8), and a call for God to act (v. 9).

PETITION FOR PROTECTION

1 May the LORD answer you in the day of trouble;
May the name of the God of Jacob defend you;

158

2 May He send you help from the sanctuary,
And strengthen you out of Zion;
3 May He remember all your offerings,
And accept your burnt sacrifice. Selah
4 May He grant you according to your heart's *desire,*
And fulfill all your purpose.
5 We will rejoice in your salvation,
And in the name of our God we will set up *our*
banners!
May the LORD fulfill all your petitions.

Ps. 20:1–5

The psalm's opening petition on behalf of the king also serves as a blessing or a benediction: *"May the Lord answer you in the day of trouble."* This request for God's answer is a generalized thesis for the whole psalm. It also establishes the immediate context; it is a *"day of trouble,"* a day of "distress" or "pressure."

First, there is the petition-benediction for protection: *"May the name of the God of Jacob defend you."* The *"name"* bears both the authority and the presence of the person. *"The name of the God of Jacob"* refers to the God of the patriarch whose family was delivered from Egypt. Before Sinai, God speaks of Israel as "the house of Jacob" (Exod. 19:3). The request that God *"defend"* the king literally means "to set him on high," to place him in a defensible position against his enemies as the Lord did Israel in the Exodus.

We too need the Lord's protection in the *"day of trouble."* Jesus promises that His sheep will know Him and that no one "shall . . . snatch them out of My hand" (John 10:28). Here is our hiding place when we go into battle. Likewise, Paul tells us to wear the defensive armor of the gospel when we fight against "the wiles of the devil" (Eph. 6:11 ff.). Here God provides our fortress in the gospel.

The petition-benediction for provision follows: *"May He send you help from the sanctuary, / And strengthen you out of Zion."* It is from God's dwelling place on Zion that aid comes. This support would include the assurance of answered prayer and of the divine presence when David goes into battle. Similarly, Jesus is no armchair general; He also goes into battle with His troops. After Paul exhorts us to be armed for spiritual warfare, he tells us to pray "always with all prayer and supplication in the Spirit . . ." (Eph. 6:18). It is through prayer that God's presence is actualized and His provision extended. Jesus promises, "Your heavenly Father [will] give the Holy Spirit to those who ask Him!" (Luke 11:13).

Verse 3 contains the petition-benediction for the Lord to accept the king's worship: *"May He remember all your offerings, / And accept your burnt sacrifice."* This verse could mean that as this psalm is spoken, the king is actually offering a sacrifice on the altar. When Israel was facing the Philistines in battle, Samuel offered a lamb as a burnt offering to the Lord and "cried out to the Lord for Israel, and the Lord answered him" (1 Sam. 7:9). The first part of the petition is that Yahweh remember all David's offerings, that is, his faithful worship in the past. David is no fox-hole believer. He comes to the present crisis with a long history of love and devotion to God. What we do day by day in times of peace prepares us for times of war. When our devotional life is a habit we are well served for the battle. This is why we are to "pray without ceasing" (1 Thess. 5:17).

The second part of the petition is that the Lord find David's burnt sacrifice acceptable, literally, "May your burnt sacrifice find fat." Since all the fat of the offering belongs to Yahweh (Lev. 3:16), this request asks God to accept the whole sacrifice for Himself.

As we now offer our bodies to the Lord, "living sacrifices" in worship, we are transformed in order that we may do the will of God (Rom. 12:1–2). Only by this radical change will we be ready to do battle against Satan's forces. Now the provision and the protection of God are appropriated.

The next petition-benediction is that David's purpose be fulfilled: *"May He grant you according to your heart's desire, / And fulfill all your purpose."* In context, David's *"heart's desire"* is to win the battle. His *"purpose"* or *"plans"* probably refer to his battle plan.

This request is fulfilled for us as we receive gifts to go against the powers of evil. For example, we are to pray for the gift of discerning of the spirits (1 Cor. 12:10). Furthermore, we are to "test the spirits" by our confessions of Jesus so that we can expose the "false prophets [who] have gone out into the world" (1 John 4:1–3). We are to know that there are "false apostles, deceitful workers, transforming themselves into apostles of Christ" because they are sent by Satan who "transforms himself into an angel of light" (2 Cor. 11:13–14), and we are to expose the "unfruitful works of darkness" (Eph. 5:11). As we do this, God will fulfill all our purposes in doing battle in His name.

At this point there is a structural break from the petition-benediction form as thanks are promised in response to God's fulfilling David's battle plan: *"We will rejoice in your salvation."* The word for *"rejoice"* means "to give a ringing cry." It is the shout of victory. *"Salvation"* is "deliverance" from enemies or triumph in battle. The parallel clause

"And in the name of our God we will set up our banners!" gives us an image of conquest. It is the banners of victory that will be set up in Yahweh's name.

Paul too ends his exposition of our new life in God's Spirit with a ringing victory cry: "If God is for us, who can be against us?" (Rom. 8:31). He then asks, "Who shall separate us from the love of Christ? Shall tribulation, or distress, or persecution, or famine, or nakedness, or peril, or sword?" (Rom. 8:35). The answer, implied, is "of course not." The apostle continues, "Yet in all these things we are more than conquerors through Him who loved us. For I am persuaded that neither death nor life, nor angels nor principalities nor powers, nor things present nor things to come, nor height nor depth, nor any other created thing, shall be able to separate us from the love of God which is in Christ Jesus our Lord" (Rom. 8:37–39). The "angels," "principalities," and "powers" here are the fallen demonic forces against whom we do battle. Our confident hope is that as we go against these hosts of wickedness we go in the name, authority, and power of the Lord Jesus Christ. His is our victory and He gives us victory. In His name we set up our triumphal banners.

The final petition-benediction asks: *"May the Lord fulfill all your petitions."* It is as if the *"heart's desire"* and *"all your purpose"* are now turned to prayer: "May God grant your every request." With the expression of this confident hope the king and his forces are ready for battle.

CONFESSION OF FAITH

> 6 Now I know that the LORD saves His anointed;
> He will answer him from His holy heaven
> With the saving strength of His right hand.
>
> *Ps. 20:6*

With this verse, David offers his positive confession. The time reference, *"now,"* suggests a new stage in the psalm. Having received God's blessing, having offered his sacrifices in worship, David is filled with assurance. A new confidence comes to us only as we wait upon the Lord. When we offer ourselves before Him and receive His anointing for our battle against the evil one, we will reach the certainty of faith. Never go against the powers of evil unless you have prayed and can say with David, "Now I know . . ." That knowledge is not merely good theology. It is the heart-knowledge of firm assurance given to our spirits. It is the knowledge Jesus gained through prayer in the garden before He went to the cross. There is no short cut to this grace, *"Now I know . . ."*

David's confidence is that the *"Lord saves His anointed"* (cf. v. 9). The verb for *"saves"* (*yāšaʿ*) is in prophetic perfect, a form that describes a future event as completed. Through prayer David knows the battle is already won. Don't we often find the real battle is in our praying through to this assurance?

David's conviction then is that Yahweh *"saves"* or "delivers" His *"anointed."* The word for *"anointed"* (*māšîaḥ*) refers to the king (1 Sam. 16:13; cf. Ps. 2:2). God does save His king, and this promise is fulfilled for us in Christ. Since the Father has delivered the Son from all the powers of evil and made Him Lord over those powers, we too are delivered and reign in Him (see Eph. 1:19–23).

Saved from his enemies and heard by God, David acknowledges God's answer from heaven. God's *"right hand,"* the symbol of authority and power, goes into action with *"saving strength."* Thus Paul prays that we may know "what is the exceeding greatness of His power toward us who believe, according to the working of His mighty power which He worked in Christ when He raised Him from the dead and seated Him at His right hand in the heavenly places" (Eph. 1:19–20). We are made confident in knowing that the same resurrection power, the same Holy Spirit, is for us. All that is Christ's is ours (see John 17).

The Lord has been teaching me recently that He wants me not only to have His message but also to have His ministry. The command to heal the sick, cast out demons, and raise the dead was given to the apostles (Matt. 10:8). They certainly couldn't do this in their own power and authority. They could, however, do it in Jesus' power and authority. If then Jesus dwells in us as He did in them through His Spirit, we will be enabled to do His works because, in fact, He does them through us. Moreover, this is exactly what He says, "Most assuredly, I say to you, he who believes in Me, the works that I do he will do also" (John 14:12). This promise is immediately followed by the key to its fulfillment: "And whatever you ask in My name, that I will do" (John 14:13). Some of us are just now experiencing this new dimension in our ministry. As we step out in faith and pray and lay hands on the sick, there is healing; there is power. Certainly we have a long way to go in this. We can claim David's promise, however, that God will answer His *"anointed"* with *"saving strength."* We pray in Jesus' name. We minister in Jesus' name, and it is Jesus, the Mediator, whom God hears and answers with *"the saving strength of His right hand."*

162

A Conclusion of Trust

> 7 Some *trust* in chariots, and some in horses;
>   But we will remember the name of the LORD our God.
> 8 They have bowed down and fallen;
>   But we have risen and stand upright.
>
> Ps. 20:7–8

David now reflects on the two alternatives for life. Rather than cataloging his assets in military strength, his chariots and his horses, David confesses his strength in *"the name of the Lord our God."* As Paul reminds the Corinthians, "For though we walk in the flesh, we do not war according to the flesh. For the weapons of our warfare are not carnal but mighty in God for pulling down strongholds, casting down arguments and every high thing that exalts itself against the knowledge of God, bringing every thought into captivity to the obedience of Christ" (2 Cor. 10:3–5). In a spiritual war only spiritual weapons work. Thus we must surrender our chariots and horses, our pride in human weapons we can manipulate and control.

When we do this, we are wise. As David concludes, those who trust in worldly weapons *"have bowed down and fallen."* Where are the Kaiser, Hitler, and Stalin now? What has happened to Julius Caesar, Marc Antony, Pilate, and Herod? Where are Augustus and Nero? They have bowed down before death. They will also bow down before Christ when "every knee should bow" and "every tongue should confess that Jesus Christ is Lord" (Phil. 2:10–11). But those who remember the Lord's name *"have risen and stand upright."* When we fall down before the Lord, He lifts us up. Our God is the God of the resurrection. He will take us to heaven itself where we shall ever behold His face in endless day.

Call for Deliverance

> 9 Save, LORD!
>   May the King answer us when we call.
>
> Ps. 20:9

David now adds a postscript: *"Save, Lord!"* As we have seen, the verb *"save"* means "deliver," "give victory." It is as if David now gathers his troops and marches toward battle with a final cry on his lips: "God, bring your saving power now."

The response to this request, given in petition-benediction form, is somewhat difficult. The Hebrew imperative *"Save, Lord!"* may be punctuated "Save, Lord, the king." If this is the case, "the king" refers to David. In the NKJV text, "the King" refers to God.

However we take the text, the intention is clear. God is asked once again for salvation or deliverance as the answer to David's prayer. The "you" addressed to the king in verses 1–5 now becomes the "us" of king and people. The Lord's answer will be in their triumph.

As with many other psalms, the expectation of Psalm 20 is that the living God is dynamically active in the midst of His people. He answers them in "the day of trouble." He sends His protection, His provision, His power. He receives worship. He directs plans. He gives victory.

All of this is centered in his king. Deliverance and power are his, and in Christ this deliverance and power are ours. This is our future hope and our present reality. As we are united with the heart of Jesus, we will be participants in all of His benefits. Then as we go into our battles, the time of calm before the storm will be a time of anointing and worship where, submitted to the lordship of Christ and filled with His Spirit, we will be made ready for the contest and certain of its outcome. *"Save, Lord! / May the King answer us when we call."*

CHAPTER TWENTY-ONE

Song of Victory

Psalm 21

Battle imagery lies at the heart of much of the Old Testament. The reason for this is simple: Israel lived in a hostile world where her position was constantly challenged by external threat. As the hub among three continents, Asia, Africa, and Europe, and controlling the trade routes that crossed the Fertile Crescent, Israel was pressed between the power centers of Egypt and Mesopotamia. As warfare is a given of the modern state of Israel, so it was a staple in antiquity, as many nations greedily eyed the Promised Land.

At the same time, Israel was also a warlike nation. She took her land originally by armed conflict. Whole cities were put to the sword. The wars of conquest were "holy wars" bearing the judgment of God against idolatry. This judgment was not merely for the destruction of empty idols, however; it was also for the expulsion of the demonic presences behind those idols (see Deut. 32:16–17; 1 Cor. 10:20). Thus Israel's battles were God's battles against the powers of darkness.

In the New Testament, Jesus comes as the Warrior-King, taking David's throne, doing battle with the demonic powers who hold this world captive. He comes to cast out the "ruler of this world" (John 12:31). He sends out His disciples with authority to expel demons (Mark 3:15). In their ministry He sees Satan fall like lightning from heaven (Luke 10:18). Thus the battle psalms are to be seen on at least two levels. The first relates to Israel and her king holding military campaigns against neighboring peoples. The second relates to the Messiah-King's conquering God's enemies in the eschatological fulfillment of the Old Testament. From this we may even derive a third level—we share in the Messiah's triumph in our own spiritual battles.

In the first half of Psalm 21, then, we have the strong affirmations of the king's victory in battle through the power of God. The Lord's salvation or deliverance is his. He goes to war knowing that he will live. Through God's salvation he receives glory, honor, and majesty. Here is the divine "yes" of God's mercy, power, and grace.

The second half of the psalm presents the other side, the divine "no" of God's anger in battle. His enemies are consumed along with their offspring. The king who experiences God's deliverance also necessarily experiences God's destruction of his foes. The praise goes to God alone for His "yes" and His "no" (v. 13).

In Jesus Christ we have the fulfillment of all of this. Our Lord assaulted sin on the cross. He defeated death by giving Himself to it and then triumphing over it. In destroying death, He also destroyed Satan's weapon to keep us in lifelong fear and bondage. Moreover, the risen Christ is the reigning Christ who pours out His Spirit upon us. Our salvation, our deliverance, is in Jesus. In rescuing us, however, He also brings judgment upon His foes. As we stand before the awesome conquering power of God, we cry with the king: "Be exalted, O Lord, in Your own strength! / We will sing and praise Your power."

The original setting of Psalm 21 is debated. It may be either a prelude or a postlude to battle. The principals are clear: the king (v. 1), the Lord (vv. 1, 7, 9, 13), and His enemies (v. 8). It is also uncertain whether verses 8–12 refer primarily to the Lord, to the king, or to both. This is not a critical interpretive question, however, since the Lord fights His enemies through the king. The traditional ascription of this psalm to David need not be disputed. The thought moves from God's affirmation of the king (vv. 1–7) to God's judgment on His enemies (vv. 8–12). The final verse is a response to God's power (v. 13).

GOD'S YES

1 The king shall have joy in Your strength, O LORD;
  And in Your salvation how greatly shall he rejoice!
2 You have given him his heart's desire,
  And have not withheld the request of his lips.   Selah
3 For You meet him with the blessings of goodness;
  You set a crown of pure gold upon his head.
4 He asked life from You, *and* You gave *it* to him—
  Length of days forever and ever.
5 His glory *is* great in Your salvation;
  Honor and majesty You have placed upon him.
6 For You have made him most blessed forever;
  You have made him exceedingly glad with Your
    presence.
7 For the king trusts in the LORD,
  And through the mercy of the Most High he shall
    not be moved.

                                        Ps. 21:1–7

The psalmist begins with the king's joy in God's salvation. The speakers here may be worshipers at the temple, the priests, or the king's troops. The *"joy"* of the king is "glad exultation" over Yahweh's *"strength"* or "might," which is revealed in battle. Thus David rejoices over God's *"salvation"* or "deliverance" from his enemies.

Verse 2 shows this deliverance as having been actualized by prayer that unlocks the power of God. David turns the desire of his heart for victory into a bold request to the Lord. Notice that his prayer is audible—he uses his lips.

As the Messiah, Jesus too has known God's might in deliverance. Protected in His birth and empowered in His baptism, Jesus lived and ministered under the hand of God. He only did what the Father did as He always sought the will of the Father, and He encourages us to live in the same way. Thus as we abide in Him we abide in the Father. As we pray in His name, the Father hears and answers. And as we do mighty works in His name, it is the Son who works in us through prayer.

In my own life and in the lives of those about me, I see an increasing sense of God's power through prayer for ministry. When I pray for God's salvation or deliverance to be manifested in Jesus's name, I pray according to His will. Thus as we see God's power at work we join David in joy and rejoicing in the strength and salvation of the Lord.

Verses 3–4 continue the theme of God's granting the king his *"heart's desire."* Here the king receives God's perfection or "goodness," God's kingdom (represented by a *"crown"*), and life now and forever.

The psalmist then speaks of God's meeting the king with *"the blessings of goodness." "Goodness"* (*ṭôb*) here is the perfection of God's purpose or will. Rather than being met by enemy armies or military disaster, the king is met by the divine purpose. Next, his kingdom is secure since he is crowned by the Lord Himself: *"You set a crown."* In fact, it is God's kingdom, His order and reign, that is manifested through the king established by Him. The crown He gives is of *"pure gold."* This represents the value and permanence of His kingdom.

Since God comes with His perfect will and sovereign authority to the king, the prayer for life is answered: "Yes." In fact, God gives him *"length of days forever and ever."* Not only is his life assured on the battlefield, it is assured for eternity.

As the king's *"heart's desire"* for the purpose of God, the kingdom of God, and the life of God is answered, so too all these themes find their fulfillment in Christ. It is He who comes to do the perfect will of the Father. He lives under divine necessity: "And He [Jesus] began to teach them that the Son of Man must suffer many things, and be rejected by the elders and chief priests and scribes, and be killed, and after three days rise again" (Mark 8:31). It is Christ also who bears the kingdom of God, the *"crown of pure gold"*: "But if I cast out demons with the finger of God, surely the kingdom of God has come upon you" (Luke 11:20). It is Christ who receives life from the Father and who grants life: "For as the Father has life in Himself, so He has granted the Son to have life in Himself" (John 5:26, see John 10:10). Likewise, Christ reveals to us the will of God, calls us into the kingdom of God, and implants in us the life of God.

Verse 5 continues the battle theme. It is the salvation or deliverance of God manifest in triumph over his enemies that brings glory to the king. This *"glory"* (lit., "heaviness") of praise covers him after conquest. Next, God gives him *"honor"* or "splendor" which God Himself wears as King of Israel. Psalm 104:1–2 puts it, "O Lord my God, You are very great: You are clothed with honor and majesty, / Who cover Yourself with light as with a garment. . . ." Then there is *"majesty"* or "dignity" which is worn as a royal robe. In these qualities the king shares the very glory of God. They are the fruit of divine salvation.

Beyond immediate victory, however, is enduring relationship with God: *"For You have made him most blessed forever; / You have made him exceedingly glad with Your presence"* (v. 6). Blessed by God, the king is a source of blessing to his people. He is *"glad"* or rejoices "with gladness" in God's presence (cf. v. 1). Moreover (and here the direct address to God in prayer ends), based upon his faith in Yahweh and His *"mercy"* or "covenant-love," the king will be steadfast: *"For the king trusts in the Lord, / And through the mercy of the Most High he shall not be moved."* With this final expression of confidence in God's faithfulness to His promise to Israel and her king, the "yes" of God's deliverance in battle ends. This psalm may have been employed in a temple liturgy, in which case the change in subject in verse 7 may also indicate a change in speaker.

All that we have seen in verses 5–7 finds fulfillment, once again, in Christ. God's salvation or deliverance, through Christ, in the defeat of sin, Satan, and death has brought glory, honor, and majesty to Him as the triumphant King. So when the high priest asks, "Are You the Christ, the Son of the Blessed?" Jesus answers, "I am. And you will see the Son of Man sitting at the right hand of the Power, and coming with the clouds of heaven" (Mark 14:61–62). Moreover, the blessing upon Jesus blesses us. Also, it is the presence of the Father that gives joy to the Son, and His trust in the Father and in His covenant-love makes Him steadfast. Thus it is God who sends Him into spiritual battle, who delivers Him from His enemies, and who establishes His kingdom forever. This is the divine "yes."

As we have suggested, what is true for Christ is also true for us in Him. We share in His victory. In His name, we too can defeat our spiritual enemies and take authority over them. The blessing, presence, and covenant-love of God are all ours and they give us security.

GOD'S "NO"

8 Your hand will find all Your enemies;
   Your right hand will find those who hate You.
9 You shall make them as a fiery oven in the time of
     Your anger;
   The LORD shall swallow them up in His wrath,
   And the fire shall devour them.
10 Their offspring You shall destroy from the earth,
    And their descendants from among the sons of men.
11 For they intended evil against You;
    They devised a plot *which* they are not able *to perform.*
12 Therefore You will make them turn their back;
    You will make ready *Your arrows* on Your string
      toward their faces.

Ps. 21:8–12

The positive triumph of the king has, at the same time, the negative effect of his enemies' defeat and destruction. Whether these verses are addressed to the Lord or to the king is uncertain. Our translation takes it as spoken to the Lord. The conclusion concerning this really matters little, however, because God operates through the king and is, in any case, the ultimate actor.

The psalmist begins then with the assertion that the hand of God will find His enemies. The symbol of the *"hand"* denotes action: the parallel phrase *"Your right hand"* denotes power. Here the *"enemies"* of God, namely, *"those who hate"* Him, will be grasped by God. The verb for *"find"* may also be translated "reach." No enemy is beyond Yahweh's reach.

When the Lord captures His enemies, they also will be the objects of His *"wrath"* (v. 9). They will be burned as a *"fiery oven"* burns. They will be consumed, swallowed up, and devoured by fire. The picture here may well be one of a city burning to the ground. *"Fire,"* however, is also a symbol of hell, eternal torment. Thus the devil in Revelation is cast into "the lake of fire" (Rev. 20:10).

That this judgment and triumph is complete is indicated by verse 10. *"Offspring"* here is literally "fruit" and *"descendants"* is "seed." When judgment comes the future dies. Death destroys fruitfulness for the next generation. There could be nothing more terrible to the Hebrew mind.

Verse 11 states the grounds for this judgment. *"Evil"* here includes "misery, distress, injury, and wrong." Evil intended against God's covenant people and His king is also evil against Him. The *"plot"* of the enemies, however, is unfulfilled because God has brought the fire of His judgment against them.

The psalmist graphically pictures this judgment in verse 12. Causing them to turn their backs, God defeats His enemies in battle as His arrows hit them head on and they are routed.

This then is the graphic "no" of divine judgment. As God's people are saved and delivered, those who attack them are destroyed. We cannot have one truth without the other. God's "no" is seen in the *"fire"* of His *"wrath."* This wrath, however, is not irrational anger. It is His moral and just judgment upon those who attack His people, who hate Him, who intend evil against Him.

Similarly, in the Revelation an angel pronounces judgment against anyone who capitulates to the Antichrist. If he does, "he himself shall also drink of the wine of the wrath of God, which is poured out full strength into the cup of His indignation. And he shall be tormented with fire and brimstone in the presence of the holy angels and in the presence of the Lamb" (Rev. 14:10). The manifestation of God's kingdom means the conquest of Satan's kingdom and all those who are subject to him.

OUR "YES"

> 13 Be exalted, O LORD, in Your own strength!
> We will sing and praise Your power.
>
> *Ps. 21:13*

This psalm of victory ends on a note of praise to the God who brings salvation to His king. Here is a final cry to Yahweh and a promise of worship. The call *"be exalted"* may also be translated "raise Yourself." So it would be a call for God to go into battle. It may, however, be a call for God to lift Himself up as the object of worship. Israel promises to *"sing and praise"* the divine *"power"* which overcomes her enemies and brings deliverance. This is God's "no" of judgment and God's "yes" of redemption.

In Christ we too have this power to release the saving work of God. After Jesus breathes on the disciples and says, "Receive the Holy Spirit," He promises, "If you forgive the sins of any, they are forgiven them; if you retain the sins of any, they are retained" (John 20:22–23). This is His awesome ministry in us. Only the presence and power of the risen Lord will save us from corruption and authenticate this work of "yes" and "no," grace and judgment.

CHAPTER TWENTY-TWO

My God, My God, Why . . . ?

Psalm 22

Historically, Psalm 22 has been classified as a prophetic psalm. When Jesus prayed from the cross, "My God, My God, why have You forsaken Me?" (Mark 15:34), He was not only expressing God's abandonment of Him as the sin-bearer, but also inviting us to understand His death through this psalm by quoting its first verse. Certainly the early church did just that. For example, Matthew tells us that the casting of lots for Jesus' garments took place "that it might be fulfilled which was spoken by the prophet" and then quotes Psalm 22:18 (Matt. 27:35; cf. John 19:24). It has even been supposed that Jesus meditated on Psalm 22 from the cross, thereby receiving strength to hang there because God's work of salvation, promised in the Old Testament, was being accomplished through His suffering.

Modern scholars, however, shy away from viewing Psalm 22 as prophetic. They prefer to see it as a combination of personal lament, prayer, and thanksgiving to be used in the temple as a liturgy for healing. The context is found in physical suffering which has brought the supplicant to the point of death (v. 15). As the psalm is prayed, a priestly oracle of healing is offered which reverses the person's condition, and the prayer ends with praise. How such healing could be liturgically guaranteed to all the ill by a temple ritual is not addressed, however.

But if we want to be consistent with the Bible, we will approach the understanding of the Old Testament from the center of Christ Himself. From this standpoint, there is no doubt concerning Psalm 22. It is Jesus, from the cross, who points us to it by His cry of dereliction, the very cry in verse 1. Furthermore, the application of this psalm to His death was made by the apostles in obedience to Him. Thus Luke tells us that the risen Lord interpreted the psalms to His disciples as referring prophetically to Himself (Luke 24:44). Can we doubt that Psalm 22 was among the texts He gave them?

To be sure, Old Testament prophecy must be seen in its historical context. It has, however, at least three levels of application. The first level, stressed by modern scholars, is the immediate context in which the oracle is given. The second level is the longer-range application to Christ's first coming. The third level is the ultimate application to the final consummation of God's kingdom in Christ's second coming. Each of these levels may or may not be operating in a particular passage. While not denying that Psalm 22 has its original context in the sufferings of a severely ill person, in light of the New Testament, it has infinitely greater meaning.

If we merely tip our hats to the New Testament application of Psalm 22, rather than seeing its fulfillment in Christ as its center, then we are in danger of missing much of what God has for us here. Psalm 22 was prayed by Jesus from the cross. As we study this text we will have on our hearts what was on His heart as He died. This psalm then is the doorway into the mystery of His dying horrors. We must take off our intellectual shoes. We are standing on holy ground.

Long before the Savior died, God prepared for His consolation in this psalm. Jesus came to fulfill the sickness, agony, and abandonment felt by its author. He also came to experience the triumph on the other side. God brings life out of death; beyond Calvary is Easter. This is the ultimate meaning of Psalm 22. Tradition, which we follow, holds its author to be David. The thought here moves from abandonment by God (vv. 1–8) to an affirmation of God's past care (vv. 9–11), the aggravation of suffering (vv. 12–18), an affirmation of God's present care (vv. 19–21), and ends with a commitment to witness (vv. 22–31). From a beginning in tragedy this psalm ends in triumph.

ABANDONMENT BY GOD

1 My God, My God, why have You forsaken Me?
Why are You so far from helping Me,
And from the words of My groaning?
2 O My God, I cry in the daytime, but You do not
    hear;
And in the night season, and am not silent.
3 But You *are* holy,
Enthroned in the praises of Israel.
4 Our fathers trusted in You;
They trusted, and You delivered them.
5 They cried to You, and were delivered;
They trusted in You, and were not ashamed.
6 But I *am* a worm, and no man;
A reproach of men, and despised by the people.
7 All those who see Me ridicule Me;
They shoot out the lip, they shake the head, *saying,*
8 "He trusted in the LORD, let Him rescue Him;
Let Him deliver Him, since He delights in Him!"

Ps. 22:1-8

Verse 1 speaks poignantly of abandonment. The very fact that David opens this prayer by addressing God so personally communicates an irony. Although he *feels* abandoned and although those around him *think* him abandoned, still he prays. The lamp of faith is not extinguished in God's silence or distance. To David he is still *"My God."*

At the same time, the experience of God's absence is real. Nothing is happening. God seems not to be hearing him. His prayer hits the ceiling as he asks, *"Why are You so far from helping Me, / And from the words of My groaning?"* The phrase *"from helping Me"* is literally "my salvation" or "deliverance." *"Groaning"* here means "roaring." The same word used is of lions (Zech. 11:3) and conquering kings (Ezek. 19:7). Thus the pain is audible. The volume is up; a roar of despair is the result.

Verse 2 then elaborates on unanswered prayer in its picture of perpetual praying against the leaden silence of heaven. Likewise, Jesus on the cross felt the abandonment of the Father. We will never penetrate this mystery. It has often been noted that when God laid our sin upon His Son there was a moral separation in the Godhead. In Helmut

Thielicke's phrase, "There was a pain in God's heart." Paul puts it that "[God] made Him who knew no sin to be sin for us, that we might become the righteousness of God in Him" (2 Cor. 5:21).

What we know from this is that our redemption was purchased at an awful cost. Jesus groaned—yes, roared—from the cross with the agony of our sin and His separation from the Father. He groaned in the *"daytime,"* being crucified at high noon. He groaned in the *"night season"* as the sun was darkened for three hours. On the cross, He knew "the dark night of the soul."

Next, in verses 3–5, David's memory goes to the character of God and His past faithfulness. God's holiness, His separateness (*qādôš*), and His rightful place in Israel's praise, "inhabiting" or "dwelling" (*yāšab*) in His people's worship, all add to the mystery. Since David is an innocent sufferer, why, in His holiness, is God silent?

Furthermore, in the past God's people were not disappointed. They *"trusted"* ("became secure") and were *"delivered"* (v. 4). They prayed and received answers; they were not *"ashamed"* (v. 5). Where are the answers and the deliverance now? The remembrance of God's holiness and past deliverance increases the pain. These verses, however, also serve as a reminder. "God, here's what You are. Here's what You did. Be consistent. Do it again! Do it now!"

How these thoughts must have been upon Jesus' heart as He hung between heaven and earth. It was God's holiness that had put Him on the cross and it was God's deliverance that would bring Him through. Yet, in the pain of divine silence, the temptation was for these thoughts to become accusations, weapons against God—haunting, empty memories, promises forsaken. In that Jesus "has suffered, being tempted, He is able to aid those who are tempted" (Heb. 2:18). The darkness of divine withdrawal was also Satan's final opportunity to tempt the Son of God.

God's distance is also the occasion for human accusation in verses 6–8. Suffering undercuts our self-esteem. When we are debilitated physically, depression easily sets in. We have a sense of worthlessness. The ill can easily identify with verse 6, in which the metaphor of the *"worm"* offers a picture of lowliness (see Isa. 41:14).

Not only has David lost a sense of his dignity and even his humanity, but he is now also vulnerable to the accusations of those around him. His suffering makes them laugh. There is sarcasm here, and rejection. They hold the sufferer's faith before him now as mockery. They say, *"He trusted in the Lord, let Him rescue Him"* (v. 8). Their attack here takes the position that disease and suffering are a sign of God's judgment. Certainly this man, this *"worm"* who is *"no man,"* must be rejected by God—in their view he has been justly forsaken.

It is not difficult to see Jesus hanging on the cross as we read these verses. In fact, Matthew makes exactly this connection. There are those who blaspheme the Lord, wagging their heads as they pass by (v. 7; Matt. 27:39). Then there are the mockers who cry, "He trusted in God; let Him deliver Him" (v. 8; Matt. 27:43). Like David, Jesus experienced both the silence of God and the scorn of people while He suffered at Calvary. These verses then are fulfilled in His Passion.

AFFIRMATION OF PAST CARE

9 But You *are* He who took Me out of the womb;
  You made Me trust *while* on My mother's breasts.
10 I was cast upon You from birth.
   From My mother's womb You *have been* My God.
11 Be not far from Me,
   For trouble *is* near;
   For *there is* none to help.

Ps. 22:9–11

Over against this deep sorrow, however, stands the continuing reality of God. Even in silence He is still God. Even in pain the memory of His past faithfulness is still a seed of hope. While David may feel abandoned now, he has a long history with God, going back to his birth. It was God who took him *"out of the womb."* It was God who also gave him faith; even before he was weaned, *"You made Me trust"* (note the stress on the divine initiative). At birth he was cast from the womb not upon the earth, or his parents, but upon the Lord. From the inception of life, *"From My mother's womb / You have been My God."* Several parallel statements stress God's continual presence and activity for David, starting with birth itself.

Similarly, in the birth narratives of both Matthew and Luke there is constant affirmation of the plan, providence, and power of God in Jesus' coming into the world. The virgin birth is God's miraculous work. Bethlehem, the angels, the star, and the flight into Egypt are all a part of God's will. In a very special way God took Jesus from Mary's womb and cast Him upon Himself. Like David, Jesus knows the deep security of a life lived before the one true God.

Based upon this lifelong trust, the psalmist's request is: *"Be not far from Me"* (v. 11). It is God's distance, God's silence which continues to be so overwhelming, especially in the context that *"trouble is near."* The word for *"trouble"* derives from a verb meaning "to bind, tie up, be restricted, cramped." Jesus certainly experienced this distress in the whole drama of His crucifixion. But it is not only *"trouble"* that overwhelms David. He adds: *"For there is none to help."* He is alone, abandoned.

THE AGGRAVATION OF SUFFERING

12 Many bulls have surrounded Me;
   Strong *bulls* of Bashan have encircled Me.
13 They gape at Me *with* their mouths,
   Like a raging and roaring lion.
14 I am poured out like water,
   And all My bones are out of joint;
   My heart is like wax;
   It has melted within Me.
15 My strength is dried up like a potsherd,
   And My tongue clings to My jaws;
   You have brought Me to the dust of death.
16 For dogs have surrounded Me;
   The congregation of the wicked has enclosed Me.
   They pierced My hands and My feet;
17 I can count all My bones.
   They look *and* stare at Me.
18 They divide My garments among them,
   And for My clothing they cast lots.

Ps. 22:12–18

The theme of abandonment dominating verses 1–8 and verse 11 now receives elaboration. The fearful metaphor of the *"strong bulls of Bashan"* is offered. Bashan was a high flat area east of the Jordan and south of Mount Hermon where wheat and cattle were raised. Its wild bulls present a graphic image of raging "trouble" or "distress." These panting animals *"gape . . . with their mouths."* They roar like lions. The emphasis here is on their verbal abuse.

Think again of the crucifixion. Matthew reports, "And those who passed by blasphemed Him, wagging their heads and saying, 'You who destroy the temple and build it in three days, save Yourself! If You are the Son of God, come down from the cross.' Likewise the chief priests also, mocking with the scribes and elders, said, 'He saved others; Himself He cannot save' " (Matt. 27:39–42). Are not these also the *"strong bulls of Bashan"*?

In verse 14 David vividly describes himself as physically and emotionally exhausted. He is drained, like water poured out. His bones have literally been "separated." Finally, his heart has turned to jelly. Emotionally, physically, and mentally, he is completely spent.

The theme of debilitation continues, coming to its ultimate conclusion in verse 15. David's strength is like a broken, baked piece of pottery, and his tongue cleaves to his palate—his mouth is dry. All of this means that he is at death's door, and whom does he hold responsible but God Himself?

How literally are we to take this? For David the crisis may be emotional. In light of the cross, however, here we see Jesus' full pain. He is *"poured out like water"* and His blood flows. His *"bones are out of joint"* as His body hangs from the cross. His *"heart has melted"* with the pain. His *"strength"* ebbs away and *"is dried up."* His tongue is bloated and in His thirst He is offered sour wine (John 19:28–29). Death now beckons. Its dust settles upon Him. And, wonder of wonders, this is God's doing: "Yet it pleased the Lord to bruise Him; He has put Him to grief" (Isa. 53:10).

Returning in verse 16 to the enemies gathered about him, David continues with a new metaphor—*"dogs."* These dogs prowl the streets, even eating human bodies (1 Kings 16:4). In the parallel phrase, they are the *"wicked"* who have surrounded David, and they do him in. He continues: *"They pierced My hands and My feet."* The word *"pierced"* is disputed by some scholars who feel the reading in the Hebrew may be corrupt and prefer to render "like a lion (*kā'ărî*) [at] my hands and feet." The noun, however, may hide the original text, meaning "to dig a round hole" (*kārâh*), i.e., "to pierce." Verse 17 adds: *"I can count all My bones."* This could be due to starvation, but if the verb "pierce" was original here, then the reference would be fulfilled by a crucified man looking down upon his naked body.

The theme of the wicked assembly continues in verses 17–18, as David is "stared" at and his *"garments"* are divided among those "casting lots" as if he were already dead.

Once again, all of this is clearly fulfilled by Jesus' crucifixion. The *"dogs"* around Him are the Jewish leaders and Roman authorities. They share in *"the congregation of the wicked."* He is crucified; His hands and feet are pierced. From the cross He sees both His dying body and the staring crowd. Then the soldiers cast lots for his clothes (Matt. 27:35).

AFFIRMATION OF GOD'S PRESENT CARE

19 But You, O LORD, do not be far from Me;
    O My Strength, hasten to help Me!
20 Deliver Me from the sword,
    My precious *life* from the power of the dog.
21 Save Me from the lion's mouth
    And from the horns of the wild oxen!
    You have answered Me.

Ps. 22:19–21

In verses 19–21 as in verses 9–11, the tragedy of suffering is again countered. Throughout the psalm so far, David has called upon God to intervene. He may feel forsaken, but He still prays. This faith, deeper than his pain, is his secret. Thus verse 19 begins: *"But You, O Lord."* Even in the utter hopelessness of this life there is still the divine possibility. In His condescension God is willing to be our last resort (C. S. Lewis). David now asks negatively that Yahweh not be far off and positively that He *"hasten to help Me!"* As he says this he confesses that God is *"My Strength,"* the help he needs is elaborated upon in verse 20: *"Deliver Me* [i.e., my soul, *nepeš*] *from the sword,"* that is, from violent death. Poetic metaphors in verses 20–21 for this deliverance include release from *"the power of the dog,"* *"the lion's mouth,"* and *"the horns of the wild oxen!"* (cf. vv. 12–13, 16).

When we think again of Jesus on the cross, one of His seven final words comes to mind: "Father, into Your hands I commit My spirit" (Luke 23:46).

Now at the end of verse 21 comes the great reversal in this psalm. And it comes with simple assurance: *"You have answered Me."* All of the agonized outpouring of verses 1–21 has reached the Father's throne. The work is done. "It is finished" (John 19:30).

COMMITMENT TO WITNESS

22 I will declare Your name to My brethren;
    In the midst of the assembly I will praise You.

23 You who fear the LORD, praise Him!
   All you descendants of Jacob, glorify Him,
   And fear Him, all you offspring of Israel!
24 For He has not despised nor abhorred the affliction
      of the afflicted;
   Nor has He hidden His face from Him;
   But when He cried to Him, He heard.
25 My praise *shall be* of You in the great assembly;
   I will pay My vows before those who fear Him.
26 The poor shall eat and be satisfied;
   Those who seek Him will praise the LORD.
   Let your heart live forever!
27 All the ends of the world
   Shall remember and turn to the LORD,
   And all the families of the nations
   Shall worship before You.
28 For the kingdom *is* the LORD's,
   And He rules over the nations.
29 All the prosperous of the earth
   Shall eat and worship;
   All those who go down to the dust
   Shall bow before Him,
   Even he who cannot keep himself alive.
30 A posterity shall serve Him.
   It will be recounted of the Lord to the *next* generation,
31 They will come and declare His righteousness to a
      people who will be born,
   That He has done *this*.

                                        Ps. 22:22–31

The response to God's intervention begins in verse 22. Now David tells what he will do: *"I will declare Your name."* To *"declare"* God's name means to magnify or exalt the God who has brought deliverance. Moreover, David's *"praise"* of God *"in the midst of the assembly"* is his public witness to his salvation. Sickness has ended in wholeness. Death has ended in life. His witness in worship, however, leads to a call in verse 23 for Israel to join in. Here worship includes public *"praise,"* "glorifying," and "fearing" God. *"Praise"* is boasting in God's character and His works. "Glorifying" God is magnifying Him by speaking of what He has done. "Fearing" God is being overcome by awe and reverence before His power and might. Here *"Jacob"* is the theological name for *"Israel"* (see Isa. 41:14; 48:12).

Verse 24 states the basis for such worship. The simple point is: God answers prayer. His silence is now over. No longer does He turn from David. Furthermore, the scorn of David's enemies is silenced before God's mighty acts. Thus *"when He cried to Him, He heard."*

While the doctrine of the resurrection is not revealed here, the theme is present. God makes alive, God heals, God restores, God answers. In His resurrection Jesus declared the mighty works of God to His brethren, His disciples. He "presented Himself alive after His suffering by many infallible proofs" (Acts 1:3). The Savior's witness led to their worship, and the disciples praised, glorified, and feared Him as they fell at His feet (John 20:28).

The theme of worship continues in verse 25. First, the quality of praise (cf. v. 22) is now strengthened by the promise of giving it *"in the great assembly."* That gathering would be during a main feast such as Passover when the tribes came to Jerusalem. David's praise becomes very public. His *"vows"* will also be paid. This refers to the votive offerings which had been previously promised. In Psalm 66:13–14 we read: "I will pay You my vows, / Which my lips have uttered / And my mouth has spoken when I was in trouble." The vows are verified, paid before the pious, *"those who fear Him* [Yahweh]."

The result of vows paid in verse 26 is that the *"poor"* are now fed. They *"shall eat and be satisfied."* Thus they too prosper in this sacrifice of praise as they share in the tithes (see Deut. 14:28–29). The conclusion to these acts of worship is again praise to the Lord and ends in an exhortation-blessing to the worshipers: *"Let your heart live forever!"*

The consequences of bringing life out of death for David embrace the whole earth as the nations now *"remember"* and *"turn,"* or repent (v. 27). They remember that God is their Creator and Redeemer, and they turn from their idolatry and immorality. Renouncing their sin, they *"turn to the Lord"* and *"worship,"* or literally, "bow down" in surrender. This submission is to God who is King, who *"rules over the nations"* (v. 28).

The totality of the world's submission to Yahweh is emphasized in verse 29: *"All the prosperous of the earth / Shall eat and worship; / All those who go down to the dust / Shall bow before Him, / Even he who cannot keep himself alive."* God's kingdom embraces the prosperous and the dying—all will *"worship"* Him, all will *"bow"* to Him.

These themes—worship among God's people, paying vows, feeding the poor, living forever, the nations submitting to Yahweh, the Lord's sovereign kingdom—are, for us, the benefits of Christ's passion. The

Book of Revelation is filled with such eschatological visions (cf. Rev. 21). The suffering of a single man thus brings blessing to the world. This is the prophetic message of Psalm 22 which is fulfilled in Christ.

Finally, verses 30–31 reveal that God's work of salvation will not only go throughout the earth but will also be passed down the generations. The suffering and deliverance of the forsaken will witness to the unborn. A *"posterity"* ("seed") will serve Yahweh who *"will . . . declare His righteousness"* to a people yet to be born. The *"righteousness"* of God is made clear in the psalm's final line: *"That He has done this."* God's righteousness is seen in His breaking the silence, answering the cry of the Crucified, delivering the Messiah from His enemies and bringing the nations to worship Him through His miraculous intervention.

The universal application of this psalm to the nations and the generations can only find its fulfillment in the One whose name is above every name; the One to whom every knee shall bow. Either this psalm is prophetic, pointing to Christ, or it is meaningless. But it not only points to Christ, as we have proposed; it was on Christ's heart as He hung upon the cross. He endured the silence of God in that awful moment knowing that His cry would be answered and that through His suffering the nations would be blessed.

Psalm 22 held Him in support in His hour of darkness. In Christ this psalm will hold us too. We will say with David and our Savior: "You have answered Me."

CHAPTER TWENTY-THREE

The Shepherd's Psalm

Psalm 23

We enter this life totally dependent upon our parents. We can do nothing for ourselves apart from making our needs known. Anger becomes our weapon. As we grow up, however, we move from dependence to independence. This move is neither certain nor complete. We still have basic needs for family, friends, intimacy. We still experience dependency. In our highly specialized culture we are dependent upon professionals for our education, protection, medical care, legal advice—the list grows and grows. We can also easily attach dependency needs to authority figures, from the president of the United States to our teacher or our employer or to our local pastor. We create substitute father and mother figures that meet our needs for order, direction, nurturing, and security. Some of these figures are vague and distant. Others are close and demanding. To assert that we should outgrow such dependency is absurd. The question is not whether to have these needs, but rather what to do with them. Certainly we must gain a major degree of independence by internalizing the ability to meet our security and acceptance needs for the sake of our adult health. At the same time, God calls us to shift our basic dependency from people to Himself. Psalm 23 is an exposition of our proper dependency upon the living Lord who wants to care for us in the way a shepherd cares for his sheep.

This psalm is the best loved single passage in the Old Testament. Untold millions have found comfort here in times of sorrow. The images are serene, pastoral, and timeless. The psalm evokes a mood of meditative security. It ends with a ringing triumph: "And I will dwell in the house of the Lord / Forever."

Tradition gives Psalm 23 to David because of his vocation as a shepherd (1 Sam. 16:11), and because of the intense personal relationship with God evidenced here. Scholars have categorized this psalm as a "psalm of confidence," which really tells us little new. The psalm soon turns from meditation, "The Lord is my shepherd . . . ," to the direct address of prayer, "For You are with me. . . ." The first half describes

God's provision (vv. 1–3) and the second half describes God's protection (vv. 4–6).

THE SHEPHERD'S PROVISION

1 The LORD *is* my shepherd;
  I shall not want.
2 He makes me to lie down in green pastures;
  He leads me beside the still waters.
3 He restores my soul;
  He leads me in the paths of righteousness
  For His name's sake.

Ps. 23:1–3

The personal confession with which David begins his meditation establishes the thesis for the rest of the prayer. In effect Psalm 23 answers the question: "What does it mean for Yahweh to be my shepherd?" Since David knows well how to care for sheep, he is able gracefully and powerfully to apply this metaphor to his relationship with God.

We should note the personal *"my."* The God of the Bible is Israel's God. Faith in Him, however, is not merely tribal or corporate. It is also personal. God is known in His individual relationships. He is the God of Abraham, Isaac, and Jacob (Exod. 3:6). When David was anointed king, God spoke to Samuel, "Arise, anoint him; for this is the one!" then "the Spirit of the Lord came upon David from that day forward" (1 Sam. 16:12–13). The Psalter witnesses to the intimacy of David's relationship with the Lord. Indeed, for David He is *"my shepherd."*

The mother of a young boy who was dying of cancer taught him the Twenty-third Psalm, having him repeat *"the Lord is my shepherd"* by counting these five words with his fingers starting with his thumb. His ring finger was the word *"my."* When he got to that word, his mother taught him to hold that finger in his fist, symbolizing the personal relationship which Jesus had for him. When the boy died, he was found holding his ring finger. He died in the shepherd's arms. All of us must come to the place where we can say that the Lord is *"my* shepherd."

The word *"shepherd"* is often applied to God in the Old Testament. In Psalm 80:1 God is addressed: "Give ear, O Shepherd of Israel, You who lead Joseph like a flock" (cf. Gen. 49:24; Ezek. 34:11 ff.). Israel's kings are also called shepherds. After denouncing the unfaithful shepherds of His people, God promises, "I will set up shepherds over them who will feed them; and they shall fear no more, nor be dismayed, nor shall they be lacking" (Jer. 23:4; cf. Ezek. 34:2). And Jesus identifies Himself as the "good shepherd," the Messianic King (John 10:11). His goodness is in His giving His life for the sheep.

For David to call God *"shepherd,"* therefore, is to acknowledge God as his King, his Savior, the One who meets all of his needs. Verse 1 concludes with the direct inference from confessing the Lord·as his shepherd: *"I shall not want."* Every need will be met by the guiding, providing hand of God. How then will this happen?

First, the shepherd rests His sheep: *"He makes me to lie down in green pastures."* In our frantic life God desires our rest. The Sabbath was instituted, in part, to guarantee this. If we do not follow His pattern, He may even enforce rest upon us. The place of rest is *"green pastures."* The Hebrew word used here means "fresh shoots." God does not intend to rest His sheep in hospital beds but gives them lush meadows where they can graze and enjoy soft grass. Today we are so goal-oriented and compulsive that we feel guilty when we rest. We need the delight of a personal quiet time of being in God's presence. When God rests us, there is no guilt—only the divine hand.

Second, the shepherd directs his sheep: *"He leads me beside the still waters."* The verb for *"lead"* means to "lead to a watering place." The pools of water allow the sheep to drink freely.

As our good shepherd, Jesus provides us with rest, food, and water. When we come to Him we enter His "Sabbath rest" or salvation (Heb. 4:1–11). He feeds us with Himself because He is the bread which has come down from heaven. As Jesus tells the multitudes, "I am the bread of life. He who comes to Me shall never hunger, and he who believes in Me shall never thirst" (John 6:35). Then Jesus gives us His Spirit to quench our thirst. Again He promises, "If anyone thirsts, let him come to Me and drink. He who believes in Me, as the Scripture has said, out of his heart will flow rivers of living water" (John 7:37–38). John comments, "But this He spoke concerning the Spirit" (John 7:39).

Next, David asserts: *"He restores my soul."* The verb for *"restore"* (*šûb*) includes "to return, to refresh." As the Lord shepherds us it is not merely our body which is cared for; it is our restored soul. Paul reminds us, "Even though our outward man is perishing, yet the inward man is being renewed day by day" (2 Cor. 4:16).

God promises to meet our needs and to guide our lives. When we offer our bodies to Him in worship, He transforms our minds and guides us in His will, that which is "good, acceptable, and perfect" (Rom. 12:2). Thus David continues: *"He leads me in the paths of righteousness / For His name's sake."* It is only changed people who can live changed lives. We are ready for the *"paths of righteousness"* when our souls are restored. What are those paths? For us, they are simply doing the will of God, manifesting God's rule, God's kingdom through our lives as we are submitted to Him. As Jesus teaches us to pray, "Your kingdom come. Your will be done on earth . . ." (Matt. 6:10).

Through our transformed lives the name of God is glorified. We are to walk the paths of righteousness *"for His name's sake."* When we take *"His name"* we are to do His will. We pray that the name of God may be vindicated in us: "Hallowed be Your name" (Matt. 6:9).

In Ezekiel 34, after judging Israel's corrupt shepherds, God promises that He Himself will become His people's shepherd. " '. . . so will I seek out My sheep and deliver them. . . . I will bring them . . . to their own land; I will feed them on the mountains of Israel, in the valleys and in all the inhabited places of the country. . . . They shall lie down in a good fold and feed in rich pasture. . . . I will feed My flock, and I will make them lie down,' says the Lord God" (34:12–15). Surely, *"the Lord is my shepherd."* But there is more: "I will establish one shepherd over them, and he shall feed them—My servant David" (Ezek. 34:23). Even beyond this, Jesus is the "good shepherd." This is God's provision.

GOD'S PROTECTION

    4 Yea, though I walk through the valley of the shadow
       of death,
     I will fear no evil;
     For You *are* with me;
     Your rod and Your staff, they comfort me.
    5 You prepare a table before me in the presence of my
       enemies;
     You anoint my head with oil;
     My cup runs over.
    6 Surely goodness and mercy shall follow me
     All the days of my life;
     And I will dwell in the house of the LORD
     Forever.

Ps. 23:4–6

David now turns from God's provision to God's protection. As his shepherd, the Lord protects him from *"the valley of the shadow of death,"* *"evil,"* and *"enemies."*

The "paths of righteousness" do not protect us from the valley, but it is the Lord who leads us through that depression of dark gloom. Though we are in the place of ultimate risk, where the darkness protects those who do evil and death casts its shadow, our fear is eclipsed by the presence of God. *"For You are with me."* As in all life, it is the Lord's presence alone which can give us complete comfort and security. When God sends His people from Egypt to the Promised Land He gives them one absolute guarantee: "My Presence will go with you, and I will give you rest" (Exod. 33:14).

The Lord grants us even more than His presence. He also grants us His power: *"Your rod and Your staff, they comfort me."* The *"rod"* beats off the external enemy, while the crooked *"staff"* snatches us from harm's way. Figuratively, it protects us from the internal enemy—our own wandering foolishness. In Jesus' parable, we are the lost sheep brought home on the shepherd's shoulders (Luke 15:3–7). He has the power to save and restore. Jesus is also the good shepherd, as we have seen, who even lays down His life for the sheep. Knowing that our Lord has the power to beat off our enemies gives us great comfort in this life. Jesus promises, "My sheep hear My voice, and I know them, and they follow Me. And I give them eternal life, and they shall never perish; neither shall anyone snatch them out of My hand" (John 10:27–28).

In verse 5 the metaphor changes as David deals with his enemies. Rather than being a shepherd, the Lord now becomes a host. He seats us, in the presence of our enemies, at His banqueting *"table,"* He anoints us with *"oil"* as a sign of celebration, and He fills our *"cup"* to overflowing. In the New Testament, the banquet *"table"* is a sign of salvation. Jesus promises to eat and drink with His disciples in the kingdom of God (Matt. 26:29). He leaves a banquet with them, the Lord's Supper, through which to remember Him (1 Cor. 11:24–26). The book of Revelation promises that the church will gather at the marriage supper of the Lamb when Christ comes for His bride (Rev. 19:7, 9). It was the sheer joy of the early Christians that broke the persecution of Rome. As it has been said, they knew how to outlive their enemies and they knew how to outdie their enemies. Thus, through His church, Jesus sets a banquet table before his enemies.

The anointing *"oil"* is often related to the gift of the Spirit. When

Samuel took oil to anoint David king over Israel, the Spirit of the Lord came upon him (1 Sam. 16:13). A full *"cup"* is another sign of God's fullness and blessing. This party is a genuine celebration.

Such celebration will never end as David affirms in verse 6: *"Surely goodness and mercy shall follow me / All the days of my life."* *"Goodness"* *(tôb)* is the fulfillment and perfection of God's will. *"Mercy"* (*ḥesed*) is His covenant-love, redemptive power, and faithfulness. The goodness of God and the love of God will *"follow"* or "pursue" David throughout his lifetime. Sometimes, as in David's relationship with Bathsheba, it is a severe mercy (2 Sam. 11–12), but mercy at its best—seeking God's *"goodness"* in our lives.

David ends with a final promise: *"And I will dwell in the house of the Lord / Forever."* Here the *"house of the Lord"* is God's tabernacle. Later it became the temple built in Jerusalem by Solomon. For the Christian, the temple now is the risen body of Christ through whom we have direct access into God's presence (John 2:19–22).

David will *"dwell"* or remain in God's house forever. *"Forever,"* literally "to length of days," means through all the days. For the Hebrews, eternity is not a timeless state, but endless days. Here is where David will be, before the Lord forever and ever.

Throughout Psalm 23 we have the revelation of God's provision and protection. His purpose is to bring us into His house, His presence, forever. To do that He rests us with His salvation; He feeds us with Himself; He gives us His Spirit to quench our thirst; He renews our soul and guides our steps in His way. This world, however, is fallen and evil, so the Lord protects us with His presence and power even in death's shadow. Moreover, we celebrate in front of our enemies, and are pursued by God's goodness and mercy throughout our lifetime. The goal through all is to be before Him forever.

As He goes to the cross, Jesus prays, "Father, I desire that they also whom You gave Me may be with Me where I am, that they may behold My glory" (John 17:24). Because "The Lord is my shepherd; / I shall not want," this prayer will be answered—"Yes."

Here then is healthy dependence. Such dependence upon God makes us independent in this world. When we find our identity and our security in Him, we are free to deal with life and not cave in. Our heavenly Father longs to meet our dependency needs, so that we can be mature and healthy in this world—a sign of the new humanity redeemed by our Lord and invested here for His glory.

CHAPTER TWENTY-FOUR

Worship: Enter the King of Glory!

Psalm 24

The church today longs for a renewal in worship. But what is worship? This question can be answered in many ways. The Hebrew verb "to worship" means literally "to bow down, to prostrate oneself." It reveals the attitude and position of a person subject to a reigning king. So we read in Psalm 95:6, "Oh come, let us worship and bow down; / Let us kneel before the Lord our Maker." To worship is to submit, to surrender. When we come to worship the Lord we come to surrender to Him.

The goal of our worship, however, when it is informed by Psalm 24, is the entrance of the "King of glory." As we call upon the Lord, as we submit to Him, we are inviting Him to be present in our midst in His glory. Our hearts will be satisfied with nothing less. Thus when God revealed Himself to Moses in a burning bush which was not consumed, Moses saw a glimpse of the divine glory. Later Moses asked of the Lord, "Please, show me Your glory" (Exod. 33:18). God answered him by passing by in His glory, but Moses was not allowed to see His face. Then when the tabernacle was completed, the cloud of God covered it, "and the glory of the Lord filled the tabernacle" (Exod. 40:34). Thus Israel experienced God's glory in that place.

Jack Hayford recounts the early days of his ministry at Church of the Way in California. In January of 1971, as he was leaving the sanctuary for home on a Saturday afternoon, he saw the room filled with a silvery mist. There was no natural explanation for what he saw, since there was no dust or smog in the room or sky. Checking the prayer room next door, Jack found no such phenomenon. He returned to the sanctuary and stood in the glow. Then He heard the Lord speak: "It is what you think it is." God had filled the room with His glory. The next morning the attendance almost doubled for the morning service. The Lord was visiting His people and His glory was manifest. Our worship has as its goal the glory of God. We see this glory fulfilled in the face of Jesus Christ. As John puts it, "The Word became flesh and dwelt among us, and we beheld His glory" (John 1:14).

Traditionally, Psalm 24 has been ascribed to David. One possible historical setting is the removal of the ark of the covenant to Jerusalem (2 Sam. 6:12–19). The "holy place" (v. 3) would then refer to the tabernacle, and the "gates" and "doors" (vv. 7, 9) would refer to the city entrance. Some scholars place this psalm later, in the temple, stressing the question-answer form as a clue to its usage. It has been given the form of an entrance liturgy. I believe we should accept Davidic authorship, however. The thought in the psalm moves from the confession of the Creator (vv. 1–2) to the qualifications for worship (vv. 3–6) and concludes with a welcome to the conquering king (vv. 7–10).

THE CONFESSION OF THE CREATOR

1 The earth *is* the LORD's, and all its fullness,
   The world and those who dwell therein.
2 For He has founded it upon the seas,
   And established it upon the waters.

                                                    Ps. 24:1–2

The well-known confession with which Psalm 24 begins reflects Genesis 1:1, "In the beginning God created the heavens and the earth." All creation has its origin in God and therefore belongs to Him. The *"fullness"* means all that fills creation. We now see that this belongs to Christ. For example, Paul tells the Colossians that all things have come into being through Him: "For by Him all things were created that are in heaven and that are on earth, visible and invisible, whether thrones or dominions or principalities or powers. All things were created through Him and for Him" (Col. 1:16). Since all things were created for Christ, all things have been created to serve Him, to worship Him, and all things are in Him. Paul concludes, "For it pleased the Father that in Him all the fullness should dwell" (Col. 1:19). This includes, of course, all the peoples of the planet, *"those who dwell therein."* Thus we are His.

Verse 2 reflects Genesis 1:6–13 and its story of the creation of the firmament, the division of the waters, and the appearance of dry land. According to the Old Testament, the earth rests upon the ocean (Ps. 136:6). Thus *"the waters"* (literally, plural of "river") would be the currents of the sea or underground streams.

The confession of God as Creator in verses 1–2 answers the question, "Whom do we worship?" We worship the God who has made us. We

are to come before Him with singing and "know that the Lord, He is
God; / It is He who has made us, and not we ourselves; / We are His
people and the sheep of His pasture" (Ps. 100:3). Thus God deserves
our worship because we belong to Him. The next question is "Who
may worship Him?"

THE QUALIFICATIONS FOR WORSHIP

3 Who may ascend into the hill of the LORD?
   Or who may stand in His holy place?
4 He who has clean hands and a pure heart,
   Who has not lifted up his soul to an idol,
   Nor sworn deceitfully.
5 He shall receive blessing from the LORD,
   And righteousness from the God of his salvation.
6 This *is* Jacob, the generation of those who seek Him,
   Who seek Your face.   Selah

Ps. 24:3–6

Literally, to *"ascend into the hill of the Lord,"* the mountain of Yahweh,
means to climb Mount Zion. Here is where the divine presence dwells;
here is where the Messiah will reign: "I have set My King / On My
holy hill of Zion" (Ps. 2:6).

The parallel question *"Or who may stand in His holy place?"* sharpens
the issue of who is qualified to worship. The tabernacle and ark are
in the *"holy place."* It is holy, separated, sacred because here is where
God dwells. Who dares to stand there before Him?

The first clause of verse 4 responds to the question of verse 3 with
a general thesis. To enter into the holy place we must each have *"clean
hands,"* that is, our hands must not be defiled by the corruption of
this world, and we must not touch unclean things. While this can mean
ceremonial defilement (see Isa. 52:11), it also means moral defilement.
This is clear from the next phrase demanding *"a pure heart."* Our hands
express what our heart intends. It is from the purity of our hearts that
true worship comes. As Jesus promises, "Blessed are the pure in heart, /
For they shall see God" (Matt. 5:8). We must be holy to enter the
holy place, but because of Christ, this demand does not crush us. He
is our holiness who has made peace with God through the shedding
of His blood. Through Him we "have access by one Spirit to the Father"
(Eph. 2:18).

Two specific points of application are now made. First, the one welcomed to the holy place is the one *"who has not lifted up his soul to an idol."* The worship of any so-called god disqualifies us from worshiping the living God. The first commandment is clear, "You shall have no other gods before Me" (Exod. 20:3). The temptation to worship idols is our temptation today. True, we do not personify our lust as Baal or our violence as Mars. We do not claim city-state goddesses like Athena as our guardians. Yet, we have our idols. They are abstract idols like "power," or concrete idols like "money." "Patriotism" guards our national destiny. "Self" receives our personal devotion. Indeed, Paul warned us of these times: "But know this, that in the last days perilous times will come: For men will be lovers of themselves, lovers of money, boasters, proud, blasphemers, disobedient to parents, unthankful, unholy, unloving, unforgiving, slanderers, without self-control, brutal, despisers of good, traitors, headstrong, haughty, lovers of pleasure rather than lovers of God, having a form of godliness but denying its power" (2 Tim. 3:1–5). Thus David warns us that we must not lift up our *"soul"* to any of these *"no-gods."*

Second, the one welcomed to the holy place is also the one who has not *"sworn deceitfully."* This means that we have not perjured ourselves. We have honored the commandment not to bear false witness. We are people of the truth; we walk in the light.

Thus a *"pure heart"* is one that is pure toward God in single-minded worship and toward others in honest speech and trustworthy oaths. As this person stands before God in the *"holy place,"* he is given the promise that *"he shall receive blessing from the Lord"* (v. 5). The blessing of the Lord is not just His benefits, it is His presence: "The Lord bless you and keep you; / The Lord make His face shine upon you, / And be gracious to you; / The Lord lift up His countenance upon you, / And give you peace" (Num. 6:24–26).

Third, as God grants us His presence, He also grants us His righteousness (v. 5), a promise that is ours in Christ. In the cross God demonstrates His own righteousness in judging sin. At the same time, He justifies the sinner by accepting him through the righteousness of Christ. God is not only righteous but He makes us righteous in His Son by faith.

These then are the qualifications for worship. Holy people are welcome in the holy place before the holy God. The good news for us is that by repentance, by faith in Jesus, and by the gift of His Spirit we are made holy and have access even into the ultimate holy place, heaven itself (see Acts 2:38; Heb. 10:19–22).

Finally, David concludes this section by affirming the identity of the worshipers: *"This is Jacob, the generation of those who seek Him, / Who seek Your face." "Jacob"* here, as is commonly true in the Old Testament, stands for Israel. The word for *"generation"* has the basic meaning "circle" and can also be rendered "assembly": "This is Jacob, the assembly of those who seek Him." The identification turns to the direct address of prayer in the final clause, *"who seek Your face."*

The awkwardness of verse 6 may be explained by an actual liturgical usage. The question of the pilgrims: *"Who may ascend into the hill of the Lord?"* in verse 3 would be followed by the priest's response in verses 4–5. Verse 6 might then be the pilgrim's reply. This would explain both the identification response, *"This is Jacob, the generation* [assembly] *of those who seek Him,"* and the prayer, *"Who seek Your face."* It is possible that David wrote this prayer for the bringing of the ark of the covenant to Jerusalem, and that this was the actual liturgy when the portable throne of God was carried into the city.

A WELCOME TO THE CONQUERING KING

> 7 Lift up your heads, O you gates!
> And be lifted up, you everlasting doors!
> And the King of glory shall come in.
> 8 Who *is* this King of glory?
> The LORD strong and mighty,
> The LORD mighty in battle.
> 9 Lift up your heads, O you gates!
> Lift up, you everlasting doors!
> And the King of glory shall come in.
> 10 Who is this King of glory?
> The LORD of hosts,
> He *is* the King of glory.   Selah
>
> *Ps. 24:7–10*

Psalm 24 now reaches its climax. The form is a command and a promise (vv. 7, 9), followed each time by a question and an answer (vv. 8, 10).

The call in verses 7 and 9 is to the gates and doors: *"Lift up your heads, O you gates! / And be lifted up, you everlasting doors! / And the King of glory shall come in."* In these verses we have a poetic address to the entrance of Jerusalem (or is it the tabernacle / temple?). The *"everlasting doors"* would point beyond any literal earthly reference. Here is a prophetic directive to the New Testament. "For Christ has not entered the holy places made with hands, which are copies of the true, but into heaven itself, now to appear in the presence of God for us" (Heb. 9:24). The *"everlasting doors"* are the gates of heaven which Zion only represents (cf. Rev. 21:25).

Following the command for the gates and doors to *"be lifted up"* in exaltation, there is the promise: *"And the King of glory shall come in."* This assertion evokes an immediate demand for identification. In verse 8, the question *"Who is this King of glory?"* is followed by reference to His conquests, *"The Lord strong and mighty, / The Lord mighty in battle."* In verse 10 the same question receives the answer: *"The Lord of hosts, / He is the King of glory."*

In both of these verses we have clear battle imagery. This connects with the ark of the covenant which was carried by Israel during the period of the conquest. Yahweh is the triumphant King: *"strong and mighty . . . in battle."* He leads victorious Israel in her holy war against idolatry. Yahweh is also *"the Lord of hosts."* These *"hosts"* would include Israel's armies (1 Sam. 17:45) and all the angelic forces of heaven.

Verses 7–10 then are a call to welcome the *"King of glory."* The *"King of glory"* is the Warrior-King who defeats His enemies and brings glory to Himself in His conquests. This mighty King will enter His city, His tabernacle, His temple, and become the object of our worship.

The *"King of glory"* is also the King who brings in His kingdom. Jesus proclaims that "the kingdom of God is at hand" (Mark 1:15) as He begins His public ministry. Like a warrior returning home with the spoils of victory, He has come to plunder Satan's domain in order to restore God's good creation which has been stolen from Him. Now the strong man is bound (Mark 3:27), and the demons shriek as they are cast out by Jesus' command (Mark 1:26). Jesus is the Lord of glory triumphing over the powers of evil, and He glorifies God as He completes His work on earth (John 17:4).

The consummation of worship for this psalm is the entrance of the "King of glory." We join the gates and doors of Jerusalem as we too are "lifted up" to welcome our King. The manifestation of Christ in glory is not only the eschatological goal toward which all of history moves, it is also the expectation of those who "ascend . . . the hill of the Lord" and "stand in His holy place." Right now, we too can be touched by the "King of glory." As Paul writes, "But we all, with unveiled face, beholding as in a mirror the glory of the Lord, are being transformed into the same image from glory to glory, just as by the

Spirit of the Lord" (2 Cor. 3:18). It is the Holy Spirit then who reveals the "King of glory" and it is the Holy Spirit who regenerates us and sanctifies us "from glory to glory." As the gospel is proclaimed in the power of the Spirit, the "King of glory" enters. "For it is the God who commanded light to shine out of darkness, who has shone in our hearts to give the light of the knowledge of the glory of God in the face of Jesus Christ" (2 Cor. 4:6). As we worship privately and publicly, we pray, "Enter—King of glory!"

CHAPTER TWENTY-FIVE

Decisive Discipleship

Psalm 25

Crisis is always unnerving; it shakes the status quo. Because of this we seek stability, building our protections around us. When they collapse, we feel out of control. Many people, however, enjoy *predictable* change. Travel is broadening. A new dish soap attracts us. We wait anxiously for the opera season to begin or for the next race for the pennant. When the structure of our lives breaks down, however, panic seizes us. It is this very break which is often God's opportunity. Cancer strikes, the stock market collapses, Mt. St. Helen's erupts, and we face our own mortality. Now we are ready for outside intervention. Now we are ready for God to do for us what we cannot do for ourselves.

Psalm 25 stands in the context of a double crisis that precipitates change. First, there is the external threat of enemies on the march. At the same time, there is the psalmist's internal crisis as he faces his own sins. Forced to find a new relationship with the Lord, the psalmist seeks decisive discipleship.

Commentators view this psalm as an individual lament, combining covenant and wisdom themes. Its acrostic structure (see earlier discussion on Ps. 9) suggests that it was a literary composition from the beginning.

This structure may have been employed as an aid to memory, making this a "teaching" psalm on discipleship. Issues of date and authorship are unresolved. Tradition ascribes Psalm 25 to David.

After calling upon the Lord (vv. 1–3) David asks for instruction (vv. 4–5). To reenter a relationship with God, however, will require mercy (vv. 6–7). Next, David confesses the Lord as his teacher (vv. 8–11), and describes the consequences of this in molding his character (vv. 12–15). Having reenlisted with the Lord, he makes a plea for deliverance (vv. 16–21). The final verse is a response for the nation (v. 22).

CALL IN CRISIS

1 To You, O Lord, I lift up my soul.
2 O my God, I trust in You;
   Let me not be ashamed;
   Let not my enemies triumph over me.
3 Indeed, let no one who waits on You be ashamed;
   Let those be ashamed who deal treacherously without
      cause.

Ps. 25:1–3

As David begins his prayer he opens himself up to God, lifting his soul as an offering is lifted before the altar in sacrifice. At the same time, he confesses his confidence in God. The petition in verse 2, *"Let me not be ashamed; / Let not my enemies triumph over me,"* sets the theme of the psalm. The prayer that his enemies not triumph over him literally reads, "Let not my enemies exalt ["rejoice"] at me." If God does not act in and through David, dealing first with his enemies and then with David, then in calling upon the Lord there will only be embarrassment and shame, and David's enemies will have the last laugh.

In verse 3 David's previous cry to the Lord is generalized: *"Indeed, let no one who waits on You be ashamed."* The repetition of *"ashamed"* adds emphasis. David doesn't want to have to defend God. He doesn't want to make promises for Him that He won't keep. He doesn't want to pray prayers that go unanswered. Here is the crisis of faith. In effect, David asks, "Will I be ashamed of God?" Who of us has never asked this and similar questions? Is the gospel really true? Will Jesus save, heal, or empower this person as we pray? How can I explain God's silence? Are His ways not my ways? Is the Lord indifferent? Is it a matter of timing? Is some sin holding me back?

Rather than being ashamed as he waits upon God, David prays that his enemies will be the ones who are ashamed: *"Let those be ashamed who deal treacherously without cause"* (v. 3). The verb rendered *"deal treacherously"* means "to act deceitfully" in regard to marriage relations, property rights, or covenants in general. David's enemies are those who are traitors to their commitments. Shame should come down upon their heads.

Verses 1–3 clearly show that David is in crisis. He needs a new touch from God. Moreover, his crisis opens him up to change. When we give up our ways, we are ready for God's.

APPLICATION FOR DISCIPLESHIP

> 4 Show me Your ways, O Lord;
> Teach me Your paths.
> 5 Lead me in Your truth and teach me,
> For You *are* the God of my salvation;
> On You I wait all the day.
>
> *Ps. 25:4–5*

After David offers his soul to God he is then ready to be discipled. Now he asks the Lord to *"show," "teach,"* and *"lead."* True discipleship engages the whole person.

First, God must *"show"* (literally, "make known," *yādaʿ*) His *"ways."* They must come by revelation since God is holy and infinite. " 'My thoughts are not your thoughts, / Nor are your ways My ways,' says the Lord. 'For as the heavens are higher than the earth, / So are My ways higher than your ways / And My thoughts than your thoughts' " (Isa. 55:8–9). And Moses prays, "Now, therefore, . . . if I have found grace in Your sight, show me now Your way, that I may know You" (Exod. 33:13). Although God's ways are revealed in His law (Deut. 8:6), they can be received only by repentance, forgiveness, the coming of God's Spirit, and the gift of salvation (see Ps. 51:10–12). After he has experienced all of this, David then promises the Lord, "I will teach transgressors Your ways" (Ps. 51:13). Now God's ways are fulfilled for us in Christ who *is* the way.

But to be well instructed is not enough. God's ways are only ours if we walk in them and we must see the direction we are to take. Thus David asks, *"Teach me Your paths."* Jesus, who is *the* way, shows the disciples His ministry and then calls them to imitate Him. When He sends out the twelve He orders: "And as you go, preach, saying, 'The kingdom of heaven is at hand.' Heal the sick, cleanse the lepers, raise the dead, cast out demons. Freely you have received, freely give" (Matt. 10:7–8). In other words, He tells them to do what He did. He concludes, "It is enough for a disciple that he be like his teacher" (Matt. 10:25). Indeed, Jesus is the path they are to take. When we see God's ways we are to walk His paths. Jesus calls us in order to extend His ministry through us.

David prays: *"Lead me in Your truth and teach me."* The word here rendered *"lead"* is the verb from which comes the word "way." Thus David is asking the Lord to "tread" or "march" him in the truth which is revealed and to teach him as he goes. Biblical truth is truth to be done, to be obeyed. The separation of the mind from the will is deadly. To believe God's word and to think God's word is not enough. We must do God's word, or else we are self-deceived (cf. Matt. 7:21 ff.; James 1:22).

David then offers the basis for his discipleship: God is his Savior. *"For You are the God of my salvation."* God has delivered David in order that He might manifest His character and His will through him. At the same time, David is attentive. He is ready, open, hungry. *"On You I wait all the day."* David's expectancy and availability are the themes of his life. He is on "ready" before the Lord.

PLEA FOR MERCY

6 Remember, O Lord, Your tender mercies and Your
    lovingkindnesses,
  For they *are* from of old.
7 Do not remember the sins of my youth, nor my
    transgressions;
  According to Your mercy remember me,
  For Your goodness' sake, O Lord.

                                                              Ps. 25:6–7

The foundation for discipleship is God's grace. In the crisis, and with new openness to the Lord's instruction, David calls upon God to remember His *"tender mercies."* The word *"mercies"* is a plural intensive meaning "Remember Your *full* compassion." David also asks Yahweh to remember His *"lovingkindness,"* namely, His covenant-love. God's mercy and love are also *"from of old."* The stress here is not upon God's love as ancient but as enduring. Thus in Psalm 103:17 we read "But the mercy of the Lord is from everlasting to everlasting."

While, as we have seen, David is conscious of his sins, he asks that God *"not remember"* them. The *"sins of my youth"* are probably inadvertent sins. *"Transgressions"* are willful acts of rebellion (see the ascription to Ps. 51). Rather than remembering his sins, therefore, David asks God to remember *him,* but from the vantage point of *"mercy,"* i.e., covenant-love and *"goodness."* Thus as God remembers His grace, He is to remember David in that grace: *"According to Your mercy remember me"* (v. 7). Likewise, as we spread out the Lord's Supper we remember Christ in His broken body and shed blood and pray, "Lord, remember me." It is this mercy alone which makes our discipleship possible.

CONFESSION OF A DISCIPLE

8 Good and upright *is* the LORD;
   Therefore He teaches sinners in the way.
9 The humble He guides in justice,
   And the humble He teaches His way.
10 All the paths of the LORD *are* mercy and truth,
   To such as keep His covenant and His testimonies.
11 For Your name's sake, O LORD,
   Pardon my iniquity, for it *is* great.

Ps. 25:8–11

In these verses David turns from direct prayer to meditation. Who is it who is taught by the Lord? It is those who are *"sinners"* (v. 8) and *"the humble"* (v. 9). Thus God shows that He is *"good"* and *"upright"* by discipling the errant and the broken rather than the proud and powerful who are unwilling to receive His teaching. God brings all of His wholeness and perfection to bear against our sin. But only the *"humble"* can receive it. To them God's *"way"* is unfolded. He *"guides"* them in His *"justice"* (*mišpoṭ*), in what is right.

The reason that God can only disciple the sinner and the humble is that all His *"paths"* are *"mercy"* and *"truth."* Sinners must have received mercy to give mercy. Only the humble who have had Satan's deceptions and their own illusions broken can receive the truth. Thus God's ways are open to those who *"keep His covenant and His testimonies."* They have been bound to Him by His grace and directed to obey His law, His will.

In the midst of this meditation David pauses for prayer: *"For Your name's sake, O Lord, / Pardon my iniquity, for it is great."* Here David's reflection of God's mercy is actualized in his own experience. He models for us how the word is made effective as we pray. A disciple not only knows the truth of God's mercy and his own sin, but he *prays* for *forgiveness.* Here is where the spiritual action is!

A close friend of mine, who has been a Christian for many years, was recently fired from a teaching position. For some time before that, he had lived with constant depression and self-hatred, which frequently manifested itself in egotism and a seductive manipulation of others. His inability to maintain a caring relationship toward his students brought about the loss of his job, and he finally had to face himself. In the moment of truth God humbled him, broke him, and then filled him to overflowing with His Spirit. Several friends were praying with him when this monumental event of cleansing occurred. As we prayed he sobbed deeply, sweating so heavily that his clothes became wringing wet, as if poisons were escaping from his pores. Then an amazing thing happened; he began to laugh with the joy of the Lord that came upon him. Since then, he, like David, is being taught by God really for the first time. He can say with the psalmist: *"Good and upright is the Lord; / Therefore He teaches sinners in the way."*

CHARACTER OF A DISCIPLE

12 Who *is* the man that fears the LORD?
   Him shall He teach in the way He chooses.
13 He himself shall dwell in prosperity,
   And his descendants shall inherit the earth.
14 The secret of the LORD *is* with those who fear Him,
   And He will show them His covenant.
15 My eyes *are* ever toward the LORD,
   For He shall pluck my feet out of the net.
                                           Ps. 25:12–15

The essential trait of a disciple in these verses is that he fears God. This "fear" is really a sense of reverence before God's holiness and majesty. It also includes recognition of God's awesome power. When Jesus displayed that power in calming the storm described in Mark 4:37, we are told that the disciples "feared exceedingly" (Mark 4:41).

The person who fears God will be taught by Him. His reverence and submission to God will make him teachable. As a result God will give him great blessing. He will *"dwell in prosperity"* and his posterity will *"inherit the earth"* (v. 13). His fear of God is both for himself and for his seed which follows. Thus, for David, God's blessing is seen here in material ways. The New Testament, while stressing the spiritual as enduring, records that Jesus did heal bodies as well as save souls. God cares about the totality of His creation.

David continues, saying that God will not only teach the person who fears Him, but He will also show him His *"secret"* or *"counsel."* Thus there will be new unveilings of God's truth and ways. For David this counsel is given in the covenant, God's special call and claim upon His people. Any word from the Holy Spirit to us must be consistent with that covenant, the revelation of God's call and love for us in His written word. The promise of God's counsel is ultimately fulfilled in Christ when He gives us His Spirit who "searches all things, yes, the deep things of God" (1 Cor. 2:10).

In verse 15, as in verse 11, David responds personally. He resolves to look always to Yahweh, certain that God will deliver him from the trapper's net or ambush and will give him victory over treacherous enemies.

PLEA FOR DELIVERANCE

16 Turn Yourself to me, and have mercy on me,
   For I *am* desolate and afflicted.
17 The troubles of my heart have enlarged;
   Bring me out of my distresses!
18 Look on my affliction and my pain,
   And forgive all my sins.
19 Consider my enemies, for they are many;
   And they hate me with cruel hatred.
20 Keep my soul, and deliver me;
   Let me not be ashamed, for I put my trust in You.
21 Let integrity and uprightness preserve me,
   For I wait for You.

Ps. 25:16–21

Instructed by the Lord and willing to be discipled by Him, David returns here to the double crisis that gave birth to this psalm. Now, however, he fully exposes himself. As he has known God's mercy and truth and responded to Him, it is possible that a deeper work of God has brought him to be more in touch with who he is.

In true judgment God must turn away from us, but in His grace we see His face. Thus David cries, as he did in verses 6–7, *"Turn Yourself to me, and have mercy on me."* He asks first for mercy in his emotional life. Experiencing the consequences of sin, he feels *"desolate,"* that is, alone. He is *"afflicted,"* or *"humbled."* The *"troubles"* or, literally, the constrictions of his heart have increased. *"Bring me out of my distresses!"* he cries.

One of the exciting areas of healing through prayer-therapy today is in the area of the emotions. As we pray for emotional healing, inner healing, and the healing of the memories, Jesus will often come bringing release, protection, forgiveness, and reconciliation. He is even able to move into past pain locked in our memories and manifest His presence and love there. In some cases, people have been delivered from the lock-up wards of mental hospitals through such healing prayers.

David also prays for moral healing: *"Look on my affliction and my pain, / And forgive all my sins"* (v. 18). Often release from sin will manifest itself in release from emotional and physical oppression. This may have been the case when Jesus said to the paralytic, "Son, your sins are forgiven you," and the boy was able to walk away (Mark 2:5).

After having dealt with his "inner" enemies, in verses 19–20 David deals with his "outer" enemies. So he prays: *"Consider my enemies. . . . Keep my soul, and deliver me."* Having lifted up his soul to the Lord, he vows that *"integrity and uprightness"* will hold him as he waits for God to answer and act.

THE RESPONSE OF DISCIPLESHIP

22 Redeem Israel, O God,
   Out of all their troubles!

Ps. 25:22

This final verse may have been added as a liturgical response once the psalm was incorporated into Israel's worship life. What God does for David, He will do for all His people. The healing of David's troubles foreshadows the healing of Israel's troubles.

True discipleship, then, begins in crisis. As it breaks us open, we are put in touch with our desperation and God employs this opening to teach us His ways. Our entrance into His school of faith, however, is only by His mercy as He remembers us and not our sin. It is the sinners and the humble who are taught the mercy and truth of the Lord and who reflect that mercy and truth to the world. It is the person who fears God who becomes His disciple. Now there is healing for the whole person and deliverance from the crisis, within and without, as God answers prayer.

Discipleship means a radical breaking of our pride, followed by the powerful infusion of God's mercy and truth into us. A repentant heart leads to healing and transformation as we begin to walk in God's ways. In a word, discipleship means becoming like Jesus, God's Son, in the power of the Holy Spirit. We are to manifest His character, bear His message, and exhibit His ministry. This is decisive discipleship.

CHAPTER TWENTY-SIX

Clear the Charge!

Psalm 26

Every nation and every individual will stand before Christ on the awesome Day of Judgment. Jesus Himself speaks of this when He promises that "all who are in the graves will hear His voice and come forth—those who have done good, to the resurrection of life, and those who have done evil, to the resurrection of condemnation" (John 5:28–29). Likewise, Paul tells the Thessalonians that the Lord Jesus will be "revealed from heaven with His mighty angels, in flaming fire taking vengeance on those who do not know God, and on those who do not obey the gospel of our Lord Jesus Christ" (2 Thess. 1:7–8). Moreover, John sees a great white throne where the dead "small and great" stand before God. Those whose names are not written in the Book of Life are to be "cast into the lake of fire" (Rev. 20:15). This sense of a final, universal judgment is strangely lacking among people today. Most of our pulpits are silent on the matter. Yet, every great revival in the history of the church has brought with it a renewed sense of the final Day of Judgment. As revivalists like Jonathan Edwards, George Whitfield, and Charles Finney warned their hearers to flee from the wrath to come, the word of God fell like a hammer and untold thousands turned to the Savior while there was yet time. If revival is to come to the church again today, we too must recapture the truth that all will stand before our divine Judge. This message, however, must not be given to drive us to despair; rather it must be given to drive us to Christ.

Psalm 26 helps us to think about the Day of Judgment. It is as if this psalm is a rehearsal for that final accounting. Here the psalmist presents himself and his case to the Lord. Behind his defense may lurk unspoken accusations. These are addressed boldly in the assertion of his righteousness.

Commentators debate the setting and form of this psalm. Some hold it to be an individual lament. Others see it as a liturgy for the cult or an entrance liturgy into the temple. The call for examination, however (v. 2), and the assertion of innocence (v. 6), seem to preclude a general, cultic origin, whatever the psalm's later usage. David is traditionally held to be the author. The movement of thought here is from David's presentation of his case for vindication (vv. 1–5) to his promise of worship (vv. 6–8), his petition for protection (vv. 9–10), and a concluding confession of assurance (vv. 11–12).

CASE PRESENTED

1 Vindicate me, O LORD,
  For I have walked in my integrity.
  I have also trusted in the LORD;
  I shall not slip.
2 Examine me, O LORD, and prove me;
  Try my mind and my heart.
3 For Your lovingkindness *is* before my eyes,
  And I have walked in Your truth.
4 I have not sat with idolatrous mortals,
  Nor will I go in with hypocrites.
5 I have hated the assembly of evildoers,
  And will not sit with the wicked.

Ps. 26:1–5

David's call for vindication is based, first, on his own trustworthiness, and second, on his trust in the Lord. The verb for *"vindicate"* means "to judge, to decide controversy." As David invites Yahweh to come in judgment, he appeals to the witness of his own character. David has walked his way in *"integrity"* (here meaning "completeness" in the sense of "wholeness" or "innocence") and is thus innocent of any charges brought against him.

Beyond his character is his commitment; David also trusts in the Lord, and his conclusion is certain: *"I shall not slip."*

In verses 2–5 David opens himself up to examination. Only God, his ultimate Judge, can know the truth of his claim to integrity and trust. This probing embraces both mind and heart. God is to scrutinize David throughout his being.

David turns in verse 3 to the positive assertion that he has beheld God's *"lovingkindness"* or covenant-love and walked the path of divine truth. To see God's love is to see His redemptive, saving work toward His people. To walk in God's truth is to obey His word, His law, His will. Israel was redeemed out of bondage in Egypt and brought to Sinai in order to be God's obedient people in the world. David stands in this covenant tradition.

That positive assertion is followed by a fourfold negative assertion in verses 4–5. First, David has not sat with *"idolatrous mortals,"* or, literally, "men of vanity." The word for "vanity" is often used of the idols who are empty (see Ps. 31:6). Second, David will not *"go in with hypocrites."* The word for *"hypocrites"* means "those who conceal themselves." Third, David hates the *"assembly of evildoers."* Fourth, David refuses to *"sit with the wicked."*

Since David is bound in God's covenant and walks in His truth, his way cannot be with those who deny God, deceive men, or practice evil (cf. Ps. 1:1). This then is the case David presents. It may mask charges that have been made to the contrary.

As we read these verses we may well ask ourselves: Could I call upon God to vindicate me? How free am I to say, "Examine me, O Lord"? Do I want God to know my mind and heart? How faithful have I been in God's love and truth? How do I deal with idolaters, when what they worship is money or patriotism? Do I stand with hypocrites? Do I tolerate and excuse them in the church? What is my response to evildoers? Am I willing to enter into partnership with them? If these questions cause us discomfort, good! This is a valid dress-rehearsal for the final Day of Judgment.

WORSHIP PROMISED

6 I will wash my hands in innocence;
  So I will go about Your altar, O LORD,
7 That I may proclaim with the voice of thanksgiving,
  And tell of all Your wondrous works.
8 LORD, I have loved the habitation of Your house,
  And the place where Your glory dwells.

Ps. 26:6–8

Having been examined by the Lord, David is ready to worship. Since his life is bound by God's love and truth, he is prepared to enter into the Holy Presence.

David begins by promising to *"wash [his] hands,"* a ceremonial sign of purity or *"innocence"* (cf. Exod. 29:4; Ps. 51:7). Next he will walk around the *"altar,"* offering worship to Yahweh with the *"voice of thanksgiving."* His praise is public and vocal. Worship becomes witness as David promises to tell of all of God's *"wondrous works."* The word rendered *"wondrous works"* means "surpassing, extraordinary acts of God." David recalls God's past mighty acts in a liturgy of praise, and witnesses to experiences in his own life of divine, miraculous intervention. Such direct wonders continue to be expected in the New Testament church. Luke tells us that "many wonders and signs were done through the apostles," paralleling Jesus' own ministry (Acts 2:43).

David now concludes this section by telling God how good it is to be with Him: *"Lord, I have loved the habitation of Your house."* Indeed, David loves the house because of the One who lives there, because it is *"the place where Your glory dwells."*

PETITION FOR PROTECTION

9 Do not gather my soul with sinners,
  Nor my life with bloodthirsty men,
10 In whose hands *is* a sinister scheme,
  And whose right hand is full of bribes.

Ps. 26:9–10

The *"sinners"* David prays that God will not identify him with are those who miss the "way" or the standard. Paul defines them as falling short of God's glory (Rom. 3:23). David also asks to be separated from "*bloodthirsty men*," those who "*scheme*" and accept "*bribes*" in order to pervert justice. Perhaps these are the men who are bringing false charges against David, triggering his cry for vindication.

When David asks God not to "*gather*" his "*soul*" or "*life*" with these evildoers, he is asking to be protected from their sins and their fate. He does not want to go with them under the avenging wrath of God.

FINAL ASSURANCE

11 But as for me, I will walk in my integrity;
   Redeem me and be merciful to me.
12 My foot stands in an even place;
   In the congregations I will bless the LORD.

Ps. 26:11–12

Rather than follow sinners into destruction, David now promises to continue to "*walk in* [*his*] *integrity*" so that Yahweh will continually vindicate him (cf. v. 1). With this vow David can ask God to "*redeem*" him and to "*be merciful*" toward him. The context of "*redeem*" here may be deliverance from all accusations and enemies. It also includes ultimate redemption into God's presence. The parallel request is for mercy. In Psalm 51:1 the mercy of God is His forgiveness: "Have mercy upon me, O God . . . / According to the multitude of Your tender mercies, / Blot out my transgressions."

With God's grace upon him David can now assert in conclusion that his "*foot stands in an even place*," that he is securely grounded. When God's people gather "*in the congregations*" or "assemblies" he will "*bless the Lord,*" fulfilling his destiny in worship.

This closing word also points eschatologically to the consummation of all things. The "*even place*" for us is God's kingdom in all of its fulfillment. There the redeemed will be gathered and God's name will be praised.

In his album *Saved* Bob Dylan sings of the coming judgment and asks, "Are you ready?" Every test of our hearts by God is a dress rehearsal for the final Day. Psalm 26 helps us answer, "Yes, I'm ready."

CHAPTER TWENTY-SEVEN

Faith Triumphant

Psalm 27

Today, single-mindedness is not always admired as a virtue. The media frequently criticize single-issue politicians and single-issue pressure groups. People devoted to a cause may be viewed as bigoted or narrow-minded. Congenial society tires of advocates who keep bringing the conversation around to "their point." Such "radicals" are judged fanatics or avoided as "bores."

At the same time, it is single-minded people who move history. Marx was consumed with the ideal of a classless utopia. Hitler rallied Germany with the vision of a master race and a thousand-year Reich. Paul affected history in a positive way when, in evangelizing the West, he determined to know nothing but "Jesus Christ and Him crucified" (1 Cor. 2:2).

Psalm 27 is a mountain peak of single-minded confession of trust and faith: "One thing I have desired of the Lord, / That will I seek: / That I may dwell in the house of the Lord / All the days of my life, / To behold the beauty of the Lord." Here is the supreme expression of a heart's desire—the consuming passion to be in the presence of the Lord God Himself.

This prayer appears to have been written in the context of crisis. The psalmist has been faced with the "wicked," with "enemies" and "foes," and fears a hostile "army" and "war" itself may again threaten. There are "false witnesses" who "breathe out violence." But the author's single-mindedness holds him in the midst of his battles. His confidence and communion with the Lord are antidotes to fear. As we study this psalm, we too are infected with the writer's power over his circumstances and the passion of his heart.

Tradition ascribes Psalm 27 to David, a view supported by its warfare imagery. The writer appears to be Israel's king, who will lead his troops in battle. If David is the author, the reference to the temple in verse 4 would be figurative. Several scholars challenge the unity of this psalm, breaking it between verses 6 and 7. Similar themes, however, are sustained throughout and the movement from meditation (vv. 1–6) to prayer (vv. 7–13) occurs often in the Psalter, reflecting the movement of the heart in worship.

MEDITATION: FOCUSED FAITH

1 The LORD *is* my light and my salvation;
  Whom shall I fear?
  The LORD *is* the strength of my life;
  Of whom shall I be afraid?
2 When the wicked came against me
  To eat up my flesh,
  My enemies and foes,
  They stumbled and fell.
3 Though an army may encamp against me,
  My heart shall not fear;
  Though war may rise against me,
  In this I *will be* confident.
4 One *thing* I have desired of the LORD,
  That will I seek:
  That I may dwell in the house of the LORD
  All the days of my life,
  To behold the beauty of the LORD,
  And to inquire in His temple.
5 For in the time of trouble
  He shall hide me in His pavilion;
  In the secret place of His tabernacle
  He shall hide me;
  He shall set me high upon a rock.
6 And now my head shall be lifted up above my enemies
      all around me;
  Therefore I will offer sacrifices of joy in His tabernacle;
  I will sing, yes, I will sing praises to the LORD.

Ps. 27:1–6

Verse 1 opens with an exuberant confession of faith. As in the preceding psalms David's intensely personal faith is reflected in the use of the possessive pronoun: *"my* light," *"my* salvation." Similarly we read in Psalm 23:1: "The Lord is *my* shepherd."

Biblical faith is relational at its core, as has been noted earlier. Yahweh prepares us for the incarnation, the supreme personal event of history by calling us into communion with Himself, and building a strong relationship with us as we learn of His steadfast love. The First Letter of John tells of "That which was from the beginning, which we have heard, which we have seen with our eyes, which we have looked upon, and our hands have handled, concerning the Word of life" (1 John 1:1).

The Lord is defined as David's *"light"* and *"salvation."* As light God is the revealer (John 1:4–5), and as light God is also holy (1 John 1:5). Since the Lord is David's light, in His presence the darkness of his enemies and the darkness of his fears are expelled.

However, God is not just the holy revealer. He is *"salvation."* The word used here includes the ideas of "deliverance" and "rescue" and is the same word from which the name of Jesus is derived. The thought of Yahweh as Savior leads David to this rhetorical question: *"Whom shall I fear?"* Since the Lord will rescue him from his foes, there is no reason to be afraid.

Next, David confesses: *"The Lord is the strength of my life."* The word *"strength"* may mean "refuge" from the root ʿwz or "stronghold" from the root ʿzz. In either case, the point is the same; Yahweh protects him. Again, his confession is followed by a rhetorical question: *"Of whom shall I be afraid?"*

Faith or fear—these are our ultimate options. Either we can know the living God as our *"light," "salvation,"* and *"strength,"* or we are condemned to anguish as we move toward our final hour. The atheist philosopher Bertrand Russell put it, "The older I get, the more nervous I become." In contrast, two weeks before his death, Pope John XXIII said, "My bags are packed. I'm ready to go."

In verses 2–3 David now turns to his enemies. As God delivers him from them, he is delivered from the source of his fear as well. He remembers, *"When the wicked* [my enemies and foes] *came against me, they stumbled and fell."*

Now in verse 3, when he is faced by an *"army"* and *"war"* rising against him, his *"heart"* (or, "mind") will not be gripped with fear. Enemy troops may march, but if such a threat should come, and it often did in David's life, he will be confident. The word for *"confident"* here means to "feel secure, be unconcerned." This security comes from the Lord, confessed in verse 1 as David's light and salvation.

Beyond the deliverance of the Lord, however, is the Lord Himself, and David now turns in verse 4 to his single-minded longing. He describes the passion of his heart in three ways. He wants to *"dwell"* in the Lord's *"house,"* he wants to *"behold"* the Lord's *"beauty,"* and he wants to *"inquire"* of the Lord. David's attitude as he comes is both that of a supplicant (he desires or "has asked from the Lord") and a seeker (he will "seek to secure" or "inquire"). The language is emphatic; he pursues his passion with vigor as he seeks a threefold response to his single-minded quest. To live where God lives, to spend his life in His presence will allow him consistent worship, prayer "without ceasing" (1 Thess. 5:17). This desire is fulfilled for us in Christ who calls us to abide in Him and who promises to abide in us (John 15:4). The Greek verb for "abide" means "to dwell, to remain." When we come to Jesus and receive His Spirit we live before Him, we dwell in Him, and His presence remains with us for eternity. This is the "abundant" life (John 10:10) which He gives to us. Paul asserts that life for him is Christ (Phil. 1:21). To dwell in the house of the Lord for us, then, is not to live in the tabernacle or the temple in Jerusalem. It is to open our heart's door to Christ and to allow His Spirit's presence to fill us unceasingly. As Jesus promises us, the Comforter, the Holy Spirit, will "abide with you forever . . . for He dwells with you and will be in you" (John 14:16–17).

The second response that David seeks is *"to behold the beauty of the Lord."* The noun for *"beauty"* also means "delightfulness, pleasantness." Where can we see such beauty but in the face of Jesus? And when we see His beauty we see the beauty of the Father. This is the beauty of His gracious love; the delight that is on His face toward us, His smile, His outstretched hand. The point of living with the Lord—for David and for us—is to *"behold"* Him. Tragically, our churches are filled with people who dwell in His house, but fail to behold His beauty. No wonder they are the "gray" people (Bruce Larson). It is only in beholding Him that we are changed to be like Him (see 2 Cor. 3:18); it is only in beholding Him that praise comes alive, devotion is real, and prayer is precious. Here, indeed, is focused faith.

The third response that David seeks is *"to inquire in His temple."* To *"inquire"* may mean "to receive oracles or prophecies." Without defining God's means of response, however, it does mean waiting for His word. One of the newer experiences of my Christian walk is to wait after spoken prayer for God to speak. If I just chatter at Him and then walk away, how can I be concerned that He never seems to speak to me? I'm never listening. When I take the time in open responsiveness to Him, often a clear word will come, inscribed upon my mind.

It may be a prophetic message; it may be a word or phrase from Scripture; it may be an impression or a picture. God speaks when we *"inquire"* of Him.

The sequence in verse 4 is crucial. We must first dwell with the Lord and He with us. Next, we must behold His beauty in worship and praise. Then and only then are we ready to inquire of Him when our hearts are open to hear His word rather than the mere echo of our own prayers.

In verse 5 David sees the consequences of His being before the Lord: *"For in the time of trouble / He shall hide me in His pavilion . . . His tabernacle."* God does not block us from trouble by denial. He protects us from the results of trouble. The words *"pavilion"* or "booth" and *"tabernacle"* or "tent" indicate God's dwelling place. They apply to the temple and, ultimately, to heaven itself (cf. 1 Kings 8:27). Not only is the *"tabernacle"* or temple the place to see the beauty of the Lord, it is also a place of security, or refuge. David adds: *"He shall set me high upon a rock."* Worship is no escape from battle, but it equips us for battle, for as we seek the Lord's face we are hidden in Him and our enemies cannot reach us there. As Paul tells the Colossians, "For you died [to sin and your old life], and your life is hidden with Christ in God" (3:3).

The results of the presence of God and the protection of God (v. 6) are, first, David will triumph over his enemies. This is the meaning of his head's being *"lifted up."* Second, David will *"offer sacrifices of joy"* before the Lord—a shout of triumph, a victory cry. Here is robust worship. Third, David promises to *"sing praises to the Lord."* Singing praise to God for battle triumph fills the Psalter and finds its classic expression in Exodus 15, the Song of Moses after the defeat of Pharaoh's armies. In heaven, the saints sing to the Lamb because they have been redeemed to God by His blood (Rev. 5:9). These songs of victory follow God's liberating, delivering work for us. True worship rings with the joy of those delivered from sin, Satan, and death.

PRAYER: SEEKING GOD'S FACE

7 Hear, O Lord, *when* I cry with my voice!
  Have mercy also upon me, and answer me.
8 *When You said,* "Seek My face,"
  My heart said to You, "Your face, Lord, I will seek."

> 9 Do not hide Your face from me;
>   Do not turn Your servant away in anger;
>   You have been my help;
>   Do not leave me nor forsake me,
>   O God of my salvation.
> 10 When my father and my mother forsake me,
>   Then the LORD will take care of me.
> 11 Teach me Your way, O LORD,
>   And lead me in a smooth path, because of my enemies.
> 12 Do not deliver me to the will of my adversaries;
>   For false witnesses have risen against me,
>   And such as breathe out violence.
> 13 *I would have lost heart,* unless I had believed
>   That I would see the goodness of the LORD
>   In the land of the living.
>
> *Ps. 27:7–13*

David now turns from his meditation on the Lord to conversation with the Lord. From this we learn the "how-to's" of devotion. After we have reflected on the character of God and expressed our single-minded desire for Him, we need to address Him directly. So, David prays: *"Hear, O Lord, when I cry with my voice!"*

In calling God by name, as David does, we enter into direct relationship with Him. Note also that David prays aloud, *"with my voice."* Early in my Christian life I learned that when I prayed vocally I could concentrate on my prayers far more easily than with silent prayer. One of the strengths of the church in Korea is the vocal prayer of the gathered congregations. Individual believers are literally caught up in a sea of prayer. Next, David asks for mercy: *"Have mercy also upon me, and answer me."* The mercy of God will be given as He answers David's prayer.

In verse 8 David enters into actual prayer-dialogue with God: *"When You said, 'Seek My face,' / My heart said to You, 'Your face, Lord, I will seek.'"* The translation here is difficult because the divine command, *"Seek My face,"* is in plural form, addressed to more than David. The call to all to seek the Lord's face is, in the idiom of the day, the call to seek His favor. As we read in Psalm 34:15–16, "The eyes of the Lord are on the righteous. . . . The face of the Lord is against those who do evil." David responds in kind to the divine command / invitation when he prays, *"Your face, Lord, I will seek."*

In asking God to turn His face toward him, David entreats the Lord not to respond with rejection. He prays: *"Do not hide Your face from me."* In a parallel clause, he then asks the Lord not to be angry. In this request, David is conscious of his sin. Certainly God has a right to judge him. It is only by His mercy that He will continue to look upon David with favor. In asking God not to be angry, David also identifies himself as God's *"servant."* He prays in humility, in submission to God as his master.

Next, David reminds God of His past goodness: *"You have been my help."* Then the request for God not to abandon him is repeated, followed by the direct address *"O God of my salvation."* This phrase echoes the confession of the Lord as David's "salvation" in verse 1. Indeed, this is true because God delivers him from his enemies and brings him into His presence.

Verse 10 completes the thought of abandonment as David adds, *"When my father and my mother forsake me, / Then the Lord will take care of me."* The abandonment by family was a death experience in ancient tribal Israel. Even in our individualistic world it is still the same ultimate, personal loss. Whatever David's actual experience (parental death?), beyond the love and security of his family is the provision of Yahweh. As Moses promises Joshua, "The Lord your God, He is the One who goes with you. He will not leave you nor forsake you" (Deut. 31:6). This is David's "bottom line" as well.

David turns now to a prayer for God's ways to be known to him (vv. 11–13). The worship of God leads to doing the works of God. Thus David prays, *"Teach me Your way, O Lord, / And lead me in a smooth path, because of my enemies."* The theme of opposition returns as David has spoken of enemies and armies in verses 2–3. He has mentioned a "time of trouble" in verse 5 and of his head's being lifted up above his enemies in verse 6. His prayer for the Lord not to abandon him is also related to God's using his enemies as instruments of judgment. Here then David prays for the *"way"* of God, His path and direction, to be made clear. To be led in that way means for David to be taught by the Lord and to be guided on a *"smooth path,"* through the opposition of those enemies who can defeat him.

From the positive request of verse 11 David moves to the negative cry: *"Do not deliver me to the will* [or, "greed"] *of my adversaries."* Why might God do this? The answer is that these enemies lie about him, they are *"false witnesses"* and have *"violence"* as their intention. But because David seeks the Lord's face and the Lord's will, his heart's desire and action expose the deception in these attacks upon him. For

God to deliver David to these enemies would be an improper judgment upon him. To be delivered from them, as he asks, will be a sign of mercy.

David's confidence in God, witnessed to in verse 13, is based on his faith that he will *"see the goodness of the Lord / In the land of the living."* Here God's *"goodness"* consists of the *"good things"* in the land, including prosperity and peace. The *"land of the living"* is Israel right now, not some future life. Through the attack of his enemies David is held by the hope of God's intervention on his behalf and ensuing goodness.

Lesslie Newbigin, a missionary-statesman who spent many years in India, suggests that the terminal illness of the West today is its loss of hope. He finds this clearly in Europe among the masses who have given up on the future and are living meaningless lives on the edge of despair. With the exception of pockets of Christians he senses an atmosphere of doom in the air. The shocking thing about this is that only a generation ago the West pulsated with the hope that reason and technology would solve our problems and bring in the millennium. Today, however, this hope is gone. We, like David, need a renewal of faith so that we may again see God's goodness, His kingdom in our day, in the land of the living. "Thy kingdom come, Thy will be done on earth. . . ."

EXHORTATION: WAIT ON THE LORD

14 Wait on the LORD;
   Be of good courage,
   And He shall strengthen your heart;
   Wait, I say, on the LORD!

Ps. 27:14

As we have seen, David has the single-minded desire to "behold the beauty of the Lord." Thus in the midst of his trials he turns to the God who has called him to seek His face. With his own faith renewed he can now invite Israel to join him in waiting *"on"* or *"for"* the Lord. To "wait for" Yahweh is to expect His answer in His action (see v. 5). Here, for David, to wait for Yahweh is to see Him destroy his enemies and at the same time grant him the security and sanctity of His temple.

Confident that God hears and answers, David exhorts us to wait for the Lord with *"good courage / And He shall strengthen your heart"* or, literally, "be strong and let your heart be strong." For emphasis, David then repeats his exhortation as he ends the psalm: *"Wait, I say, on the Lord!"*

The thesis of this psalm, as we have seen, is the single-mindedness of David's desire to behold the beauty of the Lord. The final clause reveals how he will achieve his aim: by waiting on the Lord. The God who wants us to be with Him will take us there. As we wait on Him we will commune with Him and grow to trust Him. David's single-minded goal demands single-minded means. Thus he waits for God to fulfill His promise and usher him into His presence. This is faith triumphant.

CHAPTER TWENTY-EIGHT

Conflict Resolution

Psalm 28

It is always God's way to bring life out of death. He continually surprises us by reversing our values and expectations. After Abraham and Sarah had lost all physical capability of producing an heir, Isaac was born. After Joseph was sold into Egypt as a slave, he was elevated to a position next to Pharaoh himself. Moses, the fugitive murderer, brought Israel out of bondage. David was the youngest of eight sons, but he was anointed king of Israel. Saul, persecutor of the church, became Paul, the apostle to the Gentiles. It was only through death that Jesus was raised from the dead. Indeed, out of death to ourselves, God brings life (Gal. 2:20). Psalm 28 teaches us a similar truth.

The whole mood of the first half of this psalm is the fear of judgment and death, the fear of God's not hearing or answering the psalmist's prayer. The risk of prayer is always the risk of faith: As I speak is anyone listening? In God's silence, the psalmist fears being lost with those who are evil. Thus he asks God to judge them but not him.

Suddenly, midway through the prayer his mood changes, and in verses 6–7 the presence and power of God rush in. This leads to bold petition as the prayer ends.

Commentators hold this psalm to be an individual lament or a prayer of confidence. Tradition, accepted here, ascribes it to David. Support for this view includes the militaristic references to God as "Rock" and "shield," mention of the king as God's "anointed," and God as Israel's "Shepherd." The structure is simple: first conflict, then resolution. This is also often the structure of real, living prayer.

THE CONFLICT OF FEAR

1 To You I will cry, O LORD my Rock:
  Do not be silent to me,
  Lest, if You *are* silent to me,
  I become like those who go down to the pit.
2 Hear the voice of my supplications
  When I cry to You,
  When I lift up my hands toward Your holy sanctuary.
3 Do not take me away with the wicked
  And with the workers of iniquity,
  Who speak peace to their neighbors,
  But evil *is* in their hearts.
4 Give them according to their deeds,
  And according to the wickedness of their endeavors;
  Give them according to the work of their hands;
  Render to them what they deserve.
5 Because they do not regard the works of the LORD,
  Nor the operation of His hands,
  He shall destroy them
  And not build them up.

                                        Ps. 28:1–5

As David's *"Rock,"* God is his security and fortress in battle. When doubts assail him, the Lord is his stronghold. David's request, as he begins to pray, is simple: if God will speak once again, he will know that Yahweh is the living and true God. If God remains silent, however, David will *"become like those who go down to the pit"*; that is, he will be like the heathen who hear no word from God and are destined to death. He will also be like those who repose in eternal silence; they do not speak, and God does not speak. As Psalm 115:17 puts it, "The

dead do not praise the Lord, / Nor any who go down into silence."
True life is lived only in communion with the living God. When David
cries out to Him as he prays, his expectation is that God will speak.

Only recently have I had similar expectations that God will speak
to me as I pray. I have always looked for answers to prayer in events,
but I have not really expected to hear God's voice. Now, however, as
I both pray and wait in silence upon God to answer, I am beginning
to hear Him speak. For me, God's speech is not audible, although I
know people who hear Him in this way. As I listen for Him, His address
comes back to me, written across my mind, and a real dialogue begins.
At times His speech comes in the form of Scripture, but at times it
also comes as impressions or thoughts. In public worship God often
speaks through words of knowledge or prophetic utterances (see 1 Cor.
12:8; 14:1 ff.). Thus we can pray as David prayed, *"Do not be silent to
me,"* and God will answer.

Now David expands on his cry, with added emotional intensity. He
asks God to hear his voice (he prays aloud) as he brings his requests,
his *"supplications"* to Him. Here he repeats the thought of crying to
the Lord and adds his posture for worship: *"When I lift up my hands
toward Your holy sanctuary."* David prays with "body language." His
uplifted hands are the universal sign of surrender, evidence of his readiness to receive from God. As he prays he also faces the place where
the divine presence dwells. David throws his whole self into his prayer.
He doesn't know much of "silent prayer" or "unspoken requests." David's voice, hands, and body all are engaged before the Lord. Do we
have a similar posture and expend real energy when we pray? One of
the great secrets of the effectiveness of Charles Finney's evangelism
in the revivals of the nineteenth century was the prayers of Father
Nash, a gifted intercessor. At times people were offended when they
passed by a house where he was laboring in prayer, shouting to the
Lord. David, however, would have fully understood. They both know
how to "pray through."

With verse 3 David begins to detail his supplications to the Lord.
He fears that he will be taken away with the *"wicked,"* the *"workers
of iniquity."* These are hypocrites, those who deal treacherously. They
"speak peace to their neighbors, / But evil is in their hearts." Like fishermen,
they have attractive lures hiding their hooks. Hustle is the name of
their game. David knows that they will be destroyed, but he wants
to live before God rather than die.

With a sense of righteous indignation David prays in verse 4 for
judgment upon these wicked people: *"Give to them according to their*

deeds . . . / Render to them what they deserve." "The wickedness of their endeavors" deserves God's wrath.

The grounds for their judgment include both their evil actions and their disregard for *"the works of the Lord"* (v. 5). By the *"work of their hands"* (v. 4) they deny *"the operation"* (or the "work") of God's *"hands"* (v. 5). The outcome is clear: *"He shall destroy them / And not build them up."* The verb *"destroy"* means "to tear down." Thus its opposite is "to build up." Like an enemy fortress, those who disdain the Lord's works, His mighty deeds, and His kingdom will be bulldozed to the ground.

The opening of this psalm, then, reflects David's crisis. In the silence he wants to hear God speak. He wants to see God judge human evil. His expressed fear, however, is that God will remain silent toward him and that he will be carried away in the silence of death with the evil-workers. We can easily identify with David's anguish, expressed in the petition *"Do not be silent to me."*

A young girl in our church recently died of leukemia. When we prayed for her healing, there was only a little relief. In the final moments of her life, however, she told her parents that she saw Jesus standing with her, taking her hand. His radiance was upon her face. While God did not grant her physical healing in this life, He granted her His presence. ("Death is the ultimate healing before Christ's return"—Francis Mac-Nutt.) The silence was broken as Jesus stepped in. We sense there will be a similar response for David.

THE JOY OF RESOLUTION

6 Blessed *be* the LORD,
    Because He has heard the voice of my supplications!
7 The LORD *is* my strength and my shield;
    My heart trusted in Him, and I am helped;
    Therefore my heart greatly rejoices,
    And with my song I will praise Him.
8 The LORD *is* their strength,
    And He *is* the saving refuge of His anointed.
9 Save Your people,
    And bless Your inheritance;
    Shepherd them also,
    And bear them up forever.

Ps. 28:6–9

Abruptly, the whole mood has changed. Notice the new words: *"Blessed," "strength," "shield," "trusted," "helped," "rejoices," "song,"* and *"praise."*

David now praises God; his prayer has "gotten through." God is not silent but has spoken, and David blesses Him. (See verse 2.)

With heaven now open, David experiences the security of the Lord, as God gives him power and protection: *"The Lord is my strength and my shield"* (v. 7). As a result of the trust that inaugurated this prayer, David is helped, and joy now comes like a flood.

Resolution for David also brings resolution for Israel. When God touches the king he touches the nation. This is also true today. When God changes a pastor he changes a people. Thus the Lord also gives strength to Israel as He gives protection to the king.

A renewed David now makes supplication for Israel, for it is Yahweh who is the real King of His people: *"Save Your people / And bless Your inheritance"* (v. 9). And it is Yahweh who will guide and guard them: *"Shepherd them also, / And bear them up forever."* His care is for time and eternity.

In Psalm 28, out of conflict comes resolution. Out of death comes resurrection. In the darkness of God's silence David cries to the Lord. Then God speaks and the joy returns. It is only when we die to ourselves that we can live to God. No cross, no Easter. This is always God's way.

CHAPTER TWENTY-NINE

God's Commanding Voice

Psalm 29

Natural revelation continues to be a theological issue. Does creation reveal the Creator? Do the heavens declare the glory of God? While the Biblical answer is obviously yes, the problem still isn't solved. If creation communicates something of God's attributes, why do so many

people live in such spiritual darkness? Now the issue shifts from God
to us. Perhaps the problem isn't with God or the natural world, but
with people. Paul seems to say as much in Romans 1:20–24. Perhaps
we aren't seeing the clues scattered across the planet. Perhaps we are
missing the messages coming to us.

Psalm 29 calls upon heaven and earth to join in worshiping Yahweh
as He reveals Himself in creation. He is to be praised because His voice
commands the "many waters," the "cedars of Lebanon," and the "Wilderness of Kadesh." Thus the areas north, south, and west of Israel
are under His command. God is heard in the "thunders," in the storm,
in the earthquake, and in the birth of a deer. As He commands His
world, so He will care for His people.

Behind this psalm may stand an attack upon the fertility gods for
whom the claim to rule the seas, nature, and the nations was made.
Over these lesser gods, who are no gods, stands the voice of Yahweh.
The reference to "Lebanon" may reveal Phoenician ideas lurking behind
the psalmist's thought. It is also possible that the identification of "the
Flood" with chaos is a metaphor for battle. Whether any of this is
true or not, Psalm 29 celebrates God's reign over all the earth. Since
seven is the Biblical number of perfection, the sevenfold, thematic repetition of the phrase "the voice of Yahweh" suggests that God is comprehensive and complete in His sovereignty over all things. He is in charge.
Chaos cannot overcome those who trust in Him. "Strength" and "peace"
belong to His people.

Many commentators hold this psalm to be one of the oldest in the
Psalter. Its parallels to extra-Biblical literature contribute to this view.
It may be that David, traditionally held to be author, reworked preexist-
ing material into its present form, a hymn celebrating the power of
Yahweh. The thought moves from a call to worship (vv. 1–2) to God's
voice over the waters (vv. 3–4), over the nations (vv. 5–7), and over
the wilderness (vv. 8–9); it concludes with God's reign (vv. 10–11).

CALL TO WORSHIP

1 Give unto the LORD, O you mighty ones,
  Give unto the LORD glory and strength.
2 Give unto the LORD the glory due to His name;
  Worship the LORD in the beauty of holiness.

                                                        Ps. 29:1–2

The call to *"worship"* invites the heavenly court, *"you mighty ones,"* to join in the praise of Yahweh. The phrase rendered *"mighty ones"* literally means "sons of gods." It probably refers to the angels who make up Yahweh's heavenly court (see Ps. 89:6; Job 1:6). Thus these angelic beings are commanded: *"Give unto the Lord glory and strength,"* that is, *"the glory due to His name."*

"Worship" is defined here as giving to God, not getting from God. The worshipers are to offer *"glory"* to God, that is, praise for His majesty and triumph. They are also to offer *"strength,"* the ascription of might or power. To *"give"* these praises is to voice them in God's presence. It is similar to shouting "Long live the Queen" to Elizabeth II, or addressing her with the title "your Majesty." Thus we read that "in His temple everyone says, 'Glory!' " (v. 9). The call in verses 1–2 then is for the heavens to shout *"glory"* and *"strength"* in the presence of Yahweh. In so doing, the worshipers reflect to Him essential aspects of His being and character.

Having told the divine beings what to offer to God in worship, David now tells them how to worship: The word for *"worship"* means "to bow down," "to surrender." Those who so submit are to do so *"in the beauty of holiness."* *"Beauty"* here means "splendor" or "holy adornment." *"Holiness"* here means "apartness, sacredness." These worshipers are to submit to Yahweh in the adornment of being separated from their sin, rebellion, and idolatry.

The call to worship then pictures the holy angels, garbed in sacred beauty, bowing before Yahweh and shouting "Glory," "Strength." This praise is His due; it is *"the glory due to His name."*

Do we in our churches in any way reflect this heavenly worship? We should. We too are called to surrender to the Lord in worship (Rom. 12:1), and to offer praises to His name (Heb. 13:15). Moreover, we are to worship the Lord *"in the beauty of holiness."* Our holiness is Jesus Christ Himself who clothes us in His righteousness and makes us, through His Spirit, what we are, "but as He who called you is holy, you also be holy in all your conduct, because it is written, 'Be holy, for I am holy' " (1 Pet. 1:15–16).

GOD'S VOICE OVER THE WATERS

3 The voice of the LORD *is* over the waters;
  The God of glory thunders;

> The Lord *is* over many waters.
> 4 The voice of the Lord *is* powerful;
> The voice of the Lord *is* full of majesty.
>
> *Ps. 29:3–4*

The God whom we worship is the God who speaks creation into existence, who orders all things according to His word, and who commands this fallen world into submission to Himself. The voice of Yahweh, the theme of this psalm, is *"over the waters,"* even *"over many waters."* God's voice *"thunders,"* expressing His power and *"majesty."*

Whether the *"thunder"* is God's *"voice"* or represents His *"voice"* matters little. In the rolling *"thunder,"* the power and *"majesty"* of God is heard. I recall being awakened from a dead sleep in Wichita, Kansas, one summer by the explosion of lightning hitting near the house where my wife and I were staying. This was followed by the crack of thunder. My body involuntarily shook from the shock. Here was raw power. My trembling reflected my awe at the majesty displayed.

The point in verse 3 is that through His *"voice"* God rules the *"waters"* (Gen. 1:21). In the New Testament Jesus silences the storm (Mark 4:35–41). For the Bible, the storm of this psalm and of the Gospel account may also represent demonic chaos behind nature's attack or the chaos of the nations. God, however, commands the waters and they submit to Him (cf. Exod. 15:8–10).

Since God is called *"the God of glory,"* and His *"voice . . . is powerful"* and *"full of majesty,"* giving "glory" and "strength" to His name is simply reflecting back to Him the appropriate response to who He is (see vv. 1–2).

GOD'S VOICE OVER THE NATIONS

> 5 The voice of the Lord breaks the cedars,
> Yes, the Lord splinters the cedars of Lebanon.
> 6 He makes them also skip like a calf,
> Lebanon and Sirion like a young wild ox.
> 7 The voice of the Lord divides the flames of fire.
>
> *Ps. 29:5–7*

Not only does God command the sea to the west of Israel, He also commands the nations to the north. His voice breaks the *"cedars of Lebanon"* by His flash of lightning. This is probably what is meant by the *"flames of fire"* in verse 7. In Isaiah 2:12–13 the cedars of Lebanon are a symbol for lofty pride. This may also be the thought behind these verses since the magnificence of the cedars was proverbial. Thus God brings the pride of the nations low. At His command *"Lebanon and Sirion" "skip like . . . a young wild ox."* They act like silly calves because their power is ended when they hear Yahweh's voice (cf. Ezek. 31:3–18). *"The voice of the Lord"* controls nature (vv. 3–4) and nations (vv. 5–7).

It is hard for us today to hear God's voice over the pride of East and West. This is true partially because in His passive wrath, God has given us up to our sin. It is also true because in this age of grace He holds back His hand of judgment, "not [being] willing that any should perish" (2 Pet. 3:9). Prophetic signs, however, reveal that God is still in charge of the nations (see Mark 13:1 ff.). The appeal of Hal Lindsey's *The Late Great Planet Earth* has been to show that prophecy and our history are intertwined; the world is not chaotic. God is still in charge and will bring all things to their proper fulfillment in His time.

GOD'S VOICE OVER THE WILDERNESS

8 The voice of the LORD shakes the wilderness;
  The LORD shakes the Wilderness of Kadesh.
9 The voice of the LORD makes the deer give birth,
  And strips the forests bare;
  And in His temple everyone says, "Glory!"

Ps. 29:8–9

God's voice also commands *"Kadesh"* to the south of Israel. He *"shakes the wilderness."* The verb for *"shakes"* here means to "dance" or to "writhe in pain" as in childbirth. It is used again in verse 9: *"The voice of the Lord makes the deer give birth,"* literally, "makes the deer writhe in pain." Here David pictures God's voice as an earthquake ripping across the wilderness, stripping *"the forests bare"* in judgment, but also bringing new life as a fawn comes into the world.

These manifestations of God's power evoke a proper response. *"In His temple everyone says, 'Glory!'"* The *"temple"* is the "palace" where the king dwells. Here it refers to God's heavenly abode where His angels worship Him (see vv. 1–2; cf. Mic. 1:2–3). This is then reflected in the earthly worship of Israel.

As we also see God's sovereign power commanding nature and the nations, and as we hear His voice and see His glory, we must bow in worship and cry, *"glory!"* in response to such majesty and might. In our worship we too reflect the worship of heaven. Thus in the Book of Revelation John hears heaven and earth join in one accord: "Blessing and honor and glory and power / Be to Him who sits on the throne, / And to the Lamb, forever and ever!" (Rev. 5:13).

GOD RULES

> 10 The LORD sat *enthroned* at the Flood,
>   And the LORD sits as King forever.
> 11 The LORD will give strength to His people;
>   The LORD will bless His people with peace.
>
> *Ps. 29:10–11*

Yahweh sits above the *"Flood,"* above the chaos. There He is enthroned, ruling and using the "waters" in judgment (see Gen. 6–9). *"The Lord sits as King forever"* over creation and history.

As King, God empowers His people Israel, giving them *"strength"* from His strength. This may mean strength to battle against the forces of chaos. Then He blesses them *"with peace"* (*šālôm*) or "wholeness." No wonder all praise should be offered to Him.

In Psalm 29 God is King. He is the sovereign Lord. While chaos and pride challenge His rule, His voice, His word prevails. Are we listening to the voices of chaos or pride? They will fail. Listen to the voice of God. Shout "Glory!" In this worship your heart will be tied to heaven.

CHAPTER THIRTY

Joy in the Morning

Psalm 30

Sickness is often a time for sorrow. Physical debilitation can sink our spirits. Anger over being set aside results in depression. Dependency upon others and mounting financial strain contribute to despair. And the pain caused to loved ones causes us pain. Illness may bring false guilt because we did not choose it (Paul Tournier), but it is guilt just the same. Where healing comes, however, there is a new beginning. Strength returns. We are free to move about. The feelings of childish dependency are forgotten. We live again.

It is in this context of sickness and recovery that Psalm 30 is written. Here is an expression of praise after healing. The psalmist has been close to death: "You [God] have brought my soul up from the grave." In his illness there has been weeping, the sense of God's absence, and mourning. Now, however, all of this is past. The healing of God has turned sorrow into joy.

Commentators describe this psalm as an individual psalm of praise. It is traditionally ascribed to David. The sequence of thought moves from a personal expression of joy for healing (vv. 1–3) to a call for communal thanksgiving (vv. 4–5). This praise is predicated upon the crisis of sickness (vv. 6–10) and the relief of restoration (vv. 11–12).

In Praise of Healing

1 I will extol You, O Lord, for You have lifted me up,
   And have not let my foes rejoice over me.
2 O Lord my God, I cried out to You,
   And You healed me.
3 O Lord, You brought my soul up from the grave;
   You have kept me alive, that I should not go down
      to the pit.

Ps. 30:1–3

225

David begins by praising God. To *"extol"* is "to exalt, to raise up." David lifts God up because God has lifted him up. To be sure, God is already lifted up, but now David lifts Him up in his thoughts and his praise. His worship is in response to God's bringing him back from death's door (see v. 3). By this David's foes have been silenced. Clearly David's enemies held that his sickness was God's wrathful response to his sin. However true this might be (see v. 5), in his healing God's life is now poured out upon David, and the basis for his enemies' joy has been demolished. David has a twofold reason then for extolling the Lord: he has been healed and his enemies have been confounded. When we experience God's healing in our lives the same things happen to us. We are restored and our enemies: Satan, and his demonic hordes, the power of sin in us, the unbelieving world, and even our unbelieving hearts, are silenced.

In verse 2 David is lifted up because he cried out to Yahweh and was healed. Notice the personal address here: *"O Lord my God."* Out of intimacy David can come to the Lord. His cry is not general, but a literal cry for help. As a result, David experiences God's healing: He knows, as did Moses, that the Lord is his healer (Exod. 15:26). Moreover, it is through prayer that he has experienced the healing power of God. There is a certain mystery here, but God's word makes it clear that we have to ask for healing. Jesus healed those who cried out to Him in faith. James 5:14–15 exhorts us, "Is anyone among you sick? Let him call for the elders of the church, and let them pray over him, anointing him with oil in the name of the Lord. And the prayer of faith will save the sick."

I well remember the first time I saw Francis MacNutt pray for the healing of a back injury. Before he began to pray he said, "Notice, nothing is happening. Now I'm going to pray and something will happen." And it did; it was just that pragmatic, and the injured man was healed.

In verse 3, God's healing has brought David back from the brink of death. The Hebrew for "grave" is Sheol (šĕ'ôl), denoting the underworld abode of the dead. It is a place characterized by silence (see v. 9; Ps. 94:17) and darkness (Ps. 143:3). Those who are there have no fellowship with God (Ps. 88:5). *"The pit"* is often used in parallel to Sheol (see Ps. 88:3–6). Literally, the word means a cistern or a well, so it can also mean a grave. God, however, has kept David among the living. The grave is not his end.

JOIN THE JOY

4 Sing praise to the LORD, you saints of His,
   And give thanks at the remembrance of His holy
      name.
5 For His anger *is but for* a moment,
   His favor *is for* life;
   Weeping may endure for a night,
   But joy *comes* in the morning.

Ps. 30:4–5

Based upon his testimony of healing and his extolling of Yahweh, David invites those around him to join in worship: The word for *"saint"* (*ḥāsîd*) here in verse 4 means "kind, pious." It appears often in the Psalter. Here it probably refers to David's fellow worshipers.

Their praise is not focused on David's healing, however, but on remembering God's *"holy name,"* or, literally, His "holiness." God does what He does because of who He is. Thus His wrath passes quickly: *"For His anger is but for a moment."* Indeed, in the age of grace God's wrath is meant to lead us to repentance and healing: *"His favor is for life."* The word *"favor"* here means "acceptance, good will." In this acceptance life is to be found. "For God so loved the world that He gave His only begotten Son, that whoever believes in Him should . . . have everlasting life" (John 3:16).

Again, in the parallel phrase, *"weeping"* lasts merely for the night, *"But joy comes in the morning."* The word for *joy* means a "ringing cry," a "shout." Here is the proper response of those who know Yahweh's holiness and who experience His favor.

THE CRISIS OF SICKNESS

6 Now in my prosperity I said,
   "I shall never be moved."
7 LORD, by Your favor You have made my mountain
      stand strong;
   You hid Your face, *and* I was troubled.
8 I cried out to You, O LORD;
   And to the LORD I made supplication:
9 "What profit *is there* in my blood,
   When I go down to the pit?

Will the dust praise You?
Will it declare Your truth?
10 Hear, O Lord, and have mercy on me;
Lord, be my helper!"

Ps. 30:6–10

David now reflects on his past history. He states, *"Now in my prosperity I said, / 'I shall never be moved.' "* This presumptuous thought could continue through the first part of verse 7 with the meaning, "My mountain will last forever." Like David, self-sufficient people at times even attribute their strength to God's favor. How often we see people claim that their prosperity proves that "God is good" while their hearts are far from Him. The content here is similar to Jesus' parable about the rich fool who built bigger barns and then said to himself, "take your ease; eat, drink, and be merry" (Luke 12:19). God, however, called him a fool and required his soul that very night.

A shadow falls across David's presumption as he continues: *"You hid Your face, and I was troubled."* God turns away in His wrath, and the consequence of divine displeasure is that David is *"troubled,"* or "dismayed, terrified." His world falls in as it did when his health failed (vv. 2–3).

Harry Blamires notes that in the modern state, crisis is moved to the edges of our lives. The government promises us everything, and we are numbed by it. Sickness, however, still turns our attention to God. Think of how cancer, heart disease, or AIDS grip us with fear. Suddenly, our mortality is before us. We, like David, are troubled or, better, "shattered," "terrified."

Now, David responds to his new circumstances. He cries out to the Lord, making his *"supplication"* to Him. In his sickness, David tells God that in death, if he goes *"down to the pit"* he will not be able to *"praise"* Him or to *"declare [His] truth."* While at this point David did not have the full revelation about eternal life, what he says is true. When he is dead, he will not be able to worship or witness in this world. This is reason enough for his life to be spared. Here then David bargains with God for healing. How often in praying for the sick we are tempted to offer all kinds of reasons why God should intervene. The fact is, however, that God heals simply according to His will and our faith. As Mark says of Jesus' ministry in Nazareth, "Now He could do no mighty work there, except that He laid His hands on a few sick people and healed them. And He marveled because of their unbelief" (Mark 6:5–6).

After the argument there is simply the cry: *"Hear, O Lord, and have mercy on me; / Lord, be my helper!"* David's focus moves from himself to Yahweh and he asks for *"mercy"* or "grace." This is really all God wants to hear from us. We see this again and again in Jesus' ministry. As blind Bartimaeus cried, "Jesus, Son of David, have mercy upon me!" (Mark 10:47). In the context of this psalm, mercy comes as healing.

THE RELIEF OF RESTORATION

11 You have turned for me my mourning into dancing;
   You have put off my sackcloth and clothed me with
   gladness,
12 To the end that *my* glory may sing praise to You
   and not be silent.
O LORD my God, I will give thanks to You forever.
                                        Ps. 30:11–12

Now, in an abrupt transition, there is a shift back to the joy of verses 1–3. Having remembered his illness and God's healing, David rejoices in what the Lord has done. Using the image of death (representing the seriousness of his illness), David contrasts *"mourning"* and *"sackcloth"* (a garment of penitence) with *"dancing"* and *"gladness."* He has experienced an explosion of joy.

Not only does David dance, he also sings, filled with *"praise"* and *"thanks."* His *"glory"* is himself, now renewed and "glorious." His *"praise"* is everlasting, *"forever."*

As God heals people today, the experience witnessed to in Psalm 30 becomes theirs. I have seen some critically ill patients brought back from death's door by healing prayer. The flush of joy returns to their faces. Their desire to worship flourishes. They witness with David: "O Lord my God, I cried out to You, / And You have healed me" (v. 2).

CHAPTER THIRTY-ONE

Nevertheless, I Live!

Psalm 31

Jesus died with Psalm 31:5 upon His lips: "Into Your hand I commit My spirit" (see Luke 23:46). As He spoke this prayer He called God "Father," using the name of deepest intimacy. Concerning His special relationship with God, in John's Gospel, Jesus says, "For the Father loves the Son, and shows Him all things . . ." (John 5:20). The fact that Jesus prayed from Psalm 31 in His final moments of agony suggests that as we study this prayer we are also studying the heart of our Lord. Here, indeed, the themes of suffering and triumph are wedded together so that this is a psalm of death and resurrection.

The psalmist faces enemies who seek to entrap him. They slander him and want him dead: "They scheme to take away my life." Undoubtedly Jesus must have reflected upon these themes as He concluded His public ministry and went to Jerusalem to die.

The psalmist also knows great inner anguish. He cries for God's mercy because his soul and body are "spent with grief" (v. 10). He is rejected by friends and enemies (v. 11). He is "like a dead man, . . . a broken vessel" (v. 12). Again, Jesus' own experience is illumined by these verses. The one exception is the psalmist's admission of his iniquity and the physical consequences of his own sins. Here we see the prophetic power of the Old Testament and at the same time, its limitations.

Into this deep and serious darkness the light shines. God comes to "save" and "deliver" (v. 2). God redeems the psalmist from the trap set for him by his enemies. Beyond all the trauma he trusts in God, and God's goodness and protection are his. Thus the psalmist turns to the Lord and "breaks through" in prayer. He knows from experience that with God, after death there is life.

Commentators refer to Psalm 31 as an individual lament or a psalm of thanksgiving. Some see it as composite. It is accepted here in its unity and its traditional ascription to David.

The psalm begins with a cry for help (vv. 1–5). This is followed by a confession of confidence in God (vv. 6–8), which leads to the heart of the prayer: despair (vv. 9–13) and deliverance (vv. 14–18). With the resolution of faith, David concludes, certain of God's protection (vv. 19–20) and calling upon Israel to join him in loving the Lord (vv. 21–24).

CRY FOR DELIVERANCE

1 In You, O LORD, I put my trust;
  Let me never be ashamed;
  Deliver me in Your righteousness.
2 Bow down Your ear to me,
  Deliver me speedily;
  Be my rock of refuge,
  A fortress of defense to save me.
3 For You *are* my rock and my fortress;
  Therefore, for Your name's sake,
  Lead me and guide me.
4 Pull me out of the net which they have secretly laid
      for me,
  For You *are* my strength.
5 Into Your hand I commit my spirit;
  You have redeemed me, O LORD God of truth.

Ps. 31:1–5

David comes to God with a confession of confidence. This is the basis upon which the rest of the psalm is built. Because David is seeking God's intervention, he prays that he not be shamed by unanswered prayer (cf. v. 17; Ps. 25:2–3). Moreover, knowing God's *"righteousness"* or "justice" (*şĕdaqâh*) granted in the covenant, David asks for deliverance. Reinforcing this thought, he asks God to hear his prayer: *"Bow down Your ear to me,"* and to act: *"Deliver me speedily."* Thus salvation includes both the negative, David's deliverance from his enemies, and the positive, security and protection where Yahweh will be his *"rock"* of refuge, his *"fortress"* of defense.

David can ask God to be his *"fortress"* because he already knows that this is who God is: *"For You are my rock and my fortress."* When we call upon God to act, we are asking Him to manifest to us that which He already *is.* David also draws upon his past experiences of God's saving work as he now asks Him to intervene again. When he appeals to the Lord to *"lead"* him and *"guide"* him *"for Your name's sake,"* he is asking God to vindicate the power of His name by answering his prayer.

Now David's request becomes specific. He wants deliverance from the schemes of his enemies. These plots are represented by an animal trap into which he has fallen. God will be David's *"strength"* by releasing him. Thus he puts his spirit, the very breath of his life, into God's hands with the confession: *"You have redeemed me, / O Lord God of truth."* The verb for *"redeemed"* means "ransomed" or "purchased" from bondage. It is God who sets David free.

Notice the urgency here. The trap is set and David is in it. His very life is at stake (see v. 13). Yahweh, however, is his deliverer, his rock, his fortress, his savior, his strength, and his redeemer. Yahweh is righteous and true. He will lead and guide David. Verses 1–5 show that although the hour is late and the crisis severe, God is fully able to respond by His abundant grace. In the context of these verses celebrating the saving power of God, no wonder Jesus prayed, *"Into Your hand I commit my spirit."*

CONFIDENCE IN GOD

6 I have hated those who regard useless idols;
   But I trust in the LORD.
7 I will be glad and rejoice in Your mercy,
   For You have considered my trouble;
   You have known my soul in adversities,
8 And have not shut me up into the hand of the enemy;
   You have set my feet in a wide place.

                                                    Ps. 31:6–8

David now presents himself as a man who hates idolaters and who trusts in Yahweh. The first and second commandments of the Decalogue are on his heart. It is God alone whom he worships and serves (see Exod. 20:3–6). Thus David is *"glad"* and rejoices in Yahweh's *"mercy"* (*ḥesed*), His "goodness" and "covenant-love" in saving him from his enemies.

God's *"mercy"* is specifically seen as He considers David's *"trouble."* Moreover, He has *"known [his] soul in adversities."* The verb "to know" (*yādaʿ*) here means that God has had intimate fellowship with David in the midst of his suffering.

Thus, David has not been *"shut . . . up into the hand of the enemy,"* that is, he has not been held in his powerful grip. Instead, he has been set *"in a wide place,"* that is, a place free from constriction.

David's confidence in God, then, is based on his trust and on God's action (vv. 7–8). God shares his troubles. He is neither distant nor aloof. God also moves on David's behalf and gives him the *"wide place"* of salvation. No wonder David can commit his spirit to Yahweh, and no wonder Jesus also does the same thing. In the midst of the unbelief of His disciples and the hounding of His enemies, surrounded by chattering demons and the jaws of hell, Jesus knew intimacy and power with the Father. The devil's hand could not catch Him or snuff Him out. He was not protected *from* adversity but He was protected *in* adversity. Even on the cross He could pray, "Father, into Your hands. . . ."

THE CRISIS: DESPAIR

9 Have mercy on me, O LORD, for I am in trouble;
   My eye wastes away with grief,
   Yes, my soul and my body!
10 For my life is spent with grief,
   And my years with sighing;
   My strength fails because of my iniquity,
   And my bones waste away.
11 I am a reproach among all my enemies,
   But especially among my neighbors,
   And *am* repulsive to my acquaintances;
   Those who see me outside flee from me.
12 I am forgotten like a dead man, out of mind;
   I am like a broken vessel.
13 For I hear the slander of many;
   Fear *is* on every side;
   While they take counsel together against me,
   They scheme to take away my life.

Ps. 31:9–13

Now David gives us a comprehensive picture of pain. Having expressed his cry to the Lord and his confidence in the Lord, he turns to his crisis, the despair which overwhelms him.

First, he calls out for new *"mercy"* because he is in *"trouble."* This *"trouble"* consumes his whole self. He weeps with a *"grief"* which engages his *"soul"* or "self" (*nepeš*) and his *"body."* Verse 10 underscores these points. David's *"life"* is *"grief";* he groans through his years. Weakened, his *"strength fails"* because of his *"iniquity"* or "guilt." Moral failure leads to physical collapse: *"my bones waste away."* Here is a picture of a seriously ill man. Whatever his violation of God's will has been, it has led to emotional pain and bodily weakness. David's grief endangers his life itself.

Not only is David critically ill, he also is faced with the rebuke and rejection of enemies and friends alike. He is a *"reproach"* among his *"enemies"* and *"especially among [his] neighbors."* Insult is added to injury: he is even *"repulsive"* ("fearful") to his *"acquaintances."* His physical bearing seems to be so hideous that *"those who see me outside flee from me."*

Clearly the universal conclusion is that God has abandoned David. People view him as a *"dead man."* They put him out of their minds. He is *"like a broken vessel,"* worthless, to be discarded.

He has not fully lost his position or power in this massive rejection, however. For he endures *"slander,"* *"fear* [or "terror"] . . . *on every side,"* and the plots of his enemies to *"take away [his] life."*

David's grief comes, then, from the sense of his own guilt and the rejection of those around him. His body breaks under the strain. Can we hear some of Jesus' sorrow in David? He grieved not for His own sins, for He had none, but for ours. He too was rejected and His life demanded of Him. Indeed, "He is despised and rejected by men, / A Man of sorrows and acquainted with grief" (Isa. 53:3).

THE RESOLUTION: DELIVERANCE

14 But as for me, I trust in You, O LORD;
   I say, "You *are* my God."
15 My times *are* in Your hand;
   Deliver me from the hand of my enemies,
   And from those who persecute me.
16 Make Your face shine upon Your servant;
   Save me for Your mercies' sake.
17 Do not let me be ashamed, O LORD, for I have called
      upon You;
   Let the wicked be ashamed;
   Let them be silent in the grave.
18 Let the lying lips be put to silence,
   Which speak insolent things proudly and
      contemptuously against the righteous.

                                          Ps. 31:14–18

In this crisis, David throws himself upon the Lord: *"But as for me, I trust in You, O Lord."* The confession of verse 6, *"I* trust in the Lord," now turns to prayer. Furthermore, Yahweh is David's God. Notice the personal relationship: *"You are my God."*

David's *"times"* are in God's *"hand."* He controls David's life and destiny. Because he is held in God's hand, David can pray, *"Deliver me from the hand of my enemies."* Either God's hand or our enemies' hand holds us. To be out of his enemies' hand is for David to be free from those who *"persecute"* him, or *"pursue"* him.

David asks to be delivered into the Lord's presence: *"Make Your face shine upon Your servant; / Save me for Your mercies' sake."* David asks to see God's face like the sun, breaking through the clouds of his depression. The Old Testament ends with this promise: "But to you who fear My name / The Sun of Righteousness shall arise / With healing in His wings" (Mal. 4:2). Here David is the object of that healing. Also, since God is merciful, he asks for mercy: *"Save me for Your mercies' sake"* (cf. 9).

Next, David asks God to answer his prayer and to save his from shame: *"Do not let me be ashamed, O Lord."* Since he has prayed, he will be *"ashamed"* if God fails to answer. David asks, rather, that this happen to his enemies: *"Let the wicked be ashamed."* Their shame will be their death under divine judgment. Thus they will be *"silent in the grave,"* and their *"lying lips"* will also be silenced. Thus their insolence and pride *"against the righteous"* will end.

In verses 14–18, then, David confesses his trust in Yahweh. He expects God's deliverance and presence. Shame will come to the wicked, but David will not be ashamed as God answers his prayer.

Although this psalm was upon Jesus' heart as He died, He is strangely silent about divine retribution toward His enemies. In fact, He prays for their forgiveness, rather than for their doom (Luke 23:34). On the cross Jesus bears our shame. It is this that rightly makes us ashamed. He allowed the Father's face to be darkened toward Him, in order that the Father's face might shine upon us.

PROTECTION AND PRESENCE

19 Oh, how great *is* Your goodness,
    Which You have laid up for those who fear You,
    Which You have prepared for those who trust in You
    In the presence of the sons of men!

20 You shall hide them in the secret place of Your
    presence
From the plots of man;
You shall keep them secretly in a pavilion
From the strife of tongues.

Ps. 31:19–20

Having asked God to intervene by delivering him from his enemies, David now praises Him for His goodness and His presence. Here it is clear that he has experienced a breakthrough in prayer.

David delights in the Lord's *"goodness"* which is given to those who *"fear"* Him and *"trust"* in Him. To *"fear"* God here is to have awe before His mercy and might. To *"trust"* God is to take Him at His word, knowing that he will be true to what he says. The *"goodness"* of God then will be made public, revealed to all: *"In the presence of the sons of men."* David now knows this *"goodness."*

At the same time, those who *"fear"* and *"trust"* God will be kept in His *"presence."* They will be hidden there from people's schemes, *"the plots of man,"* and their accusations, the *"strife of tongues."* Furthermore, they will be kept by Him in a *"pavilion"* ("shelter").

It is important to see here that it is God's *"presence"* which reverses all the ills David has experienced. His enemies may vanish and his health may improve, but his heart will still be empty. It is the *"presence"* of the Lord for which he longs. Here is his defense against the *"plots of man"* and the *"strife of tongues."*

Even though on the cross, as our sin-bearer, Jesus knew the absence of God for a moment, He was sustained through those awful hours by the Father's presence. Thus the cry of dereliction was addressed to Him: "My God, My God, why have You forsaken Me?" (Mark 15:34). That cry was also a quote from Psalm 22 which, like Psalm 31, ends in triumph. It is certain by His use of the psalms that our Lord meditated deeply on the passages about sickness and healing, suffering and joy, death and life. Thus as He was dying, He was held by the goodness of God.

SUMMONS TO WORSHIP

21 Blessed *be* the LORD,
    For He has shown me His marvelous kindness in a
        strong city!

22 For I said in my haste,
   "I am cut off from before Your eyes";
   Nevertheless You heard the voice of my supplications
   When I cried out to You.
23 Oh, love the LORD, all you His saints!
   For the LORD preserves the faithful,
   And fully repays the proud person.
24 Be of good courage,
   And He shall strengthen your heart,
   All you who hope in the LORD.

Ps. 31:21–24

Knowing God's presence, David is now ready to worship, as God's grace is upon him. The *"strong city"* is a city of siege-works, a fortified city. This may be a poetic picture for the secure context in which God's covenant is honored. In Revelation, the holy city of New Jerusalem is the church made up of God's people. Here God dwells and worship abounds (Rev. 21:2).

While in verse 22 David thought himself *"cut off"* from the Lord, he was too "hasty" or "alarmed," for God heard his *"supplications"* when he *"cried out"* to Him.

With his prayers answered, David is ready to summon Israel to worship. The *"saints"* ("pious") in verse 23 are probably his fellow worshipers. The basis for this call to love God is that Yahweh *"preserves the faithful."* At the same time, the *"proud"* are also fully repaid for their arrogance.

The exhortation continues, *"Be of good courage"* ("be strong"), and is followed by the promise, *"And He shall strengthen your heart, / All you who hope in the Lord."* When we take courage, God gives us courage; He strengthens our hearts.

Certainly Jesus could have identified with the conclusion of Psalm 31. He knew God's covenant-love and fulfilled it by the new covenant in His blood (1 Cor. 11:25). His death led to resurrection, and from His glory He now calls us to love God, be strong, and *"hope in the Lord."* Likewise, in Galatians, Paul witnesses to death and resurrection. From this psalm David could say with him: "Nevertheless, I live . . ." (Gal. 2:20). This is authentic spiritual experience. No death, no resurrection. But beyond grief and guilt and enemies, stands the hand of the living God.

Lloyd Ogilvie, who has a powerful personality and an eloquent presence, tells about being in Scotland as a theological student. One day he was confronted by Thomas Torrence, the noted theologian. Torrence said to him, "Ogilvie, you've got to die." Lloyd was startled until he realized it is only in the surrender of death to self that we can give our spirits to God. Then the darkness vanishes, and His face shines upon us.

CHAPTER THIRTY-TWO

Prescription for Revival

Psalm 32

In a recent book D. Martyn Lloyd-Jones points out that until the early part of this century the evangelical church expected revival. Such revivals shaped the Reformation, produced the Puritans, brought the Wesleys before England, fostered the Great Awakening, and sent rivers of spiritual fire across nineteenth-century America and Great Britain. Similar movements of God have occurred in Korea, Wales, the Congo (Zaire), and East Africa in this century. For most modern evangelicals, however, revival as an unexpected, direct, mighty work of God has been replaced by the well-organized evangelistic campaign. When church life grows cold, the evangelistic training program or crusade is offered as the answer. Here is the difference between "program evangelism" and "power evangelism" (John Wimber). Lloyd-Jones also asserts that while those involved in program evangelism are advocates of the gospel, those who are swept up in power evangelism are *witnesses* to it in the New Testament sense of the term. They have been endowed with "power from on high" (Acts 1:8), and that power is direct, verifiable, and experiential.

The need of the church today is not for new, slick programs of evangelism. The urgent need of the church in all her division, worldliness, and impotence is for revival—a fresh breath of God's Spirit blowing across His people, unleashing joy and power, and sweeping sinners under conviction into God's kingdom.

If this is so—and I believe it is!—how then can we be prepared for such a movement of God? While revival is the sovereign act of God, there is a heart condition upon which He can work. It was said of our Lord that He could do no mighty works in Nazareth because of its people's unbelief. If our hearts are open to God and our faith is alive, we may expect to see revival even in our secular, lifeless, "me" generation. Psalm 32 is a prescription for revival because it witnesses to a heart open to the living God.

This psalm is identified by some commentators as an individual psalm of thanksgiving or a wisdom psalm because the language in verses 1–2 and 9–10 reflects the wisdom literature of the Old Testament. Others classify it as a penitential psalm. Tradition attributes its authorship to David. The historical context of the meditation and prayer is seen in verses 3–5 where David has gone from rebellion to repentance. In this he experienced both spiritual release and physical healing which are the gifts of true forgiveness from the Lord. The thought here progresses from the blessing of forgiveness (vv. 1–2) to the release from burdens (vv. 3–5) to prayer and protection (vv. 6–7), ending with God's response in guidance (vv. 8–9) and our response in worship (vv. 10–11).

THE BLESSING OF FORGIVENESS

1 Blessed *is he whose* transgression *is* forgiven,
  Whose sin *is* covered.
2 Blessed *is* the man to whom the Lord does not impute
    iniquity,
  And in whose spirit *there is* no deceit.

Ps. 32:1–2

The meditation begins: *"Blessed is he whose transgression is forgiven, / Whose sin is covered."* Here David opens by pronouncing a blessing upon the person who has dealt with his *"transgression," "sin,"* and *"iniquity."* Thus there is no greater "blessing" or "happiness" than to experience God's cleansing power.

The first clause, then, speaks of the forgiveness of transgression. The noun *"transgression"* means rebellion against divine authority. God "forgives" our transgression by literally "bearing" it or "carrying" it away. When we feel God in His mercy lift the load of our guilt from us, we know that a great weight has been taken. John Bunyan's Pilgrim goes to the cross where his burden rolls from his back. This is the marvelous liberty of the children of God. "If the Son makes you free, you shall be free indeed" (John 8:36).

The second clause speaks of *"sin"* being *"covered."* *"Sin"* means missing the mark or standard. Paul defines it as falling short of God's glory (Rom. 3:23). God "covers" our sin the way we would cover something offensive to us. Thus the sacrifice of Christ now stands between the holiness of God and our moral failure.

Verse 2 speaks of iniquity not imputed. *"Iniquity"* means straying from the straight path. The verb for *"impute"* means "to consider, to reckon." When we repent, God no longer views us as perverse or straying. In fact, when we accept His promise of forgiveness, He imputes His own righteousness to us (see Rom. 4:3–8).

This kind of forgiveness, real and deep, breaks us. It forces us to be honest about our own perversion. We cannot hide when we face our sin. The shame and deceit, the hypocrisy under which we have lived, like the false fronts on a Hollywood movie set, are all exposed. The grief over our sin and the gift of God's righteousness then make us guileless. Thus David concludes verse 2 with the blessing of those *"in whose spirit there is no deceit."* When God catches us, exposes us, and forgives us, He also frees us from pretense. At last we can be honest.

I remember attending my first Alcoholics Anonymous meeting with a friend and hearing each member introduce himself or herself. "I'm Carol, I'm an alcoholic." I thought to myself, "What would happen in the church if we all used the same kind of pattern to introduce ourselves, 'I'm Don, I'm a sinner'?" The pretense would be gone, and we would be blessed.

BURDEN AND RELEASE

3 When I kept silent, my bones grew old
  Through my groaning all the day long.
4 For day and night Your hand was heavy upon me;
  My vitality was turned into the drought of summer.
  Selah

> 5 I acknowledged my sin to You,
>   And my iniquity I have not hidden.
>   I said, "I will confess my transgressions to the LORD,"
>   And You forgave the iniquity of my sin.   Selah
>
> *Ps. 32:3–5*

David here reflects upon his condition prior to experiencing the power of forgiveness. The silence he speaks of in verse 3 is the silence of the unrepentant. As he harbors his sin he feels its physical effects in his bones. The verb for "grow old" also means "to wear out, to waste away." This could well be a metaphor for depression. David felt like an old man. Moreover, this happened as he groaned *"all the day long."* The *"groaning"* suggests continual emotional pain, perhaps repressed anger.

In his sin David is against himself, and God is also against him. Thus he continues, saying, *"Day and night Your hand was heavy upon me"* (v. 4). There was no relief. The heaviness of his body and spirit becomes more intense because he senses that God's anger is also upon him. In Karl Barth's phrase, God's wrath is His no against our sin.

David concludes his thought by recalling that his vitality withered and dried up as he kept silent. The picture here is of the summer heat. When the rains are over, the landscape of Israel becomes parched and dry. This is David; he is limp with exhaustion.

Unrepentance and unforgiveness bring depression, emotional pain, alienation from God, and physical weakness. It is worth noting that untold millions live in this condition; they even accept it as normal or inevitable.

One of God's gifts to the church today is the ministry of inner healing. A key element in this spiritual therapy is not only receiving forgiveness from God but also giving forgiveness to ourselves. The denial of sin, the repression of sin, and the suppression of sin are not answers. The infection continues to eat at us. I have had the experience of laboring under unforgiveness. At one time I was so depressed that I had stomach pains that would not go away. Like David I groaned *"all the day long."* Finally I went to the hospital, but there was no treatment. I needed to experience forgiveness—only in Christ did I find lasting relief—and I needed to forgive myself for participation in the pain that was mine.

In verse 5 the psalmist's burden is released. The very words for David's moral failure in verses 1–2 are now employed again. He takes his falling short of God's standard, his straying from the Lord, and his rebellion and offers them all to God: *"I acknowledged my sin to You."* The verb here means "to make known." As David brings his failure before the Lord, he is relieved of the cover-up that has kept him in spiritual and physical sickness. Now, rather than having to cover up his own iniquity, he allows God to cover it for him.

Verse 5 answers the question "How can I receive the blessing of verse 1?" The twofold response is: (1) confess your sins to the Lord and (2) accept His forgiveness. Thus David concludes: *"And You forgave the iniquity of my sin."*

In order for us to bring our sin to God we must be certain of His love and mercy. We are to see His heart in the cross. There Jesus takes our transgression and the judgment of death that we deserve. There upon the cross is the "Lamb of God who takes away the sin of the world" (John 1:29).

Most people today view God as either a distant, indifferent Creator or as a harsh judge. Both views are distorted. God in His Son is the loving Father who welcomes us home. He cleanses us with the blood of Jesus. He restores us to Himself. It has been estimated that over 80 percent of all illness today may be spiritual in origin, psychosomatic. If we will come to Christ, be freed from guilt and restored to the Father, we can be healed! The depression will be lifted, the emotional pain will be gone, and our spirits and bodies will be renewed because the heavy hand of God's no has become the light hand of His yes. As John puts it, "If we confess our sins, He is faithful and just to forgive us our sins and to cleanse us from all unrighteousness" (1 John 1:9).

PRAYER AND PROTECTION

6 For this cause everyone who is godly shall pray to
   You
   In a time when You may be found;
   Surely in a flood of great waters
   They shall not come near him.
7 You *are* my hiding place;
   You shall preserve me from trouble;
   You shall surround me with songs of deliverance.
   Selah

Ps. 32:6–7

Having shown the power and blessing of forgiveness, in verse 6 David now broadens his prayer to include us. In effect, David is saying "Because You are merciful and because we need forgiveness and healing, everyone who is *'godly'* ['pious,' namely, seeking God and belonging to His covenant] will pray to you." What is the prayer of the *"godly"*? It is the prayer of repentance. A basic truth of the Bible is that the godly know that they are ungodly. Then when they turn to the Lord, they become godly in union with Him.

The clause telling us to pray *"in a time when You may be found"* (v. 6) contains both a promise and a warning. The promise is that this is such a time. Now God's heart is open to us in His Son. The warning is that this time will pass. The door will shut and those outside will be outside forever.

Such a prayer of repentance and God's forgiveness leads to assurance. Thus David continues: *"Surely in a flood of great waters / They shall not come near him."* Here David gives us a picture of God's protection. When the raging floods come, we will not be swept away; God will keep us secure in Himself. In the next verse David becomes personal: *"You are my hiding place."* God is the refuge and fortress where he is protected from his enemies. God is also his keeper who preserves him from *"trouble"* or *"distress"* and surrounds him with *"songs"* or shouts *"of deliverance."* God is the Warrior-King who fights David's battles to victory. Here David ends on a note of worship and joyful praise.

Verses 6–7 complete the thought of the blessing pronounced in verse 1. When we confess our sins to the Lord and receive His cleansing and healing, we are not doomed to repeat the cycle. God will defend us from evil and the Evil One. The prayer Jesus teaches us, "deliver us from evil" (or as here in the NKJV, "the Evil One"), is not in vain. God answers that prayer and gives us *"songs of deliverance."* This is revival!

DIVINE RESPONSE: GUIDANCE

> 8 I will instruct you and teach you in the way you
>   should go;
>   I will guide you with My eye.
> 9 Do not be like the horse *or* like the mule,
>   *Which* have no understanding,
>   Which must be harnessed with bit and bridle,
>   Else they will not come near you.
>
> Ps. 32:8–9

Now God speaks. He is the living God. He is the voice of prophecy. His address here need not be through some temple priest. God speaks directly to David and God promises to speak to us. So David records God's word in verse 8: *"I will instruct you and teach you in the way you should go; / I will guide you with My eye."*

God is our triumphant King and God is our teacher. When the Lord brings Israel out of Egypt He gives His people the law. Redemption is for obedience. We are "saved to serve." God promises instruction and teaching to David. This teaching is for living, walking in the Lord's ways. But God not only shows us the way, He also guides us in it. His *"eye"* is upon us as a watchful Father. We always live and walk before Him. He looks upon us and does not turn His face from us.

Verse 9 contains a warning that contrasts with the positive teaching in verse 8. We are not to be like a *"horse"* or *"mule"* who needs a *"bit"* and *"bridle"* for control. We are to be responsive to God, obedient to His word, and anxious to walk in His ways. We are to "keep in step with the Spirit" (Gal. 5:25, NIV). Then we will not be like a rebellious, dumb animal which must be forced to do the will of its owner.

This warning is fulfilled only after Pentecost. Now with the Holy Spirit alive in us, we no longer struggle against the demands of the law but we walk in the Spirit (Rom. 7, 8). It is only in the power of the Spirit then that the "righteous requirement of the law" is fulfilled in us (Rom. 8:4). Indeed, God's eye is upon us through His Spirit.

Human Response: Worship

> 10 Many sorrows *shall be* to the wicked;
>   But he who trusts in the Lord, mercy shall surround
>   him.
> 11 Be glad in the Lord and rejoice, you righteous;
>   And shout for joy, all *you* upright in heart!
>   *Ps. 32:10–11*

David contrasts the wicked with the faithful in his conclusion. The noun for *"sorrows"* literally means "pain." In his unrepentant state David knew this pain. Now, however, with his trust in the Lord renewed, he knows the *"mercy,"* the covenant-love of God. This mercy surrounds him like the songs of deliverance of verse 7.

David's ending exhortation speaks of the *"righteous,"* the *"upright in heart,"* namely those who have repented and have been renewed. They are now called to worship. They are to *"be glad in the Lord,"* in Yahweh, who provides *provision* for sin (vv. 1–5), *protection* from enemies (vv. 6–7), and His *presence* through life (vv. 8–9). Israel's *"joy"* is to be expressed in shouting; it is to be vocal and verbal. It is the cry of delight from those who stand in the presence of the God of their salvation. It is the only valid expression of those who see the Lord: *"Shout for joy, all you upright in heart!"*

Here we see that Psalm 32 is the high road to revival. Revival will come when we no longer tolerate sin or repress sin and all of its sickness in the Body of Christ. Revival will come when we confess and acknowledge our sin; then and only then will the blessing of God come to us again. Our mourning will turn to joy before the Lord, and we as a church will find our depression and the "drought of summer" over. Sam Moffett, missionary to Korea, notes that great, sustained revival there came in 1904 when a few half-hearted converts began to pray seriously. It then exploded into "waves of wailing and weeping and writhing in agonies of confession." This terrified the missionaries, but they could not stop it. They were frightened because of the "presence of a Power which could work wonders," as an observer described it. Today Korea is on its way to having a majority Christian population.

The encouragement of Psalm 32 is that we pray "in a time when You may be found." Let us hold fast to that promise and seek the favor and the face of the Lord. Perhaps we too may know a "Power which can work wonders."

CHAPTER THIRTY-THREE

Our God Speaks and Sees

Psalm 33

God speaks. This is the heart of Biblical revelation. In this He is contrasted with the "dumb idols" (1 Cor. 12:2). "Thus says the Lord" dominates the Old Testament books of the prophets. "Truly, truly, I say unto you" introduces Jesus' sayings. The gift of prophecy brings God's living voice to the church, as does the gift of preaching. Throughout the Bible and the history of the church God is speaking, and we are called to listen. The open Bible is an essential symbol of our faith. The book is open—accessible and available, calling us to study, to listen, and to obey. Moreover, it is written in our tongue. In His divine condescension God chooses to speak through human words, our words. Calvin says that God "lisps His word to us as a mother lisps to her newborn infant."

Not only does God speak, He also sees. His eye is upon us; we are under His gaze. This means, of course, that our ways are known to God. Our lives are reviewed by Him, and He is present with us. The word without the eye can keep God distant, as the eye without the word can keep God silent and unknown. But the living God "speaks" us into relationship with Himself and then superintends that relationship as He watches for our response.

Psalm 33 is a meditation upon the word of God and the eye of God. Only at the very end is there a spoken prayer. God's word is affirmed as trustworthy and powerful. He speaks His creation into being. Then He pursues His plans in this world. Before the divine word all else is vanity. The counsel of the nations is nothing, but God's counsel "stands forever."

Next, God looks upon the earth and sees us. He is in intimate relationship with each person on the planet, "He fashions their hearts individually." Security is not to be found in kings or armies, but in the watchful eye of the Lord.

The author of Psalm 33 is not identified in the Hebrew Bible. The psalm is ascribed to David in the Septuagint, and Davidic authorship is accepted in our discussion. This psalm, as we have seen, takes the form of a meditation. Many commentators identify it as a hymn. The thought moves from a call to worship (vv. 1–3) to an affirmation of God's word (vv. 4–5), the work of the word in creation (vv. 6–9), the word among the nations (vv. 10–12), God's omniscience (vv. 13–15), the vanity of human might (vv. 16–17), and confidence in divine mercy (vv. 18–19). It ends with a final confession of submission (vv. 20–22).

INVITATION TO WORSHIP

1 Rejoice in the LORD, O you righteous!
   For praise from the upright is beautiful.
2 Praise the LORD with the harp;
   Make melody to Him with an instrument of ten
      strings.

3 Sing to Him a new song;
Play skillfully with a shout of joy.

Ps. 33:1–3

David begins with an imperative. The verb for *"rejoice"* means to "shout for joy," and it portrays a public, ringing celebration. It is the *"righteous"* who are summoned here to worship because they have been separated from the heathen, cleansed, and called to know the living God. Their praise is *"beautiful"* or "fitting," in harmony with the God who has ordained it. By God's decree they are now "a kingdom of priests and a holy nation" (Exod. 19:6).

Having told us *who* is to praise God, David tells us *how* to praise God. Here the praise of God is to be through song accompanied by the *"harp,"* an instrument of ten strings. The music is to be made to God, not to the congregation: *"Make melody to Him."* Worship is not a performance simply for our inspiration or entertainment. Worship is the vehicle through which we bring our *"praise"* and our *"joy"* to the Lord. We thank Him for who He is and for what He has done for us.

The singing is to be with a *"new song."* It is not to be simply traditional or familiar. It is to reflect our creative joy before the Creator and our response to the ever-new acts of God. This song anticipates the new song of redemption in the Book of Revelation (Rev. 5:10). Also, our music is to be played *"skillfully."* This is not amateur hour. We are to offer our very best to God. Our worship is to be joyful, beautiful, and boisterous. It includes a *"shout of joy."* But what is the basis for this *"new song"*?

THE WORD CREATES WORSHIP

4 For the word of the LORD *is* right,
And all His work *is done* in truth.
5 He loves righteousness and justice;
The earth is full of the goodness of the LORD.

Ps. 33:4–5

In verses 4–5 David shows us that worship is Israel's response to God's word. *"For the word of the Lord is right"* (v. 4). The adjective for *"right"* has the sense of "upright" or "straightforward." There is no deception in what God says. Since it is through the word that the Lord does His work, His works are *"done in truth,"* or "in trustworthiness"; we can count on them. The power and authority of God's *"word"* and *"work"* are consummated in Jesus, the "Word-Worker" (John Wimber; see John 3:34; 10:32). God's word through His Son, the living Word, in the power of the Holy Spirit, is a life-changing word. It reveals, illumines, and delivers. It rolls back the kingdom of Satan. It "breaks the power of cancelled sin" (Charles Wesley).

Now David elaborates upon the works of God. They include *"righteousness,"* moral purity in relationships; *"justice,"* true judgments; and *"goodness,"* covenant-love. God loves these works because they are the expressions of His character. Indeed, *"the earth is full of the goodness of the Lord."* His love is manifest everywhere (cf. Matt. 5:43–48).

This then is the basis of our worship. God has spoken; God has acted; He makes Himself known as righteous, just, and loving. Now— "Rejoice in the Lord."

THE WORD IN CREATION

6 By the word of the LORD the heavens were made,
   And all the host of them by the breath of His mouth.
7 He gathers the waters of the sea together as a heap;
   He lays up the deep in storehouses.
8 Let all the earth fear the LORD;
   Let all the inhabitants of the world stand in awe of
      Him.
9 For He spoke, and it was *done;*
   He commanded, and it stood fast.

Ps. 33:6–9

As David meditates here upon the word of God in creation, the text presupposes Genesis 1. First, God speaks the heavens into being (v. 6). Then, the heavenly *"host"* is created *"by the breath of His mouth."* The *"host"* refers to all the angelic beings. God's *"breath"* (*rûaḥ*) is His Spirit which brings the *"host"* into existence (cf. Gen. 2:7; Ezek. 37:6–14; see also Acts 2:2–4). God also "heaps up" the waters and puts the oceans or underground waters into *"storehouses"* (v. 7; cf. Gen. 1:9–10). Thus He controls and provides for all of His creation.

Before the glory of the Creator and His powerful word *"all the earth"* should bow in *"fear."* To fear God is to stand *"in awe of Him,"* to be humbled before His power and majesty, His word and His work. *"For He spoke, and it was done."* God creates *ex nihilo;* at His command everything stands. Also through the word, God sustains the world. Since in the New Testament the creative word of God is revealed as the Son, our worship of the Creator is fulfilled as we bow before Jesus (John 1:1–14; Col. 1:16–17). Here in verses 6–9 the heavens and their host and the sea and its "deeps" are to evoke wondrous fear before our God. Thus we are to bow before the power of His word.

THE WORD AMONG THE NATIONS

10 The LORD brings the counsel of the nations to nothing;
   He makes the plans of the peoples of no effect.
11 The counsel of the LORD stands forever,
   The plans of His heart to all generations.
12 Blessed *is* the nation whose God *is* the LORD,
   The people He has chosen as His own inheritance.

Ps. 33:10–12

Not only does the creation exist by the word of God, the nations are also judged by that same word. Thus verses 10–11 contrast the vain *"counsel"* and *"plans"* of the nations with God's own *"counsel"* and *"plans."*

In their pride, the *"nations"* ("Gentiles") claim a false autonomy. They offer their worldly *"counsel"* ("advice, wisdom") and they make their *"plans."* They live on the horizontal, employing politics as the "art of the possible." Their devices are "balance of power," "the dictatorship of the proletariat," "pro-choice," the New Deal, the thousand-year Reich, NATO, the Warsaw Pact, the Alliance for Progress, and so on. Their *"counsel"* and *"plans,"* however, are a passing show. Thus God brings the autonomy of the nations, which is their idolatry, *"to nothing,"* *"of no effect."* He breaks their rebellious spirit. On the other hand, *"the counsel of the Lord stands forever"* and His *"plans"* last through the *"generations,"* for this *"counsel"* and these *"plans"* come from the eternal God who speaks His word and who does His work in righteousness and truth.

A nation submitted to Yahweh, a *"nation whose God is the Lord,"* is blessed. This, of course, refers to Israel, *"the people He has chosen as*

His own inheritance" (v. 12). The Jews are called to be God's servant and to carry out His will in the world (see Deut. 7:6–8; Isa. 44:1 ff.). This promise, however, is now extended to God's new Israel, the church (Gal. 6:16; cf. Rom. 9–11).

GOD SEES ALL

> 13 The LORD looks from heaven;
> He sees all the sons of men.
> 14 From the place of His dwelling He looks
> On all the inhabitants of the earth;
> 15 He fashions their hearts individually;
> He considers all their works.
>
> *Ps. 33:13–15*

David turns now from meditating on the word of God to the eye of God: *"The Lord looks from heaven"* (cf. v. 18). God both speaks and sees. Even though He is exalted in heaven, His watchful eye assures us of His attention and presence. When Solomon dedicated the temple, he prayed that God's eyes would be "open toward this temple night and day . . . that You may hear the prayer which your servant makes toward this place" (1 Kings 8:29). And Hanani promised King Asa, "the eyes of the Lord run to and fro throughout the whole earth, to show Himself strong on behalf of those whose heart is loyal to Him" (2 Chron. 16:9). God then sees *"all the sons of men"* throughout the whole earth. He is no mere tribal deity, for *"all the inhabitants of the earth"* are within His gaze.

Moreover, the Lord *"fashions"* the *"hearts"* of all people *"individually,"* and He *"considers"* and judges *"all their works."* God's ultimate purpose in salvation is to bring all the nations to Himself. All are the object of His watchfulness. None can escape His judgment.

HUMAN MIGHT IS VAIN

> 16 No king *is* saved by the multitude of an army;
> A mighty man is not delivered by great strength.
> 17 A horse *is* a vain hope for safety;
> Neither shall it deliver *any* by its great strength.
>
> *Ps. 33:16–17*

Because of who God is in His creative, judging, and redeeming word, and because of His all-encompassing gaze, no one should trust in human power or might. No *"king"* is secure with his *"army."* No warrior or *"mighty man"* is *"delivered"* by his own *"strength."* No *"horse"* offers *"safety"* in battle. Both Israel and the nations must surrender such vain hopes. Moreover, history bears this out. Our God is in the business of breaking the pride of the nations. Where is Victoria's Empire now? Where is Hitler's Reich? Where is Wilson's "world made safe for democracy"? What happened to the "war to end all wars"? Our national peril is our trust in MX missiles, B1 bombers, and "Star Wars" armaments. Like the horse of old, they are *"a vain hope for safety."*

Divine Mercy Is Everlasting

18 Behold, the eye of the LORD *is* on those who fear
   Him,
   On those who hope in His mercy,
19 To deliver their soul from death,
   And to keep them alive in famine.

Ps. 33:18–19

While God sees all people as His creation (vv. 13–15), His *"eye"* is especially upon *"those who fear Him, / on those who hope in His mercy."* As we have noted, those who fear God are those who reverence Him, who bow in awe before Him. Submitted to Him in worship, they are lifted up by the expectation of His mercy, His covenant-love.

The Lord will *"deliver"* His own from *"death"* and *"keep them alive in famine"* (v. 19). He will be the master of their circumstances. While the primary reference here is temporal, we do not stray too far in seeing the ultimate references as spiritual. Thus for us it is Jesus who delivers our souls from eternal death (John 11:25–26) and who feeds us with Himself in this life (John 6:35). As He says to His disciples, "Do not labor for the food which perishes, but for the food which endures to everlasting life, which the Son of Man will give you" (John 6:27).

Confession of Submission

20 Our soul waits for the LORD;
   He *is* our help and our shield.

251

21 For our heart shall rejoice in Him,
   Because we have trusted in His holy name.
22 Let Your mercy, O LORD, be upon us,
   Just as we hope in You.

Ps. 33:20–22

David ends his meditation on the God who speaks and sees by an inclusive confession of openness in verse 20. The true God who creates all things, is above all things, and sees all things will come and will do His work. He is especially our deliverer, our *"help"* and our defense, our *"shield."* Therefore, our trust in Him, in *"His holy name,"* brings the joy of worship. He will not let us down.

Finally, David asks the Lord to turn our hope for mercy into the experience of mercy by letting His *"mercy . . . be upon us."* This fresh baptism of divine love will result in the "new song" of worship (v. 3) as God's people rejoice in Him.

Psalm 33 clearly affirms that the word creates worship. The word is not given to create theology, institutions, or church programs. It is given to create and to recreate us, to bring us the mercy of God, and to turn us into worshipers filled with the joy of God's Spirit. The word delivers us from the vanity of our own plans and power. It casts us upon the Lord so that His plans and power may become ours. We then live under His gaze, with His eyes of mercy upon us. He will keep us through this life and usher us at last into His presence.

One final question may be asked: how can the substance of this psalm become our experience? The key lies in verse 22: meditation must turn to prayer. My own experience is that often I think about the Lord but fail to talk to Him; just as often I may talk to Him but neglect thinking about Him. In Psalm 33 there is massive reflection upon God's character and power and the contrasting vanity of this world. However, David doesn't leave it there. At the end He cries for mercy. From this I learn that I must take my largest thoughts about God and turn them into prayers, fully expecting to experience more and more of Him as I wait before Him.

CHAPTER THIRTY-FOUR

Meditation and Instruction on the Fear of the Lord

Psalm 34

In Romans 3 Paul gives a brief summary judgment upon this fallen world in a catalogue of Old Testament texts. He concludes with the indictment "There is no fear of God before their eyes" (Rom. 3:18 = Ps. 36:1). Certainly this charge stands against our modern age as well.

A symbol of our arrogance is found in the epigram carved over a saloon door on the Titanic: "Not even God can sink this ship," a blasphemy that still rots at the bottom of the Atlantic. Today also we have no fear of God. Instead our list of fears includes nuclear arsenals, cancer, the sun's radiation, budget deficits, the Hong Kong flu, the Mediterranean fruit fly, and AIDS, but most of us view God, at best, as the retired chairman of the board (David MacInnes). He has a position of honor, but no power. He is to be saluted, memorialized, and ritualized, but we are convinced He really can't or won't act in our lives.

Psalm 34 tells us just the opposite. This psalm witnesses to a God who has delivered "this poor man" (v. 6). The immediate context of this rescue is a military campaign. In his history, now, at the moment of writing, the psalmist has seen not only the presence of God, but also the power of God, and that power leads him to fear. Thus when Peter's nets are filled with fish at Jesus' command, he cries out, "Depart from me, for I am a sinful man, O Lord!" (Luke 5:8). Jesus responds, "Do not be afraid" (Luke 5:10). The miracle evokes awesome wonder, and Peter falls at Jesus' knees.

According to tradition, which we accept, this psalm is written by David (at least at its core). It is acrostic in its structure, following the Hebrew alphabet except for the lack of a verse beginning with the letter *wāw*. A final verse (beginning with *pē*) follows the verse starting with the last letter of the Hebrew alphabet. Commentators identify the psalm as an individual lament. Its overall structure includes meditation (vv. 1–10) and instruction (vv. 11–22). The theme is the "fear of the Lord" (see v. 9). The thought moves from an invitation to worship (vv. 1–3), to confession (vv. 4–6), exhortation (vv. 8–10), and instruction (vv. 11–14), and it concludes with encouragement (vv. 15–22).

INVITATION TO PRAISE

1 I will bless the LORD at all times;
    His praise *shall* continually *be* in my mouth.
2 My soul shall make its boast in the LORD;
    The humble shall hear *of it* and be glad.
3 Oh, magnify the LORD with me,
    And let us exalt His name together.

Ps. 34:1–3

The meditation begins with a call to worship. This individual expression of intent also becomes an invitation for us to identify with David (v. 3).

The content of verse 1 is blessing and praise. The object of such worship is *"the Lord,"* Yahweh; and the time element is continuous, *"at all times."* Life is found and lived in the praise of God. As Paul writes to the Colossians, "And whatever you do in word or deed, do all in the name of the Lord Jesus, giving thanks to God the Father through Him" (3:17).

David begins very personally, *"I will bless."* The verb for *"bless,"* which may share a common root with "kneel," voices appreciation and gratitude. It also promotes respect for the one being blessed. The synonym here is *"praise,"* which includes thanksgiving (Ps. 35:18), giving glory (Ps. 22:23), and magnifying God (Ps. 69:30). Thus the worship and praise of Yahweh is David's continual disposition.

The praise of the Lord is always in David's *"mouth"* (v. 1) because his words reflect his heart. Verse 2 deepens the thought: *"My soul shall make its boast in the Lord."* David engages in worship out of the totality of his being.

Such worship becomes witness: *"The humble shall hear of it and be glad."* The thought is a commentary on the public, corporate nature of David's praise. As he worships, the *"humble"* are encouraged and rejoice with him. These "pious poor" or "meek" always welcome such worship, and it is to them that the gospel is preached (Luke 4:18). Thus when they hear David extol God, they are *"glad."* His joy is infectious.

Now, David turns to exhortation, offering an invitation to worship that intensifies his praise and draws us in (v. 3). We too are included!

To *"magnify"* the Lord is to call Him great. Psalm 48 expands on this meaning, beginning with its first verse: "Great is the Lord, and greatly to be praised." God is great because He is the great King who reigns in Zion. He is the Creator; He is above all gods; He is the judge of all the earth. No wonder we should *"magnify"* Him *"together."*

A parallel thought concludes Psalm 34:3. To *"exalt"* God's name is to raise it up in praise; it is the name above all others.

David's invitation for us to worship is no call to bland, sterile formalism but rather to verbal, public, personal praise. It is a call to continual worship that lifts the hearts of others, drawing them into this spontaneous, robust chorus of delighting in the name of the living and true God. Next, David turns to God's deliverance as he meditates on the consequences of his prayers.

CONFESSION OF FAITH

4 I sought the LORD, and He heard me,
    And delivered me from all my fears.
5 They looked to Him and were radiant,
    And their faces were not ashamed.
6 This poor man cried out, and the LORD heard *him,*
    And saved him out of all his troubles.
7 The angel of the LORD encamps all around those who
        fear Him,
    And delivers them.

Ps. 34:4–7

Having called us to worship, in these verses David confesses his faith in the Lord whom he has praised. His God is the living God. Verse 7 pictures a battlefield setting, in which *"the angel of the Lord"* makes his camp around the faithful and *"delivers"* them. The word *"deliver"* here means "to snatch or tear away, to rescue." God not only rescues David from his enemies but also from his *"fears,"* from being *"ashamed,"* and from *"troubles."*

David asserts in verse 4 that he *"sought the Lord."* The Hebrew verb here means "to ask of, to inquire." He continues *"and He heard me."* The verb for "to hear" literally means "to answer or respond." David asks; God answers in an action: *"He . . . delivered mè from all my fears."* Likewise, when Samuel cries out to the Lord, God answers by sending thunder to confuse the Philistines (1 Sam. 7:9–10). Thus when David is *"delivered"* from all his *"fears,"* he is also *"delivered"* from his enemies, the source of those fears.

David's companions also experienced deliverance. Their *"radiant"* faces symbolize joy, and they also reflect the glory of God as they are turned to Him. Moreover, when we are *"radiant,"* shame is excluded. Thus *"their faces were not ashamed."* As our *"faces"* are turned to the Lord, the shame of defeat is gone. Indeed, "We are more than conquerors through Him who loved us" (Rom. 8:37).

Once again, in verse 6, God's answer to the cry of distress is action. Verse 7 makes the source of this deliverance clear: it comes from *"the angel of the Lord"* who camps around David and his men. Supernatural aid was also experienced by Joshua when he prepared to lead Israel into the Promised Land. As he stood before Jericho he was confronted by a man who came as "Commander of the army of the Lord" (Josh. 5:13–15). In the context, this commander is an angelic figure or a theophany of God Himself.

Who are the delivered? Those who *"fear"* the Lord. Here a basic theme of this psalm is introduced. The angelic visitation creates a proper fear or reverence before God's glory, and the angelic visitation comes to those who have a proper *"fear"* or reverence for God's glory. Those who have seen God's power moving upon people will find that the best reaction is to fall on their faces in the same fear that the disciples had on the mount of transfiguration (Mark 9:6). As Paul reminds the Corinthians, he was with them "in weakness, in fear, and in much trembling. And my speech and my preaching were . . . in demonstration of the Spirit and of power, that your faith should not be in the wisdom of men but in the power of God" (1 Cor. 2:3–5).

EXHORTATIONS TO TEST AND FEAR THE LORD

   8 Oh, taste and see that the LORD *is* good;
     Blessed *is* the man *who* trusts in Him!
   9 Oh, fear the LORD, you His saints!
     There is no want to those who fear Him.
  10 The young lions lack and suffer hunger;
     But those who seek the LORD shall not lack any good
      thing.

                           Ps. 34:8–10

In this section David calls us twice and comforts us twice (vv. 8, 9). The call to *"taste"* is the call to test. We are not just to believe in the Lord's goodness; we are to experience that goodness. God's goodness includes both His deliverance (vv. 4–7) and His gifts (vv. 9–10). His goodness to us is the expression of His character.

Henrietta Mears used to invite skeptical students to take the test of faith. As a former chemistry teacher, she would ask them into the spiritual laboratory to find out if Christ is real. She described this according to the analogy of finding a chemical unknown. She would encourage students, "Commit your life to Him and He will prove Himself real to you." As current advertising would put it, "Take the taste test."

David follows the call with comfort: *"Blessed is the man who trusts in Him!"* The word *"blessed"* means "happy." True happiness comes from surrender to the living God.

David's second call (v. 9) is to *"fear,"* picking up the theme from verse 7.

His second word of comfort is that those who live in reverence before God will *"not lack any good thing."* Jesus confirms this promise, "Therefore I say to you, do not worry about your life, what you will eat or what you will drink; nor about your body, what you will put on. Is not life more than food and the body more than clothing? . . . But seek first the kingdom of God and His righteousness, and all these things shall be added to you" (Matt. 6:25, 33).

In contrast to those who *"fear the Lord"* are the *"young lions [who] lack and suffer hunger"* (v. 10). Even these predators can go hungry, but *"those who seek the Lord"* will always be satisfied.

In the famine and disaster of our world, it is hard to believe this verse literally. Certainly our Lord knew suffering and Paul often went to bed hungry (2 Cor. 11:24–27).

We are not immune from the assaults of the devil and the consequences of the Fall. Nevertheless, we have the promise of God's protection and provision. He saves our souls, He heals our bodies, He provides for our needs. It is true that we do not experience all of His kingdom fully in this life. Yet, the signs of His goodness are also here. Is there not a real solution to the problem of suffering in verse 8: *"Taste and see that the Lord is good"*? The Lord is good in His benefits, but more than that, the Lord is good in Himself. When we *"taste"* Him we are filled. Jesus' fulfillment and Paul's fulfillment were not found in lives of ease. They were found in knowing the Lord and doing His will. Paul puts it this way: "For to me, to live is Christ, and to die is gain"

(Phil. 1:21). To lack Christ is to lack everything. To have Christ is to have everything. Thus *"those who seek the Lord shall not lack any good thing."*

Instructions for a Godly Life

11 Come, you children, listen to me;
    I will teach you the fear of the Lord.
12 Who *is* the man *who* desires life,
    And loves *many* days, that he may see good?
13 Keep your tongue from evil,
    And your lips from speaking deceit.
14 Depart from evil and do good;
    Seek peace and pursue it.

Ps. 34:11–14

It is David's intention in this psalm not only to worship the Lord and witness to His goodness, but also to teach us to fear Him (v. 11). Adopting the style of instruction used by the court scribes of the Ancient Near East, David calls upon his students to listen. This "courtly style" is most closely identified with Solomon in the Old Testament. However, Joseph in Egypt is also a type of the man of wisdom (von Rad). This wisdom teaching, like all the other streams of tradition in Israel, is fulfilled in Christ who became for us "wisdom from God" (1 Cor. 1:30).

Here David's invitation, *"Come, you children,"* places him in the stance of the father instructing his sons in the proper way of life. The summons to be as children includes accepting the authority of the teacher, submitting to his teaching, and being open and ready to learn. Only one who has been taught by the Lord can teach others. Since David knows the fear of the Lord, he can teach the fear of the Lord from what God has shown him through his own experiences.

After the invitation to instruction, David projects a call for the person who is ready to receive it: *"Who is the man who desires life, / And loves many days, that he may see good?"* (v. 12). This description is also motivational. It is as if David asks, "Do you want to live long and well?" Most of us do, of course. "Then hear this."

The instruction proper begins with verse 13. In its parallel phrases is the first ideal for the wise person who fears the Lord: he controls his *"tongue."* Thus Proverbs 8:13 reads, "The fear of the Lord is to hate evil" and, "A righteous man hates lying . . ." (Prov. 13:5). Since God is true we are to walk in the truth. Fearing Him, we are to be subject to His truth. Or, to put it another way, out of our awe and reverence for God we are to be so secure that we fear no man—and thus we will tell the truth. When we are weak before God, we will be strong before the world. When we come to love God's truth, we will hate the devil's lies.

Second, knowing the fear of the Lord, we will avoid the presence of sin in our lives. To know the fear of the Lord is to separate ourselves from whatever destroys our communion with Him. As Paul tells the Ephesians, we are to "have no fellowship with the unfruitful works of darkness, but rather expose them" (Eph. 5:11).

Our moral life, however, is not simply to be lived as a negative. Too often being a Christian has been thought of only as following a list of "don'ts." David instructs us to *do good.* The negative call to leave evil behind is for the sake of positive action. As Paul tells the Colossians, we are now "partakers of the inheritance of the saints in the light" (1:12).

"Good" is defined in the Old Testament by the law of God. It is moral living, not merely to be known or contemplated, but to be done. "If you love Me," Jesus said, "keep My commandments" (John 14:15).

Since we live in such an amoral age, we need the word of God to instruct our minds and to sharpen our consciences. Our world is filled with double-talk. Adultery and fornication are called "sexual freedom." The murder of unborn children is "pro-choice." Selfishness is "self-affirmation" or "self-realization." Thus God must tell us what evil is so that we can depart from it, and God must tell us what good is so that we can do it. To learn the fear of the Lord, then, is to learn the moral will of God. It is to guard our tongue and our behavior from evil. It is to do the good work of God in the world.

In light of the New Testament, the call to do good is not simply a call to moral living, but also to eschatological living. It is a call to do the very works of Jesus, to manifest His kingdom, restoring God's order over this fallen, disordered creation.

Verse 14 instructs us to *"seek peace, and pursue it." "Peace"* is "wholeness"—personal, social, political, spiritual. We are to inquire after wholeness in every dimension of life and go after it with energy and perseverance. As Jesus says, "Blessed are the peacemakers, / For they shall be called sons of God" (Matt. 5:9).

Having received Christ, who "Himself is our peace" (Eph. 2:14), we are both at peace with God (Rom. 5:1) and we have peace in our hearts. What God gives to us we must pass on. We are to bring reconciliation to broken lives, broken relationships, and this broken world. God calls us to manifest His kingdom by pursuing justice for the oppressed as well as by pursuing forgiveness for the sinner. What that means for the affluent church in the West must be discovered by all of us. I serve on a mission board called Floresta. Under the leadership of one of our elders we plan to reforest a substantial part of the Dominican Republic, which uses wood as the basis of its energy economy. This project will create fuel, prevent erosion, reduce dependency upon foreign imports, and provide jobs. This is one way of pursuing peace in the name of Jesus.

The fear of the Lord, then, includes moral living, kingdom power, and social justice and compassion for the poor. Those who live this way before the Holy God are seen and heard by Him.

ENCOURAGEMENT TO THE RIGHTEOUS IN GOD

15 The eyes of the LORD *are* on the righteous,
   And His ears *are open* to their cry.
16 The face of the LORD *is* against those who do
      evil,
   To cut off the remembrance of them from the earth.
17 *The righteous* cry out, and the LORD hears,
   And delivers them out of all their troubles.
18 The LORD *is* near to those who have a broken heart,
   And saves such as have a contrite spirit.
19 Many *are* the afflictions of the righteous,
   But the LORD delivers him out of them all.
20 He guards all his bones;
   Not one of them is broken.
21 Evil shall slay the wicked,
   And those who hate the righteous shall be condemned.
22 The LORD redeems the soul of His servants,
   And none of those who trust in Him shall be
      condemned.

Ps. 34:15–22

Having told us how we are to live before God, David now tells us again about the One before whom we live. Those who live in fear of the Lord are both seen and heard by Him. He is open to them and listens to their prayers. Those who do evil, however, live under the wrath of God (see Rom. 1:18 ff.). There are only two alternatives: do good and live; do evil and die. God is righteous. We are called to reflect His righteous character in the world. If we refuse to live this way He will turn from us. To be separated from God is death. If He does not remember us, we will be forgotten, driven away like the chaff (Ps. 1:4).

Having promised the righteous person God's presence in verses 15–16, David now promises answers to prayer in verses 17–18. Verses 15–16 tell us whom God hears and verses 17–18 tell us what God does when they pray to Him. Thus David continues in verse 17, *"The righteous cry out, and the Lord hears."* As we noted above, God's people cried out in Egypt. God heard, and sent Moses to deliver them. Likewise, throughout the Gospels we see Jesus responding to those who come to Him for help. As they show Him their wounds, He touches them with His healing power.

A friend of mine recently experienced the collapse of his marriage, with resulting financial woes. He was also an alcoholic and close to despair. At the same time, he knew that God was pursuing him. We had met several times to talk about the Lord, but he continued to follow his pattern of making no decision. Finally, one night as he lay in bed, anxiety-ridden, he called out to the Lord. Suddenly his room was filled with singing. It lasted for two hours. The voices rang with the phrase, "the Lord is King." As the music faded, my friend cried out, "I want to go with You!" From that moment on, the reality of Christ has been his. *"The Lord hears,"* indeed, and we are delivered from our troubles when we cry to Him.

With the promise of God's presence and His answers to our prayers, David brings this psalm to its conclusion with ringing hope (vv. 19–22): *"Many are the afflictions of the righteous, / But the Lord delivers him out of them all."* God does not promise a life of ease; He promises a life of deliverance. Sin infects us. Our flesh rebels. Satan harasses us. The world tempts us. Death threatens us. Indeed, our afflictions are many, but the Lord in Christ delivers us from *"all"* of them. First, He forgives our sins (1 John 1:9). Second, He crucifies our flesh (Gal. 2:20; Rom. 6:6). Third, He arms us against Satan (Eph. 6:16–18). Fourth, He delivers us from the world (1 John 2:15–17). Fifth, He promises us resurrection from the dead (Rom. 6:5).

Not only do we have the promises of spiritual victory; in verse 20 we also have the promise of physical protection. How literally should we take this statement? On one level, it is a concrete guarantee of

God's care. To expect no fracture of any bone throughout our lifetime would be absurd. Nevertheless, this promise assures us of God's protection for the whole person. On another level, this verse is prophetic. The hope for the righteous who are delivered and protected finds its fulfillment in Christ. On the cross His bones were not broken, so this specific promise was fulfilled in Him (John 19:36). Christ is both afflicted on the cross (v. 19) and at the same time protected (v. 20). This is the great paradox of His work of redemption.

Verse 21 pronounces the Lord's judgment: *"Evil shall slay the wicked."* The first clause of this verse restates a theme that is common in the psalms: the wicked will be caught in their own designs, for God, not evil, has the last word. His judgment is final and complete. As Jesus says in His awesome parable of the Day of Judgment, "And these [the goats] will go away into everlasting punishment" (Matt. 25:46).

The psalm ends on a note of triumph *"The Lord redeems* ["ransoms, buys back"] *the soul of His servants."* While *"evil"* cuts off the *"wicked,"* the Lord is our redeemer. He delivers the lives of those who are submitted to Him. Verse 22 applies both to the crisis of David's military campaign (vv. 6–7) and to the ultimate crisis of David's existence in this world. Moreover, the fulfillment of this promise is found on the lips of Christ: "Father, I desire that they also whom You gave Me may be with Me where I am, that they may behold My glory which You have given Me; for You loved Me before the foundation of the world" (John 17:24).

Having declared our positive hope, David uses a negative to state the same thought in contrasting terms: *"And none of those who trust in Him* ["fly to Him, seek refuge"] *shall be condemned."* Here is the gospel in the Old Testament. It is by faith that we are not condemned. It is by our faith in His promise that God is pleased (Gen. 15:6). As Paul exclaims, "There is therefore now no condemnation to those who are in Christ Jesus" (Rom. 8:1).

CHAPTER THIRTY-FIVE

When Friends Become Enemies

Psalm 35

There is probably no deeper wound than that inflicted by a trusted friend's rejection. Part of the sadness of human life is to see the fracturing of deep, caring relationships. Divorce is an obvious example of shattered lives, abandoned hopes and dreams. Its recent victims wander in depression and shock.

An experience I once had with a brother in ministry gives special significance to this psalm. We had developed a business partnership dedicated to communicating the gospel, but once the business began to prosper, his values changed and he wanted to sever the relationship. The hurt was deep and lasting, as I felt betrayed personally, and on behalf of the others with whom we had shared our Christian goals. Anger turned to grief, and the loss left a hole in my heart.

In the psalm, the writer is faced with enemies who strive with him and fight against him. They also actively pursue him, seeking his life and plotting his destruction. Their attack, however, is unjust. These enemies, who come from the psalmist's inner circle, are friends who have turned against him. They have become "fierce witnesses" and seek to confuse him. Earlier, when they suffered adversity, the psalmist's heart went out to them. He viewed them as family members. They, however, do not return kindness for kindness. During the psalmist's distress, they attack secretly and devise deceitful matters. Turning the psalmist's weakened condition to their advantage, they attack him as wolves attack the sick in the herd.

Thus the psalmist has his own Judas. In the pain of being a victim of treachery he turns to God, asking Him to act on his behalf. Refusing to take judgment into his own hands, he believes that the Lord will vindicate him.

Most commentators have identified this psalm as an individual lament. Some, however, suggest that it refers to Israel's facing the rebellion of vassal states and thus is a royal psalm. This commentary will give it an individual focus. The military, hunting, and legal language here would all support the tradition of Davidic authorship.

Psalm 35 moves from a call to Yahweh for action and judgment (vv. 1–8) to a confession of praise (vv. 9–10). This is followed by an indictment of treachery (vv. 11–16) and a call for deliverance (vv. 17–18). Once again, the adversaries' deceit is exposed (vv. 19–21). This is followed by a call for vindication (vv. 22–26), and the psalm then ends in a communal celebration (vv. 27–28).

CALL TO ACTION

1 Plead *my cause,* O LORD, with those who strive with
     me;
  Fight against those who fight against me.
2 Take hold of shield and buckler,
  And stand up for my help.
3 Also draw out the spear,
  And stop those who pursue me.
  Say to my soul,
  "I *am* your salvation."

Ps. 35:1–3

David's first words evoke a courtroom scene as he asks God to be his defense attorney: *"Plead my cause, O Lord, with those who strive with me."* The image shifts quickly to battle language, which is then sustained through verses 2–3. Here David asks God to take up a *"shield"* (*māgēn*), *"buckler"* (*ṣinnâh*), and *"spear."* The *"buckler"* is also a type of shield, larger than the *māgēn*, probably rectangular, made of wood and leather, covering the whole body. The shield and buckler are for defense and the spear is for offense. David asks God to take the spear and *"stop those who pursue me."*

Here then as an attorney by word and as a soldier by deed, David calls upon Yahweh to be his *"salvation,"* his "deliverer" (*yĕšû'âh*). David wants God to say to him, to his *"soul,"* "I *am your salvation."* In other words, he wants the comfort and assurance of this personal word from the Lord.

Do we expect such a direct address from the Lord today? Certainly we have it in the Bible, His written word. But in the Bible God speaks through many means: angels, visions, dreams, tongues, prophecies, words of knowledge and wisdom (see the Book of Acts and 1 Cor. 12). Recently God has increased my expectation that He will speak to me directly as I listen for His voice. Such speech will always be in conformity to the written word, and it may well employ any of the many means revealed there. Shouldn't we, like David, ask the Lord to speak to our souls?

CALL TO JUDGMENT

> 4 Let those be put to shame and brought to dishonor
>   Who seek after my life;
>   Let those be turned back and brought to confusion
>   Who plot my hurt.
> 5 Let them be like chaff before the wind,
>   And let the angel of the LORD chase *them.*
> 6 Let their way be dark and slippery,
>   And let the angel of the LORD pursue them.
> 7 For without cause they have hidden their net for me
>   *in* a pit,
>   *Which* they have dug without cause for my life.
> 8 Let destruction come upon him unexpectedly,
>   And let his net that he has hidden catch himself;
>   Into that very destruction let him fall.
>
> *Ps. 35:4–8*

Here David becomes explicit about what he wants God to do with his enemies, with those who *"plot"* his *"hurt."* He wants them to *"be put to shame and brought to dishonor."* This will happen when they are routed in *"confusion"* just as a phalanx is broken in battle. Further, he wants them destroyed: *"Let them be like chaff before the wind"* (cf. Ps. 1:4). He asks that they be chased by God's avenging *"angel"* (cf. Josh. 5:13–15; Judg. 2:1 ff.). As they retreat, he prays that their *"way"* will be *"dark and slippery"* so that they will not be able to see where they are going and will fall before the *"angel"* who pursues them.

The reason for invoking this judgment becomes clear in verse 7. David's enemies have plotted against him *"without cause."* Like hunters they have set a trap for him, digging a hole for his *"life"* (or "soul"). In a shift from the plural to the singular in referring to his enemy, David asks that he be caught by his own treachery. He prays that the trap be sprung *"unexpectedly, / And let his net that he has hidden catch himself."* This will bring *"destruction."* The Hebrew noun used here means "devastation, ruin"; thus God's judgment will be complete.

Here we see again that for David divine retribution comes both by God's active intervention and by the inevitable self-destruction of those who do evil.

CONFESSION OF PRAISE

> 9 And my soul shall be joyful in the LORD;
>   It shall rejoice in His salvation.
> 10 All my bones shall say,
>   "LORD, who *is* like You,
>   Delivering the poor from him who is too strong for
>   him,
>   Yes, the poor and the needy from him who plunders
>   him?"
>
> *Ps. 35:9–10*

Anticipating God's action against his foes, in verse 9 David turns to praise. He will be *"joyful in the Lord"* and *"in His salvation,"* or "deliverance." We must beware when we worship the Lord only for His benefits and not for Himself. David's whole frame (*"all my bones"*) will confess the uniqueness of Yahweh: *"Lord, who is like You . . . ?"* That God delivers the *"poor"* from the clutches of the *"strong,"* namely, those who plunder the *"needy,"* shows Him to be the living, true, and merciful God. Any idol can look good with the rich and powerful. A popular religious science pastor gathered the young and affluent "movers" around her in San Diego by telling them, "Prosperity is your divine right." This was exactly what they wanted to hear. Yahweh, however, gives grace to the weak and the oppressed. In this He shows His love and also glorifies Himself. As the Lord tells Paul, "My grace is sufficient for you, for My strength is made perfect in weakness" (2 Cor. 12:9). Moreover, it is ever God's way to choose the foolish of this world to confound the wise (1 Cor. 1:27).

ADVERSARIES' TREACHERY

> 11 Fierce witnesses rise up;
>   They ask me *things* that I do not know.
> 12 They reward me evil for good,
>   *To* the sorrow of my soul.
> 13 But as for me, when they were sick,

My clothing *was* sackcloth;
I humbled myself with fasting;
And my prayer would return to my own heart.
14 I paced about as though *he were* my friend *or* brother;
I bowed down heavily, as one who mourns *for his*
      mother.
15 But in my adversity they rejoiced
And gathered together;
Attackers gathered against me,
And I did not know *it;*
They tore *at me* and did not cease;
16 With ungodly mockers at feasts
They gnashed at me with their teeth.

Ps. 35:11–16

The tragedy of David's situation is now made clear. These *"fierce witnesses"* (v. 11) who attack him were once his intimates. He loved them, identifying with their distress: *"when they were sick, / My clothing was sackcloth"* (v. 13). Moreover, David *"humbled"* himself, *"fasting"* on their behalf. Even with such sympathetic sorrow his prayers seemed impotent: *"And my prayer would return to my own heart."*

Furthermore, David treated these former friends as intimates, as family: *"as though he were my friend or brother."* He mourned for them as he would for his own *"mother."* These verses may imply that David is faced with a *palace revolt,* with the *traitorous* loss of companions. Those who know us intimately can hurt us the most severely. Our very vulnerability opens us up to abuse. This is the threat of close relationships; it is the risk of genuine love.

As David experiences such pain, his former friends delight in his *"adversity."* The word used here for *"adversity"* literally means "stumbling," perhaps indicating a sudden change in David's situation, or some illness. Weakened, he was attacked by his enemies when he was ignorant of their plots. They *"tore"* at him like wild beasts. This is probably a metaphor for slander that continued unabated. His *"attackers"* became like Judas. Court intrigue, rebellion, civil war—these are what David receives from those he loved and trusted.

CALL FOR DELIVERANCE

17 Lord, how long will You look on?
Rescue me from their destructions,
My precious *life* from the lions.

18 I will give You thanks in the great assembly;
I will praise You among many people.

Ps. 35:17–18

Now David calls upon the Lord in his distress. He expresses frustration with God's inactivity: *"Lord, how long will You look on?"* Certainly God sees his calamity. It is enough! So he prays: *"Rescue me"* or, literally, "Restore my soul." Here David asks to be delivered from his enemies' *"destructions."* They are pictured as *"lions."* His response to God's intervention will be worship and witness. He promises that he will give *"thanks"* to God *"in the great assembly,"* probably during one of the feasts. Here David's *"praise"* for what the Lord has done will be public.

ADVERSARIES' DECEIT

19 Let them not rejoice over me who are wrongfully my
enemies;
Nor let them wink with the eye who hate me without
a cause.
20 For they do not speak peace,
But they devise deceitful matters
Against *the* quiet ones in the land.
21 They also opened their mouth wide against me,
And said, "Aha, aha!
Our eyes have seen *it.*"

Ps. 35:19–21

Again, as in verses 11–16, David returns to a description of his enemies. In doing so, he asks for both deliverance and protection from them: *"Let them not rejoice over me . . . / Nor let them wink with the eye."* Here his enemies are those who *"hate"* him unjustly, that is *"without a cause."* Also, *"they do not speak peace, / But they devise deceitful matters,"* or, literally, "words of deceit." The noun for "deceit" means "treachery." Thus David's enemies plot against him secretly. This also explains the phrase *"wink with the eye."*

Moreover, they mock him, opening *"their mouth wide against"* him (see Isa. 57:4). Their taunt, *"Aha, aha!"* is followed by the claim that they have seen David's misfortune (see v. 15). The description in these verses then leads again to a call for divine intervention (cf. vv. 17–18).

CALL FOR VINDICATION

22 *This* You have seen, O LORD;
    Do not keep silence.
    O Lord, do not be far from me.
23 Stir up Yourself, and awake to my vindication,
    To my cause, my God and my Lord.
24 Vindicate me, O LORD my God, according to Your
       righteousness;
    And let them not rejoice over me.
25 Let them not say in their hearts, "Ah, so we would
       have it!"
    Let them not say, "We have swallowed him up."
26 Let them be ashamed and brought to mutual confusion
    Who rejoice at my hurt;
    Let them be clothed with shame and dishonor
    Who exalt themselves against me.

                                              Ps. 35:22–26

The theme of this section is *"vindication"* (*mišpot*, "judgment," in vv. 23, 24). For David God is the true witness to his heart: *"This You have seen, O Lord"* (v. 22). God has also witnessed the machinations of his enemies. Thus David calls upon Him to speak: *"Do not keep silence"*; to come near: *"O Lord, do not be far from me"*; and to arouse Himself for *"vindication."* We could paraphrase verse 23 as David's saying, "Get up and wake up!" This anthropomorphic language displays the intimacy which he feels toward Yahweh.

David's call for the Lord to judge him *"according to [His] righteousness"* (v. 24) attests to his certainty of innocence before the divine decree. David also wants the traitors' lies and plots to cease. He prays that their conclusions and their judgments will not stand: *"Let them not say, 'We have swallowed him up,'"* or in other words, "We have destroyed him" (cf. Jer. 30:16).

Likewise, David asks that when his enemies' plans against him fail, they will be *"clothed with shame and dishonor"* (v. 26).

CALL FOR CELEBRATION

27 Let them shout for joy and be glad,
    Who favor my righteous cause;

269

And let them say continually,
"Let the LORD be magnified,
Who has pleasure in the prosperity of His servant."
28 And my tongue shall speak of Your righteousness
And of Your praise all the day long.

Ps. 35:27–28

When David is vindicated, those who stand with him, who *"favor"* his *"righteous cause,"* will cry out. *"Let them shout for joy and be glad."* Their *"shout"* will be a "ringing cry" of exultation, manifesting their gladness. The content of their cry, however, is not to be praise for David. They are to praise God *"continually,"* saying, *"Let the Lord be magnified, / Who has pleasure in the prosperity of His servant."* David wants only to be seen as God's servant who has been vindicated by Him.

Finally, David too will join in the witness and worship. He will *"speak of"* God's *"righteousness"* in vindicating him and *"praise"* God *"all the day long."*

We may experience difficulty in our understanding of this psalm as we relate it to Jesus' command to His disciples to love their enemies and to do good to those who persecute them (Matt. 5:43–44). David, however, prays not for redemptive justice, but for punitive justice. The good news of the gospel is that now, in Christ, God's wrath is redemptive, designed to bring us to the Savior. This, however, is not so for those who reject the Son. The day will come when God's judgment will be final for them. He, not we, will be vindicated. His enemies will be ashamed, to their eternal loss. Jesus Himself says: "For whoever is ashamed of Me and My words in this adulterous and sinful generation, of him the Son of Man also will be ashamed when He comes in the glory of His Father with the holy angels" (Mark 8:38). In light of this verse, Psalm 35 is a solemn warning to those who deny God, plot against His people, and plunder the poor and needy. We presume upon God's grace to our eternal peril.

CHAPTER THIRTY-SIX

When Humanism Fails

Psalm 36

When God reveals who we are, humanism fails. Thus as the psalmist meditates, God puts an oracle in his heart concerning the wicked. This word shows us our darkness. At the same time, there is also the revelation of God's light which illumines our path. We will either live in our darkness or in His light. There are no alternatives.

The themes of human depravity and divine grace reach us today like messages from some other age. We are still enamored with the myths of progress, evolution, the survival of the fittest (which by definition, of course, must be the best), and the power of human reason and initiative. Regardless of how bloody our century has been, we cling to our conviction that we can achieve a perfect world on our own rather than seeing our darkness and falling at Jesus' feet. The Bible speaks to those with shattered illusions and abandoned dreams; it is here for us when humanism fails.

Psalm 36 is described by commentators as an individual lament. It contains wisdom meditation like that of Psalm 1 (vv. 1–4), hymnic elements (vv. 5–9), and prayer (vv. 10–12). The movement of thought within these forms is clear. First, there is the revelation of our darkness (vv. 1–4). Next, there is the revelation of God's light (vv. 5–9). Finally, there is a prayer for protection (vv. 10–12). Tradition, which we follow, ascribes this psalm to David.

REVELATION OF HUMAN DARKNESS

1 An oracle within my heart concerning the
   transgression of the wicked:
There is no fear of God before his eyes.
2 For he flatters himself in his own eyes,
   When he finds out his iniquity *and* when he hates.
3 The words of his mouth *are* wickedness and deceit;

> He has ceased to be wise *and* to do good.
> 4 He devises wickedness on his bed;
> He sets himself in a way *that is* not good;
> He does not abhor evil.
>
> *Ps. 36:1–4*

Psalm 36 begins with a "preface." Literally, David describes what he is about to write as "an oracle of transgression of the wicked within [his] heart." The word for *"oracle"* means an "utterance" and is usually linked to God as its source (cf. Rom. 3:2). David receives this *"oracle"* in his *"heart,"* meaning "mind" in Hebrew thought. God may make His word available to our minds in audible or visible "speech." Thus Jeremiah both hears and sees God's word (Jer. 1:4, 11).

Certainly today we "see" God's word in the Bible. We can also "hear" and "see" God speak to our minds through His Spirit. This may come as words of knowledge, prophetic utterances, or visions (1 Cor. 12:8–10; Acts 2:17).

The *"oracle"* David receives reveals *"the transgression of the wicked."* Here the *"wicked"* are known by what they do. They are the bad trees that bear their bad fruit (Matt. 7:17–20). To know such evil requires revelation. God must show us what evil really is in order to break through our human rationalizations and illusions. Thus Jesus declares Himself to be the "light of the world" and then shows us the evil of our sin and Satan's domain. His light exposes the darkness.

The wicked person is first revealed by his presumption: *"There is no fear of God before his eyes."* All sin flows from this. The Hebrew word used here for *"fear"* means "dread" rather than "awe." It is the fear of judgment. Thus in Romans 3:11–18 when, from the Old Testament, Paul catalogs sin he climaxes his list with this verse. It is the final, irrefutable argument for our being transgressors.

Moreover, rather than loving and worshiping God, the wicked man *"flatters himself in his own eyes"* (v. 2). The rest of this verse is difficult to translate. It literally reads "to find his iniquity to hate (it)." Probably the meaning is that the flattery the wicked person engages in is so great that he believes God will not discover his sin or judge it. Thus he is vain; he is narcissistic. In his pride he has ruled God out of his life.

Furthermore, his words no longer contain the truth. They are *"wickedness"* and *"deceit,"* a cover for evil intentions. Wise thoughts and good actions have deserted him. In their place he plots wickedness when he is alone, *"on his bed,"* and walks in an "evil way." Rather than fleeing evil, he traffics in it. His conscience is seared.

These verses present a comprehensive picture of human darkness engaging mind, heart, and will. When we no longer see ourselves standing before God as our judge, we become perverted. Our ego is inflated. Flattery replaces truth. Our minds are grasped by wickedness and we deceive others. The path that we walk is evil. The result is a self-centered and self-consumed person who has no authentic relationship with God, himself, or others. Flattery, illusion, and deception determine his life. Only the word of God and the Holy Spirit's conviction can reveal to us such depths of human sin, *"the transgression of the wicked."*

REVELATION OF GOD'S LIGHT

5 Your mercy, O LORD, *is* in the heavens;
  Your faithfulness *reaches* to the clouds.
6 Your righteousness *is* like the great mountains;
  Your judgments *are* a great deep;
  O LORD, You preserve man and beast.
7 How precious *is* Your lovingkindness, O God!
  Therefore the children of men put their trust under
    the shadow of Your wings.
8 They are abundantly satisfied with the fullness of
    Your house,
  And You give them drink from the river of Your
    pleasures.
9 For with You *is* the fountain of life;
  In Your light we see light.

Ps. 36:5–9

With the above oracle given to him, David now sees clearly the goodness of God. In the darkness the light shines all the more brightly, and David's mind soars to the Lord. First, he thinks of God's *"mercy,"* His covenant-love, which is transcendent and eternal—"heavenly." So also is His *"faithfulness,"* His "trustworthiness," which is so great that it goes all the way to the *"clouds."* Next, God's *"righteousness,"* His right relationship to us, is as firm and steadfast as *"the great mountains,"* and God's *"judgments"* ("justice") are as deep as the ocean depths. As David looks at the created world he thus sees metaphorical signs of the greatness of God. The *"heavens,"* the *"clouds,"* the *"mountains,"* and the *"deep"* all remind him of the *"mercy,"* the *"faithfulness,"* the

273

"righteousness," and the justice of Yahweh. In His character God holds all creation together: *"O Lord, You preserve man and beast."*

In verse 7, David returns to the mercy or *"lovingkindness"* of God. He calls it *"precious."* It is this covenant-love that is beyond comparison. With it we can be like chicks protected by a mother hen. We can nestle *"under the shadow of [the Lord's] wings"* (cf. Matt. 23:37).

Furthermore, to come into God's *"house"* is to be *"satisfied"* by its *"fullness"* (v. 8). *"Fullness"* here is literally *"fat."* The word denotes oil and rich food and can be a metaphor for full spiritual blessings. There is also *"drink from the river of Your pleasures."* This *"river"* is parallel to the *"fountain of life"* in verse 9 (cf. Ezek. 47:1 and Rev. 22:1). Moreover, there the light of God dwells, along with the light of His word, His law. The light of God's presence is revealing: *"In Your light we see light."*

The contrast between living as a transgressor and living before God could not be clearer. Rather than the darkness of conceit and self-consumption, the light of God's mercy, faithfulness, righteousness, and justice is given to us. Furthermore, the Lord comes as a mother hen to protect us. He welcomes us into His *"house"* where His goodness overflows in rich food and thirst-quenching drink. Here are *"fullness"* and *"pleasures,"* indeed, the very *"fountain of life."* Welcome home!

PRAYER FOR PROTECTION

10 Oh, continue Your lovingkindness to those who know
    You,
    And Your righteousness to the upright in heart.
11 Let not the foot of pride come against me,
    And let not the hand of the wicked drive me away.
12 There the workers of iniquity have fallen;
    They have been cast down and are not able to rise.

Ps. 36:10–12

With the strong contrast before him between our evil and God's light, David now asks God to sustain His mercy, His covenant-love, to those who know Him. He further prays that the *"upright"* may know God's *"righteousness."* In the context of God's love and righteousness, those who know Him will be protected from evil.

Now David concludes by asking that his enemies may not be able to cut him down and place *"the foot of pride"* on his neck (see Josh. 10:24). He also asks that their *"hand"* may not *"drive* [him] *away"* from God's house (cf. v. 8). Looking beyond the moment, David sees the wicked as *"fallen,"* *"cast down,"* and *"not able to rise."* God's judgment against them will be final and certain.

In this psalm we see again that naive humanism is only overcome by divine revelation. The myths of progress and worldly achievement are exposed when God makes our true condition known. The masks are torn off. The play is over.

When our darkness is exposed, we become light in the light of God (Eph. 5:8). This is true humanism, humanity as we were created to be.

CHAPTER THIRTY-SEVEN

The Wicked and the Righteous

Psalm 37

Early in my walk with Christ I was introduced to verse 5 of Psalm 37: "Commit your way to the Lord, / Trust also in Him, / And He shall bring it to pass." This was one of the cardinal verses of the great Christian educator Henrietta Mears. This verse is a summary of how to live life as a believer. First, there is the decision: "Commit!" Then there is faith: "Trust also in Him." Finally, there is the Lord's work: all that we do is what He does in us. "He shall bring it to pass." This text, like John 3:16, is undamaged when it is lifted from its context. Yet, the context is illuminating. The author is an old man (v. 25). From the vantage point of a lifetime of experience he meditates on the fate of the wicked and the righteous. While he has seen the wicked in great power (v. 35), he has also seen them pass away. The righteous, however, are secure because they are held in the hand of God (vv. 23–24). Since the destruction of the wicked is sure (vv. 34–36), the righteous are not to fret over their fate (vv. 1, 7, 8).

This psalm is written to give assurance to the righteous. This assurance comes not only theologically, because God is on the side of the righteous; it also comes experientially. Over his lifetime the psalmist has seen the wicked come to a bitter end (vv. 36, 38). Psalm 37 offers real wisdom and perspective on the age-old question of the prosperity of the wicked and the suffering of the righteous in its triumphant call to trust the judgment and salvation of the living God.

Now Psalm 37:5 takes life. The verse is written by a man who has walked with the Lord throughout his life. In his maturity he has learned the meaning of commitment and trust. He has seen and rejected the alternative to this life of faith. He has also seen God intervene and act during his own crises again and again. When he promises that God will "bring it to pass," this truth is carved in his life experience. There is an integrity here that is born of the Holy Spirit and a life lived to the sunset years with the true and faithful God.

Tradition ascribes this psalm to David. Most commentators reject this because the psalm is a wisdom psalm whose author is a teacher imparting his learning to the next generation (v. 25). Such wisdom teachers, however, were also found in the courts of the Ancient Near East. They carried on a tradition of teaching which long preceded David's reign and to which he himself was exposed. Nevertheless, we will not offer a definitive judgment on the issue of authorship here.

Psalm 37 has the structure of an alphabetic acrostic (cf. Psalms 9–10). Its collection of wise sayings contrasts the wicked and the righteous. While it is difficult to outline, the psalm's major points are clear. God keeps the righteous. The wicked may appear to succeed for a moment but they will fade away. Though the righteous may stumble, Yahweh will continue to hold them. Their ultimate destiny is assured by Him.

THE DESTINY OF THE WICKED

1 Do not fret because of evildoers,
  Nor be envious of the workers of iniquity.
2 For they shall soon be cut down like the grass,
  And wither as the green herb.

Ps. 37:1–2

The psalmist begins with consolation: *"Do not fret because of evildoers."* The verb for *"fret"* is strong, meaning "to burn with anger." The anger that is warned against comes from envy toward *"the workers of iniquity"* because of their apparent success in this world. As the psalmist later says, "I have seen the wicked in great power, / And spreading himself like a native green tree" (v. 35). Nevertheless, this should not cause the righteous anxiety. Whatever power the *"evildoers"* now have, it will be gone in a moment. They will be *"cut down"* like mowed *"grass"* and *"wither as the green herb"* dies in the hot summer sun. The *"evildoers"* are simply among those with no anchor in eternity, with no ground beyond themselves. They are like the grass that withers when God's breath blows upon it (Isa. 40:7).

THE RESPONSE OF THE RIGHTEOUS

3 Trust in the LORD, and do good;
    Dwell in the land, and feed on His faithfulness.
4 Delight yourself also in the LORD,
    And He shall give you the desires of your heart.
5 Commit your way to the LORD,
    Trust also in Him,
    And He shall bring *it* to pass.
6 He shall bring forth your righteousness as the light,
    And your justice as the noonday.

    Ps. 37:3–6

Rather than worrying about the wicked the psalmist exhorts the righteous to trust in Yahweh and obey Him: *"Trust* ["have security"] *in the Lord, and do good."* They are to live in His promised land (Canaan) and be nourished by His character. They are to *"feed on His faithfulness."*

Moreover, beyond *"trust"* there is *"delight"* (v. 4). The verb for *"delight"* means "to be of dainty habit, to take exquisite delight." As the righteous *"delight"* in Yahweh, the *"desires"* of their hearts will be given to them. This does not mean that our selfish desires will be granted, although God promises to care materially for His people. It does mean that as we delight in the Lord He will change us and the desires of our hearts will be in conformity to His will. So Jesus promises, "If you abide in Me, and My words abide in you, you will ask what you desire, and it shall be done for you" (John 15:7).

Not only are the righteous to *"delight"* in the Lord, they are also to walk in His ways. So the psalmist continues, *"Commit your way to the*

Lord" or, literally, "Roll your way upon Yahweh." As the righteous walk they are to *"trust also in Him."* The promise then follows: *"And He shall bring it to pass"* or, literally, "He will do it." Our job then is to surrender. God will *"bring forth [their] righteousness as the light, / And [their] justice as the noonday,"* and we will shine with His character. Luther, commenting on this thought, says that when we come to Christ we are married to Him by faith. Like a bride we give Him all we have, namely, all our sin—and He gives us all He has, namely, all His righteousness.

THE ATTITUDE TOWARD THE WICKED

7 Rest in the LORD, and wait patiently for Him;
    Do not fret because of him who prospers in his way,
    Because of the man who brings wicked schemes to
        pass.
8 Cease from anger, and forsake wrath;
    Do not fret—*it* only *causes* harm.
9 For evildoers shall be cut off;
    But those who wait on the LORD,
    They shall inherit the earth.
10 For yet a little while and the wicked *shall be* no *more;*
    Indeed, you will look carefully for his place,
    But it *shall be* no *more.*
11 But the meek shall inherit the earth,
    And shall delight themselves in the abundance of
        peace.

Ps. 37:7–11

The righteous are to *"rest in the Lord"* or, literally, "be silent," and *"wait"* for Him to act (v. 7). Their attitude is to be one of patience before God. They are not to *"fret"* over the prosperity of the wicked: The psalmist exhorts: *"Cease from anger, and forsake wrath; / Do not fret—it only causes harm."* In harboring anger the righteous may become rebels against the Lord.

Verse 9 reminds the righteous to be patient because *"evildoers"* will be destroyed, *"cut off"* (see vv. 2, 15, 20, 22, 28, 36, 38). *"But those who wait on the Lord . . . shall inherit the earth,"* or "possess the land" (Canaan). Verse 10 expands on this thought; the *"wicked"* and his *"place"* quickly pass away (cf. vv. 35–36). Verse 11 repeats the thought of verse 9: *"But the meek shall inherit the earth"* (cf. Matt. 5:5), *"And shall delight themselves in the abundance of peace,"* that is, total security, plenty, and wholeness. The new thought here is that it is the *"meek,"* the *"poor, humble, or afflicted,"* who end up with the land and receive its bounty. This comes, however, not by their taking it but by Yahweh's gift. He is the author of salvation; "He shall bring it to pass."

Does this mean that Nietzsche was right in accusing Christianity of a "slave ethic"? Are the poor to do nothing? Yes and no. Yes—salvation is God's gift given to the humble. No—since God is on the side of the poor, we must be too, anticipating His kingdom in ministering to them, knowing that in our spirits we are all poor and that we are a sign of the kingdom coming as we live in this world caring for God's people. Our treasure is in heaven. When the kingdom comes we shall inherit the land.

THE JUDGMENT OF THE WICKED

12 The wicked plots against the just,
   And gnashes at him with his teeth.
13 The Lord laughs at him,
   For He sees that his day is coming.
14 The wicked have drawn the sword
   And have bent their bow,
   To cast down the poor and needy,
   To slay those who are of upright conduct.
15 Their sword shall enter their own heart,
   And their bows shall be broken.

Ps. 37:12-15

The psalmist expands in these verses on the theme of the *"wicked"* person's schemes and his fate. Although the righteous may quake in fear at the wicked man's plotting and scoffing, the *"Lord laughs"* in disdain because He sees that *"his day is coming"* and that the very weapons they take up will destroy them. When we violate God's moral order we violate ourselves. History is littered with illustrations of this truth. When Judas sold Jesus for thirty pieces of silver he really sold his own soul.

THE ADVANTAGES OF THE RIGHTEOUS

16 A little that a righteous man has
   Is better than the riches of many wicked.

17 For the arms of the wicked shall be broken,
But the LORD upholds the righteous.

Ps. 37:16–17

The advantage of the righteous person is the focus of these two verses. Although he may have *"little"* of this world's goods in comparison to *"the riches of many wicked,"* he is really better off. He will endure while the wicked person, whose *"arms . . . shall be broken,"* will not be able to use what he has. However, *"the Lord upholds the righteous."*

Notice here that the psalmist does not assert that it is simply good for the righteous to have little. If they are righteous and have much that is one thing. However, it is better to have little rather than to have much in wickedness, because the judgment of God is coming.

THE WICKED PASS AWAY

18 The LORD knows the days of the upright,
And their inheritance shall be forever.
19 They shall not be ashamed in the evil time,
And in the days of famine they shall be satisfied.
20 But the wicked shall perish;
And the enemies of the LORD,
Like the splendor of the meadows, shall vanish.
Into smoke they shall vanish away.

Ps. 37:18–20

The psalmist elaborates here upon the theme of the previous stanza. First, Yahweh knows *"the days of the upright,"* namely, He remembers them, He keeps them in mind. They have an eternal *"inheritance."* Second, when judgment comes, *"in the evil time . . . in the days of famine,"* they will neither *"be ashamed"* nor go hungry. Yahweh will keep them. *"The wicked,"* however, *"shall perish."* They will *"vanish"* *"like the splendor of the meadows"* swept by fire (cf. v. 2). This final image finds vivid illustration in the summer fires of Southern California. In the dry months the hills often burn, incinerating expensive homes. A quiet, affluent neighborhood one day may be charred ruins the next. Like the *"wicked,"* *"into smoke they . . . vanish away."* The Lord's judgment is swift and complete.

The righteous are not promised here a trouble-free life. What they are promised is that God will keep them and that His judgment on the wicked will not fall on them too. For us, in Christ, this has been fulfilled in that the judgment we deserve has fallen on Him. In Revelation 3:10, God promises the church militant, "Because you have kept My command to persevere, I also will keep you from the hour of trial which shall come upon the whole world."

THE MERCY OF THE RIGHTEOUS

21 The wicked borrows and does not repay,
   But the righteous shows mercy and gives.
22 For *those* blessed by Him shall inherit the earth,
   But *those* cursed by Him shall be cut off.
23 The steps of a *good* man are ordered by the LORD,
   And He delights in his way.
24 Though he fall, he shall not be utterly cast down;
   For the LORD upholds *him with* His hand.
25 I have been young, and *now* am old;
   Yet I have not seen the righteous forsaken,
   Nor his descendants begging bread.
26 *He is* ever merciful, and lends;
   And his descendants *are* blessed.

Ps. 37:21–26

While the wicked actually steals as he borrows because he *"does not repay,"* the righteous gives out of *"mercy"* to those who have not. In these acts the covenant blessings and cursings now operate (see Deut. 27–28). The blessed who show mercy *"inherit the earth"* (the land). The cursed who steal are *"cut off."*

Furthermore, *"the steps of a good man are ordered by the Lord"* (v. 23). The verb for *"ordered"* means "to make firm, to establish." The way the righteous walk is directed and confirmed by Yahweh. *"And He delights in his way."* Or, perhaps better, keeping the parallelism, "And he [the righteous] delights in His [Yahweh's] way."

Moreover, if the righteous *"fall,"* the situation is not terminal; *"he shall not be utterly cast down."* The Lord will uphold *"him with His hand."* So we read in Jude 24, "Now to Him who is able to keep you from stumbling, / And to present you faultless / Before the presence of His glory. . . ."

To these thoughts, the psalmist now adds his personal witness. Once *"young"* and now *"old,"* over a lifetime he has *"not seen the righteous forsaken"* (v. 25). Nor are his descendants left *"begging bread"* in poverty. To the contrary, the righteous person has money to be *"merciful"* and *"lends"* it. Thus *"his descendents are blessed."* Here we have a Hebraic picture of a full and happy life which extends to the generations to come. It is a life in which the theme is *"mercy."* The righteous person's hand is both full and open. As Jesus commands us, "Freely you have received, freely give" (Matt. 10:8).

EXHORTATION TO THE RIGHTEOUS

27 Depart from evil, and do good;
   And dwell forevermore.
28 For the LORD loves justice,
   And does not forsake His saints;
   They are preserved forever,
   But the descendants of the wicked shall be cut off.
29 The righteous shall inherit the land,
   And dwell in it forever.

Ps. 37:27–29

Based on the above observations, the psalmist now turns to exhortation: *"Depart from evil, and do good."* The result will be the possession of God's *"land."* There the righteous will *"dwell forevermore"* (see also v. 29). The basis for this moral action is that *"the Lord loves justice"* (v. 28). To *"do good,"* then, is to act justly, in accord with God's will. Moreover, beyond mere obedience, the Lord grants His presence to *"His saints"* and He preserves them *"forever."* The wicked, however, find that their progeny perish: they *"shall be cut off."* But *"The righteous shall inherit the land, / And dwell in it forever."*

Why then should we live moral lives? Why should we be just? First, because the just receive the *"land"*; they *"inherit"* eternal life. Second, because *"the Lord loves justice"* and *"His saints"* want to please Him. Third, because the just know the presence and power of God to keep them through this life. The hope for eternal life, *"the land,"* may be self-serving. However, it is God's delight that we be with Him *"forever."* He has placed in our hearts the longing for eternity. This then becomes a part of the Biblical moral imperative. "Without a pinch of apocalyptic there are no ethics" (Karl Barth).

WISDOM OF THE RIGHTEOUS

30 The mouth of the righteous speaks wisdom,
   And his tongue talks of justice.
31 The law of his God *is* in his heart;
   None of his steps shall slide.

Ps. 37:30–31

Next, the psalmist defines the righteous person as the one whose *"mouth . . . speaks wisdom."* Thus this psalm comes in the context of wisdom teaching, that is, wise instruction about practical living. This *"wisdom,"* however, is not merely the proverbial deposit of the Ancient Near East. It is *"wisdom"* paralleled with *"justice"*; it is *"wisdom"* baptized into the covenant. It is wisdom which begins with the "fear of the Lord." Moreover, it is the word of God written on the heart (Deut. 6:6); it is internalized. This wisdom guarantees the walk of the righteous person: *"None of his steps shall slide."*

PROTECTION OF THE RIGHTEOUS

32 The wicked watches the righteous,
   And seeks to slay him.
33 The LORD will not leave him in his hand,
   Nor condemn him when he is judged.

Ps. 37:32–33

The oppression of the righteous, and especially the poor, is a common theme in the Old Testament. For example, Amos addresses those "who oppress the poor, / Who crush the needy" (Amos 4:1). God brings His judgment against those who "tread down the poor" (Amos 5:11). He warns, "You afflict the just and take bribes; / You divert the poor from justice at the gate" (Amos 5:12), and he concludes, "it is an evil time" (Amos 5:13). Similar oppression probably is in mind in verses 32–33. The promise that the land will belong to the meek (v. 11) suggests that the wicked are trying to take their inheritance from them. Land schemes have always been a weapon for the oppression of people and nations. *Bury My Heart at Wounded Knee* is a sad commentary on this theme in American history as the native Indians were robbed of a vast wilderness.

PROVISION FOR THE RIGHTEOUS

34 Wait on the LORD,
   And keep His way,
   And He shall exalt you to inherit the land;
   When the wicked are cut off, you shall see *it.*
35 I have seen the wicked in great power,
   And spreading himself like a native green tree.
36 Yet he passed away, and behold, he *was* no *more;*
   Indeed I sought him, but he could not be found.
37 Mark the blameless *man,* and observe the upright;
   For the future of *that* man *is* peace.
38 But the transgressors shall be destroyed together;
   The future of the wicked shall be cut off.

                                             Ps. 37:34–38

Now the psalmist exhorts the righteous to *"wait on the Lord"* (see v. 9). To wait on God means to wait for God to act (v. 5). It means to be before Him in silent expectancy (see v. 7). But it also means to obey God's will: to *"keep His way."* The promise is that the righteous will be exalted *"to inherit the land."* At the same time, they will see *"the wicked . . . cut off"* or destroyed. The fulfillment of this verse for us will finally take place when the kingdom of God is realized in the "new heaven" and the "new earth" (Rev. 21:1).

The psalmist's assurance that the final judgment will come for the wicked is based on his present experience of seeing the rich and powerful fade away. Although the wicked person had *"great power"* spreading like a large *"tree,"* he *"passed away . . . he could not be found."*

"The blameless man," the man who is complete, morally sound, by contrast has a destiny of *"peace." "Peace"* here means "complete security and well-being" (cf. v. 11). Nevertheless, the *"transgressors,"* those who violate God's will, will *"be destroyed."* Their end is death.

SALVATION FOR THE RIGHTEOUS

39 But the salvation of the righteous *is* from the LORD;
   He is their strength in the time of trouble.
40 And the LORD shall help them and deliver them;
   He shall deliver them from the wicked,
   And save them,
   Because they trust in Him.

                                             Ps. 37:39–40

The psalmist now concludes with the triumph of *"salvation"* for the *"righteous."* *"Salvation"* is God's gift; it is *"from the Lord."* He is their *"strength,"* and they can flee to Him. He also gives *"help"* and deliverance. The righteous will be saved from the wicked and be made secure, *"Because they trust in Him,"* or "seek refuge" in Him. So Psalm 37 ends sounding the gospel.

Throughout this psalm, only two categories of people are seen to be in the world: the righteous and the wicked. Biblical faith is antithetical faith (Francis Schaeffer; see also the comments on Ps. 1). While the wicked may prosper for a moment due to unjust gain, their judgment is certain and final. It is the righteous who are held, kept, and saved by Yahweh. They commit their way to Him, trust in Him, and wait for Him to act. They inherit all of God's promises of peace and prosperity in the land. The wicked, however, pass away abruptly. They burn like the grass. They have no substance. They are grounded only in time, and time comes to an end. The righteous find their substance in the Lord. They are grounded in Him and He does not pass away. He assures their place in His kingdom. God Himself will resolve "the problem of evil." His justice is swift. Then the righteous will shine forever, as the noontime sun.

CHAPTER THIRTY-EIGHT

The Road to Healing

Psalm 38

A theme of Alcoholics Anonymous is that "you are only as sick as your secrets." The deep moral and spiritual secrets which we carry leave us in emotional and physical pain. Often those secrets are also secrets to us. They lie buried in our unconscious. For example, some excessively dependent adults may be seeking in their relationships the parental love they failed to receive as children. Or, confusing approval for love, some spend their lives working for approval but come up empty-handed so far as love is concerned. Repressed anger toward parents, which we are afraid to admit for fear of losing their love, may be the cause of chronic depression. Then there are our conscious secrets: sexual sin, consuming jealousy, self-protecting lies, and spiritual hypocrisy. How do we break these chains? What is the road to healing? This psalm is here to help us by bringing our secrets into the light.

In Psalm 38 the author experiences virtually total rejection and despair. At issue is some major sin (vv. 3 and 18) which is now a burden too heavy to bear. As a result, the psalmist feels God's wrath. His body also collapses in physical pain. Moreover, his spirit languishes in deep depression. Now his friends stand aloof and his enemies plot against him, but he is too sick to respond. He can only cry out to God in his pain.

Here we encounter a man who holds on to God by a thread. As he bares his soul, we learn the steps toward healing. This psalm is effective therapy, and it speaks to the deep places in us.

Traditionally, authorship of Psalm 38 is ascribed to David, and there is no overwhelming reason to dispute this view. The form of the work is described by commentators as an individual lament. The thought moves from a recognition of God's anger (vv. 1–2) to a confession of sickness (vv. 3–5), a recognition of illness and depression (vv. 6–8), the assurance that God knows (vv. 9–10), a lament over rejection (vv. 11–12), another confession of depression (vv. 13–14), and a confession to God (vv. 15–20), concluding with a call for intervention (vv. 21–22).

GOD IS ANGRY

> 1 O Lord, do not rebuke me in Your wrath,
>   Nor chasten me in Your hot displeasure!
> 2 For Your arrows pierce me deeply,
>   And Your hand presses me down.
>
> *Ps. 38:1–2*

David's opening plea to God graphically portrays his feelings as being like those of God's enemy, shot through by His *"arrows"* which *"pierce [him] deeply."* This is no mere flesh wound. The pain goes right to his heart. At the same time, God's *"hand presses [him] down,"* much as a parent might discipline a child by restraining him physically from moving away. Thus David feels weighted down under the heavy *"hand"* of God.

Interestingly enough, David begins his prayer addressing the real problem, his sense of alienation from God. His sickness, guilt, and hostile human relationships are all secondary to the primary issue. If David's relationship with the Lord can be healed, all other areas of his life will be open to healing as well. On the other hand, if he merely deals with the other problems, he will experience fleeting results. It is clear from verses 1–2 that the foremost need on the road to healing is to deal with our relationship with God.

I Am Sick

> 3 *There is* no soundness in my flesh
> Because of Your anger,
> Nor *any* health in my bones
> Because of my sin.
> 4 For my iniquities have gone over my head;
> Like a heavy burden they are too heavy for me.
> 5 My wounds are foul *and* festering
> Because of my foolishness.
>
> *Ps. 38:3–5*

Next, David turns to his physical and moral condition. His body is unhealthy as a result of God's rejection. The Hebrew word used here for *"flesh"* (v. 3) can simply signify human beings as a whole (see Gen. 6:12, "all flesh"), or it can also denote the whole person or the self (see Isa. 40:6–7). The flesh for the Bible is not evil in itself because it is a part of God's good creation. It is, however, a point where sin can enter human life (see Rom. 7:14). It then becomes sinful (see Rom. 8:3). Thus David's *"flesh"* here has lost its wholeness and is under God's "wrath," God's heavy "hand." This physical reaction has a moral basis. David continues, saying he is sick *"because of [his] sin"* ("missing God's way"). Here we see that God's "wrath," His moral indignation, and our *"sin"* all go together. It is our *"sin,"* our disobedience, however, which provokes divine "wrath." This then may lead to physical illness which can be caused by "wrath" or *"sin"* interchangeably.

David goes on to elaborate on his moral and physical problems. His *"iniquities"* submerge him like a flood, having gone *"over [his] head."* He is drowning in them. Moreover, they are a crushing *"burden . . .*

too heavy for [*him*]." He also has infected sores, *"foul and festering."* They are ugly to the nose and to the eye. The reason for this moral pain and physical horror is his *"foolishness."* In Proverbs, folly is sin (see Prov. 24:9). Thus David's *"foolishness"* here is parallel to his *"iniquities"* in verse 4. Some commentators take these physical symptoms as indicating leprosy; however, this cannot be proven. Any number of diseases could produce these results.

How much of this applies to us today as we seek God's healing? There is do doubt that sin and physical illness can be intimately related, especially when sin is denied or covered up. There are also some sins which may bring illness with them, for instance, sexual promiscuity may bring venereal disease. But what about God's wrath? Is illness a sign of His displeasure? We must be cautious in our answer. According to Romans 1:18–32 we live in a world where, in His wrath, God has given impenitent man up to his sin by standing back and letting it run its course. Indirectly we are all subject to this fallen world and the consequences of God's withdrawal. For the Christian, however, God's wrath has been placed upon Jesus. This means that we are no longer the objects of His judgment or His withdrawal. His grace is upon us and His hand is open to heal us. Where we do experience God's discipline it is corrective rather than punitive (Heb. 12:5–11). Thus we may now come boldly to God through Jesus and ask for healing, knowing that He is smiling upon us in His love.

I AM DEPRESSED

6 I am troubled, I am bowed down greatly;
   I go mourning all the day long.
7 For my loins are full of inflammation,
   And *there is* no soundness in my flesh.
8 I am feeble and severely broken;
   I groan because of the turmoil of my heart.

Ps. 38:6–8

Not only does David experience physical pain, he also knows emotional pain. Verse 6 suggests that he is deeply depressed. *"I am troubled"* translates literally, "I am bent." He continues, *"I am bowed down greatly."* His posture represents his spiritual and emotional state: *"I go mourning all the day long."* This *"mourning"* comes both from his sense of alienation from God and the burden of his guilt and deteriorated physical condition.

Furthermore, David relates that his *"loins are full of inflammation"* (literally, "burning"). He concludes that *"there is no soundness in [his] flesh."* Again, he is weak, *"feeble,"* and broken,*"* and groans *"because of the turmoil* [groaning] *of his heart."* Here then we have a combination of moral, emotional, and physical sickness. Much of this sounds like depression manifesting itself in grief, a sense of loss. This would explain the groaning of David's *"heart."*

GOD KNOWS

> 9 Lord, all my desire *is* before You;
>   And my sighing is not hidden from You.
> 10 My heart pants, my strength fails me;
>   As for the light of my eyes, it also has gone from
>   me.
>
> *Ps. 38:9–10*

As David prays, he presents his condition fully to God. He knows David's *"sighing,"* his panting *"heart"* (anxiety?), his exhaustion *("my strength fails"),* and the darkness in his *"eyes."* This final phrase gives away the depths of David's despair. As Jesus says, "The lamp of the body is the eye. If therefore your eye is good, your whole body will be full of light. But if your eye is bad, your whole body will be full of darkness" (Matt. 6:22–23).

Here, however, is the beginning of healing. David discloses his condition to the Lord, holding nothing back. He knows that emotional and physical stress begin to lift when we expose them to God in prayer. If we are "as sick as our secrets," then we are as well as our disclosures. This is especially true when those disclosures are made to a loving, powerful, heavenly Father who wants us well (see 1 Thess. 5:23).

PEOPLE REJECT ME

> 11 My loved ones and my friends stand aloof from my
>   plague,
>   And my relatives stand afar off.

289

12 Those also who seek my life lay snares *for me;*
   Those who seek my hurt speak of destruction,
   And plan deception all the day long.

Ps. 38:11–12

Here David experiences human rejection along with divine anger. His *"loved ones," "friends,"* and *"relatives"* are *"aloof."* They withdraw from his *"plague."* The noun for *"plague"* can be translated "stroke," "heavy touch," "plague-spot," and thus "leprosy." The meaning of the word here is probably more general than "leprosy." David is avoided because of his cumulative condition, and this rejection contributes to his depression.

David's illness is also an invitation to his enemies to attack him. They seek his life, laying *"snares"* for him as though he were a wounded animal. They *"speak of destruction"* and *"plan deception."* The word for *"plan"* literally means "meditate." Thus they "chew over" their plots *"all the day long."*

Here we have a picture of total rejection. Family, friends, and enemies all "jump ship." David experiences the abandonment that many AIDS victims receive today. No one wants to be near him or to touch him.

I AM DEEPLY DEPRESSED

13 But I, like a deaf *man,* do not hear;
   And *I am* like a mute *who* does not open his mouth.
14 Thus I am like a man who does not hear,
   And in whose mouth *is* no response.

Ps. 38:13–14

One way to view these verses is as testimony to the depths of David's depression. Rather than rallying against rejection, he shuts people out. His emotional life "closes down." *"Like a deaf man,* [David does] *not hear."* He blocks out verbal communication. Also, his *"mouth"* is sealed. *"Like a mute,"* he refuses to respond. Verse 14 then reiterates these thoughts for emphasis.

Another possibility is that David is deaf and dumb in a passive-aggressive state. This would mean that his deaf-mute condition is not a response to his sickness but to the rejection which he describes in verses 11–12. If this is true, it connects well to verses 15–20. It means that David does not hear people or speak to them; now he speaks to God alone.

CONFESSION TO GOD

15 For in You, O Lord, I hope;
   You will hear, O Lord my God.
16 For I said, *"Hear me,* lest they rejoice over me,
   Lest, when my foot slips, they exalt *themselves* against
      me."
17 For I *am* ready to fall,
   And my sorrow *is* continually before me.
18 For I will declare my iniquity;
   I will be in anguish over my sin.
19 But my enemies *are* vigorous, *and* they are strong;
   And those who hate me wrongfully have multiplied.
20 Those also who render evil for good,
   They are my adversaries, because I follow *what is*
      good.

Ps. 38:15–20

David deals here with two adversaries: his *"sin"* and his *"enemies."*
Turning to the Lord with a glimmering of hope, he is aware that God
cares and hears, and that he is still able to talk to Him even if he can
talk to no one else. When hope dies, we die. After all human hope is
gone, however, there are still God's promises to us. "And now abide
faith, hope, love, these three . . ." (1 Cor. 13:13).

First, David asks God to protect him from his enemies: *"lest they
rejoice over me, / Lest, when my foot slips, they exalt themselves."* For his
foot to slip means for David to stumble from God's path, the way in
which he should walk (cf. Ps. 37:5). Since this has already happened
(see v. 4), the opportunity has come for David's enemies to exalt themselves by depreciating him. Moreover, in verse 17 he is poised for greater
catastrophe. In light of the description of David's condition, he could
well refer here even to death itself.

Second, in this crisis moment David confesses his sin and sorrow
to the Lord (v. 18). Here he is at the root of his problem. If David
can experience God's mercy and the return of divine favor, he will be
on the road to healing (cf. Ps. 51:7–8).

At the same time, David's enemies are *"vigorous"* and their number
grows. However, they *"hate* [him] *wrongfully."* The word for *"wrongfully"* means "falsely, fraudulently." Although David isn't sinless, his
enemies have used his sickness to their advantage. They also *"render
evil for good,"* and they oppose him because he seeks Yahweh's will,

he pursues *"good."* Regardless of his sin, he knows what is right and desires to *"follow"* it. This is no contradiction. It is because of his sense of righteousness that David languishes in such depression and despair.

In verse 18, then, we see a crucial step in David's healing. Previously he has been conscious of his sin and felt its weight (vv. 4–5). Now, however, he declares his *"sin."* He feels *"anguish"* over it. Apart from such deep, heartfelt confession neither we nor David will know healing. In a somewhat different context, James encourages us to confess our sins to each other and to pray for each other "that you may be healed" (James 5:16). Here, as in Psalm 38, confession and healing are wedded.

Again and again in ministering to the sick I have seen honest confession of sin begin the healing process. I have seen people pour out their hearts to God and then experience deep relief and an infusion of joy in the Holy Spirit. There is no other route to health or sanity. We all need to be cleansed. This is humbling, breaking. But in Christ, after death comes resurrection.

CALL FOR INTERVENTION

21 Do not forsake me, O LORD;
   O my God, be not far from me!
22 Make haste to help me,
   O Lord, my salvation!

Ps. 38:21–22

Psalm 38 ends with a call for God to act. First, David asks for God's presence and then he prays for the Lord's saving power to come quickly. And who is the one to whom David prays? *"O Lord, my salvation!"* It is the Lord who will deliver him from his own wrath and from David's sin, sickness, and enemies.

This prayer is not a prayer of victory (cf. Ps. 51), yet, as we have seen, it demonstrates the road to healing. It includes an honest description of David's moral, emotional, and physical illness and its relational consequences. It deals forthrightly with the rejection he feels from God, family, and enemies. In his despair, David cries out to the Lord. The fact that this psalm was written down and cherished is an eloquent witness that his prayer was heard.

CHAPTER THIRTY-NINE

The Passing Show

Psalm 39

The passing of time is an issue for us all, not just for the elderly. A good friend of mine used to sit and look out of his bedroom at the lengthening shadows of the afternoon when he was still in high school. He thought about the fact that time was speeding by so quickly, and that he had so many things that he wanted to do. He also thought about God. The passing of time gives us a heart for eternity.

Our culture is engaged in a massive denial of time and aging. We remove the elderly to "retirement villages." We employ cosmetics to keep us young looking. We pluck or dye gray hairs. We pay for facelifts and cosmetic surgery to reverse the aging process—but it is all in vain. Time marches on and so do we. If we add to this any sense of our own sin and God's judgment, then, indeed, life seems empty at best.

Psalm 39 expresses a deep awareness that this world is passing away. Overwhelmed by its temporal nature, especially in light of divine judgment, the psalmist breaks his silence to question God. This issue is severe because of his own sin and God's displeasure. This makes him sense the futility of life all the more. Thus he feels like a "stranger" toward God. If God won't lift His wrath, then the psalmist will just vanish away.

Traditionally this psalm has been attributed to David. The assumption that he writes as an old man is unnecessary. The form is an individual lament, which includes both direct prayer and meditation. The psalm reflects wisdom teaching. Its thought moves from breaking the silence (vv. 1–3) to the question of life's meaning (vv. 4–6) and the call for forgiveness (vv. 7–11), and it concludes with the assurance of answered prayer (vv. 12–13).

MY SILENCE BREAKS

1 I said, "I will guard my ways,
    Lest I sin with my tongue;

> I will restrain my mouth with a muzzle,
> While the wicked are before me."
> 2 I was mute with silence,
> I held my peace *even* from good;
> And my sorrow was stirred up.
> 3 My heart was hot within me;
> While I was musing, the fire burned.
> *Then* I spoke with my tongue:
>
> *Ps. 39:1–3*

The opening verses are a preface or prelude to the psalm proper. Here David has vowed to keep silence, like the wise men of his court. He refuses to *"sin"* with his *"tongue"* and thus muzzles, or bridles his mouth (cf. James 3:5–10). Next, he gives the reason for his restraint: *"The wicked are before me."* Perhaps David doesn't want them to hear his complaint to the Lord or his confession of sin. Or maybe he restrains himself from cursing them.

While he was silent and even refused to speak *"good,"* much less evil, his *"sorrow* [pain] *was stirred up."* Then his *"heart"* became *"hot."* Moreover, he continues, *"While I was musing* [murmuring in meditation], *the fire burned,"* namely, his heart, hot like a coal, burst into flame. *"Then I spoke with my tongue"* (cf. Jer. 20:9).

Thus David's silence turns to speech because the sorrow or the pain which has been turning over and over in his heart finally overpowers him. Engulfed in an emotional torrent, he can contain himself no longer.

WHAT IS MY END?

> 4 "LORD, make me to know my end,
> And what *is* the measure of my days,
> *That* I may know how frail I *am*.
> 5 Indeed, You have made my days *as* handbreadths,
> And my age *is* as nothing before You;
> Certainly every man at his best state *is* but vapor.Selah
> 6 Surely every man walks about like a shadow;
> Surely they busy themselves in vain;
> He heaps up *riches*,
> And does not know who will gather them.
>
> *Ps. 39:4–6*

The questions that have agitated David's heart and he now addresses to the Lord are issues of death and life. The *"end"* (v. 4) means the end of a definite time period rather than a goal; it is another word for "death." This *"measure"* of David's *"days"* refers to the span of his human life in this world. When he knows the time of his death and the length of his life he will *"know how frail I am."* As we shall see, these questions are pressing because of David's sin and resulting sickness.

In verses 5–6, in effect, David answers his own request. First, his *"days"* are *"as handbreadths,"* the width of the hand measured at the base of the fingers, about four inches. Thus they are brief and fleeting. Furthermore, his *"age is as nothing before [God]."* It is a mere blink or blip compared to eternity. The brevity of life is true for all people. Thus *"certainly every man at his best state is but vapor,"* that is, "breath." We read in James 4:14: "For what is your life? It is even a vapor that appears for a little time and then vanishes away." David also pictures each person as being *"like a shadow."* The conclusion to this meditation is that merely busying ourselves in gathering *"riches"* is futile. We may *"heap"* them up, but someone else *"will gather them"* (cf. Matt. 6:19–20; Luke 12:13–21).

In sum, David tells us: First, human life is frail; we are like vapors and shadows. Second, time is fleeting; for each of us it is like a few handbreadths. Third, wealth as the goal of life is futile; if we spend our days gathering it, someone else will spend it when our days are gone. Now David knows his *"end,"* his death, and *"the measure of* [his] *days,"* his life. Armand Nicholi, the Harvard psychiatrist, says that only when we are ready to die are we ready to live. David here accepts both his death and his life in light of his death. Now he is ready to move to the deeper issues before him.

REMOVE MY SIN AND YOUR ANGER

7 "And now, Lord, what do I wait for?
My hope *is* in You.
8 Deliver me from all my transgressions;
Do not make me the reproach of the foolish.
9 I was mute, I did not open my mouth,
Because it was You who did *it*.
10 Remove Your plague from me;
I am consumed by the blow of Your hand.

11 When with rebukes You correct man for iniquity,
You make his beauty melt away like a moth;
Surely every man *is* vapor.   Selah

Ps. 39:7–11

When David acknowledges that his hope is in God, he is ready to deal with the Lord. First, he asks for God to *"deliver [him] from all [his] transgressions."* *"Transgressions"* are the moral violations of God's will. They are acts of rebellion, or law-breaking. For God to *"deliver"* him means for Him to both forgive David's guilt and to free him from the consequences of his actions. The results will be that he will not be subject to *"the reproach of the foolish."* They hold that God won't listen to him or do anything in his life because of his sin. God's action, however, will silence them.

In verse 9 David recalls verse 2. He was *"mute"* because God *"did it."* What God did was bring judgment against David's sin until his *"sorrow"* was so *"stirred up"* that he had to speak. Now David asks God to *"remove"* His wrath evidenced in the *"plague"* on him. The Hebrew word for *"plague"* means "stroke, mark, or plague-spot," and can thus signify the mark of a disease sent as God's judgment. It overwhelms David: *"I am consumed by the blow of Your hand."* Furthermore, the divine judgment is also disciplinary: *"with rebukes You correct* ["admonish"] *man for iniquity"* (v. 11).

Here David reveals the problem of sin and judgment. Awareness of the transitoriness of life is intensified by his severe sickness. With his health gone, he sees himself as a mere *"vapor"* or *"shadow."* Thus David asks the Lord to *"remove"* his *"transgressions"* and to lift the resulting *"plague."* How then are we to understand these points?

First, life is a passing show and our illnesses and weaknesses remind us of our mortality. This is all to the good.

Second, sin often leads to sickness. Thus when sin is forgiven, the root of many ills is broken. If, as has been estimated, over 80 percent of all hospital beds are filled by people who have diseases of psychogenic origin, then our health problems often have a spiritual basis. Grace is the true medication we need.

Third, sickness is often viewed in the Bible as a sign of God's judgment (see Exod. 9:3). It can also be a result of Satan's work (see Job 1:12). While sickness in our lives may come from the disorder of the fall or may be a consequence of Satan's work in us, God comes in Jesus to heal the sick. David simply saw God bringing the *"plague"* of His wrath upon him and cried out for deliverance. When we come to Christ, we receive God's forgiveness, knowing that He has borne the wrath of God on the cross, and that there is now no condemnation for those who are in Him (Rom. 8:1). This means that in Jesus God comes to heal us rather than to punish us. The Holy Spirit has anointed Him to preach the gospel to the poor, to heal the brokenhearted, to deliver the captives, to give sight to the blind, to liberate the oppressed, and to announce "the acceptable year of the Lord" (Isa. 61:1–2; Luke 4:18–19). Thus we can say with even more assurance than did David, "My hope is in You."

HEAR MY PRAYER

12 "Hear my prayer, O LORD,
   And give ear to my cry;
   Do not be silent at my tears;
   For I *am* a stranger with You,
   A sojourner, as all my fathers *were.*
13 Remove Your gaze from me, that I may regain
      strength,
   Before I go away and am no more."

Ps. 39:12–13

David now holds his sorrow before the Lord, pleading with Him to speak: *"Do not be silent at my tears."* He identifies himself to Yahweh with the humble titles *"stranger"* and *"sojourner."* Under Biblical law the *"stranger"* is a protected resident alien. The *"sojourner"* is an alien passing through the land. Provisions were made for both of these groups to be incorporated into Israel's life (cf. Exod. 12:48–49). Here David stands with them, as did his ancestors, *"all my fathers."*

The psalm concludes with a plea for God to take His *"gaze"* from David, literally, to "look from" him so that his *"strength"* may return. Normally God looks away in His wrath; here, however, God's gaze is the gaze of judgment and brings the plague. David begs for that look to lift. If it doesn't, he will be a dead man; he will *"go away"* and be *"no more,"* like the "vapor" of verse 5.

This psalm in its reflection on human life, focuses on its ephemeral and passing nature. Sickness only adds to our sense that this world is fallen and we are fallen with it. Nevertheless, David's hope is in God. This is the evening star that guides and encourages him. Apart from the eternal God, all of life is meaningless, and despair will over-whelm us.

CHAPTER FORTY

From Clay to Rock

Psalm 40

Smooth waters mean smooth sailing. Rough waters, however, test what we are made of and who commands the ship. Will our faith hold in the hour of trial? Will God's promises stand? Part of our ability to answer these questions rests on what we have experienced of God in the past. A new convert has the advantage of a fresh faith, but a mature Christian has the advantage of an enduring faith. What God has been to us in the past is the promise of what He will be to us in the future, and more. We must always anticipate surprises from God since He is the living God whose ways are not our ways (Isa. 55:8).

Psalm 40 bears clear witness to what God has done in the past. He has delivered the psalmist from the "horrible pit" and given him a "new song," and he is bold in his public witness concerning the character of God. Now, however, as new evils have come upon him, his sins are suffocating him and his enemies are in hot pursuit. The psalmist needs a new touch of God's forgiveness and a new experience of God's freedom from those who wish him evil. He sees himself as "poor and needy," and he eagerly calls upon the Lord to deliver him.

This psalm is in two parts, thanksgiving (vv. 1–10) followed by personal lament (vv. 11–17). The fact that verses 13–17 are also Psalm 70 means that either the psalmist borrowed Psalm 70 as a previous literary tradition or that this section was later detached for liturgical use and then became a separate psalm. The latter possibility seems to be the likely one.

As far as authorship is concerned, tradition ascribes this psalm to David. The attitudes toward sacrifice and the law, however, are used as arguments against early authorship (see vv. 6–8). This is problematic, especially in light of Psalm 51:16–17. Here we accept the Davidic tradition.

The movement of the psalm goes from a witness to what God has done and the response of public worship (vv. 1–10) to a cry for deliverance from sin and enemies (vv. 11–15), an exhortation to worship (v. 16), and a final call for help (v. 17).

DIVINE DELIVERANCE

1 I waited patiently for the LORD;
And He inclined to me,
And heard my cry.
2 He also brought me up out of a horrible pit,
Out of the miry clay,
And set my feet upon a rock,
And established my steps.
3 He has put a new song in my mouth—
Praise to our God;
Many will see *it* and fear,
And will trust in the LORD.

Ps. 40:1–3

David begins with a confession of his past experience. As with Abraham, it is likely that as he *"waited patiently"* his faith grew (see Rom. 4:20–21). Thus Jesus tells us to keep on asking, to keep on seeking, and to keep on knocking, in present imperatives (Luke 11:9). We will get our answer as David got his.

When God hears, God acts. David was rescued from, literally, "the pit of tumult" or "roaring." This probably refers to roaring waters which suggest the chaos of death. Since the pit is often a metaphor for death (see Ps. 30:3), the *"pit"* and the *"miry clay"* may also represent the underworld or abode of the dead. But God did not merely rescue David from death, He *"set [his] feet upon a rock,"* and *"established [his] steps."* God provided refuge, stability, and security. For David salvation is not only to be saved *from* something, it is also to be saved *for* something. Christ rescues us from sin, and He also rescues us for Himself. We are secure and established in Him.

As a result of God's work David has a *"new song."* The song is new because the work of God for him is new. Each experience of divine intervention has freshness. So David sings a *"new song"*; he puts his new wine into new wineskins (see Mark 2:22). His song is a song of gratitude, *"Praise to our God,"* for the rescue he has received.

Worship in the Bible is usually a corporate, public event and includes witness. As David praises God, *"many will see it."* They do not merely hear his praise, they *"see"* him praising. His joy before the Lord is his worship-witness. When David went to bring the ark of the covenant to Jerusalem, we are told that "then David and all the house of Israel played music before the Lord on all kinds of instruments. . . . Then

David danced before the Lord with all his might. . . . So David and all the house of Israel brought up the ark of the Lord with shouting and with the sound of the trumpet" (2 Sam. 6:5, 14–15). A witness to renewal in the church today is the kind of worship others can *see* as a sign of God's presence in our midst.

David says that when people *"see"* his worship they will *"fear,"* they will be in awe of God. They will look beyond David to the Lord and be confronted by Him, and they too *"will trust in the Lord."* The word for *"trust"* means "to find security." Those who see David's worship will find that as they join him, Yahweh will also put their *"feet upon a rock."*

The Lord Is Trustworthy

> 4 Blessed *is* that man who makes the Lord his trust,
>   And does not respect the proud, nor such as turn aside
>   to lies.
> 5 Many, O Lord my God, *are* Your wonderful works
>   *Which* You have done;
>   And Your thoughts toward us
>   Cannot be recounted to You in order;
>   *If* I would declare and speak *of them,*
>   They are more than can be numbered.
>
> *Ps. 40:4–5*

David now gives the content of his witness. He proclaims that God is trustworthy and blesses those who trust in Him. The word for *"blessed"* is the same as that in Psalm 1:1 and means "happy," "rewarded." The *"proud"* are those who stand against God. This was Satan's temptation in the fall and this is always our temptation. God isn't impressed: "God resists the proud, / But gives grace to the humble" (1 Pet. 5:5). Those who *"turn aside to lies,"* turn aside from the Lord, to illusion, to vanity, to idols, and ultimately to Satan (see John 8:44).

The *"blessed"* person will join David in praise. Here the content of David's praise focuses on God's *"works"* and God's words, or *"thoughts."* The word rendered *"wonderful works"* in verse 5 means "supernatural, extraordinary works." It identifies God's direct interventions in history rather than the orderly display of nature. Thus David praises God for the fresh manifestations of His saving power which have evoked his "new song."

David also praises God for His *"thoughts toward us."* They cannot be ordered by the human mind and they are vast in their extent, *"more than can be numbered."* As Isaiah 55:9 says, "For as the heavens are higher than the earth, / So are My ways higher than your ways, / And My thoughts than your thoughts." However vast and infinite God's mind and thoughts are, we must remember that they are *"toward us."* God is the God who reveals Himself. He speaks, and His Spirit searches even His depths and makes them known to us (1 Cor. 2:10–13).

Thus God is revealed in both His mighty works and in His word. The two must go together. The work is interpreted by the word, and the word is verified by the work.

HEART WORSHIP

> 6 Sacrifice and offering You did not desire;
>   My ears You have opened.
>   Burnt offering and sin offering You did not require.
> 7 Then I said, "Behold, I come;
>   In the scroll of the book *it is* written of me.
> 8 I delight to do Your will, O my God,
>   And Your law *is* within my heart."
>
> Ps. 40:6–8

Next, David contrasts true worship with false worship. He denotes the *"sacrifice,"* a communion offering eaten by the people; the *"offering,"* either a grain or an animal offering of any kind; the *"burnt offering,"* a male animal wholly given to Yahweh, consumed by fire on the altar; and the *"sin offering,"* an expiatory sacrifice. None of these offerings, however, is desired or required by God, as he has *"opened"* David's *"ears"* to understand. What He does desire (v. 8) is a *"delight to do [His] will"* and His *"law"* written upon the *"heart."*

Is this then an attack upon the cult (priestly liturgy) as such? While many modern interpreters have taken these verses in this way, it is doubtful that this is David's intention. Thus verse 9 continues with the assertion that he has witnessed to God "in the great congregation," that is, in the festival gatherings of Israel. The contrast in verses 6 and 8 is not between *"sacrifices"* and the *"will"* of God, but between sacrifices and the right attitude and action. God cares about our *"heart"* and His *"law"* (including the laws of sacrifice for Israel) written there (see Jer. 31:33). Without our hearts, and a *"delight to do [His] will,"* including the offering of sacrifices, we are just going through motions that God neither desires nor requires. Thus He rebukes Israel through Isaiah for sacrificial worship by those whose "hands are full of blood" (Isa. 1:15). God asks, "To what purpose is the multitude of your sacrifices to Me?" (Isa. 1:11).

While verses 6 and 8 seem clear, what is the meaning of verse 7? *"Then I said, 'Behold I come; / In the scroll of the book it is written of me.' "* What would be written of David in some scroll that would determine his coming? While modern scholars puzzle over this verse, it is clear to the author of Hebrews what it means. First, in its context the full intent of David's attack upon the sacrifices is that they are not adequate to procure eternal salvation for us. "For it is not possible that the blood of bulls and goats could take away sins" (Heb. 10:4). Second, these verses become prophetic. It is Christ who is written of *"in the scroll of the book."* Moreover, it is He who comes to do the will of God (see v. 8). In offering Himself for sin, once for all, He simultaneously fulfills and abolishes the Old Testament sacrificial system. Thus verse 7, written under the inspiration of the Holy Spirit, speaks of Christ and pours ultimate meaning into verses 6–8. God does desire sacrifice, except that it must be sacrifice from the heart. Yet all sacrifices are limited, and God therefore fulfills His own desire (and demand) by giving His Son as the perfect sacrifice for sin. This is promised in the Old Testament, *"the scroll of the book,"* and fulfilled in Christ who delighted to *"do"* the Father's *"will"* and who had His *"law"* perfectly written on His *"heart."* Thus our worship is fulfilled in Christ who writes God's law upon our hearts by the Holy Spirit.

HEART WITNESS

9 I have proclaimed the good news of righteousness
  In the great assembly;
  Indeed, I do not restrain my lips,
  O LORD, You Yourself know.
10 I have not hidden Your righteousness within my heart;
  I have declared Your faithfulness and Your salvation;
  I have not concealed Your lovingkindness and Your
    truth
  From the great assembly.

Ps. 40:9–10

Now David turns to true witness; what is written on the heart must be spoken to the world. The verb paraphrased *"proclaimed the good news"* means to "bear tidings," "preach," or even "evangelize" (James Muilenberg). David's message then is God's *"righteousness,"* which is the perfect will of God manifested in true relationship with Him. This includes, of course, God's delivering David (v. 3). Thus as David worships, he also witnesses when Israel gathers *"in the great assembly,"* possibly during one of the great festivals. David then adds for emphasis that he has not restrained his lips and appeals to God as his witness: *"O Lord, You Yourself know."*

In verse 10 David again repeats the thesis of verse 9: *"I have not hidden Your righteousness within my heart."* This time, however, he elaborates upon his witness and includes God's *"faithfulness"* or "truthfulness," His *"salvation"* or "deliverance," His *"lovingkindness"* or "covenant-love," and His *"truth"* or "trustworthiness." All of these attributes he declares before God's people.

As we have seen, part of this psalm is prophetic. As Jesus comes to do the will of God in sacrificing Himself for our sins, so He also is the evangelist. He preaches the *"good news"* of God's *"righteousness,"* the gift of salvation which He offers to us. Thus Christ is God's righteousness to us and for us (Rom. 3:22). He is God's faithfulness (Rom. 8:38–39), salvation (Rom. 5:9–10), love (Rom. 5:8), and truth (Rom. 9:1). Thus, like David, when we think of Him we do not "restrain our lips."

CRY FOR MERCY

11 Do not withhold Your tender mercies from me, O
     LORD;
   Let Your lovingkindness and Your truth continually
     preserve me.
12 For innumerable evils have surrounded me;
   My iniquities have overtaken me, so that I am not
     able to look up;
   They are more than the hairs of my head;
   Therefore my heart fails me.

                                                    Ps. 40:11–12

As David witnesses to God's righteousness in all of its dimensions he is also struck by his own sin and prays for God's *"tender mercies"* to be upon him. The noun for *"tender mercies"* means "compassion," the motive behind God's actions to uphold His covenant. Thus God's *"tender mercies"* are expressed to David by His *"lovingkindness"* and *"truth."*

The reason for this call is that once again David experiences *"innumerable evils,"* which come as a result of his *"iniquities"* or *"wrongs"* that have caught up with him. They are vast, *"more than the hairs of my head."* His eyes are downcast: *"I am not able to look up"* and his *"heart"* faints.

The only answer is for God again to move upon him in mercy. Keith Miller, some years ago, wrote a book entitled *The Second Touch.* He built his thesis on the progressive healing that a blind man experienced from Jesus. First his eyes were opened, but he saw people "like trees, walking" (Mark 8:24). Then, after Jesus touched him again, his eyesight was fully restored. David needs this "second touch" from the Lord. The good news is that it is available to all of us again and again. Francis MacNutt observes that in the healing ministry, when praying for the sick, often it is not "all or nothing," but "more or less." Much healing is progressive. We are all sinners needing continual cleansing and healing.

CRY FOR DELIVERANCE

13 Be pleased, O LORD, to deliver me;
   O LORD, make haste to help me!
14 Let them be ashamed and brought to mutual confusion
   Who seek to destroy my life;
   Let them be driven backward and brought to dishonor
   Who wish me evil.
15 Let them be confounded because of their shame,
   Who say to me, "Aha, aha!"

Ps. 40:13–15

David needs deliverance again. Not only is he faced with his own sins, there are also those who seek to kill him. They wish him evil and taunt him; thus David calls upon God to go into a battle on his behalf. He asks that his enemies be *"driven backward"* into retreat and that they be dishonored. *"Let them be ashamed. . . . Let them be confounded because of their shame."*

RESOLUTION OF FREEDOM

16 Let all those who seek You rejoice and be glad in
     You;
   Let such as love Your salvation say continually,
   "The LORD be magnified!"
17 But I *am* poor and needy;
   Yet the LORD thinks upon me.
      You *are* my help and my deliverer;
      Do not delay, O my God.

Ps. 40:16–17

Finally, David prays that all who *"seek"* the Lord may find His joy. The verb for *"seek"* means to "inquire" of the Lord, to ask of Him. Since God will answer, they will *"rejoice and be glad in [Him]."* Their joy becomes a worship of praise as they *"say continually, 'The Lord be magnified.' "* They bask in His *"salvation."*

David too wants the joy of his salvation. So, confessing that he is *"poor and needy,"* and certain that Yahweh still *"thinks upon"* him, he prays that God will act quickly since He is his *"help"* and his *"deliverer."* The God who brought him out of the "horrible pit" and the "miry clay" will do it again. David is right where he needs to be for God to act. As Jesus says, "Those who are well have no need of a physician, but those who are sick. I did not come to call the righteous, but sinners, to repentance" (Mark 2:17). David is ready to hear and heed that call.

Often we, like David, feel stuck in life—by our past, by our circumstances, by our sin, by our enemies. God wants to set us free. He pulls us up from the clay. He plants us on a rock. All that we can do is to wait patiently and cry to Him. He will do the rest.

CHAPTER FORTY-ONE

Raise Me Up!

Psalm 41

The psalms are life-experience commentaries on how fallen and evil this world is. When the church experiences her life here and now she is the church suffering and the church militant (Luther). The psalms are not written for times of peace, but for times of war. They witness to "fighting without and fear within" (2 Cor. 7:5). They challenge the naïve humanistic idealism of the liberal West. But they also have a sense of glory about them because in the midst of the battle God is King. He is the triumphant leader of Israel's armies and He is the one before whom all enemies must fall. There is a certain "realized eschatology" (C. H. Dodd) here which comes to fulfillment in the New Testament.

In Psalm 41 the writer speaks of a man facing illness and enemies, then reveals that he is that man. He has sinned, he is hounded by enemies, he is sick. His close friend has even turned against him. Now he calls upon God for mercy, asking for healing so that he can deal with his enemies and verify God's faithfulness to him.

Tradition, which we follow here, ascribes this psalm to David. The form contains elements both of thanksgiving and individual lament. The movement of thought progresses from a general blessing of the pious (vv. 1–3), to a description of need (vv. 4–9) and a cry for help (vv. 10–12), and concludes with a blessing of God (v. 13).

BLESSING FOR THE PIOUS

1 Blessed *is* he who considers the poor;
  The LORD will deliver him in time of trouble.
2 The LORD will preserve him and keep him alive,
  And he will be blessed on the earth;
  You will not deliver him to the will of his enemies.

3 The LORD will strengthen him on his bed of illness;
You will sustain him on his sickbed.

Ps. 41:1–3

David begins with general statements in the third person singular: *"Blessed* ["fully happy"] *is he who considers the poor."* This man will be considered by God. The reason for this is that God commands Israel to care for the poor (Deut. 15:7–11). Doing so is thus a sign of piety. The person who fulfills this command is close to God's heart, but when this command is disobeyed Israel is subject to God's wrath (see Jer. 5:28–29; Ezek. 18:12–13).

The promise of verse 1 evidences itself in preservation and blessing *"on the earth"* or, *"in the land."* Negatively, this blessing is manifest in that God *"will not deliver him to the will of his enemies." "The will of his enemies"* is, literally, "the greed of his enemies." That greed would be seen as they take his land.

Next, David says, *"The Lord will strengthen* ["support"] *him on his bed of illness."* Moreover, and here David turns to the direct address of prayer, *"You will sustain him on his sickbed."* The verb rendered "sustain" is poorly translated; it means "to turn, overturn, overthrow, change, transform." Thus David is saying that God "transforms" the pious person *"on his sickbed,"* namely, He restores him to health. The Lord is able to grant both His presence and power to the sick (cf. vv. 4, 10). These then are the full blessings of God: the godly are kept *"alive"* and *"blessed"* in the land; they are delivered from their *"enemies"* and healed from their diseases.

God doesn't promise us that we won't be sick in this fallen world. He does promise, however, not to desert us in our sickness. He is there to *"strengthen"* us with His presence. Moreover, He will transform us and heal us by His power. These promises change our attitudes toward illness. Disease is never a sign of blessing. God doesn't make us sick to give us rest or to teach us a lesson or to have us spend more time with Him. If we wanted to discipline our children, we wouldn't give them cancer! (Judith MacNutt). Sickness is evil. It is the absence of blessing. It is a part of the curse. God then comes against this enemy with His presence and power to heal. The church must not abandon healing to the medical profession or the Christian Science practitioner. God is in the healing business. He comes to help us improve and to make us well. We need to pray to these ends.

MERCY IN MISERY

4 I said, "LORD, be merciful to me;
  Heal my soul, for I have sinned against You."
5 My enemies speak evil of me:
  "When will he die, and his name perish?"
6 And if he comes to see *me,* he speaks lies;
  His heart gathers iniquity to itself;
  When he goes out, he tells *it.*
7 All who hate me whisper together against me;
  Against me they devise my hurt.
8 "An evil disease," *they say,* "clings to him.
  And *now* that he lies down, he will rise up no more."
9 Even my own familiar friend in whom I trusted,
  Who ate my bread,
  Has lifted up *his* heel against me.

                                                    Ps. 41:4–9

The generalizations concerning the person who "considers the poor" now become specific as they are applied to David. He needs the blessing of God for healing soul and body. Also he needs deliverance from his enemies. He prays first that God's mercy be manifested in forgiveness: *"Heal my soul, for I have sinned against You."* True healing begins in our relationship with God. Thus Jesus forgives the paralytic before He commands him to get up and walk (Mark 2:5–12). This is not to say that sin causes all disease. It does mean, however, that where sin has invaded our lives, it must be cleansed before its consequences can be removed. Merely to cure symptoms while their cause remains is ultimately futile.

Next, David turns to his enemies, who are using the occasion of his illness, assuming that sin is the cause, to attack him. They *"speak evil of me."* They desire his death, that *"his name perish."* In verse 6 David changes from the plural "enemies" to the singular "enemy." He describes a man's coming to visit him in his illness and speaking vain or empty words. *"His heart gathers iniquity"* as he surveys David's condition. Then he leaves and spreads lies about him.

This evokes the response of all David's enemies. They *"whisper together against me . . . they devise my hurt"* or, literally, "devise evil for me." The word *"disease"* in verse 8 is literally "a thing of ruin or worthlessness," "a Belial thing." This could be a curse which David's enemies utter against him, especially if "Belial" refers to the powers of chaos (that is Satan, see 2 Cor. 6:15). This curse would be the curse of death: *"he will rise up no more."*

Even David's trusted friend (literally, "my man of peace") who ate bread with him (the sign of intimacy, hospitality) has turned on him, a final experience of treachery that is also prophetic of Jesus' betrayal by Judas (see John 13:18). Thus David's experience of attack becomes Jesus' experience since He is David's son (Mark 10:47; Rom. 1:3), fulfilling David's reign and kingdom in His messianic work.

CRY FOR HELP

10 But You, O LORD, be merciful to me, and raise me
      up,
   That I may repay them.
11 By this I know that You are well pleased with me,
   Because my enemy does not triumph over me.
12 As for me, You uphold me in my integrity,
   And set me before Your face forever.

                                                      Ps. 41:10–12

With all of this evil upon him, David pleads again for mercy. Here God's mercy will be in David's physical healing, subsequent to the spiritual healing for which he has already prayed. As David experiences both forgiveness from sin and freedom from illness, he will *"repay"* those who plot against him, for his enemies are God's enemies.

With his healing comes assurance: *"By this I know that You are well pleased with me, / Because my enemy does not triumph over me,"* or, literally, "my enemy does not shout over me." The "shout" is that of a victorious army. The sign of God's favor is David's relief from his oppressors.

As far as David is concerned God *"upholds"* him in his *"integrity,"* which is the *"integrity"* of his trust in Yahweh, and restores him to divine favor: *"And [You] set me before Your face forever."* Here is full healing, to be in the presence of the Lord.

BLESSING UPON GOD

13 Blessed *be* the LORD God of Israel
   From everlasting to everlasting!
   Amen and Amen.

                                                      Ps. 41:13

Certain that his prayer is answered, David blesses the covenant God. He is to be praised through all eternity: *"From everlasting to everlasting!"* David then adds: "Amen and Amen," that is, "Yes and Yes again."

In Psalm 41 David expects God to act for him in the midst of his sin and suffering. He asks for deliverance, healing, protection, and the eternal presence of the Lord. These are his expectations and experiences. As this psalm was added to the Psalter, these same expectations and experiences became those of God's people. Is this true also for us? Do we expect God's healing? His deliverance? Is forgiveness a doctrine or an experience?

This psalm stands in judgment upon a sick and unbelieving church until we join in David's acceptance of the mercy and power of God.

CHAPTER FORTY-TWO

A Soul Thirsty for God

Psalm 42

Augustine has said that all of us have a "God-shaped vacuum" which only He can fill. Most people, unfortunately, deny this in their pride of wanting to control their own lives. In their rebellion they want their will rather than God's will to be done. They look for human, worldly power rather than the power of God's Spirit. They seek beauty rather than the One who creates both beauty and our ability to perceive it. They pursue a chemical rather than a spiritual high. Thus rather than worshiping the Creator, they worship the creation (Rom. 1:25)—that which is finite rather than infinite and that which is passing rather than that which is lasting. And yet, the God-shaped vacuum can only be filled by God. It rejects all substitutes. This creates a heart-hunger, a gnawing spiritual emptiness that prepares us for Psalms 42–43. Like the psalmist's soul, our souls begin to pant for God.

Here then the psalmist is in agony. He longs to know the presence of God. He also longs to be delivered from his enemies. This will lift his grief and his cast-down soul. His memory goes back to happier days worshiping in the temple, and he longs to experience this again. In the midst of his tears, however, he also has hope as he concludes, "For I shall yet praise Him." Then his panting soul will be satisfied again.

Psalms 42 and 43 need to be taken together. The repetition of the refrain in 42:5, 42:11, and 43:5 suggests that they were originally one. Then, too, the sense of God's silence (42:3, 9–10; 43:2), the oppression of enemies (42:9–10; 43:1–2), and the longing for temple worship are themes that are common to both (42:4; 43:3–4). They are treated as one work here.

The author of these psalms is unknown. Tradition ascribes the first one to the "sons of Korah," who were probably a family of temple singers (see *Introduction*). With Psalm 41 we end the first formal grouping or "book" of the psalms which, with the exception of Psalms 1–2, 10, and 33 are attributed to David. Psalm 42 begins the Elohistic Psalter in which God is addressed, not as Yahweh but now as Elohim (referring to the Hebrew names). The form of these psalms is an individual lament.

The psalm (speaking of 42 and 43 as a unit) opens with an expression of spiritual hunger made more severe by the haunting memory of temple worship and hope (42:1–5). This is followed by an exposition of the psalmist's problems (42:6–10) and a call for hope and vindication (42:11–43:2). This will result, once again, in restored worship (43:3–5).

Spiritual Hunger

1 As the deer pants for the water brooks,
　So pants my soul for You, O God.
2 My soul thirsts for God, for the living God.
　When shall I come and appear before God?
3 My tears have been my food day and night,
　While they continually say to me,
　"Where *is* your God?"

Ps. 42:1–3

The psalmist begins with a compelling and beloved image. He thirsts for God as a deer thirsts for water in the desert. The *"water brooks"* are springs which flow continually from subterranean rivers. In John 7:37–38 Jesus promises that those who come to Him and drink will have these streams flowing from their hearts. By this He meant the Holy Spirit who would be given to believers (John 7:39).

Verse 2 then repeats the thought. The psalmist's *"soul"* is himself, and the living God will satisfy him in the same way that streams of water satisfy the deer. Do we have this same thirst? Do we pant for God? Or do we pant for sex, drugs, and rock-and-roll? Do we pant for Jaguars, holidays on the Riviera, and certificates of deposit? The psalmist's thirst is no vague spirituality. His soul pants for the *"living God."* Here is an elemental need that must be met. Thus Jesus promises: "Blessed are those who hunger and thirst for righteousness, / For they shall be filled" (Matt. 5:6).

The longing for God provokes a question in verse 2. The intent of the question is, "When shall I come to the temple where God dwells and see His face?" (cf. 42:4; 43:3–4).

However, in God's absence and in the inability to go up to Jerusalem and worship, the psalmist grieves. His tears feed him *"day and night,"* that is, continually. They are his elemental *"food"* ("bread"). He is also strung by hostile people around him who ask mockingly, *"Where is your God?"*

HAUNTING MEMORY

> 4 When I remember these *things,*
> I pour out my soul within me.
> For I used to go with the multitude;
> I went with them to the house of God,
> With the voice of joy and praise,
> With a multitude that kept a pilgrim feast.
>
> *Ps. 42:4*

As the psalmist's mind goes back to happier days, his memory only reinforces his sadness and longing. What he remembers is worship, his procession *"with the multitude"* to God's *"house."* He hears echoing in his mind the *"voice of joy and praise."* The noun for *"joy"* here is "ringing cry." Psalm 100:1 exhorts us, "Make a joyful shout to the Lord, all you lands." This is the appropriate way in which to come into the Lord's house. The psalmist also remembers the *"multitude"* gathered with him, keeping a *"pilgrim feast,"* or a "pilgrimage."

This picture of the sense of deep loss raises questions about worship.

Do we even remember our worship? If it were taken from us would we experience grief? How do we go into God's house? Many of our churches today contain more spectators than participants. In some there is a cold formality rather than expressed joy. The presence of other people even seems to bother us rather than help us communally to celebrate before the Lord. Church renewal today begins with the renewal of worship. The good news is that this is happening across the world.

CONFIDENT HOPE

5 Why are you cast down, O my soul?
   And *why* are you disquieted within me?
   Hope in God, for I shall yet praise Him
   For the help of His countenance.

Ps. 42:5

The memory of worship now provokes an introspective question: *"Why are you cast down, O my soul?"* As Kierkegaard notes, our greatness and our pain is that we can transcend ourselves and become self-conscious of our own being. This happens here to the psalmist as he reflects on his grief and depression. He continues: *"And why are you disquieted within me?"* The verb for *"disquieted"* means "to murmur, growl, roar." His soul is *"cast down"* in discouragement and turbulent or agitated at the same time. Next, the psalmist exhorts his soul: *"Hope in God."* In this hope he knows that *"praise"* will return because he will receive *"the help of His countenance"* or, literally, the "salvation" or "deliverance" of His face. To paraphrase the thought, God will restore him, delivering him from his brokenness, and manifest His face to him once again; this is his salvation (cf. 42:11; 43:5).

ADDRESS TO GOD

6 O my God, my soul is cast down within me;
   Therefore I will remember You from the land of the
      Jordan,
   And from the heights of Hermon,
   From the Hill Mizar.
7 Deep calls unto deep at the noise of Your waterfalls;
   All Your waves and billows have gone over me.

8 The LORD will command His lovingkindness in the
    daytime,
  And in the night His song *shall be* with me—
  A prayer to the God of my life.

Ps. 42:6–8

The turn in the meditation to direct prayer is important. In seeking comfort the psalmist again taps into his memory, not of the temple, but of those other places where God has met him in the past: the land of the Jordan (Israel), Mount Hermon (in Lebanon), and the unknown Hill Mizar. In all these places, the psalmist says, *"I will remember You"* or, "I remember You."

However, *"Deep calls unto deep at the noise of Your waterfalls"* (v. 7). Thus the depths of the psalmist's depression call to the depths of God's *"waterfalls"* and His *"waves and billows"* which have all *"gone over him."* This suggests that the psalmist's sense of loss and of God's absence comes from the divine wrath represented by chaotic engulfing waters (cf. 42:9; 43:2). Therefore, while he remembers where God has met him with His "yes," (v. 6), he also now feels the divine "no."

Nevertheless, the psalmist trusts that God's *"lovingkindness,"* His covenant-love, will be his *"in the daytime"* and God's *"song"* will take him through the *"night."* The final sentence, *"A prayer to the God of my life,"* may refer to the song in the previous clause. Thus it would translate: "His song shall be with me—even a prayer to the God of my life."

Here then the psalmist gives us clues for dealing with the sense of God's absence, His no. First, we must remember when God has met us in the past. Second, we must trust His love for the future; even in the night, He will give us a song. In Christ, however, we may add a third point: God's *"waves and billows"* have been placed upon His Son. Therefore, when we flee to Christ we flee into the open arms of the Father and there is a "welcome home" party for us (Luke 15:11 ff.).

QUESTION TO GOD

9 I will say to God my Rock,
    "Why have You forgotten me?
  Why do I go mourning because of the oppression of
    the enemy?"

10 *As* with a breaking of my bones,
   My enemies reproach me,
   While they say to me all day long,
   "Where *is* your God?"

Ps. 42:9–10

Having addressed God, the psalmist now questions Him. God is his *"Rock,"* his "security." His security, however, has become his insecurity, and he is in *"mourning because of the oppression of the enemy."* During God's absence and silence, the enemy has come upon the psalmist with scoffing and reproach, asking continually, *"Where is your God?"* When he remembers God, why does God forget him? Why this grief before his enemies? How is he to deal with their reproach which mocks and haunts him, unnerving him as if all his *"bones"* were broken?

CONFIDENT HOPE

11 Why are you cast down, O my soul?
   And why are you disquieted within me?
   Hope in God;
   For I shall yet praise Him,
   The help of my countenance and my God.

Ps. 42:11

The oppression of the psalmist's enemy, the silence of God, and David's grief over both lead to a repetition of the refrain from verse 5. Why is his soul cast down? Clearly the answer is God is absent. Yet the psalmist cries, *"Hope in God."* He still has a future because God is the living God: *"I shall yet praise Him."* The final clause is changed from "For the help of His countenance" to *"The help of my countenance and my God."* Thus he will praise God for the *"help"* of his *"countenance"* or "face," namely, for the salvation of himself, and he will praise God for God Himself.

CHAPTER FORTY-THREE

A Soul Thirsty for God (Continued)

Psalm 43

CALL FOR VINDICATION

1 Vindicate me, O God,
   And plead my cause against an ungodly nation;
   Oh, deliver me from the deceitful and unjust man!
2 For You *are* the God of my strength;
   Why do You cast me off?
   Why do I go mourning because of the oppression of
      the enemy?

Ps. 43:1–2

Taking courage from the refrain in 42:11, the psalmist now calls upon God: *"Vindicate me, O God."* The word for *"vindicate"* is a legal term, calling for judgment. Next, the psalmist wants God to be his defense attorney: *"Plead my cause against an ungodly nation."* The *"ungodly nation"* is a nation of covenant breakers, namely, the Jews. The parallel line continues: *"Oh, deliver me from the deceitful and unjust man!"* The word for *"man"* may be a collective noun and thus be equivalent to *"men."* These enemies are *"deceitful and unjust"* in their attacks upon the psalmist (42:3; 42:10).

Since God is his *"strength"* (cf. 42:9, *"my Rock"*), why, he asks, is he now *"cast . . . off"*? Why the grief over his oppression? Again, the *"oppression"* is, for him, a sign of God's rejection which is sustained by God's silence.

CALL FOR RESTORATION

3 Oh, send out Your light and Your truth!
   Let them lead me;
   Let them bring me to Your holy hill
   And to Your tabernacle.

4 Then I will go to the altar of God,
   To God my exceeding joy;
   And on the harp I will praise You,
   O God, my God.

Ps. 43:3–4

Here the psalmist asks God to act, sending His *"light"* and *"truth."* They will then lead him back to Mount Zion, God's *"holy hill"* in Jerusalem (see Ps. 2:6) where God's house or *"tabernacle"* stands. *"Light"* illumines the way, just as the pillar of fire led Israel through the wilderness. *"Truth"* defines the way, or is the way itself (Ps. 25:4–5). God sends His *"light"* and His *"truth"* to lead us to Himself. Thus His Son is the light and the truth, and we come to the Father by Him.

The psalmist's goal is to be able to enter again into the presence of God. Thus when he gets to God's *"tabernacle"* he *"will go to the altar,"* where he will meet God, his *"exceeding joy."* As worship is restored there, his *"joy"* at God's presence will be expressed in praise on the *"harp"* or "lyre" (a stringed instrument with three to twelve strings). God will again be personal for him. To the psalmist, He will be *"my God."*

Only God's *"light"* can dispel the darkness of grief, depression, and our opponents' cynical taunts. This "light" brings deliverance, healing, and guidance back into God's presence where we can worship once again.

The most miserable Christians are those who know Christ but are not living in Him. They have the worst of both worlds. They can no longer be satisfied in their old life, yet neither are they satisfied in the Lord. Over the years, however, I have seen many of them restored. Then, in the presence of God, the joy comes, and the work of restoration leads to an outburst of worship. This is the ministry of the Holy Spirit in renewing God's people to "joy inexpressible" (1 Pet. 1:8).

CONFIDENT HOPE

5 Why are you cast down, O my soul?
   And why are you disquieted within me?
   Hope in God;
   For I shall yet praise Him,
   The help of my countenance and my God.

Ps. 43:5

The final refrain now becomes a refrain of strength. There is no reason for the psalmist's soul to be *"cast down."* God's "light" will come. Hope will not be disappointed. Praise will be his in the presence of God.

Throughout these two psalms, the use of the refrain builds. In 42:4, there is memory of lost worship and then the refrain. In 42:9–10, there are the attack of the psalmist's enemies and God's silence and then the refrain. Finally, in 43:3, there is the cry for "light" and "truth" and then the refrain. Thus we see the quenching of spiritual thirst by the memory of God's past goodness, honesty in grief and disappointment, and then prayer for light and truth to take us back to Zion. There, like the deer, we will be restored at the "water brooks" of God's Spirit and presence.

CHAPTER FORTY-FOUR

Boldness in Prayer

Psalm 44

Often in God's work to be faithful is not to be successful. The clearest example of this is in the ministry of Jesus. He was faithful in preaching the good news of the kingdom, in healing the sick, in delivering the possessed, in teaching the multitudes, and in training His disciples. Yet all rejected Him at the end and His enemies crucified Him. By sundown on that first Good Friday as Jesus' followers limped away in despair, it seemed that Satan had won.

Again and again in the history of the church, those faithful to God have experienced similar defeat. Even in our own times untold numbers of Christians died in Hitler's gas chambers or now languish in Russia's *gulags*. Other nations have made Christians the objects of military and police massacres. To be faithful is not necessarily to be successful.

Psalm 44 is written in the context of Israel's faithfulness and defeat. A military campaign has been lost. The enemy has taken the spoils, sold captives as slaves and deported them to "the nations." The king, who is also the commander of the army, has been dishonored, and the battle has resulted in great slaughter.

While the memory of past triumphs remains, and the hope for fresh victories has not died, the hard fact is that God's people are defeated and Israel's weakness brings reproach among the nations.

This psalm does not carry a spirit of repentance brought about by God's judgment upon Israel's sin. Rather, it justifies Israel before God. She knows that victory is only in the strength of Yahweh. At the same time, the claim is made that God's people have remained true to Him. The question is: If Israel is faithful, why is she not successful? How can a faithful people be overrun?

One possible answer is that although Israel has walked with God, she has not waited upon Him, and thus she has gone into the wrong battle at the wrong time. Whether this is true or not cannot be demonstrated. The fact is, however, that God has not gone into battle with her and success has been denied.

This psalm is described by commentators as a communal lament. Its author is the king and thus, the commander of Israel's army. "We" refers to Israel or to her troops. The date of composition is unknown.

The psalm itself moves from the historical memory of past victories (vv. 1-3) to a call for victory again (vv. 4-8). All this is a prelude to an extended complaint over defeat (vv. 9-22) followed by a final call to action (vv. 23-26).

You Gave Victory of Old

1 We have heard with our ears, O God,
   Our fathers have told us,
   The deeds You did in their days,
   In days of old:
2 You drove out the nations with Your hand,
   But them You planted;
   You afflicted the peoples, and cast them out.
3 For they did not gain possession of the land by their
       own sword,
   Nor did their own arm save them;
   But it was Your right hand, Your arm, and the light
       of Your countenance,
   Because You favored them.

Ps. 44:1-3

The psalmist begins by reminding God that the present generation has heard of the great deeds of Yahweh as they were told by *"our fathers,"* that is, orally transmitted and publicly read through the generations in a chain of tradition. The *"days of old"* are identified in the following verses as the time of Israel's entrance into the Promised Land.

First, God *"drove out the nations with [His] hand."* The verb for *"drove out"* means "to dispossess." Second, Israel was *"planted"* in the land in their place. Thus, in Isaiah Israel is God's vineyard (5:1 ff.) and God's "trees of righteousness, / The planting of the Lord" (61:3). *"You afflicted the peoples, and cast them out"* may also be rendered "You afflicted the peoples, but spread them [Israel] out" (like the branches of a tree; see Gen. 49:22). This sustains the parallelism of verse 2.

The stress on God's action continues in verse 3. God's people did not take the land *"by their own sword,"* nor were they saved (or "delivered" from their enemies in the land) by *"their own arm."* It was God's *"right hand,"* the hand of power, His strong *"arm,"* and His presence—*"the light of [His] countenance"* that gave them the land and protected them. Thus Moses' request was fulfilled when he told God, "If Your presence does not go with us, do not bring us up from here. For how then will it be known that Your people and I have found grace in Your sight, except You go with us?" (Exod. 33:15–16).

The reason for these works of God is stated in verse 3: *"Because You favored them."* The verb for *"favored"* means "to accept, to be pleased with." It was simply because of God's love that He blessed Israel (Deut. 7:7–8).

Like Israel, the church must make the same confession. Our victory over our enemies, our entrance into God's land of promise, is all by His word, not ours. "For by grace you have been saved through faith, and that not of yourselves; it is the gift of God, not of works, lest anyone should boast" (Eph. 2:8–9).

GIVE US VICTORY AGAIN

4 You are my King, O God;
  Command victories for Jacob.
5 Through You we will push down our enemies;
  Through Your name we will trample those who rise
    up against us.
6 For I will not trust in my bow,
  Nor shall my sword save me.

7 But You have saved us from our enemies,
    And have put to shame those who hated us.
8 In God we boast all day long,
    And praise Your name forever.   Selah

Ps. 44:4–8

What was true in the "days of old," the psalmist argues, ought to be true now. God is still the sovereign ruler of Israel: *"You are my King, O God."* As King, God is also the commander of Israel's armies: *"Command victories for Jacob."* The Hebrew plural, *"victories,"* signifies that they are full and complete. *"Jacob"* is a poetic name for Israel.

What triumphs are being requested are specified in verse 5: *"Through You we will push down our enemies; / Through Your name we will trample those who rise up against us."* The prepositional phrases *"through You"* and *"through Your name"* mean "by Your power and Your authority." The verbs *"push down"* ("gore") and *"trample"* suggest that God is like a bull goring and stomping on his enemy.

Moreover, the psalmist refuses to trust in his own *"bow"* or *"sword"*; it is God whom he trusts, for it is He who has *"saved"* Israel from her foes and sent her *"enemies"* off in the *"shame"* of defeat. Israel's response to God's work now is worship: *"In God we boast* ["praise publicly"] *all day long, / And praise* [give thanks to] *Your name forever."*

How do we handle defeat? At this point the psalmist has employed memory of past victories and hope for future triumphs. Moreover, his hope is not wishful thinking but is based upon what the Lord has done—His word and His work. In our darkness we have the same resources. As Bob Munger often says, "Don't doubt in the darkness what God has shown you in the light."

COMPLAINT OVER DEFEAT

9 But You have cast *us* off and put us to shame,
    And You do not go out with our armies.
10 You make us turn back from the enemy,
    And those who hate us have taken spoil for
        themselves.
11 You have given us up like sheep *intended* for food,
    And have scattered us among the nations.
12 You sell Your people for *next to* nothing,
    And are not enriched by selling them.

13 You make us a reproach to our neighbors,
    A scorn and a derision to those all around us.
14 You make us a byword among the nations,
    A shaking of the head among the peoples.
15 My dishonor *is* continually before me,
    And the shame of my face has covered me,
16 Because of the voice of him who reproaches and
        reviles,
    Because of the enemy and the avenger.
17 All this has come upon us;
    But we have not forgotten You,
    Nor have we dealt falsely with Your covenant.
18 Our heart has not turned back,
    Nor have our steps departed from Your way;
19 But You have severely broken us in the place of
        jackals,
    And covered us with the shadow of death.
20 If we had forgotten the name of our God,
    Or stretched out our hands to a foreign god,
21 Would not God search this out?
    For He knows the secrets of the heart.
22 Yet for Your sake we are killed all day long;
    We are accounted as sheep for the slaughter.

                                                    Ps. 44:9–22

The psalmist is a realist. Despite memory and hope he now turns to the sting of failure. At this moment there is no victory. God's people are shamed by defeat, not their enemies. The basis for this is divine rejection: *"But You have cast us off."* Israel has gone to war without God: *"And You do not go out with our armies."*

If it is true, as the psalm suggests, that Israel has been faithful to God and doesn't deserve defeat for her sins (see vv. 17–22), then is it possible that she has gone to fight the wrong war, presuming upon God's presence rather than waiting for His will and *then* His presence? As we have already seen, Moses demands the presence of God before he moves. Are not Israel and the church, however, quite willing to assume God's blessing and then launch ahead with battles, plans, and programs? Too often we, like the disciples, come up empty-handed. We have to say with Peter that we have fished all night and caught nothing. This report could be inscribed over many a church and many a Christian work. Idealism, pressing need, even scriptural justification are not enough. Has God told us to move? Has He mandated our ministry? If not, He won't *"go out with our armies."*

With God absent from the battle, Israel runs away in defeat. The psalmist sees this as God's doing. *"You make us turn back from the enemy."* Moreover, Israel is despoiled by those who *"hate"* her. The plunder is theirs. God has made His people *"like sheep intended for food"* (v. 11), *"sheep"* being docile and dumb (see Isa. 53:7). Thus Israel is *"scattered,"* deported, and dispersed into slavery *"among the nations."* God sells His *"people for next to nothing."* They are worthless, and God gets nothing in return: *And [You] are not enriched by selling them."*

Adding to her shame, Israel is now a *"reproach"* to the nations around her. They *"scorn"* and deride her. Her name is like a bad joke: *"You make us a byword among the nations."* A *"byword"* here is a "proverb"; Israel is proverbial for her disgrace. People shake their heads in a taunting manner. Here are early roots of anti-Semitism.

To this disgrace, the psalmist, whom we hold to be the king, now adds his own witness. The noun for *"dishonor"* in verse 15 means "insult, reproach." Also, his *"face"* is covered with *"shame."* The twofold source is verbal taunts—*"the voice of him who reproaches"*—and violent enemies.

The whole situation is black. God has abandoned His people. All other degradations come from this as Israel is defeated by her enemies. This includes her goods being plundered and her people being deported, sold into slavery. Now she is reproached by those about her and her king is disgraced.

Once again, there is an analogy here to much Christian work. If God's blessing is not upon it, however much emotional enthusiasm there may be, the enemies (the world, the flesh, and the Devil) will triumph. Towers will be half built (Luke 14:28–30) and in the end, Christian supporters will be dispersed and leadership discredited.

Nevertheless, despite defeat, the psalmist protests in verse 17 that Israel has not turned from God. Moreover, God's people continue to keep his *"covenant,"* that is, they fulfill their convenant obligations (see Exod. 19:4–6; 24:7–8). The psalmist assures God (v. 18) that their obedience has come from the heart (that is, mind). Then, too, the *"steps"* or walk that Israel takes through life is in God's "way," that is, the way of "revelation," or Torah (see Ps. 1).

Nevertheless, God has not responded favorably. The *"place of jackals"* in verse 19 is the desert (see Isa. 34:13–14). Either Israel's armies have been defeated here, or the land has now been made a desert. Also death's *"shadow"* is upon them.

In verses 20–21 the psalmist denies apostasy: *"If we had forgotten the name of our God, / Or stretched out our hands to a foreign god, / Would not God search this out?"* To remember God's *"name"* is to worship Him and obey Him. To forget His *"name"* is to deny Him. Stretching out the hands is a familiar position of worship, surrender, and praise (1 Kings 8:22; Heb. 12:12; 1 Tim. 2:8). If God's people, however, had turned to other gods in worship, certainly God would have known because *"He knows the secrets of the heart."*

Despite their faithfulness, then, Israel is *"killed all day long; / We are accounted as sheep for the slaughter"* (v. 22). Here the psalmist is not referring to just one military defeat; Israel is in a time of profound suffering (cf. v. 11). Paul employs this verse in Romans 8:36 to make the point that although Christians may suffer, they are secure in Christ's love.

Thus in verses 9–22 Israel remains faithful to God in the midst of national disaster. Similarly, Paul tells the Corinthians that in Asia he despaired of life itself. Then he adds, "Yes, we had the sentence of death in ourselves, that we should not trust in ourselves but God who raises the dead" (2 Cor. 1:9).

CALL FOR INTERVENTION

23 Awake! Why do You sleep, O Lord?
   Arise! Do not cast *us* off forever.
24 Why do You hide Your face,
   And forget our affliction and our oppression?
25 For our soul is bowed down to the dust;
   Our body clings to the ground.
26 Arise for our help,
   And redeem us for Your mercies' sake.

Ps. 44:23–26

The charge that Yahweh sleeps (v. 23) is a bold, chiding one. It comes in anger and despair, but also in trust. God is still King and can bring victory. The psalmist pleads for Israel not to be rejected forever. Next he asks why God hides His *"face,"* forgetting the *"affliction"* of defeat and the *"oppression"* by Israel's enemies. But it is God's custom in judgment to hide His face and His forgetting means rejection (cf. v. 20).

Behind these questions is the present despair. To be in the *"dust"*

(v. 25) is to be humiliated, defeated, and judged (Gen. 3:14; 1 Sam. 2:8). Only God can help. Thus in verse 26 the psalmist ends by calling upon God to act. The word for *"mercies"* is the same word used for covenant-love. Here then is an appeal for help and deliverance based on the covenant. No longer is the faithfulness or merit of Israel the basis for appeal; now God's faithfulness to His own commitment is simply addressed: "Be true to Yourself."

Like the Book of Job, Psalm 44 faces the issue of righteous suffering. Theology says that if Israel is faithful God will act. What happens when this theology doen't work?

Our response is soul-searching introspection: we think we must be in sin. Another response is recognition of the power of the enemy: Satan is the god of this world—we must be better armed for battle. Still another response, the one in this psalm, is to call boldly upon God: "We are true to You. Why aren't You true to us?" In the Bible, God loves people who contend with Him. They knock at midnight demanding bread (Luke 11:5–8). They refuse to let Him go until He blesses them (Gen. 32:22–32). They are brash in prayer (Luke 11:8).

In this psalm Israel has the experience of being faithful but not successful. We may find ourselves in similar circumstances. What of the pious Christian whose children are on drugs? What of the missionary who makes few converts? Psalm 44 tells us to be bold in prayer. Don't be afraid to confront God. Don't hide your anger; He knows your heart.

As you confront Him you may discover that you went off to war in His name, but He didn't tell you to go and thus He didn't go with you. You must wait on Him and for Him. In His time, He will act.

CHAPTER FORTY-FIVE

The King's Wedding Psalm

Psalm 45

Not surprisingly, this psalm has been seen by many as referring to Christ, and His bride—the church. As David's son, standing in his royal line, Jesus inherits his throne, his kingdom, and all the promises which God made to him (see 2 Sam. 7:8–16). Thus as David is the ideal king for Israel, Jesus consummates his kingdom.

At the same time, the Old Testament as a whole is prophetic and eschatological: history moves under the sovereign will of God's fulfilling His purposes. Thus all of it finds its goal in the New Testament as it points beyond itself and Israel to the final consummation of God's kingdom, His reign, and rule through His Messiah.

Psalm 45 is composed to celebrate the king's wedding. After a description of his royal glory and kingdom his bride, the queen, is introduced. She is encouraged to forget her people and her father's house. The king is now her Lord. Finally, she is described in all her glory as she is brought into the royal household. The oriental court poetry here includes both prophetic and wisdom motifs ("Listen, O daughter, / Consider and incline your ear." Cf. Prov. 4:1; 14:1). Its purpose is to praise the king and it includes instruction for the new queen to help her enter his palace as his bride. If this is true, there will also be instruction for the church which becomes Christ's bride and is married to Him by faith (Luther).

Commentators describe this psalm as a royal psalm. Its author is unknown. It is traditionally ascribed to "the sons of Korah" (see chap. 42) and called "a song of love." The movement of thought is from the king (vv. 1–9) to the queen (vv. 10–17). In verses 1–5 the king is praised and in verses 6–9 his relationship to God's kingdom is extolled. Following this, the preparation and presentation of the queen are described in verses 10–15. The psalm ends with a prophetic word about sons in verses 16–17.

Praise to the King

1 My heart is overflowing with a good theme;
  I recite my composition concerning the King;
  My tongue *is* the pen of a ready writer.
2 You are fairer than the sons of men;
  Grace is poured upon Your lips;
  Therefore God has blessed You forever.
3 Gird Your sword upon *Your* thigh, O Mighty One,
  With Your glory and Your majesty.
4 And in Your majesty ride prosperously because of
    truth, humility, *and* righteousness;
  And Your right hand shall teach You awesome things.
5 Your arrows *are* sharp in the heart of the King's
    enemies;
  The peoples fall under You.

Ps. 45:1–5

Verse 1 stands as a preface to the entire psalm, telling us who is writing, what he is writing about, and how he writes. Here the author introduces himself as a court scribe who has composed this psalm for the king's wedding. He speaks from his *"heart,"* or *"mind," "overflowing with a good theme."* The verb for *"overflowing"* means "to stir or bubble over," referring to the overflow of his heart. The *"theme"* is *"good"* and is defined as *"concerning the King."* The composition is oral, it is recited, and the psalmist's *"tongue is [his] pen."* He identifies himself as a *"ready writer"* or "scribe," the word for *"ready"* probably meaning "skilled."

The thesis of the psalm is the supremacy of the king: *"You are fairer than the sons of men."* The word for "fair" means "beautiful." The king is the ideal of humanity. He towers above all others.

His greatness is because *"grace is poured upon Your lips."* The word *"grace"* here may denote how the king speaks or what the king says, or, probably, both. He speaks graciously because he is gracious. His graciousness leads us to conclude that he has divine blessing: *"Therefore God has blessed You forever."* So Christ, our King, is full of grace and truth (John 1:14), and He gives us grace from His fullness (John 1:16).

The king's greatness also comes from his power in battle as a warrior. This is pictured by the sword that he puts on: *"Gird Your sword upon Your thigh, O Mighty One"* (v. 3). Here he is called *"Mighty One"* and bears *"glory"* and *"majesty."* The adjective *"Mighty"* here serves as a title and means "strong, valiant." Thus his *"glory"* and *"majesty"* sur-round him and are manifested as his *"enemies"* are defeated. So Jesus, our King, bears the very glory of God (John 1:14). He, too, is armed with the sword of God's word from His mouth (Rev. 1:16), which He employs in battle (Rev. 19:15). As our divine King, Jesus is worshiped in heaven by a numberless host who give Him *"glory"* and *"majesty,"* saying, "Worthy is the Lamb who was slain / To receive power and riches and wisdom, / And strength and honor and glory and blessing!" (Rev. 5:12).

Next, the king rides in his *"majesty,"* *"prosperously"* ("successfully"). However, he does not wield raw power, but is prosperous *"because of truth, humility, and righteousness."* His success then is directed by his character. He is true and trustworthy, humble, pious, and righteous. He upholds the covenant relationships. Jesus rides into Jerusalem as our King, fulfilling Old Testament prophecy. He comes sitting on a donkey. This expresses His humble character. He is also true and trust-worthy, and fulfills all righteousness.

The king's *"right hand"* teaches him *"awesome things."* The word for *"awesome things"* means "mighty acts" and refers to the great deeds that the king does. The *"right hand"* symbolism refers to the king's might in battle. When he draws his bow, his arrows find their mark; they *"are sharp in the heart of the King's enemies"* (v. 5). Thus, under his authority and judgment, nations fall.

Once again, this picture is fulfilled by Jesus, who reigns at God's right hand, exercising the very victory, authority, and power of God. The arrows of His word broke the power of His enemies in His public ministry. At the command of Jesus, men followed Him, the sick were healed, and demons were cast out. This ministry is to go on in His name in the church today. The Book of Acts witnesses to this extension as the kingdom of Christ moves out into the world.

GOD'S KINGDOM AND HIS KING

6 Your throne, O God, *is* forever and ever;
  A scepter of righteousness *is* the scepter of Your
    kingdom.
7 You love righteousness and hate wickedness;
  Therefore God, Your God, has anointed You
  With the oil of gladness more than Your companions.

8 All Your garments are scented with myrrh and aloes
   and cassia,
Out of the ivory palaces, by which they have made
   You glad.
9 Kings' daughters *are* among Your honorable women;
At Your right hand stands the queen in gold from
   Ophir.

Ps. 45:6–9

We come now to a central issue and text in this psalm. *"Your throne, O God, is forever and ever"* (v. 6). To whom are these words addressed? If they are addressed to God then the problem becomes the sudden change in subject matter from God to the king without any transition. If they are addressed to the king, however, how can he be called *"God"?* Some have proposed that the king here is deified, after the Egyptian manner. This is impossible in light of the rest of Scripture, however. Others have proposed emending the text. For Hebrews 1:8 the solution is simple: this verse is prophetic and messianic; it is addressed to the Son of God, here called *"God."*

The real solution may be that verse 6 is addressed to God, Elohim, and verse 7 is addressed to the reigning king in the original context. There is no transition, however, because verse 6 is also prophetically addressed to the Son of God, the coming messianic King, as is also verse 7. Often in Old Testament prophecy, there is a double meaning; there are both immediate application and long-term fulfillment, points that are closely connected. When verses 6 and 7 are fulfilled by Christ, they apply equally to Him. God's *"throne"* in heaven is eternal, *"forever and ever."* Moreover the sign of His kingdom, His *"scepter"* (the Hebrew word probably denotes a military weapon) is a *"scepter of righteousness"* ("uprightness, justice"). His reign is exercised in righteousness.

The earthly king and the Messiah both *"love righteousness and hate wickedness; / Therefore God, Your God, has anointed You / With the oil of gladness."* This anointing is probably a reference to the coronation of the king. The *"oil of gladness"* is used in the ceremony itself and is also connected with the Holy Spirit. When David was anointed king by Samuel, oil was poured on his head and the Spirit came upon him (1 Sam. 16:13). In Jesus' baptism, as well, He was both called into His messianic ministry and anointed with the Holy Spirit (Matt. 3:16–17). Often the Holy Spirit is also identified with joy or *"gladness"* (see Gal. 5:22). Here the king receives an extravagant portion of oil, *"more than Your companions."*

Having described God's (and the king's) throne and scepter and the king's anointing, verse 8 now pictures his garments. They are *"scented with myrrh,"* a solid or gum resin from a thorny shrub; *"aloes,"* a substance from the sandalwood tree used for perfumes and incense; and *"cassia,"* an aromatic bark used in perfumes. The garments also come from *"ivory palaces,"* namely palaces decorated with ivory. The final phrase, *"by which they have made You glad,"* is best re-translated: "The stringed instruments have made you glad."

The mention of *"myrrh"* reminds us of the wise men's gift to the Christ-child. Also Jesus was anointed with costly oil before His death, and His body was anointed with spices when He was buried.

The psalmist describes the king's attendants, who include the *"kings' daughters,"* the ladies of the harem, and the *"queen"* who stands in the place of honor at the king's *"right hand."* She is adorned with *"gold from Ophir"* (see 1 Kings 10:11). *"Ophir"* is probably in Saudia Arabia today.

If we look at this passage in light of both Old and New Testament theology, the following points can be made. First, the earthly king simply represents and manifests the heavenly King, God Himself. Thus verse 6 speaks of God's throne where His sovereignty, His scepter, reveals itself in righteousness. Likewise, the earthly king is to manifest God's righteousness in his reign. So Jesus proclaims the presence of God's kingdom in His ministry and makes that kingdom known by defeating demonic enemies and restoring broken spirits and bodies (see Mark 1:15 ff.). Second, based upon God's righteousness, the king loves righteousness and hates wickedness. We see this demonstrated throughout Jesus' ministry. Third, the king is also anointed with oil as Jesus was anointed with God's Spirit, and the king smells of rich spices, which also played a role in Jesus' life. Finally, next to the king stands the queen, sharing his authority and beauty. Jesus' queen is His church. He has purchased His bride to "present it to Himself a glorious church, not having spot or wrinkle or any such thing, but that it should be holy and without blemish" (Eph. 5:27). The church too shares His authority; it is seated with the reigning Christ (Eph. 2:6).

PREPARATION OF THE QUEEN

10 Listen, O daughter,
    Consider and incline your ear;
    Forget your own people also, and your father's house;

11 So the King will greatly desire your beauty;
   Because He *is* your Lord, worship Him.
12 And the daughter of Tyre *will come* with a gift;
   The rich among the people will seek your favor.

Ps. 45:10–12

As the psalmist now turns to the queen's preparation for marriage, he adopts a wisdom-teaching mode, characteristic of the court: *"Listen, O daughter."* The first point made to the new queen is that she *"forget"* her *"own people"* and her *"father's house."* If her *"own people"* refers to another nation, this means that the queen is a foreigner. It may, however, simply refer to her tribe or extended family. She is called upon to make the break with the old identity and the old ties (cf. Gen. 2:24). Thus when we as the church come to Christ, there must be a death to the past, to the point of hating father and mother and even our own selves, in order to be His disciples (Luke 14:26).

The king will long for his bride. The verb for *"greatly desire"* means "to be passionate for," that is, the king will want to consummate the marriage. The queen, in return, will submit to the king as her *"Lord"* and *"worship* [bow down to] *Him."* Similarly, when we come to Christ as His bride we bow in worship before Him. Thus Thomas submitted to the risen Lord confessing, "My Lord and my God!" (John 20:28).

The queen will be courted by rulers and powerful *"people."* The *"daughter of Tyre"* will bring a *"gift"* and *"the rich . . . will seek your favor."* *"Daughter"* here either means a princess from the great trading center north of Israel or it may be symbolic for the "people of Tyre" (cf. Ps. 9:14). Thus into the New Jerusalem, which is Jesus' bride, the church, "the kings of the earth [will] bring their glory and their honor" (Rev. 21:24, 26). Again, it is the church, made up of the meek, that will inherit the earth.

PRESENTATION OF THE QUEEN

13 The royal daughter *is* all glorious within *the palace;*
   Her clothing *is* woven with gold.
14 She shall be brought to the King in robes of many
     colors;
   The virgins, her companions who follow her, shall
     be brought to You.

15 With gladness and rejoicing they shall be brought;
   They shall enter the King's palace.

Ps. 45:13–15

Now the queen, the *"royal daughter,"* is ready for the presentation. She is *"all glorious"* in *"her clothing . . . woven with gold."* She also wears *"robes of many colors"* as she is *"brought to the King."* Her attendants, *"virgins, her companions who follow her,"* enter the king's palace *"with gladness and rejoicing."*

Likewise, the church wears robes, but they will be white and spotless, washed in the blood of the Lamb (Rev. 7:14). The church too is made ready to be married to Christ. Thus at the end of the age, there is great rejoicing in heaven "for the marriage of the Lamb has come, and His wife has made herself ready" (Rev. 19:7). Verse 15 of the psalm well expresses not only the wedding of Israel's king, but also the union of Christ and His church.

Prophetic Word about Sons

16 Instead of Your fathers shall be Your sons,
   Whom You shall make princes in all the earth.
17 I will make Your name to be remembered in all
      generations;
   Therefore the people shall praise You forever and ever.

Ps. 45:16–17

The prophetic word from God given through the psalmist contains the promise to the king and queen that the royal line will continue for generations to come. *"Fathers"* pass away. In their stead they will have *"sons"* who will become *"princes in all the earth."* This verse is clearly eschatological (see 2 Sam. 7:16). There will be a day, yet to come, when the Messiah's followers will inherit the earth.

Moreover, God *"will make [the king's] name to be remembered in all generations"* and he will be praised by *"the people"* (or "all peoples"; the Hebrew noun is plural). Here the plural represents fullness. Their thanksgiving will be endless, *"forever and ever."*

So in the Book of Revelation (1:5–6), John proclaims to the church that Jesus is the "ruler over the kings of the earth," and He has "made us kings and priests to His God and Father, to Him be glory and dominion forever and ever. Amen." In the deepest sense, this wedding psalm celebrates the final King to come who will claim His bride forever.

As a pastor, I have performed hundreds of weddings. It is always exciting to have the rehearsal and then to gather for the main event. All of the participants appear in their finest clothes. The bride is always radiant, glowing and a bit nervous as she prepares to walk down the aisle to her groom. Often there are tears of joy as the procession begins. This is the crowning moment—all the hopes, fears, plans, and promises of the engagement period are now climaxed as the wedding takes place. It is as if every wedding is a dress rehearsal for that day when we as Christ's bride are with Him "face to face," married for eternity.

Here then is a "good theme," indeed, and our hearts overflow. The one remaining question with which we as the church must search our hearts is this: Are we ready?

CHAPTER FORTY-SIX

Security in the Storm

Psalm 46

We speak naïvely of terra firma. It isn't. Geologists have discovered that the continents are actually afloat, continuing to be built and changed by moving plates. Volcanoes are earth's heat vents lying near the plate perimeters, which are also earthquake prone. What we have then is a dynamic, living, changing planet set in an exploding, expanding universe. Creation as pictured by deists—like a clock that has been wound up and then left to tick along on its own—just doesn't work. In fact, creation is a great natural drama that seethes with the unexpected, but has a meaningful purpose that will reach culmination. Psalm 46 describes it exactly in this way (see vv. 2–3). But if earth is not our fixed position, then where can we be anchored?

Psalm 46 answers this question by celebrating God's strength and our security in Him. The crisis that evokes this meditation (vv. 1–9) and God's response (v. 10) is not a specific incident, but a general sense of the instability and insecurity of this life. This is seen in nature: "Therefore we will not fear, / Though the earth be removed" (v. 2); and history: "The nations raged, the kingdoms were moved; / He uttered His voice, the earth melted" (v. 6).

Beyond this creation is the power and will of the sovereign Creator. Beyond human leaders and events stands the power of God who "made desolations in the earth" (v. 8), and who also "makes wars cease to the end of the earth" (v. 9). He brings judgment, and He brings peace.

It is God who is in charge. He is to be worshiped and praised. His word is final; His presence is security. All other hopes dissolve before Him.

Tradition ascribes this psalm to the sons of Korah (see chap. 42). Its form is mixed, although it may best be described as a hymn. The psalm moves from our meditation (vv. 1–9) and God's response (v. 10) to its conclusion (v. 11, repeating v. 7).

OUR CONFESSION

1 God *is* our refuge and strength,
  A very present help in trouble.
2 Therefore we will not fear,
  Even though the earth be removed,
  And though the mountains be carried into the midst
    of the sea;
3 *Though* its waters roar *and* be troubled,
  Though the mountains shake with its swelling.   Selah
                                             Ps. 46:1–3

The psalm begins with a confession of faith made by the people of Israel (note the plural): *"God is our refuge and strength."* The noun for *"refuge"* means "shelter." When the rains come God protects us. Isaiah promises that after Israel is cleansed the Lord will guard Zion with a pillar of cloud by day and a pillar of fire by night, as in the exodus. He continues, "For over all the glory there will be a covering. And there will be a tabernacle for shade in the daytime from the heat, for a place of refuge, and for a shelter from storm and rain" (Isa. 4:5–6).

God is also our *"strength,"* that is, His might is exerted against His foes (Exod. 15:13; Ps. 21:8). Thus God both protects us as our shelter and fights for us; He is both our shield and our sword. Moreover, He is always with us: *"A very present help in trouble."* The noun for *"trouble"* means, literally, "distress, cramped quarters, a constricted feeling." God is here to help when the pressure mounts, when the world closes in upon us.

The consequence of this confession is: *"Therefore we will not fear."* Our *"fear"* is gone because of the provision and presence of God. Verses 2 and 3 describe a fearsome disaster. *"We will not fear, / Even though the earth be removed, / And . . . the mountains be carried into the . . . sea."* Here is the return to primeval chaos. The verb for *"removed"* means "changed." It could describe an earthquake or an eruption such as happened at Krakatau near Java in 1883 when five cubic miles of matter exploded and a mountain vanished.

Verse 3 continues, *"We will not fear"* though the ocean's *"waters roar and be troubled, / Though the mountains shake with its swelling."* Hurricane and tidal wave cannot touch us and neither can earthquake or avalanche. Through it all, God, the Creator and sustainer of this lively planet, holds us fast.

God's Presence and Power

4 *There is* a river whose streams shall make glad the
   city of God,
   The holy *place* of the tabernacle of the Most High.
5 God *is* in the midst of her, she shall not be moved;
   God shall help her, just at the break of dawn.
6 The nations raged, the kingdoms were moved;
   He uttered His voice, the earth melted.

                                          Ps. 46:4–6

Over against the watery chaos of verse 3 is God's *"river"* of verse 4: *"There is a river whose streams shall make glad the city of God."* This *"river"* is a perennial stream watering Zion (see Ezek. 47; Rev. 22:1). It is the river of God's mercy and His Spirit, and it makes His people glad.

In the midst of God's city, Jerusalem, there is *"the tabernacle of the Most High"* (the name for God among the Jebusites; see Gen. 14:18–24). *"God is in the midst of her, she shall not be moved"* (cf. Rev. 21:3). Since God lives in Jerusalem, He is her stability. Moreover, when the sun rises and the nations march into battle, God is Jerusalem's security.

The thought continues: *"The nations raged, the kingdoms were moved."* The verb for *"raged"* is the same word used to describe the waters roaring in verse 3, and the verb for *"moved"* also is applied to the mountains in verse 2. Like nature, then, history also has its chaos. The voice of God, however, is greater than the noise of this planet. The statement that *"He uttered His voice, the earth melted"* may be metaphorical (the earth melts in fear). If it is literal, it may refer to Peter telling us that on the Day of the Lord, "the heavens will pass away with a great noise, and the elements will melt with fervent heat; both the earth and the works that are in it will be burned up" (2 Pet. 3:10).

God, however, is our stability and security. When we dwell in Jerusalem, the chaos of history with the din of battle cannot carry us away.

God's Protection

> 7 The LORD of hosts *is* with us;
> The God of Jacob *is* our refuge.   Selah
>
>   *Ps. 46:7*

The promise of security continues in the confession: *"The Lord of hosts is with us."* The *"hosts"* are angelic retainers (Ps. 103:20–22). But the God who rules His angelic armies is also the God of Israel, the God of Jacob, "our" God, and *"our refuge"* ("high place"). Thus He sends His angels to aid us in battle and promises to be our place of retreat.

I recall hearing Professor Otto Piper of Princeton tell of being expelled from Nazi Germany in the 1930s. He was alone and penniless on the streets of London. Suddenly, from nowhere, a man came up to him, gave him an address to go to, and vanished. The address turned out to be a place of employment for him as a teacher of theology. By Professor Piper's witness the "man" on the street was an angel. Indeed, *"the Lord of hosts is with us."*

God's Peace for the World

> 8 Come, behold the works of the LORD,
> Who has made desolations in the earth.
> 9 He makes wars cease to the end of the earth;

He breaks the bow and cuts the spear in two;
He burns the chariot in the fire.

Ps. 46:8–9

The psalmist now invites us to see *"the works of the Lord."* God brings His judgments, His *"desolations"* ("waste"). He stops war; *"He breaks the bow and cuts the spear,"* and *"burns the chariot."* This picture of God defeating His enemies is eschatological: *"He makes wars cease to the end of the earth."* Isaiah 2:4 sees the day when swords will be beaten into plowshares, and Revelation 20:4 promises the millennial reign of the Lord. Here the chaos of history becomes the cosmos of God.

GOD'S PEACE FOR THE HEART

10 Be still, and know that I *am* God;
I will be exalted among the nations,
I will be exalted in the earth!

Ps. 46:10

God now speaks a direct prophetic word. As He brings peace to the earth so He brings peace to the heart. We can experience *now* that eschatological reality: *"Be still, and know that I am God."* To *"know"* that God is God is to experience Him in the quiet of our hearts. This is relational, not merely theological knowledge. It is letting God's peace settle down upon us. It is knowing Him as our security and stability in the storm.

Now we are ready for God's next word: *"I will be exalted among the nations, / I will be exalted in the earth!"* The word for *"exalted"* means "to be lifted up, to be raised high." We can think of a victorious coach being carried from the field by his team, receiving the praise of the fans. God will be raised high, and both creation and history will bow to His sovereign will and give Him glory. We know that this will take place when Christ comes to manifest the fullness of God's kingdom. Remembering Philippians 2:10–11 ("Every knee should bow . . . and every tongue should confess that Jesus Christ is Lord, to the glory of God"), we pray, "Thy kingdom come. . . ."

A CONCLUDING REFRAIN

11 The LORD of hosts *is* with us;
The God of Jacob *is* our refuge.   Selah

Ps. 46:11

The psalm ends with a repetition of verse 7 as a refrain.

Is God big enough to deal with our personal problems? Is He big enough to deal with East-West crises? Racial violence in South Africa? Religious violence in Northern Ireland? Volcanoes? Hurricanes? Shifting plates? Comets?

The God of Psalm 46 commands angelic hosts, volatile nature, expanding creation, historical chaos, wars, and rumors of wars. He is the Lord of Hosts. He will be exalted in the earth. No wonder then that this psalm inspired Luther's "A Mighty Fortress Is Our God." Indeed, God is our refuge, our fortress. In Him we are safe and secure.

CHAPTER FORTY-SEVEN

Our God Reigns

Psalm 47

The Bible is a book of battles. Since the Fall, murder and killing are thematic to life. General Douglas MacArthur was fond of quoting Plato: "Only the dead have seen the end of war." Cain murdered his brother. Moses and Joshua were military commanders, as were the judges and the kings of Israel. What unfolds in the Bible, little by little, is the spiritual battle raging behind our earthly struggle. Thus the demons control the idols (Deut. 32:16–17). This means, as in Satan's temptation of Jesus, that spiritual powers rule the nations and their false gods. If this was true in the ancient world, it can be just as true today.

The Christian then is called into spiritual battle. His enemies are more subtle in their disguises because they don't come as marauding barbarians against fortified cities, but they are, nevertheless, just as real. The Lord calls us, too, into battle. We, like Israel of old, need to know how to fight. While the answer is complex (see Eph. 6:12–18), Psalm 47 gives us a central imperative: fight in praise, for our God reigns. While the weapons of our warfare "are not carnal" (2 Cor. 10:4) we must employ them, all the same. In our spiritual struggle against the hosts of wickedness praise will help us to overcome: "Rejoice in the Lord always. Again I will say, rejoice!" (Phil. 4:4).

Psalm 47 is a war psalm. It celebrates God's triumphant reign before the battle: "He will subdue the peoples under us, / And the nations under our feet." It celebrates God's triumphant reign in the battle: "God has gone up with a shout." And it celebrates God's triumphant reign after the battle: "For the shields of the earth belong to God."

The psalm presupposes a world in revolt against the Lord. He goes into battle and subdues the nations, and Israel now celebrates His triumph.

Tradition ascribes this psalm to the "sons of Korah" (see chap. 42). Commentators see it as either written for temple worship during one of the great festivals or as a victory psalm composed to honor a recent triumph. Some hold it to be an enthronement psalm celebrating Yahweh's kingship. In its form it is a hymn of praise.

PRAISE GOD BEFORE THE BATTLE

1 Oh, clap your hands, all you peoples!
  Shout to God with the voice of triumph!
2 For the LORD Most High *is* awesome;
  He is a great King over all the earth.
3 He will subdue the peoples under us,
  And the nations under our feet.
4 He will choose our inheritance for us,
  The excellence of Jacob whom He loves. Selah
          Ps. 47:1–4

The psalm begins with a call to worship. The psalmist's expectation here is for a high volume of praise—clapping and shouting. The first clause indicates the quantity of praise: *"all you peoples."* The second clause indicates the quality: *"Shout . . . with the voice of triumph."* The eschatological reference to *"all you peoples"* suggests that ultimately all nations will praise Yahweh. *"The voice of triumph"* is, literally, the voice of "shouting" ("a ringing cry"). It is an appropriate response to the presence of God in the midst of His people: "Cry out and shout, O inhabitant of Zion, / For great is the Holy One of Israel in your midst!" (Isa. 12:6).

In verses 2–4 the psalmist enumerates the reasons for worship. First, God is *"the Lord Most High."* He is the personal God of Israel, "Yahweh," *"The Lord"* (Exod. 3:15). He also bears the name of God used by the Jerusalem Jebusites (Gen. 14:18–24), the *"Most High."* Thus He is over all other gods ("demons," 1 Cor. 10:20) and nations.

Second, God is *"awesome."* He is to be reverenced and feared for His mighty power, the revelation of His numinous presence (Rudolf Otto). Thus when Isaiah sees Him in the temple and hears the seraphim cry, "Holy, holy, holy is the Lord of hosts; / The whole earth is full of His glory!" he responds, "Woe is me" (6:3–5).

Third, He is a great King, a sovereign ruler. His word and will are absolute. Again, in his vision of God Isaiah sees his sin and the sins of Israel and he then cries out in woe, as he says, "For my eyes have seen the King, / The Lord of hosts" (6:5).

Fourth, God is *"over all the earth."* His reign is universal. He alone is Creator and Redeemer (see Rev. 4:11; 5:9–10).

Next, God is to be worshiped for what He does: He leads us in victory over the peoples and nations. In the statement *"He will subdue the peoples under us, / And the nations under our feet"* we have a picture of military victory, where the commander puts his foot on the defeated enemy's neck (see Josh. 10:24). Ralph Winter has pointed out the difference between *"peoples"* and *"nations."* *"Peoples"* are ethnic groups. *"Nations"* are political entities. In the Great Commission we are told to take the gospel to all "peoples," that is, to all cultural and ethnic groups. Our task in spiritual warfare is not done until all peoples hear the gospel. This includes all tribes and cultural groups, many of whom are hidden in the larger political divisions. Our enemies then will be won, conquered by the power of love, as the power of Satan over them is broken.

God not only gives victory in battle, He also gives His people an *"inheritance."* Thus we have a future. For Israel this was the Promised Land. For us it is the new heaven and the new earth (Rev. 21:1). The *"excellence* [or pride] *of Jacob"* is synonymous with the *"inheritance"* in the previous phrase and also refers to the Promised Land. *"Jacob"* here again stands for Israel.

For all these reasons, we are to shout our joy to God for who He is and for what He has done. In this *"shout"* of *"triumph"* we are ready for battle. This is the locker room meeting before the game, the prayer meeting before the evangelistic crusade, our worship before preaching and ministry.

One of the most important things that God is presently teaching us at our church is that worship prepares us to receive the Spirit's ministry because worship opens us up to the living God. As we praise Him through His Son our faith grows. Now we are ready for battle, or to put it better, now the first battle over our own apathy and flesh has been won.

PRAISE GOD IN THE BATTLE

5 God has gone up with a shout,
  The LORD with the sound of a trumpet.
6 Sing praises to God, sing praises!
  Sing praises to our King, sing praises!
7 For God *is* the King of all the earth;
  Sing praises with understanding.

Ps. 47:5–7

Next, the psalmist describes God's going to war: *"God has gone up with a shout, / The Lord with the sound of a trumpet."* The verb for *"gone up"* (v. 5) means "to ascend, to climb," and can be taken to mean in the cultic sense that God has gone up to the temple. The verb is also a technical term for going to war (Judg. 1:1; 1 Sam. 7:7); thus in Isaiah 36:10 the governor or chief of staff of the King of Assyria asserts that he has "come up" against Judah with Yahweh's blessing. He tells King Hezekiah's servants, "Have I now come up without the Lord against this land to destroy it? The Lord said to me, 'Go up against this land and destroy it.'" In the context of verses 3 and 9, then, we take God's "going up" with *"a shout"* and *"the sound of a trumpet"* as His going into battle for Israel. The *"trumpet"* (*šōpār*, "ram's horn") is used to summon troops for battle and to direct them in battle (see Judg. 6:34; 2 Sam. 2:28).

In response to Yahweh's fighting for her, Israel is called to praise Him. God's people are to *"sing praises to God,"* who is their *"King"* and *"the King of all the earth."* The imperative *"sing praises"* is repeated five times for emphasis. Israel is also to sing to God *"with understanding,"* that is, skillfully.

Praise goes with a battle already won. God is to be worshiped in the battle because He is the universal, sovereign King and will therefore win. His enemies must fail, and we are victorious in Him. For this reason, Paul and Silas, having been beaten and jailed in Philippi, prayed and sang to the Lord at midnight with their feet in the stocks (Acts 16:23–25). This is the faith that cannot be broken. This is faith in the midst of the battle.

GOD IS EXALTED AFTER THE BATTLE

8 God reigns over the nations;
　God sits on His holy throne.
9 The princes of the people have gathered together,
　The people of the God of Abraham.
　For the shields of the earth *belong* to God;
　He is greatly exalted.

Ps. 47:8–9

The psalmist confesses again God's reign. The *"nations"* are His subjects and He sits before them *"on His holy throne."* It is holy or "separated" because He is holy. Then the leaders of the *"princes of the people"* (plural, "peoples"; see v. 3) gather. They are joined by the *"people* [or "nation"] *of the God of Abraham,"* that is, the Jews who belong to Abraham's covenant (see Gen. 17:7). All, both Jew and Gentile, submit to the sovereign King, surrendering their *"shields."* With all peoples and nations before Him, *"He is greatly exalted."*

Psalm 47 prepares us for our battles. If we begin in praise, we will end in praise. Our God reigns; He breaks the revolt against His sovereign will. He is the great Warrior-King who rolls back Satan's darkness. Thus we can "shout with the voice of triumph" (v. 1), for "we are more than conquerors through Him who loved us" (Rom. 8:37).

CHAPTER FORTY-EIGHT

God Dwells in Zion

Psalm 48

For the Bible, cities can be centers of pride and corruption, as Babylon symbolizes (see Rev. 17–18). However, a city can also be a center of strength and worship. Jerusalem on Mount Zion symbolizes this (see Rev. 21). Of course, physical Jerusalem never fulfilled her earthly destiny to be the city of God. Rather, the Gentiles destroyed her in 586 B.C. and again in A.D. 70. Thus prophets such as Ezekiel look for a new city and a new restored temple. For the New Testament this city is now the church. Therefore, Paul tells the Ephesians that they have been made members "of the household of God" and they are a building "under construction" (Marcus Barth) growing "into a holy temple in the Lord, in whom you also are being built together for a dwelling place of God in the Spirit" (Eph. 2:19–22).

When John has his final vision in the Book of Revelation he sees the New Jerusalem, God's city, which is also the bride of Christ. This city is His church (Rev. 21:9–11).

Psalm 48 celebrates the greatness of Jerusalem on Mount Zion. Here Zion is great because God is great and dwells in His city and in His temple, in the midst of His people. The immediate context of the psalm is probably that of worshipers going up to Jersualem for one of the major festivals. It is likely that this psalm was employed in the actual course of worship. Thus verse 9 reflects, "We have thought, O God, on Your lovingkindness, / In the midst of Your temple" and verse 12 calls for a processional: "Walk about Zion, / And go all around her."

As we study Psalm 48, however, we need to see that the fulfillment of this picture of Jerusalem lies in the future. In this sense the psalm is eschatological. It will be the glorified church, made up of Jew and Gentile, which in the end will become God's purified, redeemed, restored place of habitation.

This psalm is attributed to the "sons of Korah" (see chap. 42). Its form is a hymn where God is praised in the context of Zion. After the call to worship, Zion is identified as beautiful, terrible, eternal, joyful, and faithful.

CALL TO WORSHIP

1 Great *is* the LORD, and greatly to be praised
   In the city of our God,
   In His holy mountain.

Ps. 48:1

The call to worship tells us who is to be worshiped and where He is to be worshiped. It is the *"Lord,"* Yahweh, who is *"to be praised"* because He is *"great."* The adjective *"great"* when applied to God means great in His works (Deut. 11:7), His glory (Ps. 21:5), His name (Jer. 10:6), His mercy (1 Kings 3:6), His goodness (Neh. 9:25), and His compassion (Isa. 54:7–8). Because God is great, He does great things: "How great thou art!" Great praise is appropriate to a great God. He is *"greatly to be praised."*

Verse 1 also tells us where God is to be worshiped. He is *"to be praised in [His] city,"* Jerusalem, and *"in His holy mountain,"* Zion. The mountain is *"holy"* ("separated," "other") because the holy God dwells there.

ZION BEAUTIFUL

2 Beautiful in elevation,
   The joy of the whole earth,
   Is Mount Zion *on* the sides of the north,
   The city of the great King.
3 God *is* in her palaces;
   He is known as her refuge.

Ps. 48:2–3

The rest of this psalm is a meditation on the greatness of Zion. Zion is *"beautiful in elevation."* It is *the* "high place" because here the transcendent God meets us. It also brings *"joy"* to *"the whole earth."* *"Joy"* here means "exultation" or "rejoicing" expressed in praise. Thus the blessing of Zion comes to all people. A similar thought appears in Isaiah 2:2–4 where "the mountain of the Lord's house" is "exalted above the hills" and "all nations shall flow to it." The law then goes out from Zion and peace comes to the earth.

Zion is also *"on the sides of the north"* or, better, "the heights of Zaphon." "North" (*ṣāpôn*) is the mythological name for the mountain of the gods. Zion now displaces this ancient pagan idea. The true Zaphon is Zion; Zion is the true *"north"* where God dwells (cf. Isa. 14:13). Zion is also *"the city of the great King"* (see Ps. 47:2). No earthly king makes God's city great. He himself is there. *"God is in her palaces; / He is known as her refuge."* The noun for *"palaces"* can also be rendered "citadel" or "stronghold," which is a better parallel to *"refuge."* God is Zion's fortification and defense.

Zion is exalted, blessing the earth. It is both the dwelling place and fortress of the *"great King."* The presence and the power of God are to be found there. This description is now being fulfilled by the church, the Body of Christ. United to Christ, we are sharing His resurrection life and reign. As Paul put it, "[God] raised us up together, and made us sit together in the heavenly places in Christ Jesus" (Eph. 2:6). We are *"beautiful in elevation."*

The church is also *"the joy of the whole earth."* It is the church which has borne the message of salvation to the nations. Thus Isaiah's prophecy of light to the Gentiles bringing joy (Isa. 9:1–3) increases through her mission. Moreover, the church is where God dwells through His Holy Spirit (Eph. 2:19–22) and He is her protection, her *"refuge."*

ZION TERRIBLE

4 For behold, the kings assembled,
   They passed by together.
5 They saw *it, and* so they marveled;
   They were troubled, they hastened away.
6 Fear took hold of them there,
   And pain, as of a woman in birth pangs,
7 *As when* You break the ships of Tarshish
   With an east wind.

Ps. 48:4–7

While Zion is beautiful to the believer, it is terrible to the unbeliever. Thus the rulers of the nations come and see it, *"the kings assembled"* and *"they passed by together."* It is as if they have come together to attack the city. However, when they saw Zion they *"marveled,"* they were *"troubled,"* and they *"hastened away."* To "marvel" is to be "astounded." Either the kings were astounded at Zion or, more likely, at the presence of Yahweh in her midst. Their astonishment turned to being *"troubled"* ("dismayed" or "terrified"), which led to flight. Indeed, they *"hastened away."*

Their terror is documented with the use of two metaphors. The kings feel *"fear"* and *"pain, as of a woman in birth pangs."* They also experience the dread of sailors who see *"an east wind"* break up *"the ships of Tarshish."* The identity of *"Tarshish"* is debated. It may refer to the Phoenician city of Taressus in Spain.

Thus in verses 4–7 that which gives believers courage and confidence causes unbelievers to fear and to flee. When Jesus came, the common people heard Him gladly. The religious leaders, however, disdained to follow Him. The same is true for Christ's teachings today—beautiful to the body of believers, terrible to those whose minds are darkened (see 2 Cor. 4:3–4).

ZION ETERNAL

> 8 As we have heard,
>   So we have seen
>   In the city of the LORD of hosts,
>   In the city of our God:
>   God will establish it forever.   Selah
>
> *Ps. 48:8*

For believers, what was once merely *"heard"* has now been *"seen."* Faith has turned to sight. Thus the *"city of the Lord of hosts"* (God's angelic court, Ps. 103:20–21), the *"city of our God,"* has been established *"forever."* The verb for *"establish"* means "to be firmly fixed, secure, certain." All else will pass away, but Zion will stand. She is held by the eternal God. Of this city John writes, "There shall be no night there: They need no lamp nor light of the sun, for the Lord God gives them light. And they shall reign forever and ever" (Rev. 22:5).

ZION JOYFUL

> 9 We have thought, O God, on Your lovingkindness,
>   In the midst of Your temple.
> 10 According to Your name, O God,

> So *is* Your praise to the ends of the earth;
> Your right hand is full of righteousness.
> 11 Let Mount Zion rejoice,
> Let the daughters of Judah be glad,
> Because of Your judgments.
>
> *Ps. 48:9-11*

The psalmist now turns from meditation to prayer, addressing God directly. His mind is filled with God's *"lovingkindness,"* His *"name,"* His *"righteousness,"* and His *"judgments."*

Having entered the temple he now joins the other worshipers who think ("imagine") or have an image in their minds of Yahweh's *"lovingkindness,"* His covenant-love. The symbols of the covenant are about him as he stands in the holy place, at the center of Israel's faith. Here prayers are prayed, sacrifices are offered, hymns are sung, and the ark of the covenant rests in the Holy of Holies—with its mercy seat, its angelic guards, and the tablets of the law housed within it. No wonder Israel remembers God's love in Zion.

Next there is the thought of God's *"name,"* which bears the person, the presence, and the power of God. The greatness of God's *"name"* is seen in the praise offered to it throughout the world: *"According to Your name, O God, / So is Your praise to the ends of the earth"* (v. 10). The particularity of God always bears within it His universality. Thus He calls Abraham to Himself in order to bless the nations (Gen. 12:1–3).

Now the thought turns to God's *"right hand . . . "* full of *"righteousness."* He is not capricious. He always acts according to His promises and commands given in the covenant. God is "right, true, straight" in all His dealings.

Now the city and its inhabitants, *"the daughters of Judah,"* are to *"rejoice,"* and *"be glad"* because of *"Your judgments."* God's judgments include His just decisions based on His *"righteousness"* and His acts of judgment against Israel's enemies.

Here, thought and reflection on God's character lead to a call for worship. Whenever we tap into our memory of who God is and what He has done for us, we are ready to praise Him. Moreover, all of the divine attributes are fulfilled in Christ who offers us a new covenant that satisfies God's righteousness and judgments so that we may be forgiven and enter into a new relationship with Him (see Jer. 31:31–

34). Thus, the church is now the *"daughters of Judah"* who are to *"rejoice"* and *"be glad."*

ZION FAITHFUL

12 Walk about Zion,
   And go all around her.
   Count her towers;
13 Mark well her bulwarks;
   Consider her palaces;
   That you may tell *it* to the generation following.
14 For this *is* God,
   Our God forever and ever;
   He will be our guide
   Even to death.

Ps. 48:12–14

The psalm ends with a call for a procession around Jerusalem: *"Walk about Zion, / And go all around her."* As the worshipers walk, they are to *"count her towers"* on the walls, *"mark well her bulwarks,"* and *"consider her palaces"* (or "citadels"). Some distant sense of this experience can still be ours in visiting the old walled city of Jerusalem today. The purpose of the procession is to see how strong and well defended Zion is, and to remember that God is her true citadel and "refuge."

The purpose of surveying the city is not merely to strengthen the faith of the pilgrims. They must now *"tell . . . the generation following."* They are responsible for educating their children in their faith. Thus they must give witness to what they see.

The testimony to their children and the point of the psalm is then summarized in verse 14: *"For this is God, / Our God forever and ever,"* or, "For this God is our God. . . ." The "great" Lord, the "great King," the "Lord of hosts," who is loving, righteous, and just is *"our God."* He will *"guide"* His people *"even to death,"* or to the end of their lives. He will be faithful to the end.

Many Christians today say, "I love Jesus, but I hate the church." The church, however, is God's city, the New Jerusalem. She is also the bride of Christ. How can we claim to love the Husband and hate His bride? Psalm 48 will help us to love God and His city, His residence, His church. If the church is ever "great," it is because of God's greatness.

God's true church, like Jerusalem, has a temple for worship and strong defenses against the enemy. There the living God is present in love, righteousness, and judgment.

Before this church, enemies tremble in terror and the gates of hell will not prevail (Matt. 16:18). We need to know the church and her history and we need to love the church. Jesus bought her with His blood and God is in her midst.

CHAPTER FORTY-NINE

Death and Life's Meaning

Psalm 49

A few years ago, when I was teaching the college class at Bel Air Presbyterian Church, I met a couple who told me about their son Dennis. He had died at the age of twenty-three of cancer. Dennis had been a Christian for only six months when he was told he had the disease and that at the most he had three years to live. Through the ups and downs of those years Dennis's spiritual life grew as he gained increasing boldness about his faith. He said, "Cancer brought me to my knees; I had no control over my life."

In an interview at U.C.L.A. Medical Center Dennis responded to a doctor's question about life by asking him, "Do you want to live a short time for God or a long time for nothing?"

Finally, Dennis was brought home to die. His mother would come into his room and ask her sedated son, "Dennis, are you here?" His reply each time was, "Yes, Mother, I'm here." Near the end when she came in again with her question, Dennis's reply was "No, Mother, I'm going home." Looking about, Dennis cried, "Faith is a lighted room."

A plaque stands over the bed where Dennis died. It reads:

> I hear you, Christian,
> Riotous, joyful, unafraid,
> Because you know a song
> From the other side of death.

Dennis's mother told me, "He prepared us to die."

Likewise, Psalm 49 prepares us to die. A wise meditation upon the meaning of life, it especially addresses the issues of human riches and pride, all swallowed up by death. Rather than trusting in wealth, the wise in this world trust in God. Rather than fearing death, they trust in God's power to redeem beyond the grave.

Tradition attributes Psalm 49 to the "sons of Korah" (see chap. 42). It is a wisdom poem containing proverbs and "dark sayings" written to be accompanied by the harp. As wisdom is crosscultural, so this psalm is addressed to all people, in every situation of life.

After an invitation to wisdom (vv. 1–4), there is a meditation on the futility of riches when death takes all (vv. 5–12). Fools die, but God redeems the wise (vv. 13–15). Death, however, levels all (vv. 16–20).

Invitation to Wisdom

1 Hear this, all peoples;
  Give ear, all inhabitants of the world,
2 Both low and high,
  Rich and poor together.
3 My mouth shall speak wisdom,
  And the meditation of my heart *shall give*
    understanding.
4 I will incline my ear to a proverb;
  I will disclose my dark saying on the harp.

Ps. 49:1–4

The opening call to listen is an imperative to gain our attention. The whole of humanity, rather than just Israel, is addressed: *"all peoples . . . all inhabitants of the world."* Moreover, every sociological stratum is included, *"Both low and high, / Rich and poor together."* The writer speaks *"wisdom, / And the meditation of* [his] *heart"* to foster *"understanding"* (v. 3). The noun for *"wisdom"* (ḥākmâh) appears here in the plural, indicating "full wisdom," and embraces the scribal classes' practical observations on how to get through life. Here the psalmist also includes his own input, *"the meditation of my heart."* In bringing his creative effort to the wisdom tradition, his concern is not merely to impart knowledge, but to bring enlightenment.

He continues: *"I will incline my ear to a proverb"*; that is, he receives the oral tradition of the wisdom teachers. Also, he offers his own *"dark saying"* ("parable" or "riddle") as he plays the *"harp"* (or "lyre"). Similarly Jesus expresses this union of tradition and personal innovation when he says, "Therefore every scribe instructed concerning the kingdom of heaven is like a householder who brings out of his treasure things new and old" (Matt. 13:52).

Riches Cannot Redeem Us

5 Why should I fear in the days of evil,
  When the iniquity at my heels surrounds me?
6 Those who trust in their wealth
  And boast in the multitude of their riches,
7 None *of them* can by any means redeem *his* brother,
  Nor give to God a ransom for him—
8 For the redemption of their souls *is* costly,
  And it shall cease forever—
9 That he should continue to live eternally,
  And not see the Pit.

Ps. 49:5–9

In verse 5, the psalmist asks a crucial question: *"Why should I fear in the days of evil, / When the iniquity at my heels surrounds me?"* The phrase *"at my heels"* is probably better translated "my foes" ("overreacher"), thus reading "When the iniquity of my foes surrounds me." The reason for the psalmist's fearlessness in light of evil days and enemies is that those who are prideful and *"trust in their wealth"* reach an insurmountable barrier: *"None of them can by any means redeem his brother"* (v. 7). This is the basic issue of life.

The verb for *"redeem"* may also be translated "to ransom, to buy back, to purchase back." Here, then, "buying back" a *"brother"* from death by human *"wealth"* is impossible. The price is too high, as is made clear in verse 8. There is no installment plan. Moreover, this is a spiritual rather than a material matter (v. 9): *"That he* [the brother] *should continue to live eternally, / And not see the Pit"* (the grave, Sheol; cf. Ps. 16:10; 30:9).

What we learn here is that we need to be redeemed from death. Human wealth and power are meaningless now. What can we give to God to escape the Pit? Shall we write Him a check? Offer Him some stock? Our soul is at stake and apart from redemption, it bears the penalty and curse of death. Our pride is broken on this issue. Now we can begin to learn true wisdom.

DEATH TAKES ALL

10 For he sees wise men die;
   Likewise the fool and the senseless person perish,
   And leave their wealth to others.
11 Their inner thought *is that* their houses *will last*
      forever,
   Their dwelling places to all generations;
   They call *their* lands after their own names.
12 Nevertheless man, *though* in honor, does not remain;
   He is like the beasts *that* perish.

Ps. 49:10–12

The issue before us is the issue of death (v. 10). Death is the great leveler, and none of us can escape it. The author of this psalm, a *"wise"* man, will die. *"The fool and the senseless person"* will also die. The *"fool"* is the person who rejects wisdom (Prov. 1:7). The *"senseless person"* is "brutish," like an animal. All of them *"leave their wealth to others."* Thus to make *"wealth"* the object of trust is to lose everything in the end.

Verse 11 elaborates on the dangers of wealth. Material possessions have only the illusion of lasting. How often are we promised that we have a "lifetime guarantee" on a purchase? Products are marketed to us as "unbreakable," "waterproof," "rust-free." One ad even tells us that "a diamond is forever." It may be, but we're not.

Moreover, the wealthy *"call their lands after their own names,"* that is, they secure their lands legally in their own names. This, again, gives us the illusion of immortality. We think that we really possess things, but we don't. I recall, when I was younger, the shock of seeing houses which I had known my whole life being demolished in order to put in a new freeway. There was something unnerving in seeing them torn down and carted away. My stable world was shaken.

The conclusion is that we are all a part of the passing show. *"Neverthe-*

less man, though in honor, does not remain." Humanity, however honored, *"is like the beasts that perish"* (v. 12).

One of German Field Marshal Rommel's most cherished medals was the Iron Cross, which he always wore around his neck. He received this decoration for bravery in World War I. Years after his death, his biographer visited a small museum where some of his effects were kept. There, he found the cross, dusty and forgotten, in a small box. *"Man, though in honor, does not remain."*

Fools Die; God Redeems

13 This is the way of those who *are* foolish,
   And of their posterity who approve their sayings.Selah
14 Like sheep they are laid in the grave;
   Death shall feed on them;
   The upright shall have dominion over them in the
      morning;
   And their beauty shall be consumed in the grave,
   far from their dwelling.
15 But God will redeem my soul from the power of the
      grave,
   For He shall receive me.   Selah

Ps. 49:13–15

The *"way"* of the *"foolish"* and *"their posterity"* who agree with them is described in verse 13 as resembling those of sheep who *"are laid in the grave"* (*šeʾôl*, the abode of the dead, cf. v. 9). Furthermore, *"death shall feed on them,"* or better, "shall shepherd them." (The Hebrew text at this point is corrupt.) Following the translation here, the *"upright"* will rule them during their life, *"in the morning,"* and they will finally *"be consumed in the grave, far from"* their houses which they thought to be eternal.

In contrast to the *"foolish"* who die, the psalmist now gives his witness in verse 15. Here is the answer to the problem of verses 7–9. Since human wealth and pride cannot redeem a soul from death, who or what can? The answer, of course, is that redemption is God's work. He pays the "costly" price and reclaims His creation to be with Him forever. He alone can break *"the power of the grave"* or, literally, "the hand of Sheol." Thus the person who trusts in Him is received by Him. The Hebrew verb *"receive"* or "take" may indicate being taken to heaven as Enoch was (see Gen. 5:24).

For us, God's redemption has been accomplished in Christ. The promise of this psalm and the resolution to death are ours. As Paul puts it, "In Him we have redemption through His blood, the forgiveness of sins, according to the riches of His grace" (Eph. 1:7; cf. 2 Pet. 1:18–19).

DEATH LEVELS ALL

16 Do not be afraid when one becomes rich,
   When the glory of his house is increased;
17 For when he dies he shall carry nothing away;
   His glory shall not descend after him.
18 Though while he lives he blesses himself
   (For *men* will praise you when you do well for
       yourself),
19 He shall go to the generation of his fathers;
   They shall never see light.
20 A man *who is* in honor, yet does not understand,
   Is like the beasts *that* perish.

Ps. 49:16–20

The psalmist now exhorts us not to *"be afraid when one becomes rich"* or *"when the glory of his house,"* his estate and family, increases. The reason for this is that death strips us naked (v. 17) and His *"glory,"* that is, his "heaviness" or "wealth," remains behind. *"While he lives he blesses himself"* or, literally, "he blesses his soul in his life," with self-congratulations, and receives the *"praise"* of others. In death, however, when he joins *"the generation of his fathers,"* there is only darkness.

The psalmist now concludes (v. 20) that a person *"who is in honor,"* that is, enamored with the honor of this life, and who *"does not understand, / Is like the beasts that perish."* What does he *"not understand"*? He doesn't understand that he is going to die, that he can't take his *"honor"* and property with him in death. He doesn't understand that the issue of life is his soul, and that God alone can redeem him from death. Indeed, he doesn't understand at all.

Psalm 49 forces us to consider our lives and to understand that the only issue that counts is redeeming our souls from death. Once we are clear about this, we are prepared to die. This psalm has done its work.

CHAPTER FIFTY

God Comes to Judge

Psalm 50

The Christian lives in the tension between faith and obedience, worship and work. One must lead to the other or we will have half a gospel. Too often the church is charged with hypocrisy: "They don't practice what they preach."

I remember hearing of a sermon Lloyd Ogilvie preached in Bethlehem, Pennsylvania, some years ago. As he stood in the pulpit he preached the personal gospel of salvation by faith. Unknown to the congregation, he was standing on only one leg. After fifteen minutes or so, he fell over. Getting up, he launched into the topic of social responsibility, standing on only the other leg. Again, after a while, he fell. Standing up again, he made his point: we need a two-legged gospel of faith and obedience. Nothing less will bless God and bless this world.

Psalm 50 demands a faith that acts. It calls for worship that works. Here God is introduced both as the Creator and the Covenant-God of Israel. Creation is called to witness because He is coming to judge His people (v. 4). This psalm is prophetic in that it exposes Israel's sins: murder, adultery, and lying (vv. 18–20). God's stern warning of judgment, however, is followed by the promise of salvation.

Psalm 50 is attributed to Asaph, one of David's chief musicians (1 Chron. 6:39; 15:16–17). Thus it may come from the circle of temple singers. Its prophetic form and message, however, are clear. Some commentators suggest that it was written during Josiah's reform (see 2 Kings 23).

Here God comes in glory to judge His people (vv. 1–6). He judges their worship (vv. 7–15) and their obedience (vv. 16–21). Israel's Judge, however, is also her Savior (vv. 22–23).

THE CREATOR COMES IN GLORY

1 The Mighty One, God the LORD,
   Has spoken and called the earth
   From the rising of the sun to its going down.

355

2 Out of Zion, the perfection of beauty,
  God will shine forth.
3 Our God shall come, and shall not keep silent;
  A fire shall devour before Him,
  And it shall be very tempestuous all around Him.

Ps. 50:1–3

The speaker is *"the Mighty One, God the Lord"* (ʾēl, ʾĕlōhîm, ʾAdonāi). Compounding God's names gives an awesome sense of majesty. He speaks and calls *"the earth."* The call is a summons to witness His judgment (see v. 4). It is the whole *"earth"* that is to appear before Him *"from the rising of the sun to its going down."*

God speaks in *"Zion,"* His holy mountain, where His temple stands. The idealized description of Zion here in verse 2 reflects similar thoughts to those of Psalm 48. Zion is perfect because God is in her midst. In His holiness and majesty He radiates light. This is the reason Moses came from the Lord's presence on Sinai with his face shining, reflecting God's glory (Exod. 34:29).

Light is also revelation; as God shines He speaks, and as He comes there is a devouring *"fire,"* which is *"tempestuous* ["whirling"] *all around Him."* On Sinai God descended "in fire" with a great earthquake (Exod. 19:18). The manifestations of His glory are similar here. The *"fire"* and the wind suggest His holiness, the consuming fire of His Spirit in judgment (contrast Acts 2:1–3).

GOD COMES TO JUDGE

4 He shall call to the heavens from above,
  And to the earth, that He may judge His people:
5 "Gather My saints together to Me,
  Those who have made a covenant with Me by
    sacrifice."
6 Let the heavens declare His righteousness,
  For God Himself *is* Judge.   Selah

Ps. 50:4–6

Here is the call of verse 1. Heaven and earth, the whole of creation, the cosmos, supernatural and natural, are summoned because God is ready to *"judge His people,"* Israel.

The command is: *"gather My saints"* (v. 5). The *"saints"* are defined here as the people of the *"covenant."* They are *"saints,"* not because they are "saintly," but because God has called them and they have been bound to Him. They are defined as *"those who have made a covenant with Me by sacrifice."* The basis for this is the Sinai covenant in Exodus 24:1–8 where Israel promises to obey all things written in the Book of the Covenant. This is then sealed by a blood sacrifice. Thus God's people are now gathered. It is probable that the command to *"gather"* them is addressed to angelic hosts (see Ps. 103:20–21; cf. Mark 13:27).

As they come, the psalmist exhorts the *"heavens"* to witness to God's *"righteousness."* They know His nature because they dwell with Him in light. His faithfulness to His covenant relationships assures us that His judgments are just: *"For God Himself is Judge."*

With the stage set for divine court to be held, God summons the witnesses, the *"heavens"* and the *"earth,"* and the accused, His covenant people. He comes in *"righteousness"* and He Himself is the *"Judge."* Thus the outcome will be absolutely fair and true.

GOD JUDGES WORSHIP

7 "Hear, O My people, and I will speak,
   O Israel, and I will testify against you;
   I *am* God, your God!
8 I will not rebuke you for your sacrifices
   Or your burnt offerings,
   Which are continually before Me.
9 I will not take a bull from your house,
   Nor goats out of your folds.
10 For every beast of the forest *is* Mine,
   And the cattle on a thousand hills.
11 I know all the birds of the mountains,
   And the wild beasts of the field *are* Mine.
12 "If I were hungry, I would not tell you;
   For the world *is* Mine, and all its fullness.
13 Will I eat the flesh of bulls,
   Or drink the blood of goats?
14 Offer to God thanksgiving,
   And pay your vows to the Most High.
15 Call upon Me in the day of trouble;
   I will deliver you, and you shall glorify Me."

Ps. 50:7–15

Above all else, Israel's worship is on God's heart. To love Him wholly is the Great Commandment (Deut. 6:5). Thus God speaks and Israel is to listen as He testifies against them.

But first, God identifies Himself: *"I am God, your God!"* He is the covenant God. Second, He affirms their sacrifices: *"I will not rebuke you for your sacrifices / Or your burnt offerings"* (see Ps. 40:6), given in the temple *"continually."* Third, God does not need the sacrifices, but Israel does. Thus He refuses to go looking for *"a bull from your house"* or *"goats,"* when He owns all the beasts in the *"forest"* and *"the cattle on a thousand hills"* (v. 10). Moreover, He "knows" (the Hebrew also means "is in relationship with, superintends") all *"the birds of the mountains"* and *"the wild beasts of the field."* Why then if God has vast herds and flocks would He need a single bull or goat?

The absurd idea, suggested in verse 12, that God waits for the sacrifices to be offered as His supper, is rejected.

God does not need Israel to feed Him, a common notion both ancient and modern religions held toward their gods or ancestors. Thus He mockingly asks: *"Will I eat the flesh of bulls, / Or drink the blood of goats?"* Sacrifices are to be offered not for God's sake, but for Israel's, as a sign of the covenant, as an act of surrender, and as a substitute for sin.

True worship is defined in verse 14. It begins with the heart: *"Offer to God thanksgiving* [sacrifice]." True worship also includes obedience. Thus *"vows"* must be paid *"to the Most High."* A "vow" is any kind of votive offering or promised gift to God. Here He is called the *"Most High,"* the title used by Melchizedek, king of Salem, who blesses Abraham (Gen. 14:18). It means "God above all other gods."

When worship is from the heart and exhibited in obedience, God promises that His people may *"call upon* [Him] *in the day of trouble."* He will *"deliver"* them and they will *"glorify"* Him. This includes both the glory manifested in the rescue itself and the resulting praise from Israel (v. 15).

This passage has an important application for us. Often we think that God needs us. He needs our money, our time, our worship. After all, what would He and His church do if we weren't there? This attitude stands rebuked and judged for two reasons. First, it presupposes a weak God. But He is the sovereign Lord. He owns the *"cattle on a thousand hills."* He needs neither us nor our money. Second, it expresses too high a view of ourselves. Pride enters in and the proud cannot stand in the presence of the Holy God. "Behold, the nations are as a drop

in a bucket, / And are counted as the small dust on the balance. . . .
All nations before Him are as nothing" (Isa. 40:17).

GOD JUDGES OBEDIENCE

16 But to the wicked God says:
   "What *right* have you to declare My statutes,
   Or take My covenant in your mouth,
17 Seeing you hate instruction
   And cast My words behind you?
18 When you saw a thief, you consented with him,
   And have been a partaker with adulterers.
19 You give your mouth to evil,
   And your tongue frames deceit.
20 You sit *and* speak against your brother;
   You slander your own mother's son.
21 These *things* you have done, and I kept silent;
   You thought that I was altogether like you;
   But I will rebuke you,
   And set *them* in order before your eyes.

   Ps. 50:16–21

Now God addresses *"the wicked"* (singular) in judgment, rebuking
him for using His law and claiming His covenant. Only the person
with a heart turned toward God has this right. The *"wicked"* person,
however, hates *"instruction"* ("discipline") and rejects God's *"words,"*
casting them *"behind"* him. The proof of this charge is given in verses
18–20.

First, the wicked person "consents" with a *"thief."* The verb for "con-
sent," meaning "to be pleased, to accept favorably," of course, violates
at least the spirit of the eighth commandment, "You shall not steal"
(Exod. 20:15). Second, the wicked person has been *"a partaker with
adulterers."* To be a *"partaker"* here is to "have a portion" with those
who break the marriage vow, violating the seventh commandment
(Exod. 20:14). Third, the wicked person has a wicked *"tongue."* This
includes *"evil"* coming from his *"mouth,"* his *"tongue"* framing *"deceit,"*
and speaking *"against [a] brother"* in *"slander."* This violates at least
the wider application of the ninth commandment, "You shall not bear
false witness against your neighbor" (Exod. 20:16).

Thus point by point the charge that the wicked *"hate instruction"* and *"cast* [God's] *words behind"* them is documented. Formerly, God was *"silent"* over this, and the wicked took His silence as approval: *"You thought that I was altogether like you."* However, they were wrong; God has come in judgment, to terrify Israel and bring reproof. The verb for *"rebuke"* (v. 21) means to "judge, convict, correct." The judgment here then is redemptive in its intention.

The case has been made, and God has *"set"* the evidence *"in order before your eyes,"* as in a legal case. Similarly, in Romans 2:17–24 Paul accuses the Jews of knowing the law and yet disobeying it. While preaching against stealing, they steal. While claiming to abhor adultery, they commit adultery. While hating idols, they rob temples. Thus they "boast in the law" and break it at the same time. The judgment of Psalm 50:16–17 stands, "What right have you to declare My statutes . . . Seeing you hate instruction . . . ?"

THE JUDGE BECOMES SAVIOR

22 "Now consider this, you who forget God,
    Lest I tear *you* in pieces,
    And *there be* none to deliver:
23 Whoever offers praise glorifies Me;
    And to him who orders *his* conduct *aright*
    I will show the salvation of God."

Ps. 50:22–23

God's rebuke must be heard. If not, He will come against those who *"forget"* Him. He will rip the wicked apart like a wild animal and *"tear* [them] *in pieces."* No one will be able to *"deliver"* them. God's judgment will be swift, violent, and final.

However, those who worship God rightly, offering ("sacrificing") *"praise"* will glorify Him and those *"who order* [their] *conduct"* ("way") according to His law will see *"the salvation of God."*

How then can hypocrisy be banished from the church? How can we have a "whole" gospel? The answer, according to Psalm 50, is in worship and work, faith and obedience.

The renewal of the church begins with a renewal in worship. This is God's priority and this theme is addressed first here. When God restores His people, He restores them in worship: *"Whoever offers praise glorifies Me."*

John Wimber tells of the beginning of the Vineyard Church in Yorba Linda, California. When John first went to be with the congregation there, they were "walking wounded" who gathered in his home under his wife's leadership.

They were so hurt, spiritually and emotionally, having been ground down by the institutional church and the agony of life, that all they could do was worship. Here were about a hundred fifty people singing to the Lord for over an hour. There wasn't any sermon or Sunday school. They just opened their hearts to God in praise. Out of this beginning, the rest of the ministry flowed. *"Conduct"* began to be rightly ordered and God's *"salvation"* was seen (v. 23).

When we learn to worship the Lord, then we will want to work for the Lord. When our faith grows, obedience will come and God will fulfill His word: *"I will show the salvation of God."*

CHAPTER FIFTY-ONE

Prayer for Renewal

Psalm 51

How we long for renewal! Every area of our life is so easily corroded and stained. Our marriages need renewal. As Scott Peck observes, we must fall in love again and again. Our families need renewal. It is tragic that often it takes illness or death to reunite us. Our churches need renewal when liturgy becomes mechanical, the prayers rote, and programs perfunctory. But most of all, we need personal renewal—deep inner conviction of our own sin and poverty—followed by a fresh cleansing and infilling of God's Spirit.

There is no renewal apart from pain. This pain may come in moral crisis. It may come when the placid order of life is broken by illness, economic reversal, or an upheaval in relationships. It may come when we reflect upon the pace with which life passes and upon our haunting need for meaning. Carl Jung said that all of the people over forty years old coming to see him for psychiatric help were looking for some reason to continue living.

The deepest renewal is spiritual, and it has a moral base. Since God is holy and since He has given us a conscience, we cannot be renewed apart from dealing with our moral failure before Him. Try as we may, we cannot remove sin by rationalization or denial. At some point our intellectual and psychological defense mechanisms will be broken. In that moment of truth when we face our own despair, God promises to come to us. But how will we know what to do? How can we experience His cleansing and renewing power? Psalm 51 becomes a key to new life. This great psalm opens the door to a radical change for each person who is willing to pray this prayer from the heart.

Tradition ascribes this psalm to David in the context of his sin with Bathsheba (2 Sam. 11–12). Here David was really guilty of a whole chain of sin. Lust led to adultery, adultery to deception, and deception to murder. In trying to cover his tracks he only dug the pit deeper. In this sense, David was no different from us. Finally, the Lord confronted him through Nathan the prophet. The ringing words "You are the man!" (2 Sam. 12:7) brought David to his knees before God, and judgment followed swiftly. At the same time, David received mercy. When he confessed to Nathan, "I have sinned against the Lord," Nathan replied, "The Lord also has put away your sin; you shall not die" (2 Sam. 12:13). Psalm 51, then, is David's deep, prayerful, agonizing response to his catastrophe.

While some scholars do not see David as author of this psalm (and there certainly may be some reworking of an earlier prayer), we will accept the traditional view that he was the writer. Psalm 51 is a prayer of lament and belongs to the seven so-called Penitential Psalms (Pss. 6, 32, 38, 51, 102, 130, 143). As we study this prayer we are at one of the deepest points of Biblical revelation. We must prepare to be changed! The thought here moves from a cry for cleansing (vv. 1–2) to the reality of sin (vv. 3–4), the depths of sin (vv. 5–6), cleansing and communion (vv. 7–9), renewal (vv. 10–11), and restoration (vv. 12–13). After a personal conclusion (vv. 14–17), there is also a corporate conclusion (vv. 18–19).

CRY FOR CLEANSING

1 Have mercy upon me, O God,
   According to Your lovingkindness;
   According to the multitude of Your tender mercies,
   Blot out my transgressions.
2 Wash me thoroughly from my iniquity,
   And cleanse me from my sin.

Ps. 51:1–2

David's cry for *"mercy"* is a cry for release from the presence and power of sin. His willingness to call upon God in the depths of his despair is based upon God's character—His *"lovingkindness"* or covenant-love, and His *"tender mercies."* The latter phrase means "compassion" or "motherly feeling." David can count on the fullness of God's mercy both because of His covenant and because of His motherly love toward him. Paul uses a similar picture of love in describing his relationship to his converts: "But we were gentle among you, just as a nursing mother cherishes her own children" (1 Thess. 2:7). In the nouns *"lovingkindness"* and *"tender mercies"* God bears both masculine and feminine characteristics. When we come to God for forgiveness we must come as did David, calling upon the fullness of God's grace. Now, however, it is through Christ's merit that we stand before the Father. We are bold to confess our sins because the blood of Jesus has established a new covenant and "cleanses us from all sin" (1 John 1:7). Here we see the mercy of God: "In this is love, not that we loved God, but that He loved us and sent His Son to be the propitiation for our sins" (1 John 4:10).

The power of verses 1 and 2 lies in the verbs. Grace in action blots, washes, and cleanses. Thus when our sin is intersected by the love of God we are renewed. Sin cannot stand before grace. David prays first for his transgressions to be blotted out the way a debt on a ledger is erased. God's promise in Isaiah 43:25 is to do exactly this. Second, David prays for his iniquity to be washed out, in the same way that clothes are laundered. Third, he prays for his sin to be cleansed, as imperfections are smelted from precious metals (see Mal. 3:3). The nouns—"transgressions, sin, iniquity"—all indicate moral failure. *"Sin,"* as noted earlier, translates a word meaning "to miss the mark, or goal, or way." Thus to sin is to deviate from God's moral law or standard, and ultimately, to miss the perfection of God Himself, "for all have sinned and fall short of the glory of God" (Rom. 3:23). As Jesus demands, "Therefore you shall be perfect, just as your Father in heaven is perfect" (Matt. 5:48). Who then can stand in the judgment? We must join David's cry, "Blot out my transgressions."

THE REALITY OF SIN

3 For I acknowledge my transgressions,
  And my sin *is* always before me.
4 Against You, You only, have I sinned,
  And done *this* evil in Your sight—
  That You may be found just when You speak,
  And blameless when You judge.

Ps. 51:3–4

Here in David's admission of his need is further ground for cleansing. There is an odd dignity in taking responsibility for our own sin. We have a tendency to blame everyone and everything but ourselves. Finally to admit, "I'm sick," or "I did it," is the first step to healing and recovery. God's word through Nathan the prophet has brought David, who is spiritually sick, back to reality, and he acknowledges that he has sinned. His consciousness is now dominated by guilt: *"And my sin is always before me."*

I have often seen people sick under the load of their sin. Such a man came to me recently. He and his family had joined a cult and moved to the south. There he committed adultery. When this became known he was expelled, and his wife refused to ever see him again. Returning to California, he lived in agony. Depression broke his spirit. Finally he went back to the south and eventually committed suicide. The cult told him that there was no forgiveness, no restoration possible. This satanic lie pushed him to destroy his life. He knew his sin—his sin was *"always before"* him—but, unlike David, he did not know his Savior.

The road to recovery, however, lies in verse 4: *"Against You, You only, have I sinned."* When we take our sin to people often we get only condemnation. When we take our sin to God, there is absolute justice and absolute mercy. God delights in forgiving the repentant sinner.

We must realize with David that all sin is against God, because it is God who orders all of life. Breaking any part of that order is a violation of His will and is a sin against Him. When Joseph was sexually tempted by Potiphar's wife in Egypt, he responded, "How . . . can I do this great wickedness, and sin against God?" (Gen. 39:9). Adultery not only breaks the marriage vow; it also breaks the divine order for marriage and is thus sin against God.

Since God's eyes are upon David, the conclusion in verse 4 is certain: God will *"speak"* justly and *"judge"* purely or clearly. Final and true justice will be given by Him alone. Thus to fall on our faces before the Lord and say with David, *"Against You, You only, have I sinned"* is the beginning of the beginning. It is to see our sins as extensions of the sin of our rebelling against the living and true God. Next, the psalm turns to the root of sin.

THE DEPTHS OF SIN

> 5 Behold, I was brought forth in iniquity,
>   And in sin my mother conceived me.
> 6 Behold, You desire truth in the inward parts,
>   And in the hidden *part* You will make me to know
>   wisdom.

Ps. 51:5–6

When David confesses that he was *"brought forth"* or "birthed" in iniquity he does not mean that sin resides in sexual intercourse. Neither does *"in sin my mother conceived me"* mean that he was born out of wedlock. What these verses do teach is that even at birth, even at conception, sin's infection is present, that because of Adam's fall, the whole human race is sinful by nature. Thus Paul writes of Adam, "By one man's disobedience many were made sinners" (Rom. 5:19). Each of us can say, with Bob Dylan, "Stone cold dead / As I stepped out of the womb" ("Saved").

It is this inner condition that is expressed in verse 6. The Hebrew word for "desire" is strong. God is true, and He wants His character to be found in us. Therefore, He "delights in" our truth; He "takes pleasure in" it. This is the truth of our being, not simply in what we say, but in who we are. God looks for trustworthiness in us, in our *"inward parts,"* our "guts."

What God desires, He also provides, so wisdom is God's gift to us.

David committed adultery out of foolishness, but God brought him to repentance through His word. This is wisdom. Jeremiah promises (31:33) that when the new covenant comes God will write His law upon our hearts. Thus Christ is now our wisdom (1 Cor. 1:30).

CLEANSING AND COMMUNION

> 7 Purge me with hyssop, and I shall be clean;
> Wash me, and I shall be whiter than snow.
> 8 Make me hear joy and gladness,
> *That* the bones You have broken may rejoice.
> 9 Hide Your face from my sins,
> And blot out all my iniquities.
>
> *Ps. 51:7–9*

Now that David has admitted his sin, acknowledged the One against whom he has sinned, and gotten to the depths of his sin, in utter helplessness he must either despair or throw himself completely upon God's mercy. Knowing the love of God, he cries out for cleansing (v. 7).

The verb for *"purge"* is intensive here, meaning "un-sin" me, purify me from uncleanness. The word is commonly used in describing the cleansing of a leper's house. Hyssop is also used to sprinkle blood in the rite of purification (Lev. 14:52). Similarly, hyssop was the agent used in spreading the blood of the Passover lamb on the lintels and doorposts of the Hebrew households in Egypt before the plague of death (Exod. 12:22). Underlying the purging of verse 7, then, is the concept of sacrificial blood. As we pray for purification, the leprosy of sin is removed.

In a parallel phrase, David asks: *"Wash me."* The result of this cleansing will be a dazzling white garment, *"whiter than snow."* As God promises through Isaiah, "though your sins are like scarlet, / They shall be as white as snow" (Isa. 1:18).

This deep cleansing gives David boldness in praying for restoration: *"Make me hear joy and gladness"* (v. 8). He not only wants cleansing; he wants communion with the Lord. Is the *"joy"* and *"gladness"* he desires that of worshipers restored to the community of God's people? Is David praying for his deafness of sin to be healed so that he can hear praise again?

The metaphor of *"broken"* or crushed *"bones"* in verse 8 suggests that God has cut David down in conviction. Confronted by the truth, he is shattered. Yet these very *"bones"* will *"rejoice"* when God cleanses and restores. In the picture given to Ezekiel, the dry bones will live when God's Spirit blows again upon Israel (Ezek. 37:1–14).

Continuing in verse 9 to pray for cleansing, David asks God to take His *"face"* away from his sin, and David's sin away from His face. God will no longer see his sins, the evil done in His sight (v. 4), and David's *"iniquities"* (v. 2) will be stricken from the record.

Up to this point in the psalm, David has been pleading for forgiveness again and again: "Blot out," "wash," "cleanse," "purge," "wash," "hide Your face," "blot out." Repetition emphasizes the depths of David's grief and the longing for release. Jesus tells us to keep on asking, to keep on seeking, and to keep on knocking (Luke 11:9). David does just this. He is bold in prayer both because of his deep pain and because of the deeper love of God.

RENEWAL

> 10 Create in me a clean heart, O God,
>   And renew a steadfast spirit within me.
> 11 Do not cast me away from Your presence,
>   And do not take Your Holy Spirit from me.
>   *Ps. 51:10–11*

Moving beyond the cry for cleansing, David now prays for a re-creation reflecting the original creation itself, as evidenced in the word *"create."* The same Hebrew verb, *bārāʿ,* is used both here and in Genesis 1:1. David has a radical new beginning in mind, a longing ultimately fulfilled in Christ. He wants total newness so that he will not fall back into the cycle of sin.

The parallel phrase calls for a *"steadfast spirit"* to be renewed. The *"spirit"* (*rûaḥ*) is the power of life itself. We are animated by our spirits. Also, the spirit is the seat of our emotions (Isa. 26:9).

In effect, verse 10 asks for a new self—heart and spirit. Such a work can only be done by God Himself. Thus Jesus tells Nicodemus that he must be reborn or born from above. Moreover, Jesus identifies this as God's miracle when He continues, "that which is born of the flesh is flesh, and that which is born of the Spirit is spirit" (John 3:6). What David asks of God comes fully with the Messiah.

Next, David turns from a request made in positive terms in verse

10 to one in the negative in verse 11: *"Do not cast me away from Your presence."* It is David's desire to live in the *"presence"* (literally, "before the face") of the Lord. While he doesn't want God to see his sin, he does want Him to see him. To be cast from God's *"presence"* is to die. This is the ultimate loss (cf. Matt. 22:1–14).

He continues: *"And do not take Your Holy Spirit from me."* The abiding presence of the *"Holy Spirit"* is parallel to being in the "presence" of God, so David asks for the *"Spirit"* not to be taken from him. When he was anointed King of Israel, 1 Samuel 16:13 tells us, "the Spirit of the Lord came upon David from that day forward." Theologically, it is the presence of the *"Spirit"* that brings David under conviction of sin. It is also the Spirit who brings assurance and comfort.

RESTORATION TO THE JOY OF SALVATION

12 Restore to me the joy of Your salvation,
   And uphold me *by Your* generous Spirit.
13 *Then* I will teach transgressors Your ways,
   And sinners shall be converted to You.

                                                              Ps. 51:12–13

Beyond a new heart is worship and witness. As David has asked for joy in verse 8, so he now connects it to salvation: *"Restore to me the joy of Your salvation"* (v. 12). *"Salvation"* here includes deliverance from the penalty and power of sin. This is God's gift; it is not our *"salvation"* but His. As God brings this deliverance, *"joy"* will come. This is the joy of enemies defeated, of victory over death. But beyond these benefits, there is the joy of the Lord's presence. Before the cross Jesus promises His disciples that their sorrow at His death will be short-lived. "I will see you again and your heart will rejoice, and your joy no one will take from you" (John 16:22). Jesus is here; this is joy! This is true worship before Him!

The next clause, *"And uphold me by Your generous Spirit"* (v. 12), translates literally, "And with a willing spirit uphold me." The "willing spirit" here probably refers, not to the Holy Spirit, but to the renewed "steadfast spirit" in verse 10. The adjective *"generous"* or "willing" means "inclined, noble." It is a spirit ready to do the Lord's bidding.

Out of the joy of worship and his resulting readiness, David promises: *"Then I will teach transgressors Your ways, / And sinners shall be converted* to You" (v. 13). David's teaching comes from his own walking in God's ways. This psalm is a part of his teaching efforts. Because he has known transgression and sin, he can teach transgressors and sinners. He is a "wounded healer" (Henri Nouwen).

Credible witness comes from those whose lives have been redeemed from their own hell. Paul can deal so effectively with legalism because he was a legalist (see Phil. 3:2 ff.). When we witness from our own wounds, the wounded can identify with us. Also, when we witness from our wounds the glory goes to God and not to us.

A friend of mine was a heroin addict and a rock musician. Since his conversion, his life has had an important impact on a circle of rock musicians, many of whom are also involved in drugs. He can identify with them and they with him. As God has healed his life, given him joy in His salvation, and given him a re-created, willing spirit, transgressors are taught and sinners "*converted*" or "turned," "returned." For him, rock music is now a vehicle through which to communicate Christ.

PERSONAL CONCLUSION

14 Deliver me from the guilt of bloodshed, O God,
    The God of my salvation,
    And my tongue shall sing aloud of Your righteousness.
15 O Lord, open my lips,
    And my mouth shall show forth Your praise.
16 For You do not desire sacrifice, or else I would give
    it;
    You do not delight in burnt offering.
17 The sacrifices of God *are* a broken spirit,
    A broken and a contrite heart—
    These, O God, You will not despise.

                                               Ps. 51:14–17

David now brings his prayer to its climax, asking God, once again, to clear the books. The word for *"bloodshed"* in verse 14 is literally "bloods" *(dāmîm,* plural). The word signifies blood violently shed and refers to David's arranged murder of Bathsheba's husband (2 Sam. 11:15). David reinforces this final request for freedom by using the address *"the God of my salvation,"* as if he were reminding God of His grace. To paraphrase the thought: "Be true to who You are. Be my Savior, O God. Deliver me."

The vow of verse 14 is immediately followed by a request in the next verse. The verb for *"sing aloud"* literally means "to give a ringing cry." David will trumpet God's righteousness when the curse is lifted. But if David is to worship rightly, God must work within him, by grace. Grace forgives us and grace evokes our response. Our *"praise"* not only reflects God's work; it is God's work. The Father not only seeks worshipers (John 4:23), the Father creates the worshipers He seeks.

What then will David offer to the Lord in worship? Israel was taught by God not to come to Him empty-handed. She must bring an offering to Him. Here, however, David does not follow tradition. The word for *"sacrifice"* here in verse 16 means "that which is slaughtered," a "blood-sacrifice." The parallel word *"burnt offering"* refers to the slaughtered animal consumed by fire as it is offered wholly to the Lord. But these offerings are not what God wants, because God wants David! Verse 17 acknowledges: *"The sacrifices of God are a broken spirit, / A broken and a contrite heart."*

All that David can offer to the Lord in worship then is his shattered *"spirit,"* his *"broken . . . heart,"* that is, the very center of his being, himself. Sin has *"broken"* him; judgment has *"broken"* him. But even more than this, when we discover God's mercy in His incredible love for us *in our sin*—here is the final breaking. As our heart sobs, the Lord puts His arms around us. When we see Jesus expelling demons, forgiving sins, cleansing lepers, and hanging on the cross—then we are finally *"broken."* We are among those who are forgiven much and who therefore love much (Luke 7:47).

This then is David's personal conclusion to Psalm 51. He simply comes to God just as he is. After we have tried everything else we must come the same way. There are no alternatives.

CORPORATE CONCLUSION

18 Do good in Your good pleasure to Zion;
   Build the walls of Jerusalem.
19 Then You shall be pleased with the sacrifices of
      righteousness,
   With burnt offering and whole burnt offering;
   Then they shall offer bulls on Your altar.

Ps. 51:18–19

Many scholars view these verses as a later addition to this psalm since they call for a renewal of Jerusalem and the sacrificial system. This appears to contradict verse 16. Such a view is modern and unnecessary. The Old Testament holds together interior spirituality and established liturgy. We need not choose between the prophet and the priest.

As king, David now prays for the nation. The restoration of the king will lead to the restoration of Israel. Broken leaders mean broken people. I recall hearing Stanley Collins tell pastors that if he were the devil he would do two things to the church: "Discourage the leaders and divide the Body." A renewed leader will renew a congregation. *"Zion"* here is Jerusalem's mountain (see Ps. 2:6; 48:2).

Once the people are restored, proper worship will come from their renewed hearts. So David concludes: *"Then You shall be pleased with the sacrifices of righteousness."* The problem isn't with the sacrificial system; the problem is with us. The *"sacrifices of righteousness"* are those offerings that are made by a renewed king and a renewed people.

Psalm 51 is a prayer for renewal. Again and again, it has brought forth streams of "mercy" to crushed "spirits" and "broken hearts." Today renewal is again stirring the church. As we are "broken" before God, the walls of Jerusalem will be built and the "sacrifices of righteousness" will ascend to His praise and glory.

CHAPTER FIFTY-TWO

The End of the "Big Lie"

Psalm 52

The Bible traces the "Big Lie" from the Garden of Eden in Genesis to the Lake of Fire in Revelation.

The "Big Lie" can be understood in various ways. It is the lie that we have created ourselves; that we are gods; that we command our own destiny; that we are self-sufficient and autonomous; that the meaning of life is pleasure, self-fulfillment, or independence. When we live out the "Big Lie" we deceive and manipulate people for our own ends. We make ourselves the center of our universe. We live out one question: "What's in it for me?" Cut off from God's goodness, we become evil in our intentions, feeding on our own selfishness.

God comes to shatter the "Big Lie" that started in the Garden. When Adam and Eve fell, they did not become like gods, as Satan promised. Instead, they simply found themselves naked and jumped into the bushes, where God confronted them, showed them their sin, executed His judgment and threw them out of the Garden to wander across the earth. We are still tempted, however, to live without God, but He doesn't leave us alone. He comes with warning and then judgment to show us our alternatives. We have only two: live with Him in the truth, or live without Him in the "Big Lie." Psalm 52 addresses these alternatives.

This psalm begins by exposing the stupidity of the "mighty man" who trusts in himself and his money. He chooses evil rather than God's goodness, and loves lying. His "deceitful tongue" covers up his evil, "autonomous" heart.

God will come and destroy this man. The righteous people will be in awe and laugh at his stupidity. The psalmist will be among them in God's house, worshiping and waiting on the Lord. Rather than finding life's meaning in himself, he finds it in the mercy of God and the goodness of His name.

Tradition, which we accept, ascribes this psalm to David. In form it is both a lament and a thanksgiving hymn. The psalm divides into three sections. Verses 1–4 contain a warning description of the "mighty man" who loves "evil" and deception. Verses 5–7 describe the resulting wrath of God. Verses 8–9 contain David's intention to be among the righteous in God's house.

THE MIGHTY MAN

1 Why do you boast in evil, O mighty man?
  The goodness of God *endures* continually.
2 Your tongue devises destruction,
  Like a sharp razor, working deceitfully.
3 You love evil more than good,
  Lying rather than speaking righteousness.   Selah

4 You love all devouring words,
  You deceitful tongue.

Ps. 52:1–4

Verse 1 opens with our alternatives: human evil or God's goodness. It begins with a question: *"Why do you boast in evil, O mighty man?"* The name *"mighty man"* in the Old Testament is applied to people such as giants (Gen. 6:4), hunters (Gen. 10:9), prideful warriors (1 Sam. 2:4), and the king's bodyguard (1 Kings 1:8). It denotes a man of great physical strength and valor. The strong, powerful, assertive male boasts, however, not in the God who gave him his strength, but *"in evil."* There is immediate contrast in the affirmation, which implies that the *"mighty man"* and his *"evil"* will soon pass away (see also v. 5). It is only God and those who know His covenant-love who last.

The evil of which the *"mighty man"* boasts is vividly described in verses 2–4. *"His tongue,"* which communicates his thoughts, *"devises destruction."* The Hebrew word for *"destruction"* also denotes an "evil desire." This is expressed here in the way his tongue cuts—like a *"razor, working deceitfully,"* or working "treachery." In the New Testament James warns, "The tongue is a fire, a world of iniquity. The tongue is so set among our members that it defiles the whole body, and sets on fire the course of nature; and it is set on fire by hell" (3:6).

Behind the work of the *"tongue"* stands the *"evil"* heart: *"You love evil more than good, / Lying rather than speaking righteousness"* (v. 3). The *"mighty man"* (v. 1) has rejected God's *"goodness"* (His moral order), and God's *"righteousness"* (His covenant relationships). Instead, he loves *"evil,"* which is hidden behind a facade or smokescreen of *"lying."*

Moreover, since the mighty man loves evil he also loves the words that hide it (v. 4). *"Devouring words"* are words that destroy. They, too, are spoken by the lying *"tongue."*

When we read this description we cannot help but think of the mighty men who have strutted across our history with their armies, their parades, their salutes, their uniforms, their press releases, and their elaborate schemes for cornering the market or dominating the world. Again and again we have been shocked by our Watergates, with their tape-erasures, their spies, their "double-speak," and their new language—such as "that statement is now inoperative," rather than "that statement is a lie."

In judging this world's mighty men, however, we can learn from this psalm that we must look to the evil and deception that we may find in our own hearts. We are all "mighty men" who may withhold from each other, be afraid to speak the truth, use our tongues like razors, and deny or rationalize our own seduction by the "Big Lie" of our autonomy. We won't, however, get off forever.

GOD'S WRATH

> 5 God shall likewise destroy you forever;
>   He shall take you away, and pluck you out of *your*
>   dwelling place,
>   And uproot you from the land of the living.   Selah
> 6 The righteous also shall see and fear,
>   And shall laugh at him, *saying,*
> 7 "Here is the man *who* did not make God his strength,
>   But trusted in the abundance of his riches,
>   *And* strengthened himself in his wickedness."
>
> *Ps. 52:5–7*

David now turns from the mighty man to the avenging hand of God. The word for *"God"* in verse 5 is *ʾēl,* the generic Semitic name for Him. It may come from the root *ʾwl.* If so, it means "to be strong." Thus "the Strong One" comes to destroy the mighty man. The Hebrew for *"destroy"* means "to break down" or "demolish." Here then is total, eternal demolition.

God's action is graphically described in the rest of verse 5: *"He shall take you away"* or "seize" you. The verb here is employed for seizing cords from a fire. He will *"pluck you out of your dwelling place* [tent]" or "abduct you from home." And God will *"uproot you from the land of the living,"* the way a plant is uprooted and dies. In all of these word pictures there is a sense of violent, quick, decisive action.

God's wrath on the mighty man serves also as a warning to the "righteous," those who submit to God's covenant relationships. Thus they *"see"* God's judgment, God's action. Their response then is *"fear"*; they are in awe of what God has done. The laughter that comes may express mocking or relief that they have not suffered such a fate.

A DWELLER IN GOD'S HOUSE

> 8 But I *am* like a green olive tree in the house of God;
>   I trust in the mercy of God forever and ever.
> 9 I will praise You forever,

Because You have done *it;*
And in the presence of Your saints
I will wait on Your name, for *it is* good.

Ps. 52:8-9

David now offers his own confession. He stands with God and the righteous. He is *"like a green olive tree in the house of God."* The *"olive tree"* grew for hundreds of years, yielding about six gallons of oil on alternate years (for Israel as God's olive tree see Rom. 11:16 ff.). The metaphor suggests that David is both evergreen and fruitful. Also, he dwells in God's *"house,"* namely, he dwells with God Himself. David trusts God's eternal *"mercy"* ("covenant love") *"forever and ever."*

Knowing the *"mercy"* of God, David now worships: *"I will praise you forever."* All God's grace, love, and forgiveness in His covenant are given to lead us into worship. Thus in Romans, based upon God's mercies in Christ, Paul calls upon us to present our bodies to Him as living sacrifices. This, Paul says, is our "spiritual worship" (Rom. 12:1, RSV).

Moreover, David's *"praise"* is for God's action: *"You have done it."* There is no direct object in the Hebrew, where the text literally reads, "You have acted." David worships God for both His word ("mercies") and His work. Furthermore, before God's people, His *"saints,"* David will *"wait* [look eagerly] *on* [*His*] *name."* The name of God manifests the presence and power of God. Thus David waits for this mainfestation in the confidence that *"it is good."*

While the mighty man is destroyed for his evil and deceit, the righteous man lives before God in worship and praise *"forever and ever."*

The "Big Lie" is exposed for what it is. If we build our lives upon ourselves and seek to be autonomous, masking that evil by deceit, we will get exactly what we want. We will be carried away by God's wrath to live in loneliness throughout eternity. "Hell," Helmut Thielicke says, "is the recognition of what we have missed." When we are ultimately alone, we will recognize that we have missed a covenant relationship with God in His mercy and that we have missed each other. Why then indeed, "do you boast in evil, O mighty man?"

CHAPTER FIFTY-THREE

Variant on Psalm 14

Psalm 53

With the exception of a few details, and apart from verse 5, Psalm 53 is identical with Psalm 14, and the text has been printed in chapter 14. Probably this is a modification of Psalm 14 for a special situation which was then incorporated into the larger body of Israel's hymnody. Eventually it found its way into the Psalter as Psalm 53, perhaps through use in temple worship. If this is true, verse 5 is the key to placing this "special edition" of Psalm 14.

The context of verse 5 is the total depravity of all people (vv. 1–3) and the special depravity of the *"workers of iniquity . . . who eat up [God's] people as they eat bread."* These evil workers are, however, now *"in great fear."* With the second line of verse 5 the change begins: *"Where no fear was, / For God has scattered the bones of him who encamps against you; You have put them to shame, / Because God has despised them."* The military language suggests that this psalm was, in part, rewritten to celebrate a deliverance of Israel from an enemy who came up against God's people in battle. They were destroyed on the field: their *"bones"* were *"scattered."* Their *"shame"* was due to their defeat at the hands of God. For the rest of the exposition of this psalm, see the comment on Psalm 14.

One point of application is in order. The Psalter is a living book of praise, worship, prophecy, teaching, and devotion. As the word of God in the midst of Israel, the Holy Spirit could refashion previous writings for new occasions and take psalms that emerged in one context and use them in another. We experience this today in the preaching and teaching of the church where an old passage will "live" for us in the immediate circumstances of our lives. Thus the relationship between Psalm 14 and Psalm 53 shows us how the ever-present Holy Spirit continues to interpret the written word of God in the life of God's people.

CHAPTER FIFTY-FOUR

When the Roof Is Falling In

Psalm 54

The ancient world lived, in the phrase of the eminent religious historian Mircea Eliade, with the "terror of history," expecting disaster to strike. Without warning, marauding armies or plagues would sweep through whole populations. Earthquakes, floods, and forest fires would often follow. In their preoccupation with escaping these terrors, many myths were created by these ancient peoples. Examples are found in the Babylonian New Year's Festival, which celebrated a return to primeval times, to "stop" history. Likewise, Platonic philosophy sought an ideal world beyond the flux of this life, and mystics placed a spiritual unity outside of time and space. For example, eastern religions asserted that the phenomenal world was an illusion, and affirmed an underlying monism. This escapism was true throughout the whole ancient world except for Israel. Here alone, according to Eliade, the people were forced to face history because they believed that in its terror they would meet the living God.

In Psalm 54 then we have the reality of the "terror of history," seen, first of all, in the "strangers" and "oppressors" who have risen up against the psalmist. There is, at the same time, another reality: the expectation that God will now act. Thus history moves in the dialectic of enemies attacking and God delivering. What was true for Israel is also true for us. We are faced with our personal and historical terrors. But we can also expect God's saving, delivering, and healing power to be manifested in our midst because our God is the God who makes history.

We accept here the tradition of Davidic authorship. The form of the psalm is an individual lament, and the thought moves from a call for help (vv. 1–3) to a confession of faith (vv. 4–5) and a commitment to worship (vv 6–7).

A CALL FOR HELP

> 1 Save me, O God, by Your name,
> And vindicate me by Your strength.

2 Hear my prayer, O God;
   Give ear to the words of my mouth.
3 For strangers have risen up against me,
   And oppressors have sought after my life;
   They have not set God before them.   Selah

                                                    Ps. 54:1–3

The verb for *"save"* in David's opening cry means to "release, deliver, set in the open." To be in an open place is to be free from vulnerability to attack. This is salvation in a concrete sense. In the plea *"vindicate me,"* the Hebrew means "to judge, to plead the cause." David not only wants to be saved from his enemies, he also wants his righteousness to be established by God's judgment. Furthermore, salvation and vindication come from the *"name"* and the *"strength"* of God. Using the *"name"* of God in prayer is the means of actualizing His presence and power. Thus when Abram camped between Bethel and Ai he built an altar "and called on the name of the Lord" (Gen. 12:8). Notice that he didn't merely call on the Lord, he called on His *"name."* To know God's name is to be able to contact Him. God's *"name"* and His *"strength"* are synonymous.

David now asks: *"Hear my prayer, O God; / Give ear to the words of my mouth"* (v. 2). The repetition is for emphasis. "Salvation" and "vindication" come from God through prayer, so David prays for God's *"ear"* to be open to him. In other words, he asks God's favor toward him.

His need for intercession is now stated: *"For strangers have risen up against me."* *"Strangers"* are aliens or foreigners. The verb used for *"risen up"* probably also means "to revolt" or "to take arms" (cf. Judg. 20:5; Ps. 27:3). A military action is taking place; *"oppressors"* seek David's *"life."* As Israel's king they want him dead. He concludes that these strangers *"have not set God before them,"* that is, they do not worship God. This suggests that the *"strangers"* are idolaters.

A CONFESSION OF FAITH

4 Behold, God *is* my helper;
   The Lord *is* with those who uphold my life.
5 He will repay my enemies for their evil.
   Cut them off in Your truth.

                                                    Ps. 54:4–5

Having called upon God to deliver him, and having identified the source of his crisis, David now confesses who God is and what He will do.

First, God is David's *"helper."* In Psalm 30:1 God's help is His mercy in healing and deliverance, and in Psalm 28:7 God helps because He is David's strength and shield. Here, God helps arm for battle. He is not only with David, however; He is also with David's men, *"those who uphold [his] life."*

Second, God will act on David's behalf: *"He will repay my enemies for their evil,"* or, literally, "He will turn the evil to my enemies." The word for *"enemies"* means "those who watch stealthily; insidious watchers." David asks God to destroy them: *"Cut them off in Your truth"* or "faithfulness."

However much this final plea may offend us, it is a realistic prayer for a king facing battle. In the "terror of history" David expects God to act, to bring His vindication by delivering him and his troops and winning the battle for him.

In Christ we now know that the Savior has been *"cut . . . off"* for us so that we who deserve to die may live. In the mystery of the gospel God reveals His deeper faithfulness to us by taking our judgment upon Himself. Thus our enemies—Satan, sin, and death—are defeated by Jesus, and our deliverance and vindication are in Him.

A COMMITMENT TO WORSHIP

6 I will freely sacrifice to You;
   I will praise Your name, O Lord, for *it is* good.
7 For He has delivered me out of all trouble;
   And my eye has seen *its desire* upon my enemies.

Ps. 54:6–7

Anticipating the answer to his prayers, David vows to *"freely sacrifice"* to God. His worship, however, is not the result of some bargain made with God. He is not under obligation to pay God off for his deliverance but worships freely from his heart. David will also *"praise [God's] name"* in its goodness, which is assured because *"He has delivered me out of all trouble* [constriction, distress], / *And my eye has seen its desire upon my enemies,"* or "my eye has looked [*in triumph*] upon my enemies" (v. 7).

In this psalm David, as we see, is not fleeing from history in denial, but facing it with realism. He must deal with his enemies, but only after he has dealt with God. He expects that God will hear his prayers and answer them by going into battle on his behalf. Thus David meets God in the crisis, knowing that it is only God who can save him and vindicate him.

When life's problems are caving in upon us we can flee into escapism or we can flee to the Lord. The promise of the gospel is that He will meet us right there and together with Him we will make history.

CHAPTER FIFTY-FIVE

Fight or Flight

Psalm 55

Psychologists tell us that there are two instinctive reactions to threat: fight or flight. As human beings we are preprogrammed to respond to attack. Our bodies automatically run through this program, which heightens our responses, preparing us to enter into combat. Our pulse speeds up, our senses are more alert, our adrenalin flows. The alternative response is flight, where we avoid the threat of conflict by running away, either physically or in denial or withdrawal. This may include passive-aggressive behavior like being silent, if engagement with our opponent continues. Psalm 55 reveals both fight and flight reactions. Here the author responds with "fight" as he prays, "Destroy, O Lord, and divide their tongues" (v. 9), and later, "Let death seize them; / Let them go down alive into hell" (v. 15). At the same time, he also responds with "flight": "So I said, 'Oh, that I had wings like a dove! / I would fly away and be at rest' " (v. 6).

What precipitates these responses? The psalmist is faced with the wrath of enemies who oppress him. His reaction to this attack is deep emotional distress, followed by the desire to flee. The fight response takes over, however, resulting in a cry to God for help and a further elaboration on the crisis. Here it turns out that the psalmist's enemy is a former, trusted friend. A palace revolt is going on; there is trouble in the city. His anger is followed by a call for judgment and confidence in God's readiness to deliver. Then complaint is again offered along with confidence in God's final resolution.

Tradition, which we follow here, ascribes this psalm to David. Contributing to this view is the fact that the revolt taking place centers in Jerusalem and has upset the city. Obviously, this is a power struggle in the highest ranks. The form of the psalm is that of a personal lament. The thought moves from complaint (vv. 1–8) to a call for judgment (vv. 9–15) and a confession of faith (v. 22), and concludes with resolution (v. 23).

DAVID'S COMPLAINT

1 Give ear to my prayer, O God,
   And do not hide Yourself from my supplication.
2 Attend to me, and hear me;
   I am restless in my complaint, and moan noisily,
3 Because of the voice of the enemy,
   Because of the oppression of the wicked;
   For they bring down trouble upon me,
   And in wrath they hate me.
4 My heart is severely pained within me,
   And the terrors of death have fallen upon me.
5 Fearfulness and trembling have come upon me,
   And horror has overwhelmed me.
6 So I said, "Oh, that I had wings like a dove!
   I would fly away and be at rest.
7 Indeed, I would wander far off,
   And remain in the wilderness.   Selah
8 I would hasten my escape
   From the windy storm *and* tempest."

Ps. 55:1–8

David begins with a general, broad-based complaint, calling upon God in emphatic terms to hear his prayer: *"Give ear to my prayer, O God"* (cf. Ps. 54:2). He asks God to *"not hide"* but to *"attend to"* him and *"hear"* him. The word for "prayer" here is general. It can refer to both personal and corporate prayer and covers a wide variety of forms and issues. The word translated *"supplication,"* identifies the type of prayer as a request for a favor, however. David continues: *"Attend to me, and hear me."* The word for *"hear"* may better be rendered "answer." He wants God to give him His attention and respond.

Next, David offers a twofold reason for needing God's response. First, he is in deep trouble: *"I am restless in my complaint, and moan noisily."* The verb for *"restless"* means "to wander, to roam." We might paraphrase the thought, "I'm all over the place in my complaint." His moaning signifies inarticulate pain. Second, he has enemies who give him pain because they are articulate; they have a *"voice."* They oppress him, they *"bring down trouble upon"* him and they *"hate"* him. Here is full-on attack. No wonder David moans!

We learn later that part of the pain he feels is that of betrayal. His close associate has not only rejected him, but he now plots against him with "deceit" and "destruction." David responds to this assault by elaborating upon his agony in verses 4–5. The *"terrors"* David feels are like the terror experienced by Israel's enemies when she passed through them on the way to the Promised Land (Exod. 15:16). Such an overwhelming sense of dread leads to *"fearfulness and trembling"* and overwhelming *"horror."* The word for *"horror"* means "shuddering." David's body is out of control with fear.

In verses 6–7 David expresses his yearning for flight. If he *"had wings like a dove!"* he would flee his circumstances and vanish; like a bird, he would find refuge in some distant crag. In Jeremiah God says, "Give wings to Moab, / That she may flee and get away. . . . You who dwell in Moab, / Leave the cities and dwell in the rock, / And be like the dove which makes her nest / In the sides of the cave's mouth" (Jer. 48:9, 28).

Then, changing the image, David says: *"Indeed, I would wander far off, / And remain in the wilderness."* The *"wilderness"* has always offered the Jews a place of refuge. Again and again, David sought its solace when pursued by Saul. He is anxious to go: *"I would hasten my escape / From the windy storm and tempest."* Here his enemies are like a deluge pouring down upon him. No wonder David would choose flight.

God understands our temptation to flee pain and adversity. He also knows our broken heart when we are rejected. Even Jesus prayed, "Father. . . . take this cup away from Me; nevertheless, not what I will, but what You will" (Mark 14:36).

These verses have special meaning for me, for I have never enjoyed confrontation; I am not a fighter. My need to be loved and accepted is so strong that when confrontation comes I am ready to flee "like a dove." I have learned, however, starting with my marriage, that just to let problems lie is no solution; they come back to haunt me. What I sow I reap. For me, therefore, although flight is a temptation, it is better to fight by facing the issues.

DAVID'S CALL FOR JUDGMENT

9 Destroy, O Lord, *and* divide their tongues,
  For I have seen violence and strife in the city.
10 Day and night they go around it on its walls;
  Iniquity and trouble *are* also in the midst of it.
11 Destruction *is* in its midst;
  Oppression and deceit do not depart from its streets.
12 For *it is* not an enemy *who* reproaches me;
  Then I could bear *it.*
  Nor *is it* one *who* hates me who has exalted *himself*
    against me;
  Then I could hide from him.
13 But *it was* you, a man my equal,
  My companion and my acquaintance.
14 We took sweet counsel together,
  And walked to the house of God in the throng.
15 Let death seize them;
  Let them go down alive into hell,
  For wickedness *is* in their dwellings *and* among them.
  Ps. 55:9–15

It is David's greatness that in turning to fight he calls upon the Lord. He knows that he cannot fight alone, so he asks for help: *"Destroy, O Lord, and divide their tongues"* (v. 9; this call for judgment will be elaborated upon later in v. 15). The verb for *"destroy"* can also mean "confuse." Thus David is asking God to confuse and *"divide"* their *"tongues,"* or speech. This judgment would end their plots and disperse them as it did at the tower of Babel.

David gives reasons for asking this judgment. Jerusalem is being torn apart. Public order is breaking down. *"Day and night"* (that is, continually) David's enemies *"go around it on [Jerusalem's] walls,"* namely, they command the walls of the city, and *"iniquity and trouble are also in the midst of it." "Iniquity"* here denotes "evil schemes," and *"trouble"* includes "mischief." The city is consumed by the wicked, which results in *"destruction"* in its center, *"in its midst,"* and *"deceit"* and guile on its *"streets"* (v. 11). *"Streets"* here means "marketplace" or "plaza." Thus all this evil has gotten to the heart of the city. It may include the collusion of judges meeting in the public square.

In verses 12–14 David becomes clearly personal as to the identity of his opponent. He is not merely attacked by *"an enemy."* If he were, he *"could bear it."* Neither is the situation simply that someone who *"hates"* him is seeking to grab power. Rather, he cannot hide because his enemy knows him well. His enemy is addressed directly as *"you, a man my equal."* He is a *"companion,"* an *"acquaintance."*

David and this former friend were so close that they *"took sweet counsel together, / And walked to the house of God in the throng"* (v. 14). For Israel there could not be a more tender picture of companionship than such sharing of community and worship.

The rejection of the former relationship brings David to cry out for judgment. His anger over betrayal is clear and unequivocal: *"Let death seize them; / Let them go down alive into hell."* Here is fight reaction, asking God to bring His ultimate judgment to bear. David calls for his enemies to be taken *"alive"* into the place of the dead, rather than being allowed to live out their natural days. Verse 15 tells us that, like Achan at Ai, they deserve God's wrath for what they harbor (see Joshua 7). Their evil, however, isn't simply in their homes; it is in them.

In light of the gospel, it is hard for us to accept David's vindictiveness. However, two things may be said. First, David needs direct action to deal with the political situation he is facing. Thus his context is far different from that of most of us in the church today. Second, we all deserve the curse of verse 15 for our evil hearts, our deceptive plans, and our Judas spirit, not only toward each other but toward God. If we don't realize that we deserve to be thrown alive into hell, then we won't realize the depths of Christ's love for us (His enemies) and the amazing grace of His heart that led Him to go to hell that we may go to heaven. We deserve the curse, but we receive the blessing. This is the surprise of the gospel: What we deserve Jesus takes for us.

DAVID'S CONFESSION

16 As for me, I will call upon God,
   And the LORD shall save me.

17 Evening and morning and at noon
   I will pray, and cry aloud,
   And He shall hear my voice.
18 He has redeemed my soul in peace from the battle
   that was against me,
   For there were many against me.
19 God will hear, and afflict them,
   Even He who abides from of old.   Selah
   Because they do not change,
   Therefore they do not fear God.

                                         Ps. 55:16–19

At this point, David gives his own confession of faith, asserting that he will *"call upon"* God and be saved (v. 16). Salvation means deliverance from his traitorous enemies. His prayers will be continuous: *"evening,"* *"morning,"* and *"noon."* Mentioning evening prayer first may indicate that David's day began with sunset. The point, however, is that his prayer is consistent and continuous. It is also vocal and energetic: *"I will pray, and cry aloud."* The verb translated here as *"pray"* means "to complain," and the verb for *"cry aloud"* means "to roar or be boisterous." David bellows and gets God's attention: *"And He shall hear my voice"* (v. 17).

In verse 18 David acknowledges the result of his prayer. To be *"redeemed"* is to be "ransomed" through a price paid. The price here may be God's energy exerted on David's behalf. The result of God's liberating act is that David's *"soul"* ("self") is *"in peace,"* or "wholeness, security, and well-being."

Not only does God deliver David, but He also afflicts or, literally, "answers" his enemies. The answer is one of judgment that comes from the One who *"abides from of old."* The verb for "abide" (*yāšab*) can also mean "sits as king or judge" (cf. Mal. 3:3). God is the King-Judge *"from of old,"* or "from the beginning" (cf. Ps. 74:12).

God's judgment is deserved *"Because they do not change, / Therefore they do not fear God"* (v. 19). The moral responsibility lies with David's enemies. They have chosen the way of destruction (cf. Rom. 1:32; 3:18).

A FURTHER COMPLAINT

20 He has put forth his hands against those who were
   at peace with him;
   He has broken his covenant.

21 *The words* of his mouth were smoother than butter,
   But war *was* in his heart;
   His words were softer than oil,
   Yet they *were* drawn swords.

                                                    Ps. 55:20–21

The complaint theme returns here in a shorter form and brings a new or modified charge against David's enemy: *"He has put forth his hands against those who were at peace with him."* These former friends are identified as being bound with him in a *"covenant"* which has now been *"broken."* Those in the covenant, of course, could include David, and thus it would not be a wholly new charge. It does, however, give it a wider dimension. The violation of the *"covenant"* (or "contract") is the violation of a legally binding agreement. Because God witnesses covenants and defends them, this is solid ground for His judging David's opponent.

Moreover, this enemy is a hypocrite whose words mask his intentions. They were *"smoother than butter,"* but *"war was in his heart"* (v. 21). Though they were *"softer than oil,"* they were in reality as sharp as *"drawn swords"* (cf. Ps. 52:2). The deception here may have been revealed in the covenant-breaking of verse 20.

It is worth noting that the rupture between David and his former friend has affected the whole city and divided it. Sin is never an individual act. The circle of those affected becomes increasingly wider when it is allowed to fester.

A Further Confession

22 Cast your burden on the Lord,
   And He shall sustain you;
   He shall never permit the righteous to be moved.

                                                    Ps. 55:22

David turns again to his own confidence in the Lord. The noun for *"burden"* means "what is given you, your lot." Certainly David has fulfilled the exhortation here; he practices what he preaches. In the promise that follows, the verb for *"sustain"* means "to support, nourish." When we throw our lot, or ourselves, on the Lord, He holds us up. Moreover, *"He shall never permit the righteous to be moved"* ("to totter, shake, slip"); that is, the *"righteous"* will be steadfast. (See chap. 1 for full discussion of the "righteous.")

To be sure, David has been shaken by the deceit and destructive actions of his former companion. Yet he has fulfilled his own exhortation. He has brought to the Lord all of his emotional pain, his feelings of rejection, the turmoil in Jerusalem, and the attacks upon him. Now he is experiencing the results. God upholds him and God stabilizes him.

We can never know the release and relief of this promise until we act on it, through prayer bringing our burden to the Lord. He, in turn, sustains us and keeps us firm. This is His work. All we can do is be open and let Him do it.

THE CONFIDENCE OF RESOLUTION

23 But You, O God, shall bring them down to the pit
    of destruction;
Bloodthirsty and deceitful men shall not live out
    half their days;
But I will trust in You.

Ps. 55:23

David again confesses his confidence that God will hear and answer his prayer, and will execute His judgment. The *"bloodthirsty"* (murderers) and *"deceitful men"* (see v. 11) will die young. David, however, puts himself in God's hands: *"But I will trust in You."* Clearly the whole psalm is a commentary on this last clause.

In his anger, then, David has had the alternatives of fight or flight. In fact, he chooses neither, but throws himself upon God and places his life and his enemies in God's hands. It is God who will fight for him. Likewise, Jesus refused to flee the cross or to fight His enemies. He put Himself into the Father's hands and thereby defeated all of His foes through His submission to the Father's will.

CHAPTER FIFTY-SIX

Trial and Trust

Psalm 56

Psalm 56 has the double theme of trial and trust. The psalmist is under attack. His opposition is relentless, fighting "all day," and substantial, "many . . . fight against" him. What is the nature of this assault? Some sort of a plot is being hatched. It includes undermining what the psalmist has said and thus seeking to trap him. His enemies' goal is to do him in. In the midst of the trial the psalmist cries out to God, expecting Him to act on his behalf. He trusts in Him and in His word. God, he believes, will deliver him from "death" and from "falling." Therefore, he will praise Him and "walk before" Him "in the light of the living."

Tradition, which we accept, ascribes this psalm to David. Its form is that of a personal lament. The movement of thought begins with a cry to God (vv. 1–2). Following a confession of confidence in Him (vv. 3–4) and a complaint (vv. 5–7), there is another confession of confidence (vv. 8–11), and finally an expression of commitment (vv. 12–13).

A CRY TO GOD

> 1 Be merciful to me, O God, for man would swallow
>   me up;
>   Fighting all day he oppresses me.
> 2 My enemies would hound *me* all day,
>   For *there are* many who fight against me, O Most High.
>
> Ps. 56:1–2

David opens this psalm with the cry: *"Be merciful to me, O God"* (see Ps. 51:1). The verb *"be merciful"* also means "to give unmerited favor or grace." Thus David calls upon God's grace rather than his own merit as the basis for his prayer. The crisis is identified; David's life is in danger. The word *"man"* could mean collective "mankind" or an individual man. In the context of verses 1–2 it seems to cover both. The verb for *"swallow up"* means either to "pant after, snuff up" (so here), or "to crush." Whichever translation is chosen, the meaning is deadly. Thus: *"Fighting all day he oppresses me."* The *"fighting"* mentioned seems not to be an actual physical attack yet. At this point, there are verbal battles and plots (see vv. 5–6) which will lead to a frontal assault.

In verse 2 David elaborates on his situation. The noun for *"enemies"* means "insidious watchers" (see v. 6) and the verb for *"hound"* is the same one used for *"swallow up"* ("to pant after, snuff up"). Thus these spies are "panting after" David. He concludes: *"For there are many who fight against me, O Most High."* The word translated *"O Most High"* ("height") may be a noun referring to God, or an adverb referring to how the enemies fight, namely, "proudly."

Thus in the midst of opposition that has become hounding and lethal, David cries out to God for mercy. The press of his circumstances and his inability to deal with them throws him into the hands of God.

A Confession of Confidence

> 3 Whenever I am afraid,
> I will trust in You.
> 4 In God (I will praise His word),
> In God I have put my trust;
> I will not fear.
> What can flesh do to me?
>
> *Ps. 56:3–4*

Having asked for help, David reaffirms his faith in God. In verse 3 he speaks directly to God, while verse 4 takes the form of meditative confession.

Fear can do interesting things to us. It propels us to fight. It urges us to flee. It makes us freeze. It throws us into panic. Here, however, fear activates David's faith. He collapses upon God's faithfulness as he puts his *"trust"* in Him. The word for *"trust"* means "to rely upon God" or "to be secure in God." Jeremiah promises, "Blessed is the man who trusts in the Lord" (17:7), and Proverbs 16:20 says, "Whoever trusts in the Lord, happy is he." Those who *"trust"* in God then are refreshed, protected, surrounded by mercy, and will not fall (Prov. 29:25; Ps. 32:10; 125:1).

Verse 4 repeats the thought of verse 3 as a meditative refrain. David praises God's word because His word is His self-revelation and contains the promise of His mercy and trustworthiness (cf. Ps. 119). Moreover, the word of God creates trust through the convicting and assuring work of the Holy Spirit as it comes to our mind and goes to our heart (see 1 Cor. 2:1–5).

Since David trusts in God he now concludes: *"I will not fear. / What can flesh do to me?"* The God in whom he trusts is the God who is "merciful," the "Most High" God, the God who speaks, the God who is angry at sin (v. 7), the God who is "for" David, the God who delivers him, and the God before whom he walks. Thus the act and attitude of trust dispels fear. When David trusts God he does not fear people. He is secure in His hand.

A COMPLAINT AGAINST EVIL ENEMIES

5 All day they twist my words;
  All their thoughts *are* against me for evil.
6 They gather together,
  They hide, they mark my steps,
  When they lie in wait for my life.
7 Shall they escape by iniquity?
  In anger cast down the peoples, O God!

Ps. 56:5–7

The oppression that David is experiencing is now more specifically defined. His enemies use and abuse what David says. They confuse his words, not because of ignorance or "a failure to communicate," but because of their evil thoughts against him. The noun for *"evil"* (v. 5) means "distress, misery, injury, calamity." Thus the confusion is intentional and comes from their wicked design to bring harm upon David. This becomes clearer in verse 6, where David describes a conspiracy. His enemies are organized; they are deceptive; they stalk him and, like an animal on the hunt, wait to strike.

In response to this evil attack David asks if his enemies will "get away with it": *"Shall they escape by iniquity?"* (v. 7). Next he calls down God's wrath: *"In anger cast down the peoples, O God!"* The references to *"the peoples"* is general, suggesting that the request is a set formula of judgment. God's *"anger"* is not an irrational outburst. It is His moral response to the immorality described in verses 5–6.

CONFIDENCE IN THE POWER OF GOD

8 You number my wanderings;
   Put my tears into Your bottle;
   Are they not in Your book?
9 When I cry out *to You,*
   Then my enemies will turn back;
   This I know, because God *is* for me.
10 In God (I will praise *His* word),
    In the LORD (I will praise *His* word),
11 In God I have put my trust;
    I will not be afraid.
    What can man do to me?

Ps. 56:8–11

David now expresses his assurance that God cares for him and will act on his behalf: *"You number my wanderings."* God keeps account of his life. The noun for *"wanderings"* means the "wanderings of an aimless fugitive." The Hebrew word comes from a verb that can also mean "to show grief" and could mean "lamentations," the grief experienced by one wandering in rejection. But God keeps track of David's sorrow. Thus, *"You . . . put my tears into Your bottle."* The image is that of God collecting his sorrows and saving or remembering them. David continues: *"Are they not in Your book?"* This phrase seems to explain the metaphor of the *"bottle."* God writes down David's grief and keeps a permanent record.

Because God knows David's suffering, He responds to his prayer (v. 9). By God's action his enemies reverse their field. Notice that prayer is David's secret weapon. It is through his crying to the Lord that judgment comes. As God answers, the man who wants to devour him and the hounding opponents (vv. 1–2) turn and run in defeat.

Isn't it true for us that too often prayer is a last resort rather than a first resort? We seem to have an attitude that says: When all else fails, pray. When we are sick, for example, our instinct isn't to pray for healing, but rather to call a doctor and get some medicine. This is not a bad response. However, the question is, do we turn immediately to God for His healing power because He is also our Redeemer, or do we only call upon God when illness is terminal and all medical resources have been exhausted?

As David prays here, he expects results. When he calls on the power of God, the power of evil is broken. He is confident in his prayers:

"This I know, because God is for me" (v. 9). The verb for "to know" (*yāda*ᶜ) means to know experientially. David knows that God will act not only because he has a Bible promise to that effect, but because God has acted for him in the past, proving that His word is true. God stands on his side. God says "yes" to his prayer.

In verses 10–11 David now repeats the confession of verse 4: *"In God (I will praise His word), / In the Lord (I will praise His word)."* God is the *"Lord,"* Yahweh, and *"His word"* stands true and active. In praising God's *"word,"* David praises the God who speaks it and carries it out. To honor God's word is to honor God. Faith is our affirmation that what God says is true. God's word, however, is never to be substituted for God. We do not worship the word; it is simply a means of revelation that leads us to God Himself. Thus David concludes, *"In God I have put my trust; / I will not be afraid. / What can man do to me?"* The verb for *"trust"* means "to find security." Once he is secure in the Lord, David's fear vanishes and his enemies are crushed. No one can harm him in God's hand (cf. v. 4).

A Personal Commitment

12 Vows *made* to You *are binding* upon me, O God;
   I will render praises to You,
13 For You have delivered my soul from death.
   Have You not *kept* my feet from falling,
   That I may walk before God
   In the light of the living?

Ps. 56:12–13

David now promises to fulfill the vows he has made to God. Literally he describes them as "Your vows," not his own. Thus once he makes them, they belong to God. The word for *"vow"* may include a "votive sacrifice" (cf. Ps. 50:14). David's vows also come with *"praises to You"* as a part of his worship.

In saying *"You have delivered my soul from death,"* David may be anticipating God's action against his enemies or he may be concluding the psalm after experiencing that action. Probably he writes in anticipation. Not only does David expect God will deliver from death, but also that God will keep his *"feet from falling"* ("stumbling") even though his enemies have marked his "steps." He concludes that the purpose and result of God's action for him is *"that* [he] *may walk before God / In the light of the living."* Rather than falling into the darkness of death, David remains among the living.

David's alternatives are our alternatives. We either will fall into the darkness of death or stand in the light of God and live. As much as we may fight such an antithetical thought, it is Biblical to the core. We serve either God or the devil. We go either to heaven or to hell. "There is no fence to sit on because there is no fence" (Jim Rayburn).

In Psalm 56, then, we learn that in the midst of trials we must trust God. He has never promised that we won't have adversity in this world. He *has promised to be with us* in the midst of it, however. As we trust Him, we will experience the truth of His promise, and with David we will "praise His word."

CHAPTER FIFTY-SEVEN

Singing in the Storm

Psalm 57

One of God's greatest gifts to His saints is joy in sorrow, triumph in tears. Jesus knew that joy, the joy of God's presence and power, although He was a "Man of sorrows and acquainted with grief" (Isa. 53:3). Many are able to endure pain when they see relief coming. To have *joy* in the pain, however, is a separate matter. Paul writes that "we . . . glory [rejoice] in tribulations" (Rom. 5:3). He also reminds the Thessalonians that they "received the word in much affliction, with joy of the Holy Spirit" (1 Thess. 1:6). Joy in suffering is an eschatological gift. It represents the penetration of God's kingdom into the midst of this fallen world and the hounding of our enemies. John Wesley saw this joy on the faces of some of his fellow shipmates during a violent storm at sea. Fearful for his life, he was amazed to watch while this little band of Moravian believers experienced the grace of God and reacted with serenity as their ship was tossed about by the Atlantic's furious waves. Wesley was staggered by their faith and soon after sought them out in London. Attending their meetings at Aldersgate turned out to be the great watershed of his life.

In Psalm 57 the writer is experiencing "calamities" coming from an enemy who would devour him. It is as if he is "among lions" out for a kill. Although they have set a trap for him, he is certain that they themselves will fall into it. In the midst of the crisis, the psalmist trusts in God, hiding in the "shadow of [His] wings," knowing God will act on his behalf. Thus he praises Him, calling upon his lute and harp so that he can sing to God among the nations. Here then is a burst of song in the storm.

Commentators identify this psalm as a personal lament. Verses 7–11, in nearly identical form, also make up Psalm 108:1–5. It appears that the latter psalm, however, has borrowed from the former. Tradition, which we follow, ascribes Psalm 57 to David. The thought here moves from a cry for mercy (v. 1) to a confession of trust (vv. 2–3) and an exposition of the crisis (vv. 4–6). A commitment to worship (vv. 7–11) brings the psalm to its conclusion.

A CRY FOR MERCY

1 Be merciful to me, O God, be merciful to me!
   For my soul trusts in You;
   And in the shadow of Your wings I will make my
      refuge,
   Until *these* calamities have passed by.

                                                            Ps. 57:1

In verse 1 the repetition of the verb makes the cry for help emphatic. It is as if David says "Be merciful, *now!*" The verb for *"be merciful,"* as in Psalm 56, means "be gracious; show Your unmerited favor; say yes to me." God's mercy is a part of His covenant-love which is unconditional. David bases his call for divine grace upon his faith: *"For my soul trusts in You."* The verb for *"trusts"* (ḥāsâh) literally means "to take refuge." The thought immediately continues: *"And in the shadow of Your wings I will make my refuge"* (ḥāsâh). As in the opening verse, repeating the verb brings emphasis. God will protect David as a mother hen protects her chicks. This covering will last until the *"calamities"* which he faces *"have passed."* The noun for "calamity" means "engulfing ruin, destruction." This evil becomes more explicit later (see vv. 4, 6). Thus God's mercy is seen in His protection for David. As with the church at Philadelphia, God will "keep" him in the "hour of trial" (Rev. 3:10). Likewise, Jesus teaches us to pray to be delivered "from the evil one" (Matt. 6:13).

A CONFESSION OF TRUST

> 2 I will cry out to God Most High,
>   To God who performs *all things* for me.
> 3 He shall send from heaven and save me;
>   He reproaches the one who would swallow me
>   up. Selah
> God shall send forth His mercy and His truth.
>
> *Ps. 57:2–3*

David's confession of his trust in *"God Most High,"* a title that means his God is above all other gods, is his acknowledgment of God's sovereign authority and power. As *"God Most High,"* He is the One who *"performs all things for [David]."* The verb for *"performs"* means "to bring to an end, to complete" that is, God takes care of all our requests and finishes His work (see Phil. 1:6). What David needs in these circumstances, however, is God's transcendent intervention. God's saving act always comes from above, literally, "the heavens" as in verse 3. Paul writes, "But when the fullness of the time had come, God sent forth His Son . . ." (Gal. 4:4). Moreover, as God acts on David's behalf: *"He reproaches* [says harsh things to] *the one who would swallow [David] up."* The power of God's reproach brings salvation to David. When God speaks, things happen. His word accomplishes His work (Isa. 55:11).

What God sends from heaven to deliver David and to judge his enemy is *"His mercy and His truth."* God's *"mercy"* is His covenant-love and His *"truth"* is His "faithfulness." God will keep His covenant with David and act in faithfulness toward him. This promise is ultimately fulfilled in Jesus, the Word made flesh who comes filled with "grace and truth" (John 1:14).

Our great temptation is to take God's work into our own hands. Are we willing to wait for Him, to pray for Him to act *"from heaven"*? Dwight L. Moody said that there is one man who won't be in heaven:

the self-made man. No one will boast that he "did it himself." For me, it is hard to let God deal with my enemies; I want to go and get them myself. I want to command their exposure and demise. It is humbling to wait for God to act. Very often His timetable isn't mine. Very often, as was the case with Abraham, He builds my faith as I have to trust His promise to act when He is ready (see Rom. 4). We can, however, stand on the promise: *"God shall send forth His mercy and His truth."*

A SEVERE CRISIS

> 4 My soul *is* among lions;
>   I lie *among* the sons of men
>   Who are set on fire,
>   Whose teeth *are* spears and arrows,
>   And their tongue a sharp sword.
> 5 Be exalted, O God, above the heavens;
>   *Let* Your glory *be* above all the earth.
> 6 They have prepared a net for my steps;
>   My soul is bowed down;
>   They have dug a pit before me;
>   Into the midst of it they *themselves* have fallen.   Selah
>   *Ps. 57:4–6*

David's enemy (now in the plural) is described in metaphorical language, as he finds himself (his *"soul"*) in the midst of *"lions."* These beasts, the *"sons of men,"* are *"set on fire,"* that is, they devour him as a fire would consume him (cf. v. 3). The means of their attack are their *"teeth"* and *"tongue."* These weapons of slander are sharp, like *"spears," "arrows,"* and a *"sword."* David is in danger of being torn apart by them.

A hunted man, David then prays in answer to the attacks upon him (v. 5). If God is exalted and His glory manifest, then the lies of David's enemies will fade into nothing. Although the Pharisees twisted the truth that Jesus spoke, in His resurrection their deceptions became meaningless and empty. The ultimate answer to David's prayer, however, will be Jesus' return in glory. Then all liars and the father of lies, the devil himself, will be seen for what they are, and God's judgment will purify the earth (see John 8:44; Rev. 21:8). At the consummation, God's *"glory"* will rule over all creation. He alone will be praised and honored in that day.

David, reflecting in verse 6 upon his immediate situation, describes his enemies' action and their disposition in another metaphor. Like hunters they have laid their trap for him, and a *"net"* is ready to be sprung. His *"soul is bowed down"* by the weight of this attack. The thought may be of carrying a heavy load or of struggling with depression. Ironically, the very *"pit"* his enemies have dug for him to fall into now becomes their own trap: *"Into the midst of it they themselves have fallen"* (v. 6).

A COMMITMENT TO WORSHIP

7 My heart is steadfast, O God, my heart is steadfast;
I will sing and give praise.
8 Awake, my glory!
Awake, lute and harp!
I will awaken the dawn.
9 I will praise You, O Lord, among the peoples;
I will sing to You among the nations.
10 For Your mercy reaches unto the heavens,
And Your truth unto the clouds.
11 Be exalted, O God, above the heavens;
Let Your glory *be* above all the earth.

Ps. 57:7–11

In light of his call for God to manifest His glory (v. 5) and the self-destruction of his enemies (v. 6), David now affirms the condition of his *"heart"*: it is *"steadfast"* ("firm"). Once again, the verb is repeated for emphasis. Based on this security David is ready to worship, and he now commands himself and his instruments to respond: *"Awake, my glory!"* (v. 8). The word *"glory"* here is probably a metaphor for his "soul" or "himself" (see Ps. 16:9). He continues: *"Awake, lute and harp!"* The word translated "lute" (*nēbel*) is more often used in the meaning of "bottle" but also means "musical instrument." Here it is thought to refer to the lute because that instrument's resonating chamber has a bulging, bottlelike shape. David's intention is to *"awaken the dawn."* By his singing and praise he will bring in the sunrise.

In verse 9 David's worship becomes witness: *"I will praise You, O Lord, among the peoples; / I will sing to You among the nations."* As God renews His church today, there is a renewal in worship. Often congregations coming alive will spend close to an hour simply praising God. A

397

friend of mine told me of attending the Vineyard Church in Santa Monica where midway through their worship people began to come forward to accept Christ. The presence of God was so manifest in the praises of His people that the unconverted could delay no longer. As the world hears us sing to the Lord, God's Spirit will touch many hearts.

David's praise is based on the vastness of God's *"mercy."* It *"reaches unto the heavens"* (v. 10). The word for *"mercy"* here is the same "covenant-love" *(ḥesed)* used so frequently throughout the Book of Psalms. That love is higher than our highest thoughts and binds heaven and earth together. Likewise, God's *"truth,"* His trustworthiness, also extends to *"the clouds." "Mercy"* and *"truth"* are not human creations; they come from the divine heart.

David concludes with the refrain from verse 5: *"Be exalted, O God, above the heavens."* For God to *"be exalted"* here means for Him to be lifted up in worship. As He is praised then His *"glory"* will be seen *"above all the earth."*

As the church today is being renewed by the Holy Spirit, she is coming alive in worship. The devil hates this and wants to do all in his power to keep God's people from praising Him from their hearts; thus he sends opposition and persecution. He seeks to snatch away the word and to choke out its fruitfulness, and the storms then come. God, however, gives us songs for the storms. As our *"lute and harp"* are awakened in praise, the dawn will come and we will sing until we see the very presence of our Lord.

CHAPTER FIFTY-EIGHT

Cry for Judgment

Psalm 58

This world is a brutal place. Since the curse of Eden, violence and bloodshed have written the pages of human history. The Bible both reflects this violence and confronts it. Thus it recounts every kind of human sin and evil: murder, rape, adultery, slaughter, deception, pride, and idolatrous power. From Cain's days to the present, rebellion against God brings destruction. However much our sensibilities may be offended, the Bible is honest in its description of human sin and its consequences.

As it addresses our depravity, the Bible finds the roots of evil in the supernatural world, the world of Satan and his demonic hosts (see Eph. 6:12). It also shows us that we have stained God's good creation and are morally responsible for our actions (Rom. 2:12–16). It shows us too the Holy God who will judge sin on both natural and supernatural levels (see Rev. 18:21–24; 20:10).

It is a fearful thing to be caught in our sin. I recall cheating on a test when I was in junior high school. My sensitive mother knew that something was wrong when I came home. Finally, I confessed what I had done and she took me that night to see my teacher, who happened also to be her personal friend. I will never forget the fear, anxiety, and embarrassment that I felt as we drove toward her house. Her judgment, however, was gracious and later that night I felt tremendous relief.

In Christ, God's judgment is both severe and sweet. It is severe because it cost the Son of God the cross, and it costs us an honest encounter with our own evil. It is sweet because the Father's forgiveness reaches out to us to cleanse our hearts and to make us new. The severe side of judgment is seen in Psalm 58. Here the author exposes sin and calls upon God to move in vengeance upon it. His picture of judgment is violent, as he longs for the vindication of the righteous. What is absent here is grace—the love of enemies and the unmerited mercy of God. What is present here is the awesome holiness of God and His certain judgment to come. As we read this psalm in light of the cross we must add one thing: all that we as sinners deserve, which is so vividly portrayed here, has been laid upon our Savior. This must cause us grief. It also must give us a sense of urgency to get the gospel out before the age of grace passes and the certain vengeance of God comes to this planet.

David is traditionally accepted as author of this psalm. The violence of its imagery fits well with the warrior-king who knows the smell of battle. Commentators identify Psalm 58 as a national lament because no personal enemies are named here. The thought moves from an indictment of the wicked (vv. 1–2), to the evidence against them (vv. 3–5), to judgment and resolution (vv. 6–11).

An Indictment of the Wicked

1 Do you indeed speak righteousness, you silent ones?
  Do you judge uprightly, you sons of men?
2 No, in heart you work wickedness;
  You weigh out the violence of your hands in the earth.

Ps. 58:1–2

In verse 1 David launches into an attack upon the wicked, asking if they *"speak righteousness,"* or "rightly," in accord with God's law. The implied answer, of course, is no. The word rendered *"silent ones"* (ʾēlem) may originally have been "gods" (ʾēlîm). It could also, however, refer to the silent idols that mask the demons (see 1 Cor. 10:19–20). Thus Habakkuk speaks of "mute [or silent] idols" (2:18). If David does address the idols here, then of course they do not speak at all, nor do they metaphorically *"speak righeousness"* since they are the source of all kinds of immorality on the earth (see Rom. 1:18 ff.).

Next, David asks whether the *"sons of men"* ("human beings," see Ps. 8:4) *"judge uprightly."* Again, the implied answer is no. The word for *"uprightly"* means "equally." Thus the clause translates literally, "Do you judge with equity [or, evenness]?"

If the *"silent ones"* are the demonic idols, then verse 1 indicts the fallen heavens and the fallen earth. Both the supernatural and the natural creation have abandoned righteousness and justice. This is made clear by verse 2: *"No, in heart you work wickedness."* Here the *"heart"* contains both the mind and the will of the person. There *"wickedness"* ("injustice") is planned and executed. This results in *"violence"* being weighed out *"in the earth."* The verb for "weigh" indicates weighing on a scale, as in weighing out justice. David expresses the thought of Genesis 6:1–7 that the wicked, however, are unjust; they weigh out violence instead, and the earth is corrupted by humankind as well as by demons.

THE EVIDENCE AGAINST THE WICKED

3 The wicked are estranged from the womb;
  They go astray as soon as they are born, speaking
    lies.
4 Their poison *is* like the poison of a serpent;
  They are like the deaf cobra *that* stops its ear,
5 Which will not heed the voice of charmers,
  Charming ever so skillfully.

Ps. 58:3–5

Here David offers his case for the indictment of verses 1–2. His focus is on wicked people rather than the demonic idols. To begin with, the depths of human evil go back to the *"womb."* There the *"wicked"* are *"estranged"* ("become strangers"). This thought suggests that they do not belong to God's covenant or His people. The result is that they *"go astray as soon as they are born,"* as evidenced by their *"speaking lies."* Here is a functional description of original sin. As David puts it in Psalm 51:5, "Behold, I was brought forth in iniquity, / And in sin my mother conceived me." The *"lies"* demonstrate the absence of just judgment noted in verse 1.

Next, David employs the image of a snake to describe the evil of the wicked. The *"poison"* they release is the venom of the *"lies"* of verse 3. More specifically, the evil are like a *"deaf cobra"* (or "adder"; the Hebrew does not specify but is derived from a verb meaning "to twist"). This snake refuses to hear *"the voice of [the] charmers"* regardless of their skill. The final phrase, *"charming ever so skillfully"* probably means "a wise binder of magic spells." Thus the wicked lie from the womb and refuse to receive direction like a cobra which is deaf even to the magicians who are supposed to be able to control it. That the serpent is seen as a deceptive liar is true starting in Genesis 3:1. His poison originates from the direction of Satan who inhabits his body (Rev. 12:9).

It is hard for us to grasp the idea that we live in a fallen world shot through with a cosmic conflict between God and Satan. As John Wimber puts its, "All that happens in the natural has its origin in the supernatural." We have been trained to deny this, however. We believe in our own goodness and autonomy. Nature is neutral and if there is a devil and original sin, somehow *we* escaped. In fact, we didn't. We are corrupted and seduced. We are the cobra refusing to hear God's word, poisoning our own environment, working wickedness in our hearts.

DIVINE JUDGMENT

6 Break their teeth in their mouth, O God!
  Break out the fangs of the young lions, O LORD!
7 Let them flow away as waters *which* run continually;
  When he bends *his bow,*
  Let his arrows be as if cut in pieces.
8 *Let them be* like a snail which melts away as it goes,
  Like a stillborn child of a woman, that they may not
    see the sun.

                                                        Ps. 58:6–8

Changing his imagery, David calls for God to intervene by breaking the *"teeth"* of the wicked, now personified as *"lions."* These wild beasts are to be defanged (cf. Ps. 7:2). In invoking God's action David reveals his desperation. Only the Lord can handle this evil.

The series of images continues in verse 7 as David asks that the wicked *"flow away as waters which run continually."* They are to be like the runoff from a rain. The woman of Tekoa used the same simile when she said to David, "For we will surely die and become like water spilled on the ground, which cannot be gathered up again" (2 Sam. 14:14). Moreover, when the wicked fight with their bows, David asks that their *"arrows"* break. Their power to harm (with their lies of v. 3?) is over. Still more metaphors add emphasis in verse 8 to David's request that the Lord remove the wicked: they should be *"like a snail which melts away"* ("leaves a slimy track"), and *"like a stillborn child"* who never lives to *"see the sun."*

All of these cries to God for judgment reveal that only divine intervention can stop the wickedness, the violence, and the lies that poison this world (see vv. 2–4). The ultimate reason for this is that they find their source in the "silent ones," the demon-inspired false gods that control our fallen history (cf. Matt. 4:8–9). Spiritual battles must be fought spiritually. Too often we find ourselves employing psychological techniques or monetary power or appeals to human emotion in trying to turn back the "power of darkness" (Col. 1:13). This is all vanity. As Jesus says to His disciples when they fail to cast out a demon: "This kind can come out by nothing but prayer . . ." (Mark 9:29).

DIVINE RESOLUTION

9 Before your pots can feel *the burning* thorns,
   He shall take them away as with a whirlwind,
   As in His living and burning wrath.
10 The righteous shall rejoice when he sees the
   vengeance;
   He shall wash his feet in the blood of the wicked,
11 So that men will say,
   "Surely *there is* a reward for the righteous;
   Surely He is God who judges in the earth."
                                          Ps. 58:9–11

David is confident that God will now act quickly: *"Before your pots can feel* [touch] *the burning thorns,"* or, literally, "the green thorns burning." God's judgment will come in less time than it takes to kindle a cooking fire of green wood. Furthermore, the wicked will be gone *"as with a whirlwind,"* or "He shall sweep them away."

As the wicked vanish, then the *"righteous,"* those belonging to the covenant, will rejoice at seeing God's *"vengeance."* In a bold image David adds that the righteous person shall *"wash his feet in the blood of the wicked"* (v. 10). This is a symbol of their humiliation and destruction.

Finally, the response to God's judgment is that people will confess that the righteous, those who are morally true, are rewarded, or, literally "receive fruit." Their reward, however, is not in the destruction of the wicked, but in the vindication of God: *"Men will say, 'Surely He is God* [or, there is a God] *who judges in the earth.'"* Thus the lies and false judgments of the "silent ones" and the "sons of men" are over (see v. 1) when God answers the cry for judgment and offers final resolution.

Insofar as we can identify with those who "go astray as soon as they are born," we too deserve to have our teeth broken and to melt away "like a snail." The urgent good news, however, is that the wrath of God has been laid upon Jesus. All who now come to Him find the judgment lifted. However, the door to the Father's house will not always stand open. Those who reject the Son of God will find the judgment of this psalm to be their lasting experience. Thus it stands as a warning sign and a call to flee to the Savior while there is yet time.

CHAPTER FIFTY-NINE

Deliver and Defend!

Psalm 59

It is hard for many of us who grew up in the Eisenhower era to accept the ruthlessness and violence of life in the '80s. I was raised in a conservative community where, although Biblical authority was a distant memory, the ethics of the Bible remained. Divorce, adultery, cheating, lying—all of these contemporary commonplaces were looked upon with disdain. Norman Vincent Peale advocated the power of positive thinking, the U.S. was the only nuclear power, and the goal of my Princeton classmates was to climb the corporate ladder or to go to Wall Street and make a killing. Thus a prayer like Psalm 59 seemed to come out of the dark ages. Who could identify with the rebellion and revolt it portrayed? In my college days, our bland world was slightly shaken in 1956 when the Hungarians rose up against Russian rule and were brutally crushed. I remember one of my friends asking what we would do if Russian tanks rolled through the campus. The response offered was that we would ask the tank commanders in for cocktails; that is, we would accommodate ourselves to the new system and go on. The '60s in this country blew away this age of naïveté, and the brutality of the "workers of iniquity" and "bloodthirsty men" (v. 2) who return at night growling "like a dog" (v. 6) became our world. We have now seen our presidents attacked. Kennedy was killed; Reagan was wounded. The Pope has also been shot. Martin Luther King, Robert Kennedy, and John Lennon were murdered. George Wallace was wounded and made a cripple for life. And on and on it goes. We live in a world of the PLO, AIDS, and the KGB. Thus Psalm 59 is our psalm.

The psalmist cries out to God because of his enemies. They are those who revolt against him. They work iniquity and seek blood. They plot against him; their lips are swords that speak cursing and lying. At night they prowl the city like dogs, belching and howling. In this chaotic atmosphere, the psalmist asks God to deliver him from his enemies' oppression and to defend him from their attacks.

Commentators identify this psalm as a lament, either personal or national. Since its authorship is ascribed to David it may well be both. The reason for this is that while the king has his own troubles, they have an immediate impact on the nation and the peoples surrounding Israel. The thought here moves from a cry for deliverance (vv. 1–2) to an exposition of the crisis (vv. 3–4), a cry for judgment (vv. 4b–5), a refrain on the crisis (vv. 6–7), and a confession of faith (vv. 8–10). Following another cry for judgment (vv. 11–13) and another refrain on the crisis (vv. 14–15), the psalm ends with a final confession of faith (vv. 16–17).

CRY FOR DELIVERANCE

1 Deliver me from my enemies, O my God;
   Defend me from those who rise up against me.
2 Deliver me from the workers of iniquity,
   And save me from bloodthirsty men.

Ps. 59:1–2

In David's opening call to God, the verb translated *"deliver"* means "to tear away, to snatch away." His plea is for God to act dramatically, just in time. David's *"enemies"* are defined as *"those who rise up against me."* They revolt against his rule. Thus he wants to be defended from them or, literally, to be "set on high," that is, lifted to a high place of safety (see Ps. 69:29). God then is the One who both delivers David and defends him. Once we have been set free from attack we need the security of the Lord to keep us. David expects this from the God who is his defense (see vv. 9, 11, 16).

His enemies are *"workers of iniquity"* (the Hebrew word for *"iniquity"*

405

here means "trouble, sorrow, wickedness"; cf. Ps. 5:5) and *"bloodthirsty men."* In Psalm 28:3 the "workers of iniquity" are defined as those who speak peace to mask evil. Moreover, they are killers; they seek blood (see Pss. 5:6 and 26:9). Often, as here in verse 2, these Hebrew nouns are linked together in order to define evil people.

THE CRISIS

> 3 For look, they lie in wait for my life;
>   The mighty gather against me,
>   Not *for* my transgression nor *for* my sin, O LORD.
> 4 They run and prepare themselves through no fault
>   *of mine.*
>
> Ps. 59:3–4

Having identified his enemies, David describes their activities. They set an ambush for him. They want his *"life"* ("soul, self"). Those who stalk him are *"the mighty"* (or "mighty men").

They are not, however, the instruments of God's judgment. They do not *"gather"* righteously because of David's sin. Thus he adds that they come against him *"Not for my transgression nor for my sin, O Lord."* The word for *"trangression"* (*peša*ʿ) means rebellion against divine authority, while the word for *"sin"* (*ḥaṭṭāʾt*) denotes a faulty action, or missing the mark. David now pictures his enemies as running and preparing for the battle, through no fault of his. Their attack is unjust and God will be just in delivering him.

As David asserts his righteousness here it is in the context of this immediate attack. Jesus Christ alone, however, can pray this prayer fully. He had no transgression or sin, yet his enemies plotted and prepared to take His life. David's claim to innocence in the psalms is thus fulfilled in the Innocent One.

A CRY FOR JUDGMENT

> 4b Awake to help me, and behold!
> 5 You therefore, O LORD God of hosts, the God of
>   Israel,
>   Awake to punish all the nations;
>   Do not be merciful to any wicked
>   transgressors. Selah
>
> Ps. 59:4b–5

In light of his righteousness then, David is free to call upon God to act on his behalf: *"Awake to help me."* He doesn't mean that God is asleep. "Behold, He who keeps Israel / Shall neither slumber nor sleep" (Ps. 121:4). He does mean, however, that in God's inactivity his enemies have multiplied and become aggressive. Thus he cries, "Wake up, Lord," and adds *"behold!"* or "open your eyes, see."

Next, he identifies God as *"Lord God of hosts, the God of Israel."* God, who is the commander of *"hosts"* of angels, is also the covenant *"God of Israel,"* and this is the God David calls upon to go into battle. He asks Him to *"punish all the nations"*; he begs Him, *"Do not be merciful to any wicked transgressors."* The verb rendered *"punish"* means to "attend to" or "to test" (in judgment). The scope of God's action is universal; it covers *"all the nations."* Thus God's action on behalf of David's immediate crisis has an eschatological dimension. David doesn't merely want his own problems resolved, he wants all evil destroyed and God's justice to be fully vindicated. This means that all *"wicked transgressors"* will be judged, not receiving any mercy. The Hebrew word for *"transgressors"* describes those who are treacherous in wickedness. David wants final, punitive judgment inflicted here, and, although we are now in the age of grace, that awesome judgment will come (see 2 Thess. 1:8).

It is important for us to keep our own problems in perspective. When we experience unjust attacks, this is merely a symptom of the larger injustice throughout the world. Do we long for all corruption to cease? If so, our needs will lead us to cry out for the whole planet. We will long for God to judge all the nations, not just our particular foes.

A REFRAIN OF CRISIS

> 6 At evening they return,
>   They growl like a dog,
>   And go all around the city.
> 7 Indeed, they belch with their mouth;
>   Swords *are* in their lips;
>   For *they say,* "Who hears?"
>
> *Ps. 59:6-7*

David now describes his enemies with a powerful simile, comparing them to wild dogs returning to the city at the end of the day. Since they are evil they love the darkness of night. On their evening hunt for food they *"growl"* as they pillage the refuse dumps: *"They belch with their mouth."* What David intends by this vivid picture becomes clear in the final clauses of verse 7: *"Swords are in their lips,"* the swords being the tongue from which come violent plans and words (cf. Ps. 52:2). Later, David will speak of the sin in his enemies' mouths, their "cursing and lying." They speak freely because they think no one hears: *"For they say, 'Who hears?' "* However, they are wrong—God hears and David hears.

What we discover from this refrain (closely repeated in vv. 14–15), is that David's enemies are speaking evil of him. While they plot against his life, they are attempting to undercut his authority by their violent, verbal attacks. In all that they say and do, their evil is exposed. God, however, is a God of truth. He will judge their lies. To this theme David now turns.

A Confession of Faith

> 8 But You, O Lord, shall laugh at them;
>   You shall have all the nations in derision.
> 9 I will wait for You,
>   O You his Strength;
>   For God *is* my defense.
> 10 My God of mercy shall come to meet me;
>   God shall let me see *my desire* on my enemies.
>
> Ps. 59:8–10

In the midst of his trauma, David confesses his faith: *"But You, O Lord. . . ."* Whenever the darkness closes in, whenever the dogs growl, whenever the swords flash, there is always a solution. It lies in God Himself.

As a pastor I have hundreds of people each week evaluating and responding to what I say in my sermons. I imagine people going home and friends asking: "How was Don today?" I'm sure there are occasional swords in the questions and comments I receive, especially when people don't think their critique will get back to me. One of my comforts is to know that most of the time I have done my best. Then, too, it is God's job, not mine, to authenticate His word. I trust the Holy Spirit to take one message and bring it home to hundreds of people, each on separate pilgrimages. When the flak comes, however, my real recourse is God. I say with David, *"But You, O Lord. . . ."*

Here in verse 8 David sees God laughing at his enemies. He derides *"all the nations"* (cf. v. 5). God is above the whole earth, scoffing at the sin that presumptuously rises up against Him. God's laugh, however, is not a laugh of indifference. It is a laugh of warning and judgment. So we read in Psalm 2: "He who sits in the heavens shall laugh; / The Lord shall hold them [the kings of the earth] in derision. / Then He shall speak to them in His wrath" (2:4–5).

Verse 9 is difficult. Many Hebrew manuscripts and the Septuagint read "O my strength." The NKJV reads, *"O You his Strength,"* which is awkward but follows the Masoretic text. Clearly David is addressing God as the next clause and the context (v. 8) show. Thus he concludes, *"I will wait* [or, watch] *for You."*

David then continues his confession. God is his *"defense"* or "high place." (The Hebrew word here is the same as that translated "defense" in vv. 16, 17.) Here he finds refuge. Thus God comes to him in His mercy or covenant love, and the result of this is that God will *"let me see my desire on my enemies"* (cf. Ps. 54:7). Here then God will allow him to see his enemies judged as he desires. What David prays for, David gets. God's deliverance and defense are his.

A Second Cry for Judgment

11 Do not slay them, lest my people forget;
   Scatter them by Your power,
   And bring them down,
   O Lord our shield.
12 *For* the sin of their mouth *and* the words of their lips,
   Let them even be taken in their pride,
   And for the cursing and lying *which* they speak.
13 Consume *them* in wrath, consume *them*,
   That they *may* not *be;*
   And let them know that God rules in Jacob
   To the ends of the earth.   Selah

Ps. 59:11–13

Here, as in verse 5, David calls out for God to act. First, he tells the Lord what he wants Him to do. Then he tells Him why, and, finally, he again tells God what he wants Him to do. Thus the thought builds to its climax.

David begins with a negative in verse 11, asking God *not* to slay the wicked, as their quick destruction might make Israel forget His judgment. Rather, David requests that God use His power to *"scatter them,"* or make them "wander," homeless. Next he asks that they be brought down, namely, overthrown. Again, this request is addressed to God: *"O Lord our shield"* (compare Ps. 3:3). Reference to God's *"power"* is a reference to God as deliverer. Reference to God's *"shield"* is a reference to God as defender.

The basis for the requests is that David's enemies *"speak"* evil; there is *"sin"* in *"their mouth"* and *"words"* (v. 11; cf. v. 7). This is an expression of their *"pride"* and it includes *"cursing"* (hexes?) and *"lying."*

When David prays, *"Let them . . . be taken in their pride,"* he means, "Let their pride trap them." *"Pride"* here means rebellious self-exaltation against God. This sentence expresses a curse. Throughout the Bible, God invariably comes to judge the proud. Thus when the Virgin Mary conceives Jesus she blesses God for "He has scattered the proud in the imagination of their hearts. / He has put down the mighty from their thrones" (Luke 1:51–52). The greatest judgment, however, comes when God steps into history in the "form of a bondservant" (Phil. 2:7). In this our egos are flattened before Him.

The repetition of the verb *"consume"* ("end") in verse 13 is for emphasis. God's *"wrath,"* like a fire, will burn up his enemies. The noun for "wrath" comes from a verb root "to be hot, to burn." Thus God's anger is like a desert wind or a devouring fire. Once His wrath comes His enemies will vanish, *"that they may not be."* Furthermore, they will *"know that God rules in Jacob,"* namely, that He is King in Israel. When Israel is called *"Jacob,"* the psalmist is describing God's people theologically rather than politically. Moreover, not only does God reign among His people, His sovereignty extends *"to the ends of the earth."* In judging David's "enemies" or "the nations," then, God is acting consistently with His sovereign lordship over all things.

Verse 13 climaxes David's call for judgment. First, he wants his enemies scattered but not killed. Then he wants their own sin to find them out. But finally, he wants God to destroy them. This is the ultimate, eschatological act. From it, all will know that our God is the true and living God.

THE REFRAIN OF CRISIS REPEATED

14 And at evening they return,
They growl like a dog,
And go all around the city.

15 They wander up and down for food,
And howl if they are not satisfied.

Ps. 59:14–15

These verses with slight variation repeat the refrain found in verses 6–7. Here again David characterizes his enemies poetically. They come back at night like dogs to *"wander,"* looking for food. If they don't find it, they *"howl."*

A FINAL CONFESSION

16 But I will sing of Your power;
Yes, I will sing aloud of Your mercy in the morning;
For You have been my defense
And refuge in the day of my trouble.
17 To You, O my Strength, I will sing praises;
For God *is* my defense,
My God of mercy.

Ps. 59:16–17

David knows that God will answer his prayer and will be his deliverer and defender. Thus while his enemies prowl he worships: *"But I will sing of Your power."* His singing is vocal and public. He sings *"aloud"* or *"gives a ringing cry."* Moreover, the content of his song centers in God's *"power"* and *"mercy."* These are not just concepts; God has proven Himself to David. The Lord has been his *"defense"* and *"refuge"* in his *"trouble."* This is the basis of his joy and his victory shout.

Verse 17 repeats the thought. God is David's *"strength"* (see v. 9); thus he will *"sing praises"* to Him. God is also His *"defense"* and the *"God of [David's] mercy."* Indeed, God comes in the midst of the battle to deliver and defend him.

As I mentioned in the introduction to this psalm, during a more restrained era it was hard to identify with David's plight. Today, however, this is not true. Ultimately, the believer's enemy is not just a human opponent set out to do him in. The real enemy is Satan and his demonic hosts. He is the one who revolts against God, works iniquity, and is *"out for blood."* It is also he who growls like a dog, using his tongue like a sword to lie and deceive. He too is the source of all pride. Thus in calling upon God to deliver us and to defend us, we are really asking God to *"deliver us from the evil one"* (Matt. 6:13).

Here we have the deep assurance that the God who is our shield and our hiding place is the God who has come in His Son to overpower the devil and his minions. Thus John writes, "You are of God, little children, and have overcome . . . because He who is in you is greater than he who is in the world" (1 John 4:4). Later, he adds that because God keeps the Christian, "the wicked one does not touch him" (1 John 5:18). Indeed, "The Son of God was manifested, that He might destroy the works of the devil" (1 John 3:8).

CHAPTER SIXTY

On the Rebound

Psalm 60

Wouldn't it be great if the Christian life were one big spiritual and emotional "high"? No downs, no disappointments, no setbacks, no defeats—just a lifelong Disneyland. But would it really be so great? Wouldn't we get bored? Isn't it true that we learn through failure more than through success? Jesus' life wasn't just one Mount of Transfiguration. There were also the wilderness, the valley, and Calvary. Character is formed in conflict (Rom. 5:3–4), and our Lord learned obedience through suffering (Heb. 5:8). As C. S. Lewis observes, the Christian life consists of peaks and troughs. When we are on the peaks, it is important to remember that the troughs are coming. At the same time, when we are in the troughs we must not forget the peaks.

I have learned over the years that after preaching my heart out for three services on Sunday, I will often be depressed on Monday. I need not take this "down" feeling as a monumental attack by the devil, although it could create an opportunity for him. I need to expect to be in this valley and give myself time to recover. In my Monday trough I remember my Sunday peak.

Throughout the Old Testament there are peaks and troughs. For example, God would come in a mighty way to an Abraham, a Moses, or a David. Later, however, they would fall into troughs of disobedience, presumption, or adultery. At times, Israel would experience great revivals, such as in Josiah's reign. This would often be followed by a low point, by disaster.

Psalm 60 reflects a trough. Israel's armies have been defeated. God has not accompanied her into battle. Thus the psalmist feels "cast off" and the people have seen "hard things" and drunk "the wine of confusion." Nevertheless, there is hope. There is "a banner [for] those who fear" God. God will deliver with His "right hand." A peak is coming when God will retake the land and surrounding territories. Then Israel will march to Edom and God will "tread down" her enemies.

Commentators take this psalm as a communal lament to be used in times of distress. If verses 6–7 indicate that Northern Israel is in Assyrian hands, then the date of composition must be after 722 B.C., when Samaria fell to the Assyrian invaders. This, however, can be debated. Tradition ascribes the psalm to David, although its authorship cannot be assured. Moreover, verses 6–12 are incorporated into Psalm 108:7–13. Here is an excellent example of the living tradition of the Psalter (cf. Pss. 57:5–11 and 40:13–17). The thought moves from a lament over judgment (vv. 1–3) to a call for salvation (vv. 4–5) and the divine answer (vv. 6–8), ending with a cry for victory (vv. 9–12).

A LAMENT OVER JUDGMENT

1 O God, You have cast us off;
   You have broken us down;
   You have been displeased;
   Oh, restore us again!
2 You have made the earth tremble;
   You have broken it;
   Heal its breaches, for it is shaking.
3 You have shown Your people hard things;
   You have made us drink the wine of confusion.

Ps. 60:1–3

The psalmist begins with an agonizing groan to the Lord: *"O God, You have cast us off."* To *"cast off"* means *"to reject, to spurn."* God has *"broken"* Israel *"down"* (cf. Jer. 1:10). This rejection comes from the divine displeasure or anger which leads the psalmist to implore: *"Oh, restore [return, turn] us again!"* The military disaster which lies behind this lament (see v. 10) is now described as if it were a natural disaster: *"You have made the earth tremble"* (v. 2). The psalmist depicts an earthquake strong enough to tear the ground open and leave it shaking. While the language is poetic, it is also possible that a natural disaster accompanied the defeat in battle. This would add force to the thought that God is standing against His people. Thus He has caused Israel to see *"hard things"* (v. 3). Her armies have been routed and her land occupied—"hard things," indeed. Moreover, *"You have made us drink the wine of confusion* [reeling, drunkenness]." This cup, according to Isaiah 51:17, is the cup of God's "fury," the "cup of trembling." This is a metaphor for God's wrath. Indeed, God has judged His people. No wonder the psalmist calls out in grief and asks Him to *"restore"* Israel.

A Cry for Salvation

4 You have given a banner to those who fear You,
  That it may be displayed because of the truth.   Selah
5 That Your beloved may be delivered,
  Save *with* Your right hand, and hear me.

Ps. 60:4–5

Nevertheless, God has not abandoned His people in the midst of the disaster; His love is greater than His judgment. Thus He has *"given a banner* [standard] *to those who fear"* or stand in awe of Him. This could be a signal for flight to safety as in Jeremiah 4:6: "Set up the standard toward Zion. / Take refuge! Do not delay! / For I will bring disaster from the north, / And great destruction." It is *"displayed because of the truth"* (v. 4), the psalmist continues. The Hebrew word rendered *"truth"* (qōšeṭ) appears only here in the Old Testament. It may be the Aramaic form of the Hebrew "bow" (qešeṭ), which would mean that the banner for refuge is displayed because of the enemies' bow. This makes good sense. Thus the purpose is that Israel, God's *"beloved, may be delivered."* Note that, regardless of her sin or circumstances, she continues to be God's *"beloved."* This is true because His love is unconditional and He keeps His covenant: "The Lord did not set His love on you nor choose you because you were more in number than any other people, for you were least of all peoples; but because the Lord loves you, and because He would keep the oath which he swore to your fathers" (Deut. 7:7–8). Therefore, the psalmist knows that he can call upon God for the people's deliverance. He adds: *"Save with Your right hand, and hear* [answer] *me."* Thus his prayer is that God's judgment will be lifted and Israel's fortunes reversed. From the trough, the psalmist looks forward to a peak because he knows that God's love and faithfulness endure.

DIVINE RESPONSE

6 God has spoken in His holiness:
"I will rejoice;
I will divide Shechem
And measure out the Valley of Succoth.
7 Gilead *is* Mine, and Manasseh *is* Mine;
Ephraim also *is* the helmet for My head;
Judah *is* My lawgiver.
8 Moab *is* My washpot;
Over Edom I will cast My shoe;
Philistia, shout in triumph because of Me."

Ps. 60:6–8

God now declares His sovereignty over the land, however much it may be ravaged by enemies. He speaks *"in His holiness"* ("separateness, apartness") which denotes His awesome majesty. As God addresses the land, He says *"I will rejoice"* (or "I will exult"). Thus He delights in repossessing His property and in ordering the surrounding territories. It is God who divides or distributes the land of *"Shechem,"* the area around the city of Shechem forty miles north of Jerusalem in Samaria. God also measures out *"the Valley of Succoth,"* located on the east side of the Jordan, north of the Jabbok. *"Measure out"* ("apportion") is a metaphor for His conquest, bringing to mind a property owner surveying his land. God also claims *"Gilead"* and *"Manasseh,"* calling them *"Mine"* in verse 7. Gilead is defined by the rivers Arnon on the south and Yarmuk on the north; the Jordan valley is its western boundary and the desert is on the east. Manasseh, one of the twelve tribes, occupied the hill country of *"Ephraim"* and part of Gilead. Metaphorically speaking, Ephraim, which may denote all of northern Israel or just the hill country of Ephraim, is God's *"helmet." "Judah,"* to the south, is God's *"lawgiver"* or "scepter," the symbol of royal authority. *"Moab,"* on the east, God calls His *"washpot,"* a demeaning epithet that may have the

Dead Sea in mind. When God states, *"Over Edom I will cast My shoe,"* he uses a servant metaphor to express ownership over the land to the southeast of Israel. Finally, *"Philistia,"* to the west, is to acclaim God with shouts of *"triumph,"* as would faithful servants of a king.

Thus whatever temporary reverses in battle Israel has experienced due to divine judgment, God will *"rejoice"* to reclaim His land and its surrounding territories. God is still on the throne.

A CRY FOR VICTORY

9 Who will bring me *to* the strong city?
  Who will lead me to Edom?
10 *Is it* not You, O God, *who* cast us off?
  And You, O God, *who* did not go out with our armies?
11 Give us help from trouble,
  For the help of man *is* useless.
12 Through God we will do valiantly,
  For *it is* He *who* shall tread down our enemies.

Ps. 60:9–12

The psalmist now responds to the revelation of God's purposes in verses 6–8 by testing His promises. He asks who will bring him into the fortified city of Edom. The response in verse 10 takes the form of a question: *"Is it not You, O God, who cast us off?"* implying the psalmist's belief that God's rejection is to continue. The parallel clause identifies God as the One *"who did not go out"* to battle *"with [Israel's] armies."* This, of course, provoked her defeat.

Nevertheless, if Israel is now to regroup and take Edom, God must be with her or all will fail. Thus the psalmist prays *"Give us help [aid] from trouble."* Human help is in vain. If God is with Israel, however, *"we will do valiantly,"* because it is God who will *"tread down our enemies."* As Moses sang after the Exodus, "I will sing to the Lord, / For He has triumphed gloriously! / The horse and its rider / He has thrown into the sea!" (Exod. 15:1). God is Israel's King; He leads His troops in battle when they are righteous before Him and obey His will.

In Psalm 60 we see a trough in Israel's life. God has cut off her armies and they have been defeated. At the same time, He is still true to His covenant. He will protect His people, reclaim His land, and lead her troops again to Edom. Israel will be restored—a peak lies ahead for her.

In our Christian lives we too have our troughs, our valley times. We experience defeat and feel that the Lord is distant. He, however, offers us refuge, reclaims our lives, and promises to be with us in the future. In Asia, Paul thought that he had received the "sentence of death" and despaired of life itself. Then the Lord stepped in and he learned to trust the "God who raises the dead" (2 Cor. 1:9). When Catherine Marshall's husband Peter, the famous Scottish preacher, was felled by a heart attack, he whispered to his wife as he was carried from the house, "See you in the morning, darling." Those were his last words. Later they took on a transcendent meaning. Indeed the morning will come. We go through "the valley of the shadow of death" (Ps. 23:4), but after our night in this world, the morning dawns. "For now we see in a mirror, dimly, but then face to face" (1 Cor. 13:12). This is our ultimate rebound, our final peak.

CHAPTER SIXTY-ONE

The Rock Higher than I

Psalm 61

Mario Savio, who led the student revolt on the University of California Berkeley campus in the early '60s, said, "We demand meaning. It is our right to demand meaning." The problem for him, however, was that he went to the wrong source. Meaning is not to be found in the "multiversity" (Clark Kerr). To find true meaning we must find a transcendent purpose for our lives. This is the attraction of Marxism—it calls the individual into a history beyond himself. Since all of us are looking for some destiny, some goal, the Bible meets us at the point of our search, offering us the "rock that is higher than I."

Although the writer of Psalm 61 feels his "heart is overwhelmed," he celebrates this high rock, which is the living God Himself. In the context of worship, and especially in prayer for the king, the psalmist praises God as his "shelter" and "tower," the source of his strength. At the same time, God protects him under his "wings" and gives him a future, a "heritage." No wonder he wants to "abide in [God's] tabernacle forever." In worship there, he finds the ultimate meaning for his life.

This psalm is identified by commentators as either a personal lament because of the prayer for the king (vv. 6–7) or as a royal psalm. Thus the prayer for the king could be a prayer by the king, using the third person singular as "throne language." Tradition ascribes the psalm to David, and if verses 6–7 are by the king himself then the tradition may be accepted. Military imagery and reference to the tabernacle also support Davidic authorship. The thought here moves from a call to God (vv. 1–2) to a confession of faith in God (vv. 3–7) and a brief conclusion affirming commitment (v. 8).

A CALL TO GOD

1 Hear my cry, O God;
    Attend to my prayer.
2 From the end of the earth I will cry to You,
    When my heart is overwhelmed;
    Lead me to the rock that is higher than I.

Ps. 61:1–2

As David calls out to God to listen to him, he is far from Jerusalem and far from the tabernacle where God dwells. He makes his call *"from the end of the earth"* (v. 2) with a heart *"overwhelmed"* (or *"fainting"*). This may indicate that he is gripped by some illness. However, it probably simply represents his longing to be back home in security and peace. Thus he requests to be led *"to the rock that is higher than I."* While this *"rock"* could literally be a fortress or a defensive position, God Himself is called a rock thirty-three times in Scripture. In Isaiah 17:10 He is "the Rock of your stronghold." In Psalm 31:3 He is addressed as "my rock and my fortress." In Deuteronomy 32:15 He is called "the Rock of his [Jeshurun's] salvation." Thus David asks God to take his *"overwhelmed"* heart to Himself; to be his *"rock," "higher,"* more secure than he is.

One of the great benefits of prayer is that when we do feel overwhelmed and call out to God, we are given a peace and security which we have not known before in that situation. As a young Christian I took my first plane flight across the country to go away to college. Most of my life had been spent in Southern California. I vividly remember feeling overwhelmed when I arrived at La Guardia airport in New York, but as I prayed, a clear sense of the Lord's presence came over me. There I found at the *"end of the earth"* my *"rock"* which was *"higher than I."*

CONFESSION OF FAITH IN GOD

> 3 For You have been a shelter for me,
>   A strong tower from the enemy.
> 4 I will abide in Your tabernacle forever;
>   I will trust in the shelter of Your wings.   Selah
> 5 For You, O God, have heard my vows;
>   You have given *me* the heritage of those who fear
>   Your name.
> 6 You will prolong the king's life,
>   His years as many generations.
> 7 He shall abide before God forever.
>   Oh, prepare mercy and truth, *which* may preserve him!
>
> *Ps. 61:3–7*

Secure in the rock, David now confesses his faith to the Lord. First, God has been a *"shelter"* for him (v. 3). The noun here means a "refuge" and relates clearly to the previous cry for a "rock." The parallel clause also identifies God as a *"strong tower"* to protect him *"from the enemy."* In Proverbs 18:10 we read: "The name of the Lord is a strong tower; / The righteous run to it and are safe." Not only is God a fortress of security however; He is also the implied object of worship (v. 4). Thus David
wants to *"abide in [God's] tabernacle forever."* Later in the psalm he will tell us what he will do there. Here the theme of safety continues. David *"will trust in the shelter of [God's] wings"* and God will protect him the way a hen protects her chicks, an image found repeatedly in Psalms. True security, then, is only to be found *"before God,"* abiding in His presence. He alone is eternal and unchanging.

Next, David confesses that God has *"heard"* his *"vows"* (v. 5). The "vow" is a votive sacrifice which David has promised to offer. It expresses the certainty that God has heard and answered him (see also v. 8). The thought of his vows leads David to an affirmation that God has given him *"the heritage of those who fear [His] name."* The *"heritage"* is the Promised Land which is a part of David's inheritance. It belongs as well to all those Israelites who have *"fear"* or awe before the *"name"* of the Lord.

Now David confesses that God will give him (the king) long *"life."* His *"years"* will be *"as many generations."* This refers not only to David but also to his royal line (see 2 Sam. 7:16). The ultimate reference, however, is to the Messiah. This is fulfilled in Jesus and His resurrection since He is David's "son" (see Rom. 1:3–4).

David continues, saying that the king *"shall abide* [sit on his throne] *before God forever"* (v. 7; cf. v. 4, where he abides in the tabernacle forever). Then he asks that God may grant (*"prepare"*) *"mercy"* and *"truth"* to *"preserve"* or keep the king. Once again, these petitions are fulfilled in Christ. He is the One who abides before God forever because He is God. Also mercy and truth are His and become ours in Him. Those who submit to this King and who dwell in His kingdom receive all the benefits of His reign. Thus we receive all that Jesus is: "For in Him dwells all the fullness of the Godhead bodily; and you are complete in Him, who is the head of all principality and power" (Col. 2:9–10).

An Affirmation of Commitment

8 So I will sing praise to Your name forever,
That I may daily perform my vows.

Ps. 61:8

David becomes personal again as he ends this psalm, promising God that he *"will sing praise to [His] name forever."* Thus he will be among the eternal worshipers who delight to sing to the Lord and extol His *"name."* God's *"name"* reveals His personhood and releases His presence, His authority, and His power. Moreover, as an act of worship beyond *"praise,"* David will offer *"daily . . . vows."*

Indeed, we do need to know meaning in our lives and to find meaning beyond ourselves. David finds this in the rock higher than himself, that rock which is God. There, before the Lord, he abides forever and there, before the Lord, he sings praises forever.

Our ultimate meaning then is to be in God's presence, where we will find security as we enjoy Him. Moreover, our joy will express itself in song. The first question of the Westminster Shorter Catechism asks, "What is the chief end of man?" The answer is given, "Man's chief end is to glorify God and to enjoy Him forever." There is no higher destiny, no higher rock.

CHAPTER SIXTY-TWO

Waiting in the Silence

Psalm 62

In the political arena the candidate's immediate response to attack is to gather votes of support. Party loyalty is advocated or influential people pursued. Likewise, nations, when threatened, create "nonagression pacts" and seek to restore some balance of power by surrounding themselves with allies. When professional athletic teams are "in the cellar," the solution is to trade or buy players so that weak positions can be strengthened. A failing business may need new management or a new infusion of capital. The point to all these illustrations is that when the "crunch" comes we instinctively seek to shore up our position. Where can we find support? New votes? Extra funds? In Psalm 62 the "crunch" is on, but the writer startles us when he says, "My soul, wait silently for God alone" (v. 5).

The exact circumstances behind this psalm are unclear. Someone ("a man") is under an attack which seems to have gone on for some time. Deception is the order of the day, the goal being to remove him from his "high position." His enemies pretend to "consult" with him, but this is only a charade. Lies and curses are in their hearts. Stations in human life, however, have no lasting meaning, nor do riches obtained by oppression and robbery. Where then is security to be found? For the psalmist the only alternative is to wait on the Lord.

Commentators describe this psalm as an individual psalm of confidence. It contains meditation, wisdom-style teaching, and ends with a brief prayer. Tradition, which we follow, accepts this psalm as one of David's. The thought here moves from the security found in God (vv. 1–2) to the violence found in people (vv. 3–4) and again to the security found in God, along with an exhortation to trust in Him (vv. 5–8). After commenting on the ephemeral nature of life (vv. 9–10), it ends with a final witness and prayer concerning true power and mercy (vv. 11–12).

SECURITY IN GOD

1 Truly my soul silently *waits* for God;
  From Him *comes* my salvation.
2 He alone *is* my rock and my salvation;
  He is my defense;
  I shall not be greatly moved.

Ps. 62:1–2

David begins his meditation with a sense of serenity. The Hebrew adverb rendered *"truly"* in verse 1 can also be used with a restrictive force for contrasting other ideas. Thus it may be better in the context to take it here as "alone" or "only" (cf. vv. 2 and 5). The clause then translates literally, "Alone unto God in silence is my soul." Throughout the psalm the foolishness of trusting in men in comparison with God is maintained. Note the stress on silence both here and in verse 5. It is in the silence that God will speak.

A recent dimension of my own devotional life is not only to read Scripture and pray but also to wait and listen for the Lord. This is not mindless Eastern meditation, but rather an attitude of being open and receptive, expecting God to speak in the silence. Always as I wait, like David, I sense God's deliverance from Satan, sin, and self: *"From Him comes my salvation."* Silence before God expresses not only openness to Him, but dependence upon Him. *"Salvation"* or *"deliverance"* is His gift, by grace alone.

Verse 2 elaborates the theme of salvation, found in God Himself, as His exclusive gift: *"He alone is my rock and my salvation"* (for God as David's rock see Ps. 61:2). The wedding of *"rock"* and *"salvation"* suggests both protection (defense) and deliverance (offense). As the next clause states: *"He is my defense."* The word *"defense"* means "high place" or "fortress" (cf. Ps. 59:16–17). With such security then, the conclusion is clear: *"I shall not be greatly moved."* Notice the qualification in *"greatly"*—some movement, yes; much movement, no. Thus as David sits silently before God his mind is not emptied. Rather, it is filled with thoughts of God as salvation, as rock, as fortress, as stability, as the firm foundation for his life.

VIOLENCE IN THE WORLD

3 How long will you attack a man?
   You shall be slain, all of you,
   Like a leaning wall and a tottering fence.
4 They only consult to cast *him* down from his high
     position;
   They delight in lies;
   They bless with their mouth,
   But they curse inwardly.   Selah

                          Ps. 62:3–4

David now contrasts his security in God with the insecurity of life in this world. Someone is under attack. Pretending to consult with him, his enemies really intend to destroy him. Is it possible that this man in *"high position"* is David himself? This would explain the emphasis in verse 2 on God as his rock and fortress.

Verse 3 begins with a question: *"How long will you attack a man?"* The verb for *"attack"* means "to shout at, to rush upon with raised fists." The NKJV renders the next clause as one of judgment: *"You shall be slain, all of you."* It may also be translated: "Will you murder, all of you?" or "(that) you all may slay (him), all of you." In the context, these alternatives are probably better than the present text. Also the verb for *"slain"* means illegal murder rather than judicial punishment. *"Like a leaning wall and a tottering fence"* (v. 3) probably refers to the man who is under attack. He is shaken by those who seek his death; he is about ready to fall.

The attackers come to him pretending a consultation. This, however, is only *"to cast him down from his high position."* Thus we are dealing here with a noble man, perhaps even the king, the author of the psalm himself. The attackers *"delight in lies."* They *"bless"* this man *"with their mouth,"* they pronounce goodness upon him, but *"they curse inwardly."* The verb for *"curse"* may well include a magical or demonic use of a curse as a hex. (For curses, see 2 Sam. 16:5 ff.; 1 Kings 2:8;

James 3:9–10, 14–15.) These attackers, then, are hypocrites who deceive to destroy.

A REFRAIN OF SECURITY

> 5 My soul, wait silently for God alone,
>   For my expectation *is* from Him.
> 6 He only *is* my rock and my salvation;
>   *He is* my defense;
>   I shall not be moved.
> 7 In God *is* my salvation and my glory;
>   The rock of my strength,
>   *And* my refuge, *is* in God.
>
>   Ps. 62:5–7

Now David repeats the thoughts of verses 1–2 as a modified refrain. Rather than meditating on his soul's waiting for God, however, he addresses his soul: *"My soul, wait silently."* Also, rather than confessing that his *"salvation"* comes from God, he now confesses that his *"expectation"* (or hope) is in God. This contrasts effectively with the murderous attackers who would bring him to despair. Verse 6 is virtually identical to verse 2—God is David's *"rock," "salvation,"* and *"defense"* (or fortress). Now, however, in contrast to verse 2, his security is complete: *"I shall not be moved."*

Verse 7 adds to the refrain. David's *"salvation"* and *"glory"* ("honor") are to be found in God. Certainly, they are not to be found in humankind (see vv. 9–10). God is also *"the rock of my strength."* He is David's steadfastness. In God then he can hide. Here is his *"refuge"* ("shelter").

AN EXHORTATION TO TRUST

> 8 Trust in Him at all times, you people;
>   Pour out your heart before Him;
>   God *is* a refuge for us.   Selah
>
>   Ps. 62:8

Based upon his experience of God's protecting hand David exhorts the *"people"* to *"trust* [be secure] *in Him at all times* [continually]." As Israel's king, David is responsible for leading God's *"people."* Thus he meditates and prays not simply for himself, but also for them.

Next, they are not only to *"trust"* in God, they are also to *"pour"* their hearts out *"before Him."* The verb for *"pour"* is used to describe pouring out water or blood. It also metaphorically denotes the expression of an emotion such as anger (see Hos. 5:10). To *"pour out your heart,"* then, means to express your true self in openness and vulnerability before God. Once we are secure in Him as our "rock," we will be free to expose ourselves in this way.

In my own life I find that only before God can I express all that I am. There are times when my heart has been poured out before Him like water gushing forth from a broken dam. In a period of crisis in my life relating to people close to me, I was experiencing extreme emotional pain. I recall getting into my car and driving north for a couple of hours pouring myself out to the Lord all the while. I was so "lost" in my prayer that I was hardly aware of the freeway. God's presence came upon me in such a way that I was almost transfixed before Him. There was a profound cleansing of my inner being, and as a result, healing began to come. As I experienced God's love I could afford to become intimate with Him. This is always His gift. As David concludes, *"God is a refuge for us,"* this confession of faith reemphasizes the thought of verse 7. God is our rock and therefore we can hide in Him. When our souls have been poured out before Him, when we are the most vulnerable, He is there to embrace us in His love and hold us to His heart.

VAPOR THAT VANISHES

9 Surely men of low degree *are* a vapor,
   Men of high degree *are* a lie;
   If they are weighed on the scales,
   They *are* altogether *lighter* than vapor.
10 Do not trust in oppression,
   Nor vainly hope in robbery;
   If riches increase,
   Do not set *your* heart *on them.*

Ps. 62:9–10

Now David adopts the stance of a wisdom teacher. Such teachers existed in all the courts of the Ancient Near East. Here he reflects on the transitoriness of humankind in this world. This contrasts, of course, with the security only to be found in God. He observes: *"Surely men of low degree are a vapor, / Men of high degree are a lie."* The phrases *"men of low degree"* and *"men of high degree"* may either represent the polarities of human life or they may simply be synonyms for human beings in general (cf. Ps. 49:2). Such people are a *"vapor"* ("breath, vanity") and a *"lie"* ("falsehood, empty pretension"). When they are placed upon the scales to determine their weight, they are less than *"vapor."* There is nothing there.

C. S. Lewis in *The Great Divorce* observes that as people move farther and farther from God they become less and less real. Our true substance is spiritual and is found in our relationship with Him. Moreover, since Christ has come, we can be born anew or "from above" and have a spiritual nature created in us (see John 3:5–8). This is what puts weight on the scales.

Since humanity passes away as a *"vapor"* then (see also James 4:14), to *"trust"* in worldly plans and operations is stupid. Neither *"oppression"* nor *"robbery"* will accomplish anything lasting. To put *"trust"* and *"hope"* in them is to build on a foundation that will crumble and fall. *"Increase"* in *"riches"* is also no cause for security and in fact may bring greater insecurity. Only a heart set on God will last.

These wise observations could be illustrated at some length. Every generation passes away. Men of *"high degree"* are often revealed in their lies (e.g., the Nixon White House). Moreover, oppression simply bears the seeds of its own destruction (e.g., Hitler, Mao, and "The Gang of Four"). The more money, the more pride, greed, fear, and corruption—unless money is under the lordship of Christ. Thus David's warnings are for us as well as for ancient Israel.

TRUE POWER AND MERCY

> 11 God has spoken once,
>   Twice I have heard this:
>   That power *belongs* to God.
> 12 Also to You, O Lord, *belongs* mercy;
>   For You render to each one according to his work.
>
> *Ps. 62:11–12*

David now brings his meditation to a close with a witness and a direct prayer. God has spoken not once, but a second time, directly to him. This is the value of his waiting before Him in the silence. Commentators speak of temple oracles, cultic words, and so forth, in interpreting this verse (v. 11), displaying an implicit antisupernatural bias. But our God is the living God who addresses us in words, visions, dreams, angelic visitations, and finally in His incarnate Son. That God speaks is a basic difference between Himself and the idols. The word David receives here is simply: *"Power belongs to God."* The noun here means "strength, might." The strength or power of God is revealed in His mighty deeds. Now, in direct prayer in verse 12, David adds that *"mercy"* also *"belongs"* to God. God rewards the works of humankind, not as the basis of His mercy, however, but as the consequence of His mercy. Thus in the Exodus it is only after redemption that God demands the obedience of His people (Exod. 19:4–6). We too are saved unto good works (Eph. 2:10) and in the mystery of His grace He will reward us for them.

In the silence, then, without gathering allies or friends, David receives what he needs. As he puts it, from God comes his "salvation." Now he continues to listen to God in the confidence of divine security, and God speaks. He says, in effect, that when people attack and deceive and when oppression and robbery tempt, we are to remember that power is His. God is not only David's rock of defense against his foes, He is also his strength and power for battle with them. All of this comes to David from God's mercy because he waits for Him.

Can this also happen to us? Step into the laboratory: "My soul, wait silently for God alone."

CHAPTER SIXTY-THREE

Spiritual Satisfaction

Psalm 63

There comes a point in the lives of many of us when only an intimate relationship with God will satisfy. Many traditional Christians, including evangelicals, go through life with a low sense of spiritual vitality. Our days are largely consumed with secular pursuits. Prayer and Bible reading are one-a-day "fast food" items. "Real life" is not life in the Spirit, but life in the flesh. It is reaching here and there, doing this and that, and fitting in Christian activity largely to meet our social needs. We may close the night in prayer as a "spiritual glaze" over our real interests, but there is no manifest heart-hunger for God.

However, this can change, sometimes dramatically. A dear friend of mine who has cancer told me that this was the best thing that had ever happened to him. It stopped him short in the race of life and caused him to reevaluate everything, starting with his relationship with God. Illness and other causes may also bring us to a crisis point, throwing us, with new seriousness, upon the Lord. For some it may be a death in the family. For others it may be a major "passage" in life, a conflict in marriage, trouble with children, or a business reversal. These emotional earthquakes will break down our defenses and open us up to the Lord. What we often find then is a deep inner emptiness and a longing for God. Psalm 63 is a witness to that longing and its satisfaction.

Commentators identify this psalm as an individual lament. Tradition ascribes authorship to David, and the internal evidence—its military images and setting, its deep devotional power, its hunger for worship, and its reference to the king—supports this view. The thought moves from a longing for God (vv. 1–2) to a commitment to worship Him (vv. 3–5) and a meditation on God's care (vv. 6–8). The psalm ends with confidence in His victory (vv. 9–11).

LONGING FOR GOD

1 O God, You *are* my God;
  Early will I seek You;

> My soul thirsts for You;
> My flesh longs for You
> In a dry and thirsty land
> Where there is no water.
> 2 So I have looked for You in the sanctuary,
> To see Your power and Your glory.
>
> *Ps. 63:1–2*

As David calls out in prayer to God he also confesses his faith. This God is *his* God. He lives in a personal relationship with Him, a relationship that is the priority of his life. As he continues: *"Early will I seek You,"* David puts his whole self into his spiritual search. The Hebrew verb used here means "to seek with longing" and implies a passionate desire for God. His continuing thought, *"My soul thirsts for You; / My flesh longs for You,"* is no disembodied spirituality; the passion of his being is for God, and the verbs denote this elemental quest. Psalm 42:1–2 expresses a similar thought: "As the deer pants for the water brooks, / So pants my soul for You, O God. / My soul thirsts for God, for the living God." David's search is also *"early,"* suggesting that this is a morning prayer.

David's thirst for God is set in the context of a *"dry . . . land where there is no water."* He may well be in the wilderness or desert regions on some military campaign (cf. vv. 9–10), but the real wilderness or desert is in his heart. This is even more likely in light of the contrast in verse 2.

Note how often God speaks to people in the wilderness. It was there that Moses and Israel received most of the Pentateuch before entering the Promised Land. It was in the wilderness that the word of God came to both Elijah and John the Baptist. Even our Lord Himself, filled with the Holy Spirit, was driven into the wilderness (Mark 1:12). The wilderness strips us of our defenses and reveals our vulnerability; it quiets us before God. Now we are ready to hear Him and to do battle with ourselves, and with the devil.

Next, David remembers where his spiritual thirst has been quenched in the past. It is in the *"sanctuary"* ("holy place," "tabernacle," or "temple"). The word for *"looked for"* (v. 2) may have the sense of beholding the presence of God in a theophany or a vision. This meaning is especially possible here because in seeing God, David sees His *"power"* and *"glory."* It is clear that God manifested Himself in the tabernacle and the temple in a visual, physical presence. When Moses dedicated the tabernacle "the cloud covered the tabernacle of meeting, and the glory of the Lord filled the tabernacle. And Moses was not able to enter the tabernacle of meeting, because the cloud rested above it, and the glory of the Lord filled the tabernacle" (Exod. 40:34–35; cf. 1 Kings 8:10–11). Similarly, David has seen God's glory in the holy place.

THE WORSHIP OF GOD

3 Because Your lovingkindness *is* better than life,
   My lips shall praise You.
4 Thus I will bless You while I live;
   I will lift up my hands in Your name.
5 My soul shall be satisfied as with marrow and fatness,
   And my mouth shall praise You with joyful lips.

Ps. 63:3–5

David's worship is based on God's *"lovingkindness"* which is a greater good than *"life"* itself. This *"lovingkindness"* is His "grace," His "covenant-love," which finds David and holds him unconditionally. (The Hebrew word used here is the same word so often translated "mercy.") To be loved by God in this way is *"better than life,"* or to put it another way, it is to begin to live. Here David responds to God's love: *"My lips shall praise You. / . . . I will bless You while I live."* To *"bless"* means "to show appreciation, gratitude, and good will" which promotes respect for the one being blessed. Moreover, David will *"lift"* his *"hands"* to the *"name"* of God (cf. Ps. 28:2). Calling upon God's name in faith releases His power and presence.

The result of this worship is that David's *"soul"* ("self") is now *"satisfied"* or *"fully fed" "as with marrow and fatness"* (v. 5). By law no fat was to be eaten because it was the Lord's (see Lev. 3:16). Here, as a result of worship, God gives His own food to David and he is filled. Again he responds in praise *"with joyful lips,"* or, literally, lips "of a ringing cry."

THE CARE OF GOD

6 When I remember You on my bed,
   I meditate on You in the *night* watches.
7 Because You have been my help,
   Therefore in the shadow of Your wings I will rejoice.

8 My soul follows close behind You;
   Your right hand upholds me.

Ps. 63:6–8

David not only engages in public praise, he also seeks God *"on [his]
bed,"* where he remembers and meditates on Him. It is a good thing
for us to tap into our memory of what God has done for us. Memory
encourages faith and shows us the faithfulness of God in our lives.
Thus as Jesus extends to us the elements of the Lord's Supper He says,
"Do this in remembrance of Me" (1 Cor. 11:24).

The verb *"meditate,"* used in verse 6, also appears in Psalm 1:2. Its
primary meaning, "to moan, growl, or speak," may indicate that David's
meditation is active and verbal, thus devoting conscious energy to mull-
ing over who God is as he goes through the *"night watches,"* the several
time periods of the night (see Judg. 7:19). In memory and meditation, then, David finds security, even in the perilous hours when an
enemy could strike under the cover of darkness. Recently a dear older
woman in our church told me that when she awakens in the night
she prays for those who are on her heart. Then she is able to drop
right back to sleep. She has learned, with David, to seek God in the
"night watches."

The basis for David's meditation is that God has been his *"help."*
Protected under God's *"wings"* (for "God's wings" see chaps. 17, 36),
he will *"rejoice."* The verb here means "to shout for joy." Moreover,
because of God's protection David *"follows close behind"* Him much
as a soldier travels behind the shield that he carries. This thought also
suggests devotion and obedience to God (see Deut. 10:20). As he stays
close to the Lord, he is upheld by God's *"right hand,"* the hand of
authority and power. Verses 7–8 may also give us the content of David's
night-time meditations. He especially thinks of God's help, His protection, and His authority. Thus God keeps him safe in the warfare of
this world.

Victory in God

9 But those *who* seek my life, to destroy *it,*
   Shall go into the lower parts of the earth.
10 They shall fall by the sword;
   They shall be a portion for jackals.

431

11 But the king shall rejoice in God;
   Everyone who swears by Him shall glory;
   But the mouth of those who speak lies shall be
      stopped.

                                                          Ps. 63:9–11

David is in a battle. Enemies *"seek [his] life [soul] to destroy it."* Because
of God's help and power, however, they will be destroyed, they will
"go into the lower parts of the earth," namely, Sheol. The means of their
destruction will be that they will *"fall"* in battle *"by the sword."* God
will slay David's enemies, and *"jackals"* will eat their corpses.

Like David we too have our enemies. Paul reminds us, however, that
our real foes are not human and thus our weapons must be spiritual,
"mighty in God for pulling down strongholds" (2 Cor. 10:3–4). While
the devil seeks to destroy us, it is he who will finally go "into the
lower parts of the earth," even "the lake of fire," where he "will be
tormented day and night forever and ever" (Rev. 20:10). Knowing, in
Luther's phrase that "his doom is sure," he is all the more angry and
violent toward us in this life. Thus it is imperative that, like David,
we remember God at night and know Him as our help, our protection,
and our power. Under His "wings," we can join David and *"rejoice,"*
or *"shout for joy."*

David concludes that *"the king shall rejoice in God."* The third person
singular is "court language." It also means that this psalm applies to
the line of Israel's kings climaxing in the Messiah. Notice that David's
joy is not merely in winning the battle; it is in the God who wins the
battle for him. The danger in worshiping God for His benefits when
we are winners is that we end up worshiping the benefits and not the
God who gives them to us. Furthermore, *"Everyone who swears by Him
shall glory."* The NKJV capitalizes *"Him,"* meaning God. In the Hebrew
text, the *"Him"* could refer to the king, who, of course, represents God
to the people. In either case to "swear by" God or the king is to take
an oath of loyalty. The result will be *"glory"* or "boasting" because
such an allegiance insures that his victory is our victory. The liars,
however, will be proven wrong; their mouths *"shall be stopped"* by God's
judgment. Our King is Jesus. As He rejoices in God, so do we. His
triumph is ours and our commitment to Him evokes *"glory."*

In this psalm David's longing for God is satisfied as he worships,
meditates, and then goes into battle. The sequence is crucial. We too
must worship and meditate before we fight, because we can only fight

in the power of God. Thus we need to follow "close behind" Him and to be upheld by His "right hand." As this becomes our spiritual lifestyle, we too will see God's "power" and "glory," and our hunger for Him will be satisfied.

CHAPTER SIXTY-FOUR

God's Answer to Verbal Violence

Psalm 64

I remember studying boxing as a freshman in college. Not being much of a physical fighter, I hated the pounding I received and I certainly didn't enjoy dishing it out in return. It is true that a knockout punch may seem to come from nowhere, but there are still limited controls— the ring, the clock, the type of gloves, and officials to see that rules like no hitting below the belt are enforced. In the secret war of deception, plots, and unexpected surprises, however, there are no rules. There is a real terror in that kind of "no holds barred" competition. In our struggle with Satan we are fighting such a secret war. He knows no rules and is delighted to hit below the belt. His emissaries fight in the same way. Here then it is only God who can take care of us, because He is all-knowing and can see through the plots and disguises of the devil. John promises us that God gives us an anointing to deal with evil (1 John 2:18–20) and calls upon us to test the spirits so that we will not be deceived (1 John 4:1). Psalm 64 shows that God's power is greater than evil plots to destroy us.

The psalmist offers a prayer or meditation to God, asking to be preserved from the fear of his enemies who engage in "secret counsel," "rebellion," "laying snares," and perfecting a "shrewd scheme." These evil workers use their tongues as weapons, their words are arrows, and they shoot secretly. But God will return their fire, which will result in their stumbling, and the righteous will be glad. Here is the psalmist's answer to his enemies' verbal violence.

Commentators describe this psalm as an individual lament. Tradition holds David to be its author, and there are no internal indications to prevent us from following that tradition. The thought moves from a prayer for protection (vv. 1–4) to a description of the violent plots facing David (vv. 5–6), to God's response (vv. 7–9) and the response of the righteous (v. 10).

A Prayer for Protection

1 Hear my voice, O God, in my meditation;
   Preserve my life from fear of the enemy.
2 Hide me from the secret plots of the wicked,
   From the rebellion of the workers of iniquity,
3 Who sharpen their tongue like a sword,
   And bend *their bows to shoot* their arrows—bitter
   words,
4 That they may shoot in secret at the blameless;
   Suddenly they shoot at him and do not fear.

                                                  Ps. 64:1–4

David begins with a cry to God to *"hear my voice,"* indicating that he is speaking out loud. He addresses his *"meditation"* or his "complaint" to the Lord, asking Him to preserve him from *"fear of the enemy."* The word *"fear"* here denotes David's anxiety or terror caused by his opponents. The noun *"enemy"* in the singular may be collective and thus is best rendered "enemies" in English (cf. v. 2, *"workers of iniquity"*).

David wants God to *"hide"* him *"from the secret plots of the wicked."* To be hidden by God is to be "sheltered" or "concealed," that is, protected. The *"secret plots"* includes the plots or planning of his opponents (cf. vv. 5–6). These plots, which center on *"rebellion,"* "tumult" or "commotion," are being hatched by *"the wicked"* who are *"workers of iniquity."* These are typical parallel words used to describe those in rebellion against God and His law (see Ps. 28:3).

At present, the attack upon David consists of underhanded plots and verbal abuse. His opponents *"sharpen their tongue like a sword"* and launch their words like *"arrows"* (v. 3). Psalm 55:21 makes a similar complaint: "His words were . . . drawn swords." These words are also *"bitter,"* which could mean slanderous words or even evil incantations. The goal of the attack is to take David by surprise, so his enemies launch their arrows *"in secret"* or in ambush. The attack is sudden and fearless. This probably means that these evil workers have no fear of God (see Ps. 36:1). This picture of secret attack where *"bitter"* plots (and curses?) hit the *"blameless"* ("irreproachable") man is like today's political terrorism, which also comes from irrational, hidden sources on both the left and on the right. Satan launches his arrows at Christians in the same manner. He garbles communication, breaks down trust, awakens anxieties. He leads people to miscommunication in which the truth becomes distorted and people simply project their own irrational fears onto each other. As John Wimber reminds us, our brother is not our enemy, however misled he may be; our enemy is the devil and we must never forget that.

Violent Plots

5 They encourage themselves *in* an evil matter;
  They talk of laying snares secretly; They say, "Who
    will see them?"
6 They devise iniquities:
  "We have perfected a shrewd scheme."
  Both the inward thought and the heart of man are
    deep.

Ps. 64:5–6

In verse 5, David describes the strengthening of the opposition by mutual reinforcement. The verb for *"encourage"* means "to harden or grow firm." Thus their position becomes strong *"in an evil matter"* (or "deed") as a plot is hatched for laying out *"snares"* or traps *"secretly."* Their question *"Who will see them?"* assumes wrongly, of course, that God won't. They think David won't know anything either. But he has his informants and knows what they are about.

The thought of subversion continues in verse 6: *"They devise iniquities"* (injustice, wrong), claiming to *"have perfected a shrewd scheme,"* or literally, "a scheme well schemed." David concludes that *"the inward thought* [midpart, inside of the body] *and the heart of man are deep"* or "unsearchable."

It is out of these dark depths then that evil plans and twisted desires come. The real point here, however, is the wrongness of the assumption that no one sees them. As John says of Jesus, "and [He] had no need that anyone should testify of man, for He knew what was in man" (John 2:25). Thus God sees.

GOD'S RESPONSE

7 But God shall shoot at them *with* an arrow;
  Suddenly they shall be wounded.
8 So He will make them stumble over their own tongue;
  All who see them shall flee away.
9 All men shall fear,
  And shall declare the work of God;
  For they shall wisely consider His doing.

Ps. 64:7–9

God now will act in a manner analogous to the wicked. He too will shoot *"an arrow"* (cf. v. 3), and they also *"suddenly"* will be *"wounded"* (cf. v. 4). Furthermore, He makes them *"stumble* ["stagger"] *over their own tongue."* The tongue symbolizes the "secret counsel" and the "bitter words" which they have launched at David. That evil people are destroyed by their own words or actions has already been noted as a common theme in the psalms. (See earlier, at Ps. 5:10.) When their destruction comes then *"all who see them shall flee away."* Just as when a building falls during an earthquake, those inside are desperate to get out.

Out of their fear of God the people *"declare the work of God."* This declaration is witness, coming from a sense of awe before God's majesty and power. The people will also *"wisely consider His doing."* The verb for *"consider"* means to "ponder, give attention to." Thus the people ponder God's works to gain insight about Him and about themselves. When we see God's justice and His judgments, it is, indeed, a time for reflection. What we learn is that God is powerful and just and that wicked people and their plots will fail, dropping back down on their own heads.

The reference to *"all men"* in verse 9 probably means "all Israel." If it meant the whole earth, then the psalm would be cosmic and eschatological, but the sense of a final, ultimate judgment is absent here.

THE RESPONSE OF THE RIGHTEOUS

10 The righteous shall be glad in the LORD, and trust in
   Him.
   And all the upright in heart shall glory.

Ps. 64:10

As God judges the wicked with their own weapons, *"the righteous"* will rejoice or *"be glad in the Lord."* David says in Psalm 32:11: "Be glad in the Lord and rejoice, you righteous; / And shout for joy, all you upright in heart!" The *"righteous"* also will *"trust* [seek refuge] *in Him."* They will know that God avenges evil and is trustworthy. Moreover, *"the upright in heart"* will *"glory"* or "boast" in God. In response to God's slaying the wicked by their own sword, God's people worship Him and rest, secure in His care.

We will never know what gossip, plots, or attacks may have been launched against us. But we can know that God knows and will act in our behalf. As we have seen, irrational fear is hard to bear. In a time of relative peace it is difficult to realize that the devil is waging a secret war against us. His arrows are lies and his target is our hearts. God, however, will defend and protect us and bring his evil back upon him in the end.

CHAPTER SIXTY-FIVE

Praise the Savior and Sustainer

Psalm 65

Some years ago J. B. Phillips startled us with his charge "Your God is too small." This is certainly true for many of us in terms of our images of God. He may be a grand old man with a flowing white beard, or He may be "someone in the great somewhere," but He is not the living God of the Bible. More recently Lesslie Newbigin has pointed out that since the Reformation the church has been on a retreat from secular society. Our God is not merely too small in our way of picturing Him, He is also too small in terms of our opinion of His ability to help us cope with modern life. Little by little, Christians have turned over economics, philosophy, health-care, and education to society. We seem to have abandoned all else to the devil except for our interior piety and personal code of ethics.

Psalm 65, however, sees God as the Creator of all things and the One to whom all things belong. Moreover, He sustains His creation with active involvement in its mountains and oceans, its water supply and its harvests. Not only is He the Creator, He is also the Savior. He answers prayers and provides "atonement" for sin. God is to be worshiped and praised in Zion.

Commentators identify this psalm as a hymn of praise or as a psalm of thanksgiving. It may be that it was used at a harvest festival such as the Feast of Unleavened Bread or after the lifting of a famine. The mention of the temple, if literal, seems to undercut the tradition of Davidic authorship. The thought here moves from praise to God as Savior (vv. 1–3) to a blessing of the chosen (v. 4) and a confession of God's awesome deeds seen in His sovereignty over nature and the nations (vv. 5–8). It ends with a celebration of God's watering the earth and the resulting fruitfulness (vv. 9–13).

PRAISE THE SAVIOR

1 Praise is awaiting You, O God, in Zion;
  And to You the vow shall be performed.
2 O You who hear prayer, To You all flesh will come.
3 Iniquities prevail against me;
  As for our transgressions,
  You will provide atonement for them.

Ps. 65:1–3

The psalmist begins with an announcement of praise for God, rather than a direct expression of praise: *"Praise is awaiting You, O God, in Zion."* The Hebrew text seems literally to read. "For You silence is for praise, O God in Zion." If this is correct then the probable meaning is that the silence of resignation or surrender is the praise presented to God. The place where such an offering is made is *"in Zion."* There God dwells on His holy mountain (see Ps. 2:6). *"In Zion"* also *"the vow shall be performed"* ("paid"). This *"vow"* is either a promise made in crisis or an act of gratitude made in the confidence that prayers will be answered.

God is identified as the one who hears prayer. *"Prayer"* (v. 2) is spoken communication with God, personal or cultic. It can be merely a cry to the Lord or it can be a long formal liturgy. The content (as in the psalms) varies according to the person praying and his or her circumstances. Because God does *"hear prayer,"* He also answers it. Thus: *"To You all flesh will come."* In this verse *"flesh"* means all humanity or all Israel.

The psalmist then offers his surrender to *"God, in Zion,"* as his *"praise"* in worship. With this he brings his *"vow"* and *"prayer,"* confident that he will receive mercy. Thus he continues: *"Iniquities prevail against me"* (v. 3). *"Iniquities"* are willful acts of wrongdoing that overpower him. *"Transgressions"* ("acts of rebellion") also stand between the psalmist and a holy God. The psalmist has received good news, however: "[God] *will provide atonement for them."* The word for *"provide atonement"* means "to cover over, to appease." It signifies the removal of the barrier between humankind and God (divine wrath and our sin) through sacrifice or substitution (see Exod. 29:36; Lev. 16:10).

In sum, submission, sacrifice, and prayer are offered to God on Zion because He provides atonement. He is the Savior who welcomes us into His presence. All of this has now been fulfilled for us by Christ. He offered Himself as the final sacrifice "once for all" (Rom. 6:10). Thus "if we walk in the light as He is in the light, we have fellowship with one another, and the blood of Jesus . . . cleanses us from all sin" (1 John 1:7). It is this blood which has made atonement for us (Rom. 3:25).

BLESS THE CHOSEN

> 4 Blessed *is the man* You choose,
>   And cause to approach *You,*
>   *That* he may dwell in Your courts.
>   We shall be satisfied with the goodness of Your house,
>   Of Your holy temple.
>
> *Ps. 65:4*

The psalmist continues in meditation, reflecting on the fact that God blesses the man whom He chooses and causes to approach Him. (For God's blessing see Ps. 1.) The verb for *"choose"* refers to God's election and relates to all of Israel (Deut. 7:6), or to individuals such as David (1 Sam. 10:24). Through God's initiative alone we come into His presence. "You did not choose Me, but I chose you" (John 15:16). Thus the divine blessing is in God's call which results in dwelling in His "*courts*," namely, being in His "*house*," His "*holy temple*." The psalmist probably intends a progression here. The "*courts*" refers to the outer courtyard; the "*house*" is the actual structure where God dwells and the "*holy temple*" is the "holy place of the temple," or the inner shrine. Here is where he lives and receives all of God's "*goodness*." This may include the spiritual blessings of verses 1–3 and the sacrificial meal in the sanctuary (see Ps. 22:25–26). The ultimate blessing is to be in the presence of God Himself, in the "*temple*" where He dwells. As Psalm 16:11 says, "In Your presence is fullness of joy; / At Your right hand are pleasures forevermore."

CONFESS GOD'S AWESOME DEEDS

> 5 *By* awesome deeds in righteousness You will answer
>   us,
>   O God of our salvation,
>   *You who are* the confidence of all the ends of the earth,
>   And of the far-off seas;
> 6 Who established the mountains by His strength,
>   *Being* clothed with power;
> 7 You who still the noise of the seas,
>   The noise of their waves, And the tumult of the
>   peoples.
> 8 They also who dwell in the farthest parts are afraid
>   of Your signs;
>   You make the outgoings of the morning and evening
>   rejoice.
>
>   *Ps. 65:5–8*

As the psalmist meditates on God's answer, he is struck by His "*awesome deeds in righteousness*," His mighty acts which produce fear in His enemies and evoke praise from His people. God does not merely answer in promises; He answers in actions. He is the "*God of our salvation*," who delivers Israel. As the Savior, God is the "*confidence*" or hope "*of all the ends of the earth*," namely, the whole world, including "*the far-off seas*." Moreover, in His mighty acts He "*established the mountains*." Their strength comes from "*His strength*," as He was "*clothed with power*." The noun for "*power*" is often used in referring to the might or valor of warriors. Thus because God has a warrior's power, He does "*awesome deeds*."

God's acts are also seen in His control of *"the seas."* He brings calm to the roar of *"the waves,"* as well as *"the tumult of the peoples."* All the forces of chaos in nature and among the nations are under His sovereignty.

Moreover, nations far from Israel *"are afraid of [God's] signs,"* or mighty deeds. As God sends the plagues on Egypt He says to Moses, "And I will harden Pharaoh's heart, and multiply My signs and My wonders in the land of Egypt" (Exod. 7:3). These *"signs"* also cause the *"outgoings* [the goings forth] *of the morning and evening [to] rejoice"* ("shout for joy"). This probably means the places from which the *"morning and evening"* originate, namely, the whole earth. Fear and joy, then, are the proper responses to God's *"awesome deeds."*

Today when we stand before Yosemite Falls or gaze into the Grand Canyon we may have some sense of the Creator's majesty. His direct intervention among the nations, however, is distant for most of us. Nevertheless, as God is renewing His church, there is a new sense of God's power manifest in our midst.

CONFESS GOD'S PROVISION FOR THE EARTH

9 You visit the earth and water it,
   You greatly enrich it;
   The river of God is full of water;
   You provide their grain,
   For so You have prepared it.
10 You water its ridges abundantly,
   You settle its furrows;
   You make it soft with showers,
   You bless its growth.
11 You crown the year with Your goodness,
   And Your paths drip *with* abundance.
12 They drop *on* the pastures of the wilderness,
   And the little hills rejoice on every side.
13 The pastures are clothed with flocks;
   The valleys also are covered with grain;
   They shout for joy, they also sing.

Ps. 65:9–13

God's care for the land now becomes the focus of the psalmist's meditation. The verb for *"visit"* in verse 9 means "to attend to, to care for." As a result of God's provision, the rains come and the earth is fruitful. Thus, *"the river of God,"* which could be the rain itself, comes in abundance and the *"earth"* grows its *"grain"* in the soil God has *"prepared"* for this fruitfulness. Verse 10 continues to elaborate upon God's care.

A comprehensive picture of this blessed harvest time is given in verses 11–13. *"Crown"* (v. 11) is a metaphor for "honor." God's *"goodness"* is His completeness in blessing. The *"paths"* here may be the tracks of His chariot as it crosses the sky in the clouds bringing the rain. With the rains, the *"little hills rejoice,"* the *"pastures"* wear their grazing *"flocks"* like a garment, and *"grain"* (or "corn") covers *"the valleys."*

In Psalm 65, then, God is seen as the Savior and Sustainer of Israel, a big God who provides sacrifices for sin and rain for the land. He has not been driven out of His universe by "mother nature," nor has He been trivialized by an interior piety that removes Him from history. He performs *"awesome deeds in righteousness,"* and He commands nature and nations. Those who go to Zion to worship Him will be "blessed" in His temple and will know "the goodness of His house."

If the church is to be renewed today, she must recover this cosmic, comprehensive sense of our sovereign God, which is now to be found in the face of Jesus. As Paul puts it, "For by Him all things were created that are in heaven and that are on earth, visible and invisible, whether thrones or dominions or principalities or powers. All things were created through Him and for Him. And He is before all things, and in Him all things consist" (Col. 1:16–17). To this great Lord we must lift our prayers for revival, that He might send His Spirit as the rains and make His church fruitful with new growth once again.

CHAPTER SIXTY-SIX

God's Awesome Works

Psalm 66

Authentic Biblical faith exists in a creative tension. On the one hand, there is the corporate life of Israel and the church. On the other hand, there is the personal life of the individual. Whenever this tension is broken great damage is done. Either the individual is absorbed into the community or he or she wanders alone with a private faith. Christianity is intensely personal, but it is not individualistic. Each person finds his or her meaning within the overall plan of God for the cosmos, the planet, and all of history.

It was a great day for me when I realized that I had been called by Christ into history and now belonged to God's purpose in creation and redemption. I had been incorporated into His people, and every generation of Christians was mine. I was a part of the new Israel (Gal. 6:16) and a subject of Christ's kingdom, called into His army to do battle against the powers of darkness. I was a participant in the greatest missionary movement that the world has ever known. Thus the meaning of my life was not just in my personal salvation or my own interior spirituality but was to be found in a cause, God's purpose to unite "all things in Christ," things in heaven and things on earth (Eph. 1:10).

Psalm 66 witnesses to both the corporate and the personal nature of faith. It begins with a great confession of God's "awesome . . . works" in history. He embraces the whole earth in His plan. He has called Israel and redeemed her from Egypt. Although she has been broken in judgment, God has brought her to rich fulfillment. Suddenly, with verse 13, the psalm becomes intensely personal. The psalmist vows his intention to worship and then declares what God has done for his soul. Here, then, the psalmist sees his own relationship to God in the wider scope of all of His dealings with His people. This is authentic faith. We live in the *present* before God, we are held by the *past,* and we pursue the *future,* but all belong to Him.

Commentators describe this psalm as a hymn of thanksgiving. It has been proposed that it is a composite work in which verses 1–12 are a national liturgy to which a personal prayer (vv. 13–20) has been added. If, however, the speaker in verses 13–20 is the king, then the whole psalm may be prayed for the people and have an underlying unity. Whether verses 1–12 are a separate composition or not makes little difference. The key point for us is that the prayer starting with verse 13 only finds its meaning in the context of the larger purpose of God for His people in verses 1–12. The entire psalm is coherent in the setting of Biblical faith. The author of this psalm is unknown. The thought moves from a call to praise (vv. 1–4) to a call to see God's works (vv. 5–7) to a call to bless God for His testing (vv. 8–12). This is followed by a personal promise to worship (vv. 13–15) and witness (vv 16–20).

CALL TO PRAISE

1 Make a joyful shout to God, all the earth!
2 Sing out the honor of His name;
  Make His praise glorious.
3 Say to God,
  "How awesome are Your works!
  Through the greatness of Your power
  Your enemies shall submit themselves to You.
4 All the earth shall worship You
  And sing praises to You;
  They shall sing praises *to* Your name."   Selah
                                        Ps. 66:1–4

In the opening call to worship, the word for *"joyful shout"* means "to raise a shout" or "to blast a trumpet," and is commonly used for a war cry or a shout in triumph over enemies. It is employed in worship as well as a shout of triumph over spiritual enemies: "Oh, clap your hands, all you peoples! / Shout to God with the voice of triumph" (Ps. 47:1). When *"the earth"* joins in this cry, God will receive His due and Jesus' prayer will be fulfilled: "Your kingdom come. / Your will be done / On earth as it is in heaven" (Matt. 6:10).

In verse 2, the psalmist calls us to make singing, expressing joy, the means of worship. The content of worship is the *"honor"* or *"glory"* of God's *"name."* The word *"honor"* here means the praise or recognition given to God as His due. The *"name"* of God bears His presence, His power, and His person. When we call upon His name, we call upon Him. By His mighty acts of creation and deliverance His name is *"glorious"* or honored.

The psalmist exhorts us in verse 3 to tell God that His *"works"* are *"awesome."* The word for *"awesome"* means "fearful, dreadful, causing astonishment." Here is the overpowering sense of the numinous (R. Otto). God's *"awesome . . . works"* are seen when, *"through the greatness of Your power / Your enemies . . . submit themselves to You."* The verb for *"submit"* means "cringe." This is God's power in judgment, in battle-field victories. So great is this *"power"* that the whole "earth" will *"worship"* God (v. 4). This *"worship"* ("to surrender, bow down") will include praise and singing to the Lord's *"name."*

This conclusion is fully eschatological. It proclaims God's final triumph over all His enemies, the deliverance of the earth, and its return to worshiping and praising Him. This vision is only fulfilled in Christ's kingdom and His final triumph over sin, Satan, and death. It foreshadows the "new song" of the redeemed in Revelation 5:9. It promises "a great multitude which no one could number, of all nations, tribes, peoples, and tongues, standing before the throne and before the Lamb . . . and crying out with a loud voice, saying, 'Salvation belongs to our God who sits on the throne, and to the Lamb' " (Rev. 7:9–10). Here is the final triumph of righteousness.

CALL TO SEE GOD'S WORKS

5 Come and see the works of God;
   He is awesome *in His* doing toward the sons of men.
6 He turned the sea into dry *land;*
   They went through the river on foot.
   There we will rejoice in Him.
7 He rules by His power forever;
   His eyes observe the nations;
   Do not let the rebellious exalt themselves.   Selah
                                             Ps. 66:5–7

Having put the vision before us, the psalmist invites us now to behold God's *"works,"* to see what He has done. They are *"awesome,"* evoking wonder and terror, and they are directed *"toward the sons of men."* In verse 6, he recounts the Exodus, especially the parting of the Red Sea (*yam sûph,* literally Sea of Sledge, is more accurately translated Reed Sea) and Israel's walking through the Jordan on *"dry land."* These are the supreme examples in the Old Testament of God's awesome works, because they reveal His supreme act of redemption. Now Israel becomes

His own possession, called out of Egypt to become His son (Hos. 11:1). This mighty act of judgment against Pharaoh, displaying God's sovereignty over nature and His grace in liberating Israel and taking her into the Promised Land, leads to worship: *"There we will rejoice in Him"* (v. 6).

Through remembering what God has done and knowing that we are united to His purpose in history, we too now stand at the Red Sea and the Jordan. Ultimately we also are to stand at Calvary and the empty tomb, sharing in Christ's death and resurrection. Thus Paul can say that he has been crucified with Christ (Gal. 2:20). What Christ has done for us, He does in us when we are united to Him. By faith we return to these crucial events and know that they are for us and we are there as they happen. Thus Israel's Exodus is our Exodus, Christ's death is our death, and Christ's resurrection is our resurrection. As the Negro spiritual puts it, "Were you there when they crucified my Lord?"

The consequences of God's awesome works are that *"He rules by His power forever"* (v. 7), because He is the sovereign King. God's *"power"* is manifest when He defeats His enemies. Moreover, His reign is eternal, *"forever."* The *"nations"* (*gôyim,* "Gentiles") are under His scrutiny, and the final prayer at the end of verse 7 that the *"rebellious"* be unable to *"exalt themselves"* will certainly be answered.

CALL TO BLESS

> 8 Oh, bless our God, you peoples!
>   And make the voice of His praise to be heard,
> 9 Who keeps our soul among the living,
>   And does not allow our feet to be moved.
> 10 For You, O God, have tested us;
>   You have refined us as silver is refined.
> 11 You brought us into the net;
>   You laid affliction on our backs.
> 12 You have caused men to ride over our heads;
>   We went through fire and through water;
>   But You brought us out to rich *fulfillment.*
>
> *Ps. 66:8–12*

The psalmist now exhorts the *"peoples"* to *"bless our God,"* namely, to bless the God of Israel as the living and true God. This act of blessing is designed to promote God's honor and respect through *"praise,"* publicly and vocally.

But why should God be praised? To begin with, the psalmist says, God preserves the life of His people; they are *"among the living"* and their *"feet"* are *"not . . . moved"* (they do not "totter" or "slip") from His path (see discussion on Ps. 10:6). This is true despite God's testing them: *"For You, O God, have tested us."* The verb for *"tested"* is used regularly of proving metals. The metaphor continues: *"You have refined us as silver is refined,"* that is, the dross has been melted out. This has included God's trapping Israel in a "net" as would a hunter and afflicting her as a harsh taskmaster would a slave. Moreover, *"men . . . ride over* [their] *heads"* like an army overrunning its enemy. In sum, the psalmist recalls: *"We went through fire and through water"*—painful, dangerous means of testing. But as God promises: "When you pass through the waters, I will be with you; / And through the rivers, they shall not overflow you. / When you walk through the fire, you shall not be burned, / Nor shall the flame scorch you" (Isa. 43:2). Through the test, which could well include military defeat and captivity, God has been faithful. So the psalmist concludes: *"But You brought us out to rich fulfillment* [saturation]."

This whole passage (vv. 10–12) may presuppose the Exodus. In Egypt Israel was tested and *"refined."* She was netted in captivity. She had *"affliction"* laid upon her. However, she was delivered to *"rich fulfillment,"* to a land flowing with milk and honey.

Throughout the Bible God's people are tested and tried. Paul tells us that such testing produces character (Rom. 5:1–5). Out of the trial, glory shines. Likewise, out of death Jesus experienced resurrection, and out of our death to self we too may have a new beginning.

In my own life there has been substantial testing. During my years of higher education I was intellectually tested with regard to my faith. Then in the '60s, my white middle-class values and commitment to "the establishment" were tested and sifted. Later in life emotional wounds from the past have been tested and are being healed. Out of these tests refining has come and is coming. This life in Christ is a mixture of joy and sorrow, suffering and glory. The land, however, is before us, with its *"rich fulfillment."* Moreover, Christ's kingdom has already broken in upon us. We are not waiting merely for heavenly relief. By faith we enter that *"rich fulfillment"* now. Indeed, there is joy in the morning, and "the day is at hand" (Rom. 13:12).

PROMISE TO WORSHIP

13 I will go into Your house with burnt offerings;
　　I will pay You my vows,
14 Which my lips have uttered
　　And my mouth has spoken when I was in trouble.
15 I will offer You burnt sacrifices of fat animals,
　　With the sweet aroma of rams;
　　I will offer bulls with goats.　Selah

Ps. 66:13–15

Here the whole mood changes, as the psalmist becomes personal. His recital of God's work with Israel and his eschatological hope are completed. It is as if he asks, "Where do I fit into all of this?" The answer is in worship: *"I will go into Your house with burnt offerings"* (v. 13). Except for the hide, these animal *"offerings"* are totally consumed on the altar. They symbolize complete surrender to the Lord by giving all that is His to Him. Furthermore, the psalmist pays his *"vows"* (see chap. 65). These *"vows"* were promises of *"offerings"* which he made to the Lord in crisis, *"when [he] was in trouble."* They include *"burnt sacrifices of fat animals"* (see Lev. 22:18 ff.), *"the sweet aroma of rams,"* and *"bulls with goats."* All of these phrases are parallel and suggest in different ways the fulfillment of the vow. Thus the fat animals include rams, bulls, and goats. If the psalmist is the king we can see here why his vow is so expansive.

A WITNESS FOR GOD

16 Come *and* hear, all you who fear God,
　　And I will declare what He has done for my soul.
17 I cried to Him with my mouth,
　　And He was extolled with my tongue.
18 If I regard iniquity in my heart,
　　The Lord will not hear.
19 *But* certainly God has heard *me*;
　　He has attended to the voice of my prayer.
20 Blessed *be* God,
　　Who has not turned away my prayer,
　　Nor His mercy from me!

Ps. 66:16–20

Having committed himself to worship, the psalmist calls Israel to join him in the temple and *"hear"* of God's "awesome works." Those who come are those *"who fear God,"* who stand in reverence before Him. Before them, the psalmist makes his witness, declaring what God *"has done for [his] soul."* It is not enough to know what God has done for Israel. What has God done for you? Witness must become personal.

As is the case in so many psalms, the psalmist tells his listeners that he cried to God aloud, *"with [his] mouth."* Furthermore, God *"was extolled with [his] tongue"* or, literally, "and praise was under [his] tongue," that is, ready to burst forth.

As He worshiped and prayed, he did not hold on to *"iniquity,"* that is, he was not a hypocrite. If he were, God would *"not hear."*

The psalmist affirms in verse 19 that God *"heard"* him as he prayed. His prayer has received divine attention, and he is ready to praise God. In verse 20 he blesses God because He heard his prayer and answered with *"mercy."* The first benefit of prayer is simply that God hears. We now have a vital relationship with Him as we pray, regardless of His answer. The second benefit for the psalmist is to experience the *"mercy"* or grace of God. Assured that his offerings and vows are accepted, he gives his witness with assurance.

Psalm 66 shows us a remarkable integration between corporate faith and personal faith, between Israel and the individual. We cannot just hang around the Christian community and enjoy its benefits. If we do, we will die. It is like starving to death in a supermarket. We must eat. The great things God has done for us must be appropriated; they must become ours.

CHAPTER SIXTY-SEVEN

Call to Worship

Psalm 67

Throughout the Bible there is a tension between the particular and the universal. God calls Israel for the sake of the nations; God sends His Son to be the Savior of the world.

One of the heartbeats of the Bible is that all the nations, all ethnic groups, will come to worship the living and true God. In fact, the goal of Paul's evangelism is that all may worship: "For all things are for your sakes, that grace, having spread through the many, may cause thanksgiving to abound to the glory of God" (2 Cor. 4:15). Thus the call for all peoples to worship God is also a call to evangelism.

Are our hearts dismayed and burdened because most people curse God rather than praise Him and love Him? Does it concern us that there are so many joyless faces and empty lives? Our destiny is to be fulfilled in worship. Few are experiencing this today. Even the church is formal and apathetic. Large segments of God's people hire professional worshipers and then watch them perform. Thus the pews are filled with spectators and critics.

God, however, desires and even longs for our worship. Psalm 67 is His call to worship. Its goal is that all the peoples praise God and "sing for joy." The promise is that fruitfulness will come from worship and the blessing of God will be upon His people.

Some commentators see this psalm as a harvest prayer to be used at the time of a major feast. Others describe it as a prayer for divine blessing or a national lament. Its author is not identified. It is likely that the psalm was a part of the temple liturgy. The thought here moves from a call for blessing (vv. 1–2) to an imperative for worship (vv. 3–4) and concludes with the consequences of worship (vv. 5–7).

A CALL FOR BLESSING

1 God be merciful to us and bless us,
And cause His face to shine upon us,   Selah

2 That Your way may be known on earth,
   Your salvation among all nations.

Ps. 67:1–2

The psalmist cries out to God to *"be merciful to us and bless us."* The verb for *"be merciful"* is a word expressing sheer grace, the unmerited favor of God, His unconditional love. As God accepts us in His grace and saves us from our sins, He will also *"bless us."* Above all, this blessing is God's presence. He will *"cause His face to shine upon us."* God's shining face is His smile, His pleasure, His delight in us which, again, is a consequence of His mercy. Psalm 80:3 reads: "Restore us, O God; / Cause Your face to shine, / And we shall be saved!" Furthermore, this first verse of Psalm 67 reflects the Aaronic benediction in Numbers 6:24–26: "The Lord bless you and keep you; / The Lord make His face shine upon you, / And be gracious to you. . . ."

The consequence of God's mercy and blessing is that His *"way"* ("purpose, law") will *"be known on earth,"* and His *"salvation"* will be known *"among all nations."* Isaiah promises that the nations will flow to Zion and will say, "Come, and let us go up to the mountain of the Lord . . . He will teach us His ways" (2:3). The fulfillment of this call for God's salvation to come to the nations is now taking place as the gospel spreads. In His Son Jesus, God's face shines.

IMPERATIVE FOR WORSHIP

3 Let the peoples praise You, O God;
   Let all the peoples praise You.
4 Oh, let the nations be glad and sing for joy!
   For You shall judge the people righteously,
   And govern the nations on earth.   Selah

Ps. 67:3–4

In these verses the psalmist calls for a response to God's salvation. The second line, parallel to the first, emphasizes the universality of the gospel with the word *"all."* Again, it is important to note that this call to *"praise"* is also a call to evangelism. The Great Commission given by Jesus to the disciples begins the fulfillment of this imperative (see Matt. 28:18–20).

Furthermore, the psalmist calls for the nations to *"be glad and sing for joy"* ("give a ringing cry"; v. 4). But why should they be so happy? Because in God's coming idols will be destroyed and oppression will cease. The nations will be liberated from injustice when God takes his place as *"judge."* With the destruction of evil, He will *"govern"* ("lead, guide") all people in the perfect will of His kingdom.

These promises connect clearly with the servant songs in Isaiah. There the prophet tells of Yahweh's servant who will be filled with His Spirit. "He will bring forth justice to the Gentiles" (Isa. 42:1), and "He will not fail . . . till He has established justice in the earth; / And the coastlands shall wait for His law" (42:4). Who is this but Jesus, now Lord of the universe?

THE CONSEQUENCES OF WORSHIP

5 Let the peoples praise You, O God;
  Let all the peoples praise You.
6 *Then* the earth shall yield her increase;
  God, our own God, shall bless us.
7 God shall bless us,
  And all the ends of the earth shall fear Him.

Ps. 67:5–7

Verse 5 is an exact repetition of verse 3. This time the following verse speaks of the results of this worship—the fruitfulness of the earth. The form of the verb for *"shall yield"* (v. 6) denotes a future result of the people's praise. This rich harvest is a sign of God's blessing, His affirmation of His people. Moreover, to the people this God is *"our own God,"* namely, the God of Israel. The thought of God's blessing is now repeated in verse 7 with the conclusion that *"all the ends of the earth shall fear Him."* Again, *"fear"* is godly awe and reverence before the God who judges the nations and blesses them with His bounty.

Psalm 67 is a particularly appealing call to worship. Worship is always a response to God's initiative, His mercy and blessing. Praise is the appropriate reaction on our part to the revelation of His way and His salvation. This praise is to include ringing cries of joy for God's just judgment and government. As we praise Him, the earth will be fruitful as a sign of His blessing, and the nations will come to Him in reverence. Thus this great vision for the world to worship is also a mandate for evangelism. Wherever the gospel is going forth in power, praise is the result, and the fruitfulness of God's love and His Spirit come to us.

CHAPTER SIXTY-EIGHT

My God, My King

Psalm 68

The Biblical world view is unquestionably dynamic. God is on the move. He speaks creation into existence. He walks in the Garden with Adam. He sends the floods in judgment and puts all of life into an ark. He calls Abraham by name and later rains plagues on Egypt. At His command the Red Sea splits and Sinai thunders with the majesty of His presence. He leads His armies in battle and slaughters His enemies. He gives His people a land but later carts them away from it in chains.

Theologians, however, with at times a lethal dose of logic, have tried to organize all of this dynamic revelation of God. They created "systematic theology" in order to tie up all the loose ends. Then the Roman clerics took over with a passion to organize the church as they organized the Empire. Later, the age of rationalism posited a God who equaled nature. Since nature was a closed system of cause and effect, all that was left of the Bible were ethical values confirmed by reason (Spinoza).

In our chaotic, existential age, however, informed as it is by a dynamic universe where light can be both a particle and a wave, and where subatomic particles are indeterminate, the exploding energy of the God of the Bible may return to relevance. Moreover, as God renews His church, the dynamic power of the Holy Spirit becomes more manifest and God looks more and more like the living God.

Psalm 68 stands in this kind of context. Here God is remembered for guiding Israel through the wilderness and defeating opposing kings. He shakes Sinai and has an army of chariots who do His bidding. He also speaks oracles, wounds His enemies, and orders a procession into His temple. He "rides on the heaven of heavens" and is "more awesome than [His] holy places."

Commentators express a wide diversity of opinion about this psalm. Some hold it to be composite, containing many fragments drawn from small units. Others find it to be a guidebook for a ritual observance or a script for an actual procession into the temple. Still others propose that it is a victory psalm after battle. There is also no agreement about its literary style. While many call it a hymn, it also contains oracles

(vv. 11–13, 22–23) and a description of temple ritual. Probably it is best to note simply that this psalm contains a number of styles and themes, all witnessing to Israel's dynamic God and her dynamic life with Him.

Tradition attributes Psalm 68 to David. The reference to the temple in verse 29, however, means that at least in its present form it is later than his reign. The thought here moves from a call for judgment (vv. 1–3) to a call for praise (vv. 4–6), meditation on God's guidance through the wilderness (vv. 7–10), His victory over kings (vv. 11–14), God's holy mountain (vv. 15–18), judgment and redemption (vv. 19–23), God's procession (vv. 24–27), and God's victory (vv. 28–31). The psalm ends with a call to praise (vv. 32–35).

A CALL FOR JUDGMENT

1 Let God arise,
   Let His enemies be scattered;
   Let those also who hate Him flee before Him.
2 As smoke is driven away,
   So drive *them* away;
   As wax melts before the fire,
   So let the wicked perish at the presence of God.
3 But let the righteous be glad;
   Let them rejoice before God;
   Yes, let them rejoice exceedingly.

Ps. 68:1–3

Verse 1 is taken from Numbers 10:35, where whenever the ark of the covenant, God's portable throne, is being carried into battle, Moses cries out, "Rise up, O Lord! / Let Your enemies be scattered. . . ." The call for God to *"arise"* ("stand up") is a call for Him to get up from His throne, for His enemies are at hand.

The request in verse 2 that God drive His enemies away *"as smoke"* gives them the image of something ephemeral (this is a frequent biblical device; see Ps. 37:20). The psalmist also asks that God's enemies be like *"wax"* melting *"before the fire."* He concludes: *"So let the wicked perish at the presence of God."* The verb for *"perish"* means "to die" or "to be destroyed." The *"wicked,"* those who *"hate"* God (v. 1), are to be destroyed in battle.

The contrast is now made: *"But let the righteous be glad."* The *"righteous"* are those who are in right relationship with God in the covenant. They are to *"rejoice* [exalt] *before God."* The next clause adds emphasis: *"Yes, let them rejoice exceedingly."*

This psalm begins with a call to battle. When God acts, the *"wicked"* will vanish like *"smoke"* and *"wax."* However, the *"righteous,"* those who belong to Him, will *"rejoice."* They will see God's triumph. We join their joy when we meet Christ. In Him we know that our enemies have been vanquished on the cross and that He has won the victory in His resurrection.

A CALL FOR PRAISE

4 Sing to God, sing praises to His name;
  Extol Him who rides on the clouds,
  By His name YAH,
  And rejoice before Him.
5 A father of the fatherless, a defender of widows,
  Is God in His holy habitation.
6 God sets the solitary in families;
  He brings out those who are bound into prosperity;
  But the rebellious dwell in a dry *land.*

Ps. 68:4–6

In the context of joy, the psalmist now issues a call to *"sing praises"* to God, *"to His name."* Calling upon the name of God actualizes His presence. The psalmist continues, *"Extol* [lift up] *Him who rides on the clouds."* Since the fertility god Baal carried the title of "Cloud Rider," this phrase may have been intended as a polemic against him, by contrasting him with the true God, YAH, who rides the clouds and brings the rains. We are to *"rejoice before Him."* Here our God is the God of history and of nature. He is both Redeemer and Creator.

In verses 5–6 the psalmist relates more about the God whom we worship. First, He cares for orphans and widows. He is *"father of the fatherless"* and *"a defender of widows."* The word for *"defender"* means a judge who protects widows. The one who takes their cause is *"God in His holy habitation."* By this the psalmist means either heaven (vv. 33–34) or the temple (v. 29). Next, God cares for *"the solitary,"* the alien, the stranger, or the exile, by placing him *"in families,"* or "making

him dwell at home." Moreover, *"those who are bound"* ("captives") are
released *"into prosperity"* (e.g., in the Exodus), *"but the rebellious dwell
in a dry land"* (as did Moses' generation in the wilderness).

Thus God destroys the wicked, controls nature, and defends the poor
and oppressed. This revelation is fulfilled in Jesus who comes to defeat
the devil and his kingdom, command the chaos of nature, and minister
to the poor (see Mark 1:21–27; 4:35–41). No wonder we are to *"sing
praises to His name."*

GUIDANCE THROUGH THE WILDERNESS

7 O God, when You went out before Your people,
    When You marched through the wilderness,   Selah
8 The earth shook;
    The heavens also dropped *rain* at the presence of God;
    Sinai itself *was moved* at the presence of God, the
        God of Israel.
9 You, O God, sent a plentiful rain,
    Whereby You confirmed Your inheritance,
    When it was weary.
10 Your congregation dwelt in it;
    You, O God, provided from Your goodness for the
        poor.

Ps. 68:7–10

The psalmist now recalls how God cared for Israel in her wilderness
wanderings. This historical memory gives a basis for the assertion in
verses 4–6 that He will likewise care for us.

Thus God *"went out before"* the *"people"* as the commander of His
troops. Moses describes Him similarly in his song of triumph after the
Exodus: "The Lord is a man of war. . . . Pharaoh's chariots and his
army / He has cast into the sea" (Exod. 15:3–4). As God *"marched"*
with Israel *"through the wilderness, / The earth shook."* He is the mighty
God and nature responds to His *"presence."* Thus *"the heavens also
dropped rain"* and *"Sinai itself was moved."* We read in Exodus 19:16,
"Then it came to pass . . . that there were thunderings and lightnings,
and a thick cloud on the mountain; and the sound of the trumpet
was very loud, so that all the people . . . in the camp trembled."

The psalmist reports in verse 9 that God then *"sent a plentiful rain,"*
which probably means the autumn showers. This could also be a metaphor for the manna with which God fed Israel in the wilderness (see

Exod. 16:4). Thus through the rain God *"confirmed"* ("established") His *"inheritance."* The *"inheritance"* here is either Israel or the Promised Land, depending upon the interpretation of the *"plentiful rain"* at the beginning of verse 9. This blessing came *"when it was weary."* If "it" refers to the land this is a metaphor for dry soil. Israel *"dwelt"* in the land where she was cared for. God took this poor people and led them through the wilderness into a fruitful land. This was His grace, His gift to Israel. It is out of God's *"goodness"* ("completeness"), His bounty, that Israel lives.

VICTORY OVER THE KINGS

11 The Lord gave the word;
    Great *was* the company of those who proclaimed *it:*
12 "Kings of armies flee, they flee,
    And she who remains at home divides the spoil.
13 Though you lie down among the sheepfolds,
    You will be like the wings of a dove covered with
      silver,
    And her feathers with yellow gold."
14 When the Almighty scattered kings in it,
    It was *white* as snow in Zalmon.

Ps. 68:11–14

Now the psalmist gives a prophetic *"word"* from God concerning the destruction of *"kings"* and *"armies."* God not only leads and acts, He also speaks: *"The Lord gave the word"* ("utterance, command"). Israel responds by announcing this revelation, whose content we learn in verses 12–13. God's word is given for our edification and witness.

The content of the Lord's revelation seems to indicate the psalmist's desire to portray Him as military conqueror: *"Kings of armies flee."* He announces that Israel will be victorious over the kings in the land. The repeated *"they flee"* adds emphasis. His people will divide the spoils which are the consequence of victory. Verse 13 suffers from textual corruption and its reconstruction is speculative. The first part of the verse may be an idiomatic expression for laziness. The possible meaning here is that some of the tribes may have refused to go to war, thus they were those who *"lie down among the sheepfolds."* Nevertheless, they too enjoy the spoils of battle and are like a silver and gold statue of a dove.

The oracle of verses 12–13 receives confirmation in verse 14. Indeed, God, *"the Almighty scattered [the] kings"* as He had promised. This was as spectacular *"as snow in Zalmon."* The name *"Almighty"* (*Šadday*) is the name by which God was known to Abraham, Isaac, and Jacob (Exod. 6:3). Its root meaning is uncertain. In 2 Corinthians 6:18 the Greek for the name is *panokratōr*, "all powerful." Mount Zalmon is mentioned in Judges 9:48 as a hill near Shechem.

We see in these verses that the call to God in verse 1 to arise for battle is based on both His promise and His performance in defeating Israel's enemies as recorded here (vv. 11–14). Again history confirms faith and informs our prayers.

GOD'S HOLY MOUNTAIN

15 A mountain of God *is* the mountain of Bashan;
   A mountain *of many* peaks *is* the mountain of Bashan.
16 Why do you fume with envy, you mountains of *many*
      peaks?
   This is the mountain *which* God desires to dwell in;
   Yes, the LORD will dwell *in it* forever.
17 The chariots of God *are* twenty thousand,
   Even thousands of thousands;
   The Lord is among them *as in* Sinai, in the Holy *Place.*
18 You have ascended on high,
   You have led captivity captive;
   You have received gifts among men,
   Even *from* the rebellious,
   That the LORD God might dwell *there.*

Ps. 68:15–18

Next, the psalmist addresses Mount Bashan (note the association from one mountain to another). *"Bashan"* was situated east of the Jordan between Mount Hermon and the river Yarmuk. The verse begins, *"A mountain of God is the mountain of Bashan."* It could also be rendered, *"A mountain of the gods* is the mountain of Bashan" since the word for *"God"* here is the plural "Elohim." If this is the case, then the psalmist addresses *"Bashan"* as a mighty *"mountain of many peaks,"* presumably high enough for gods to dwell in. This would explain verse 16 where Bashan fumes *"with envy"* over God's preference for Mount Zion. The verb for *"envy"* appears only here in the Old Testament and means "to watch stealthily" or "to watch with envious hostility." God, however, will not be one among many; He does not join the idols on Bashan. His dwelling is on Zion and He *"will dwell in it forever."*

While God's mountain may not be the greatest peak, His greatness is manifest by the vast number of *"chariots"* which are with Him. There are *"twenty thousand, / Even thousands of thousands."* The *"chariot"* was a two-wheeled, horse-drawn vehicle of war, with an open back. Pharaoh pursued the people of Israel toward the Red Sea with six hundred of them (Exod. 14:7). God's chariots carry His angels, His heavenly host or army. When Elisha was surrounded by the armies of Syria, they in turn were surrounded by the armies of God: "And behold, the mountain was full of horses and chariots of fire all around Elisha" (2 Kings 6:17).

In the midst of His army of angels God dwells *"as in Sinai in the Holy Place."* The word for *"holy"* means "set apart." Thus God, who is *"holy,"* "wholly other," dwells in holiness. His place is sanctified to Him. There He has *"ascended"* after His triumph in battle, taking His captives and receiving *"gifts among men."* The *"gifts"* are tribute or offerings from vassals. These come from the *"rebellious, / That the Lord God might dwell there,"* or literally, "At the dwelling of YAH, God." Thus they come from the pagans who are jealous of God's dwelling in Zion. This is parallel to Bashan's envy in verse 16.

In Ephesians 4:8 Paul cites Psalm 68:18 and applies it to Christ's triumph over His enemies. Like Yahweh, the Risen Lord has conquered His foes and ascended to His throne. Now, however, rather than receiving tribute or gifts, He gives the trophies of His victory to His church in the form of apostles, prophets, evangelists, and pastor-teachers. Here is grace abounding as Jesus' triumph spills back upon His church. Every gift He gives is a former enemy now taken captive by Him and radically transformed for His service (see Eph. 4:7–16).

SALVATION AND JUDGMENT

19 Blessed *be* the Lord,
   Who daily loads us *with benefits,*
   The God of our salvation!Selah
20 Our God *is* the God of salvation;
   And to GOD the Lord *belong* escapes from death.
21 But God will wound the head of His enemies,
   The hairy scalp of the one who still goes on in his
      trespasses.

22 The Lord said, "I will bring back from Bashan,
   I will bring *them* back from the depths of the sea,
23 That your foot may crush *them* in blood,
   And the tongues of your dogs *may have* their portion
      from *your* enemies."

Ps. 68:19–23

The psalmist now blesses God for His *"daily"* care and His decisive intervention on Israel's behalf. God is to be praised for *"daily benefits"* or, literally, "Day by day He bears" ("to carry a load"). A similar thought appears in 1 Peter 5:7, " . . . casting all your care upon Him, for He cares for you." Jesus also offers rest for the heavy laden (Matt. 11:28). Throughout the Bible our God carries our burdens for us when we give them to Him.

While the righteous receive salvation, the wicked are judged. *"God will wound the head of His enemies."* The head wound is lethal (cf. Gen. 3:15). The parallel clause promises the same blow to *"the one who still goes on in his trespasses"* (or "offense"—the act that brings the guilt).

In verses 22–23 God again speaks a prophetic word, as He vows to return from *"Bashan,"* the high mountain of the gods, and from *"the depths of the sea,"* representing all earthly chaos, to bring judgment upon Israel's enemies. They will die under the *"foot"* of God's people, and in an ultimate retribution, the *"dogs"* will lick their *"blood"* (cf. 1 Kings 21:19).

GOD'S PROCESSION

24 They have seen Your procession, O God,
   The procession of my God, my King, into the
      sanctuary.
25 The singers went before, the players on instruments
      followed after;
   Among *them were* the maidens playing timbrels.
26 Bless God in the congregations,
   The Lord, from the fountain of Israel.
27 There *is* little Benjamin, their leader,
   The princes of Judah *and* their company,
   The princes of Zebulun *and* the princes of Naphtali.

Ps. 68:24–27

Now it is as if we are called to go up to Zion, to God's temple where He lives and reigns, so that we too can praise Him as the triumphant Lord.

Who are *"they"* of this opening section? It could be Israel, or it could be God's enemies who will bring tribute to Him (v. 29) or be scattered (v. 30). Some suggest here that the actual setting for these verses is the entrance of the ark of the covenant into the temple. Thus as the ark moves it is really *"the procession of my God, my King, into the sanctuary"* (the "holy place"). Here God is called *"King,"* a designation that has been implied throughout Psalm 68. When Israel came to Samuel demanding an earthly king, God comforted Samuel, saying, "They have not rejected you, but they have rejected Me, that I should not reign over them" (1 Sam. 8:7). Thus while God's direct rule has been compromised, He is still the true King of Israel and at the end He will establish His own King, His own Son, on Zion (Ps. 2:6).

Now the actual procession is described. There are *"singers"* who go first, followed by instrumentalists, including *"maidens playing timbrels."* The *"timbrel"* is a kind of tambourine held and struck with the hand. Then the call is given: *"Bless God in the congregations."* The plural *"congregations"* may be for emphasis: "the great congregation." God is blessed here as He is worshiped and praised by the people *"from the fountain of Israel." "The fountain"* may be the place where the procession to the temple began. *"Benjamin"* is to take the lead (v. 27). He literally "rules them," that is, the other tribes. This may indicate the line of march or express the time when Saul was king (he came from the tribe of Benjamin; 1 Sam. 10:21). The difficulty with this is the reference in verse 29 to the "temple" which was built by Solomon. Still, Benjamin could be first in the line of march by right of having produced Israel's first king. Following Benjamin are the *"princes of Judah," "Zebulun,"* and *"Naphtali."* Thus leaders from both northern and southern (Benjamin and Judah) tribes are identified.

GOD'S VICTORY

28 Your God has commanded your strength;
    Strengthen, O God, what You have done for us.
29 Because of Your temple at Jerusalem,
    Kings will bring presents to You.
30 Rebuke the beasts of the reeds,
    The herd of bulls with the calves of the peoples,

> *Till everyone* submits himself with pieces of silver.
> Scatter the peoples *who* delight in war.
> 31 Envoys will come out of Egypt;
> Ethiopia will quickly stretch out her hands to God.
>
> *Ps. 68:28–31*

The psalmist now confesses what *"God has commanded"* and calls upon Him to fulfill that command. The key thought here is *"strength,"* based on a word that means "to prevail, to be mighty." As God commands Israel to stand, then, the prayer follows: *"Strengthen, O God, what You have done for us."* It is God who by His grace fulfills His own work in us (see Phil. 1:6).

One of the things that God has done for Israel is to defeat her enemies. Thus the psalmist notes that *"kings will bring"* their tribute to Him *"because of [His] temple at Jerusalem."* This then leads to a call for God to strengthen His work by rebuking *"the beasts of the reeds"* (crocodiles, a metaphor for Egypt?) and *"the herd of bulls with the calves of the peoples,"* which probably represents another enemy of Israel. In Psalm 22:12 there is a reference to the "strong bulls of Bashan." The result of God's rebuke will be tribute of *"silver"* (v. 30) as a sign of submission. Those *"who delight in war"* will be scattered.

In verse 31 the animal figures now become historical: *"Envoys will come out of Egypt."* The word *"envoys"* renders a Hebrew word of unknown meaning. The proposed meaning is determined from the context and other translations. *"Ethiopia"* ("Cush," the land of Upper Egypt) also comes *"to God"* with her *"hands"* outstretched. The picture may be of surrender, worship, or offering gifts.

Here God strengthens His work in His people by subduing kings and scattering those *"who delight in war."* He receives tribute (v. 30) and worship (?) from the nations (v. 31). If this is the intention, the psalm now becomes eschatological, envisioning a time when Israel's enemies will flow to Jerusalem to submit to the living God (see Isa. 2:2–4).

A Call to Praise

> 32 Sing to God, you kingdoms of the earth;
> Oh, sing praises to the Lord,   Selah
> 33 To Him who rides on the heaven of heavens, *which were* of old!
> Indeed, He sends out His voice, a mighty voice.

34 Ascribe strength to God;
   His excellence *is* over Israel,
   And His strength *is* in the clouds.
35 O God, *You are* more awesome than Your holy places.
   The God of Israel *is* He who gives strength and power
      to *His* people.
   Blessed *be* God!

Ps. 68:32–35

The vision of the nations coming to the temple brings a proper call and response: *"Sing to God, you kingdoms of the earth"* (cf. v. 4). The thought is then repeated for emphasis. All the nations are to join in the praise of God.

But who is this God whom the nations are to praise? He is the one *"who rides on the heaven of heavens."* This is a similar title to the one "who rides on the clouds." He speaks with *"a mighty voice"* or "a voice of strength" (cf. v. 28). Thus Israel is to *"ascribe strength to God,"* since He has revealed His *"strength"* to her. This ascription is not vain because God's *"excellence is over Israel, / And His strength is in the clouds."* The word translated *"excellence"* means "majesty" or "pride." God is the great King and transcendent Lord who rules His people. The psalmist concludes that God is *"more awesome"* (or "fearful") than His *"holy places"* (see v. 17). Thus He is not to be identified with them nor can He be contained by them. He then is *"the God . . . who gives strength and power to His people"* out of His strength.

This vast panorama of God's work shows us a vision of the moving, living God. He scatters His enemies; He provides for His people; He takes them through the wilderness and clears the Promised Land of alien kings. Now He dwells on Zion, where He rules as King from His holy place. The nations bring Him tribute and come up to Jerusalem to worship. God gives strength and blessing to Israel. Her response is glad singing, shouts of joy, and a procession of praise into the temple.

This almighty, living God is the God for our generation too. He commands the dynamic cosmos because He is dynamic. He rules the nations and extends His kingdom where His Son is preached and loved.

As the church is being renewed today, God is breaking upon us in power and addressing His word to us. Thus our generation is adding to the mighty deeds recited in this hymn of praise. Our God is on the move and all the "kingdoms of the earth" will sing to Him.

CHAPTER SIXTY-NINE

A Fool for God

Psalm 69

What does it mean to stand with Christ in this world? There are many different answers to this question. It means to confess Him, to love Him, to grow in Him. It means to submit to His lordship, to minister in His kingdom, and to do His works and His will. It also means to love His people, to identify with them, to worship with them, to grow with them. To stand with Christ also means to bear His reproach, to share in His sufferings, and to live at His cross. To stand with Christ is to stand against this world-system. It is to do battle in His name by the power of the Holy Spirit.

Where people are willing to risk rejection, financial loss, family upset, and ecclesiastical disdain, there is a corresponding openness to the Spirit and freedom before God. Now the fresh winds of the Spirit can blow. Now God's power can be manifest in the midst of human fear and weakness.

Psalm 69 is written by a man in crisis. The waters of depression and oppression threaten his very life. While there is indication of physical illness or weakness, his real calamity comes from his enemies, who hate him "without a cause" and seek to destroy him. The elders "speak against" him; their rejection causes his broken heart and he is comfortless. Even his family turns from him. There could be no greater pain in this life.

Why is there such personal catastrophe? Rather than wrongdoing, the real source of his opposition comes from advocating God's cause. He shares the reproaches that are aimed at the Lord and His "house." Acts of self-mortification have also brought rejection. When his cries for spiritual refreshment are finally answered, at least in part, there is rejoicing because God will save him and Zion.

While this psalm arises out of personal crisis, it also is prophetic. Verses throughout the psalm find their fulfillment in Christ. For example, Jesus has "zeal for [God's] house" as does the psalmist (v. 9; see John 2:17). Also, reproaches directed toward God fell on Him (v. 9; see Rom. 15:3). And like the psalmist, Jesus was given vinegar to drink (v. 21;

see John 19:28–29). There are other allusions to this psalm in the New Testament; see, for example, verse 4 and John 15:25; verse 25 and Matthew 23:38. Moreover, themes of the psalm, such as the righteous sufferer and life out of death, are gospel themes. Clearly, there are parts of Psalm 69 that molded our Lord's sense of His ministry and destiny. This prayer needs to be read not only in the immediate context of the author, but also with an eye for prophetic passages beyond his experience.

Commentators describe Psalm 69 as an individual lament. Date and authorship will be determined, in part, according to whether the promise in verse 35 means that God will "build the cities of Judah" or that He will "rebuild" them (the verb here can be taken either way). If the meaning is "rebuild," then the psalm could be post-exilic. The mention of God's prisoners in verse 33 may also be in the context of the exile. The thought that thanksgiving is more pleasing than sacrifice may also reflect prophetic influence (vv. 30–31). All of these points, however, can be explained in other ways. Tradition ascribes this psalm to David. We will leave the question of authorship open. The thought of the psalm moves from a cry for help (vv. 1–4) to a confession of foolishness (vv. 13–18), a lament over reproach (vv. 19–20), a cry for judgment (vv. 22–28), a cry for salvation (vv. 29–33), and a concluding call for praise (vv. 34–36).

A CRY FOR HELP

1 Save me, O God!
  For the waters have come up to *my* neck.
2 I sink in deep mire,
  Where *there is* no standing;
  I have come into deep waters,
  Where the floods overflow me.
3 I am weary with my crying;
  My throat is dry;
  My eyes fail while I wait for my God.
4 Those who hate me without a cause
  Are more than the hairs of my head;
  They are mighty who would
    destroy me,
  Being my enemies wrongfully;
  Though I have stolen nothing,
  I *still* must restore *it*.

Ps. 69:1–4

The psalmist begins by calling upon God for deliverance: *"Save me, O God!"* The reason for this cry is immediately clarified. *"Waters"* are rising and are now up to his *"neck"* (*nepeš*, "soul"), and at the same time his footing is giving way: *"I sink in deep mire, / Where there is no standing."* The image of threatening waters is elaborated: they are *"deep"* and *"the floods overflow."* The psalmist is going down as the waters are going up: the peril is urgent indeed and death is near! (see v. 15).

The metaphor of waters triggers a graphic personal admission. The psalmist is *"weary with . . . crying"* ("calling out"). His *"throat is dry"* and his *"eyes"* are dim as he waits *"for my God"* (note the personal possessive pronoun). Not only is he drowning and sinking in his crisis, he is also enduring God's silence. This may well be the source of his grief. His heart is calling out for a word from the Lord and a work of the Lord.

The psalmist has enemies: *"those who hate me without a cause."* These opponents are vast, *"more than the hairs of [his] head,"* and *"mighty"* or "numerous." They are, however, unjust in their attack. They are *"my enemies wrongfully,"* or "my enemies with falsehood," that is, "lies" ("deception"). The final two clauses of verse 4 may be a proverb based on Leviticus 6:5 where the thief has to return what he has stolen. Expressed here in the negative, the sense may be: *"Though I have stolen nothing* [I am innocent], *I still must restore it* [so is the demand of my opponents]."*

As we noted, verse 4 is fulfilled in Jesus' passion: "But this happened [the world's hatred] that the word might be fulfilled which is written in their law, 'They hated Me without a cause'" (John 15:25). Here Jesus asserts that His experience fulfills the psalmist's lament. Not only is He unjustly hated, but His enemies are also vast and they charge Him falsely. Thus we can be certain that this psalm, like Psalm 22, was upon the Savior's heart as He went to the cross. Undoubtedly, He was nurtured by these prayers in accepting His calling to be the ultimate innocent sufferer. As Bonhoeffer comments, in these psalms it is Jesus who prays through Israel, and it is Jesus who fulfills these prayers. There is deep mystery here, but these verses take us into Jesus' heart. In this context, too, cannot verses 1–3 be read before the cross? There Jesus cries for deliverance as the waters of death rise and the earth gives way. As He dies He weeps for us, His throat is dry, and He waits for God.

Christians are also to accept suffering as their lot in this world. They are to share in the Savior's rejection. Thus Peter exhorts us, "Beloved, do not think it strange concerning the fiery trial which is to try you . . . but rejoice to the extent that you partake of Christ's sufferings, that when His glory is revealed, you may also be glad with exceeding joy. If you are reproached for the name of Christ, blessed are you, for the Spirit of glory and of God rests upon you" (1 Pet. 4:12–14).

A CONFESSION OF FOOLISHNESS

5 O God, You know my foolishness;
   And my sins are not hidden from You.
6 Let not those who wait for You, O Lord GOD of hosts,
      be ashamed because of me;
   Let not those who seek You be confounded because
      of me, O God of Israel.
7 Because for Your sake I have borne reproach;
   Shame has covered my face.
8 I have become a stranger to my brothers,
   And an alien to my mother's children;
9 Because zeal for Your house has eaten me up,
   And the reproaches of those who reproach You have
      fallen on me.
10 When I wept *and chastened* my soul with fasting,
   That became my reproach.
11 I also made sackcloth my garment;
   I became a byword to them.
12 Those who sit in the gate speak against me,
   And I *am* the song of the drunkards.

                                          Ps. 69:5–12

Now the psalmist confesses his *"foolishness"* to God. This is the opposite of wisdom: "A prudent man conceals knowledge, / But the heart of fools proclaim foolishness" (Prov. 12:23) God also knows his *"sins"* or "trespasses." The psalmist is innocent, yet he is conscious that God knows him more deeply than he knows himself. Thus he does not claim to be perfect. Moreover, he does not want his life to be a stumbling block to others: *"Let not those who wait for You, O Lord God of hosts, be ashamed because of me."* The offense here is probably not his "sins" but his situation (vv. 1–4). Thus this is another indirect call for God to deliver him. The *"Lord God of hosts"* is the God who commands His angelic armies (see Ps. 103:20–21). The parallel clause in verse 6 asks that those who *"seek"* God *"not . . . be confounded."* The verb for *"seek"* is often used for seeking God in worship. To *"be confounded"* is to "be humiliated."

The real *"foolishness,"* however, that the psalmist has experienced has come, not in his relationship to God, but in his relationship to people. He has borne *"reproach"* for the *"sake"* of his faith. The noun for *"reproach"* means "slander" or the "scorn" of an enemy. He continues, *"shame* [insult, ignominy] *has covered my face"* (see Ps. 44:15). Does not this verse give us a clue as to what Jesus will suffer in this world?

The psalmist also experiences the rejection of his family. He is *"a stranger"* to his *"brothers"* and *"an alien"* to his blood brothers and sisters, his *"mother's children."* The loss of family ties brings with it a loss of identity. Jesus experienced a similar loss (Mark 3:31–35) and called His disciples to the same destiny (Luke 14:26).

But why this family rejection? Verse 9 gives the positive answer: *"Because zeal for Your house has eaten me up."* The word for *"zeal"* means "ardor" or "jealousy." This may include the reformer's spirit longing to see idolatry banished from God's house, or, if this psalm is post-exilic, it may be zeal to restore the temple. As a prophetic word, this zeal is for cleansing and reformation which is fulfilled by Jesus (see John 2:16–17).

The positive reason for rejection is followed by a negative: *"And the reproaches of those who reproach You have fallen on me."* Thus the psalmist stands rejected because he bears God's rejection as his own. Paul picks up this thought in Romans 15:3 in seeing Christ's willingness to be reproached as a sign of not pleasing Himself. This then becomes the basis for the exhortation that we too ought not to please ourselves.

In his zeal for the temple and in his willingness to bear rejection, the psalmist weeps and fasts for the restoration of proper worship, a piety that brings further rejection: *"That became my reproach."* Fasting prepared Moses to receive God's revelation (Exod. 34:27–28) and it was also used to encourage God's answer (Jer. 14:12). It brings bodily appetites under control and can be a sign of grief or sorrow for sin. Thus it is accompanied by *"sackcloth,"* also a sign of mourning or repentance (see Ps. 30:11). As a result of all this, the psalmist *"became a byword"* or a "proverb." He was also attacked by *"those who sit in the gate"* (elders and judges) and was *"the song of drunkards."* Thus he is the subject of coarse humor and public rejection. Such abuse suggests that the psalmist is a prominent figure. His signs of humility and repentance, however, make him a laughingstock rather than bringing Israel to repentance. Wasn't this also true for Jesus? While the common people heard Him gladly, the rulers rejected Him, and the reproaches toward the Father fell upon the Son. This is the divine foolishness. God is in our midst and we esteem Him not.

A CRY FOR DELIVERANCE

13 But as for me, my prayer *is* to You,
   O Lord, *in* the acceptable time;
   O God, in the multitude of Your mercy,
   Hear me in the truth of Your salvation.
14 Deliver me out of the mire,
   And let me not sink;
   Let me be delivered from those who hate me,
   And out of the deep waters.
15 Let not the floodwater overflow me,
   Nor let the deep swallow me up;
   And let not the pit shut its mouth on me.
16 Hear me, O Lord, for Your lovingkindness *is* good;
   Turn to me according to the multitude of Your tender
      mercies.
17 And do not hide Your face from Your servant,
   For I am in trouble;
   Hear me speedily.
18 Draw near to my soul, *and* redeem it;
   Deliver me because of my enemies.

Ps. 69:13–18

Here is a return to the cry and themes of verses 1–4. In the crisis of near death the psalmist calls out to God: *"my prayer is to You."* His expectation is that God will answer *"in the acceptable time,"* or time of "pleasing" or "favor." It is the time of God's choosing, not his. There is a mystery here. We are the "instant" generation—we want God to be as fast as McDonald's. Often, however, He isn't. "For as the heavens are higher than the earth, / So are My ways higher than your ways, / And My thoughts than your thoughts" (Isa. 55:9). The psalmist does not presume upon God. In His time of grace, the answer will come. The basis for this confidence is the *"multitude of Your mercy."* God will be true to His commitment to Israel; He will keep His covenant. The psalmist can also claim *"the truth of* [*God's*] *salvation."* God's *"truth"* is His "firmness, faithfulness." His *"salvation"* is His "deliverance, rescue." God's covenant commitment to us is actualized as He keeps His promise and sets us free.

The psalmist now asks for deliverance from the *"mire."* The positive cry is for God to pull him out of the quicksand or the mud into which he is slipping. This is immediately followed by the negative cry: *"And let me not sink."* This metaphor for rescue now becomes literal: *"Let me be delivered from those who hate me."* This deliverance will be from the *"deep waters"* (v. 14) that are rising. That this flood bears the threat of death becomes clear. The cry that the *"floodwater"* not engulf him and the *"deep"* not *"swallow* [him] *up"* is really a cry that the *"pit"* (Sheol) not *"shut its mouth on* [him]," that is, that he not go into the grave.

After spelling out the lethal threat, the psalmist underscores His request with a fresh reminder to God of who He is: *"Hear me, O Lord, for Your lovingkindness is good,"* that is, "Your covenant-love completes or fulfills me." He then asks that God *"turn to"* him. This positive request is reinforced by its negative opposite: *"And do not hide Your face from Your servant."* The basis for this request is *"the multitude of Your tender mercies,"* your "compassion." In love God turns toward us; in wrath He turns away. The psalmist identifies himself as God's *"servant,"* a sign of humility and submission, as well as His role in relationship to Yahweh's kingship.

This request for God's attention is based on need: *"I am in trouble"* (v. 17). This *"trouble,"* of course, has been elaborated upon throughout the previous verses. In the crisis, however, the psalmist wants God's action now: *"Hear* [answer] *me speedily"* (cf. v. 13, *"in the acceptable time"*). We always live in the tension between our need and God's timing. As Jesus prayed, "Father, if it is Your will, remove this cup from Me; nevertheless not My will, but Yours, be done" (Luke 22:42). Specifically, the psalmist wants God to *"draw near"* to His *"soul, and redeem it"* ("set [it] free"). Liberation here is deliverance from his enemies' attack, the rejection of family, and, supremely, the threat of death.

My Reproach

19 You know my reproach, my shame, and my dishonor;
   My adversaries *are* all before You.
20 Reproach has broken my heart,
   And I am full of heaviness;
   I looked *for someone* to take pity, but *there was* none;
   And for comforters, but I found none.
21 They also gave me gall for my food,
   And for my thirst they gave me vinegar to
     drink.

Ps. 69:19–21

In these verses the lament continues as the psalmist builds his case against his enemies. He reminds God of his *"reproach,"* his *"shame,"* and his *"dishonor."* All of this, as we have seen, has resulted from the psalmist's identifying himself with God's cause and his zeal for the temple and its purity. God knows what has befallen him and also the state of his enemies: *"My adversaries are all before You."*

A central theme here is *"reproach,"* the stinging rebukes hurled at the psalmist: *"Reproach has broken my heart."* This engenders depression: *"And I am full of heaviness."* It is the sense of isolation and rejection, even from family, which hurts so deeply. *"I looked for someone to take pity, but there was none."* The *"comforters"* were gone. Neither was there any solace in *"food,"* for his enemies gave him *"gall for . . . food"* and *"vinegar to drink"* (v. 21). *"Gall"* is a bitter and poisonous herb. *"Vinegar"* is a sour wine. This is either a poetic expression of how food tasted in his depression, or a metaphor for the extreme insult of his enemies.

In light of the New Testament, verses 19–21 are clearly prophetic. The offering of *"gall"* and *"vinegar"* to the psalmist by his enemies is fulfilled as Jesus is offered "sour wine mingled with gall to drink" just before He is crucified (Matt. 27:34). With this key, the references to reproach, shame, dishonor, adversaries, a broken heart, heaviness, and the absence of pity or comfort all paint a vivid picture of Jesus at the cross. It is the very commitment to God's cause that took Him to His final hour. We can be certain that this psalm must have coursed through His mind as His tormentors took Him to death. It must have also offered comfort since it ends in a resolution of praise.

A CRY FOR JUDGMENT

22 Let their table become a snare before them,
   And their well-being a trap.
23 Let their eyes be darkened, so that they do not see;
   And make their loins shake continually.
24 Pour out Your indignation upon them,
   And let Your wrathful anger take hold of them.
25 Let their dwelling place be desolate;
   Let no one live in their tents.
26 For they persecute the *ones* You have struck,
   And talk of the grief of those You have wounded.
27 Add iniquity to their iniquity,
   And let them not come into Your righteousness.
28 Let them be blotted out of the book of the living,
   And not be written with the righteous.

Ps. 69:22–28

The psalmist now speaks curses upon his enemies. This is the opposite of the blessings so prevalent in the Psalter. Under the covenant there is a blessing for obedience and a curse for disobedience (see Deut. 28).

Having thought of his own diet of poison, the psalmist pronounces his opponents' *"table"* a *"snare,"* and *"their well-being* [security] *a trap."* He then calls down illness upon them, asking that *"their eyes be darkened"* (become blind), and that *"their loins shake continually."* The *"loins"* symbolize the seat of strength in the body. Continual shaking would indicate the loss of that strength through sickness or fear (cf. Rom. 11:9–10 where Paul applies these verses to God's judgment upon Israel).

Next, the psalmist calls for God's *"indignation"* to be poured out and His *"wrathful anger"* to *"take hold of,"* or overtake, his enemies. The consequences of this vengeance are that *"their dwelling place"* or "camp" ("nomadic encampment") will *"be desolate,"* their *"tents"* empty. Both his enemies and their posterity will perish. That no line will be left is the ultimate judgment.

The reason for such a severe act is that *"they persecute* [or, pursue] *the ones You have struck."* The most obvious meaning here is that God has afflicted the psalmist and that his enemies have used the occasion to unleash their attack upon him. But nowhere else in the psalm is the affliction of the writer attributed to God. To the contrary, the psalmist's affliction comes from his identification with God's cause. Thus it is likely that verse 26 applies to other sufferers who have also been attacked by his enemies. Therefore, he adds, they *"talk of the grief of those You have wounded."* Note that the plural is used here and that the first person singular is absent throughout verse 26. The point is that evil men presumptuously take God's judgment into their own hands and, like a pack of wolves, attack the wounded of the herd.

The call for judgment is again sounded in verse 27: *"Add iniquity to their iniquity."* This is appropriate justice for those who add their wounds to God's wounds. Then the psalmist prays: *"And let them not come into Your righteousness."* The word for *"righteousness"* here means "salvation," that is, "vindicated righteousness." The alternative to *"righteousness"* is then set out: *"Let them be blotted out of the book of the living, / And not be written with the righteous."* This metaphor indicates a written register of the righteous (see Rev. 13:8). Blotting out the wicked effectively destroys them, and they are forgotten.

The call for judgment is, no doubt, offensive. To wish sickness, suffering, and death to one's enemies appears mean and hot-headed—vindictive. But we must remember that the psalmist is in extreme crisis as he prays. Moreover, he experiences the attack upon God as if it were upon himself. Since God is the God of Israel He moves in both lovingkindness and judgment. This is "keeping covenant." In calling for God's judgment, then, the psalmist is calling for the vindication of God's name. There is no higher passion: "Hallowed be Your name" (Matt. 6:9).

A CRY FOR SALVATION

29 But I *am* poor and sorrowful;
   Let Your salvation, O God, set me up on high.
30 I will praise the name of God with a song,
   And will magnify Him with thanksgiving.
31 *This* also shall please the LORD better than an ox *or*
   bull,
   Which has horns and hooves.
32 The humble shall see *this and* be glad;
   And you who seek God, your hearts shall live.
33 For the LORD hears the poor,
   And does not despise His prisoners.

Ps. 69:29–33

In the psalmist's cry for judgment in verses 22–28 there is no arrogance. Thus he confesses here: *"But I am poor."* The word for *"poor"* can also mean "humble." The psalmist is a broken man. He is *"sorrowful"* ("is in pain"; cf. v. 20). His need now is for God's *"salvation"* to lift him: *"O God, set me up on high."* With this deliverance there will be song, in which he will *"praise"* God's *"name"* (which manifests His presence) and *"magnify Him with thanksgiving."* To *"magnify"* God is to make His reputation or honor great through public praise.

This worship is more pleasing to the Lord than animal sacrifices such as *"an ox or bull."* Note that the bull *"has horns"*; it is fully grown, and therefore more valuable than a calf. The intention here, however, is not to deny the sacrificial system but rather to stress the importance of the attitude behind the act. When Isaiah denounces sacrifices it is because the hands that offer them are "full of blood" (Isa. 1:15).

God's setting the psalmist *"on high"* will be a witness to the *"humble,"* who also will *"be glad."* Those *"who seek* [inquire of] *God"* will *"live"* when they see what He has done for the psalmist. The reason for this is that God *"hears the poor, / And does not despise His prisoners"* (v. 33). As noted in the introduction to this chapter, these prisoners could be the Jews in captivity. But this could also be a metaphor for those who are punished by God and then released when they seek Him.

In these verses there is a decided shift in the tone of the psalm. Heretofore, crisis has been the heartbeat. Suddenly the psalmist shifts to a focus on worship and witness. Hope breaks in. As we have noted, there are strong prophetic themes here, pointing to Christ. While the bitterness of our Lord's suffering is represented and predicted, there is another side at least hinted at. After death there is resurrection.

A CALL FOR PRAISE

34 Let heaven and earth praise Him,
   The seas and everything that moves in them.
35 For God will save Zion
   And build the cities of Judah,
   That they may dwell there and possess it.
36 Also, the descendants of His servants shall inherit
      it,
   And those who love His name shall dwell in it.

Ps. 69:34–36

Now it is as if the psalmist breaks through to release and victory. All creation including *"the seas and everything that moves in them"* is to join in shouts of worship and gladness. The reason for this over-whelming response is that *"God will save Zion"* (see discussion of Ps. 2:6). Here is deliverance for all Israel. Moreover, He will *"build the cities of Judah,"* the southern part of Israel. The result of the cities' being built is that Israel will live in them and *"possess"* the land. More-over, *"the descendants"* ("seed") of God's people, *"His servants,"* will *"inherit"* the land. Their posterity will go on, and *"those who love His name shall dwell in it."* The sign of God's salvation is that Israel holds the land down through the generations. As God promised Abraham, "Also I give to you and your descendants after you the land in which you are a stranger, all the land of Canaan, as an everlasting possession; and I will be their God" (Gen. 17:8).

As we have seen, the "foolishness" of this psalm is the author's will-ingness to have zeal for God's house and bear "reproach" for Him. The consequences have been intense suffering and rejection, even from His own family. Now the waters of death are up to his neck. But his anguished cry is answered, and the psalm ends on a victorious note.

No wonder Jesus found solace and direction from Psalm 69 for His own ministry and suffering. No wonder that the apostles also found in this psalm prophetic words concerning the Messiah's coming.

Are we willing to have a similar zeal for God and for His house? Are we willing to allow His reproaches to fall upon us? Shortly before his conversion, my friend John Wimber saw a man in downtown Los Angeles carrying a sign reading: "I'm a fool for Christ. Whose fool are you?" That thought stuck in his mind. Later John knew that he too had been called to be Christ's fool in this world. For him that meant that if Jesus told him to pray for the sick, then John would pray for the sick. And if Jesus promised the power of the Holy Spirit, then John would ask for that power. Now the leader of a continuing revival among the Vineyard Churches, John is willing to "step out of the boat" and be Christ's fool. He is also willing to bear the reproach for that. Indeed, zeal for God's house is his. Is it ours?

CHAPTER SEVENTY

Variant on Psalm 40:13–17

Psalm 70

1 Make *haste,* O God, to deliver me!
  Make haste to help me, O Lᴏʀᴅ!
2 Let them be ashamed and confounded
  Who seek my life;
  Let them be turned back and confused
  Who desire my hurt.
3 Let them be turned back because of their shame,
  Who say, "Aha, aha!"
4 Let all those who seek You rejoice and be glad in
    You;
  And let those who love Your salvation say continually,
    "Let God be magnified!"
5 But I *am* poor and needy;
  Make haste to me, O God!
  You *are* my help and my deliverer;
  O Lᴏʀᴅ, do not delay.

Ps. 70:1–5

With slight alterations in the text this psalm is a repetition, or double, of Psalm 40:13–17. Its presence here witnesses to the editing of the psalm texts and their transmission in the worship life of Israel. It is probable that Psalm 40 was the original setting and that these verses were separated for liturgical usage in the temple.

The text is a prayer for judgment on the enemies *"who seek* [the psalmist's] *life"* and the deliverance of the "poor and needy." This psalm could have been used in the context of a national crisis, perhaps by the king. It is a personal lament which also calls upon the whole congregation to join in praise.

In verse 1 the phrase "Be pleased, O Lord" of 40:13 is missing, and verse 2 lacks the word "together" (rendered "mutual" by ɴᴋᴊᴠ) of 42:14. The psalmist's request that his enemies *"be turned back because of their shame"* in verse 3 reads "Let them be confounded because of their shame" in 42:15. In verse 5 the cry for God to *"make haste to me"* reads "Yet the Lord thinks upon me" in 42:17. Apart from these minor changes the texts are identical.

What we learn from this variant is that these prayers are "living word" in Israel's life. As they were used in worship they were modified under the inspiration of the Holy Spirit to fit their times and liturgical purposes. This also helps us to understand further modifications in New Testament quotations of the psalms that may come as paraphrases, citations from the Hebrew text, or from the Septuagint.

CHAPTER SEVENTY-ONE

Lifelong Faith

Psalm 71

Young Christians often wonder if their faith will last. I remember this concern when Christ first became real to me at fifteen years of age. Am I just going through a phase? Is this merely an emotional experience? Is this a fad? These were good questions because my conversion came in the context of Young Life, a popular evangelistic ministry to high school students. Since so many of my friends were "accepting Christ" and since many were leaders in my school, was I just being carried along on a wave of teenage religion?

When I first attended Glendale Presbyterian Church one Sunday evening these questions were resolved. The pastor, Clarence Kerr, was a graying man in his early sixties. After reading the scripture, he laid aside his glasses and preached the gospel with passion. Here was no popular teen-leader. Here was a mature man proclaiming the same word I had heard in my Young Life gathering. After the service, I met Howard and Margaret Brown, a couple in their late sixties who introduced themselves to me with beaming faces. "In this church we believe that you must be 'born again,' " they said, going on to give me a brief testimony. I knew there and then that I was "home." If they were also afflicted

by a "fad," it had lasted them a lifetime. In their smiles I knew that
the God who had called me was the God who would keep me. Whatever
life might hold, He would always be there for me. This also is the
witness of Psalm 71.

The author is an old man; he is "in the time of old age." His strength
is failing as his enemies rise against him. They charge that now, at
the end, "God has forsaken him," perhaps because of some illness.
However, his faith has been lifelong. It is God who took him from
his "mother's womb" and who also taught him in his youth. Now
that he is "old and gray-headed" he calls upon the Lord not to "forsake"
him; his desire is to witness to his faith to the generation to come.
He is confident that although God has shown him "great and severe
troubles," he will be revived again and his "greatness" will be increased.
Those who attack him then will be "brought to shame" and he will
worship and witness anew. Commentators describe this psalm as an
individual lament containing several psalm types. The author is unknown. The thought moves from a cry for deliverance (vv. 1–8) to a
lament over enemies (vv. 9–11), a call for judgment (vv. 12–13), a promise
of praise (vv. 14–16), a promise of witness (vv. 17–18), a confession
of confidence in help (vv. 19–21), and a final expression of praise (vv.
22–24).

A Cry for Deliverance

1 In You, O Lord, I put my trust;
  Let me never be put to shame.
2 Deliver me in Your righteousness, and cause me to
    escape;
  Incline Your ear to me, and save me.
3 Be my strong refuge,
  To which I may resort continually;
  You have given the commandment to save me,
  For You *are* my rock and my fortress.
4 Deliver me, O my God, out of the hand of the wicked,
  Out of the hand of the unrighteous and cruel man.
5 For You are my hope, O Lord God;
  You are my trust from my youth.
6 By You I have been upheld from birth;
  You are He who took me out of my mother's womb.
  My praise *shall be* continually of You.

7 I have become as a wonder to many,
But You *are* my strong refuge.
8 Let my mouth be filled *with* Your praise
And with Your glory all the day.

Ps. 71:1–8

Verses 1–3 are nearly the equivalent of Psalm 31:1–3a. It may well be that the psalmist cites this earlier prayer from memory as he begins his prayer. He starts with a confession of faith: *"In you, O Lord, I put my trust"* ("seek refuge"). Because of this, he asks *"never"* to be *"put to shame."* Literally, the text reads, "Let me not be ashamed forever." By God's *"righteousness,"* His covenant-faithfulness and moral character, he prays to be delivered. We learn later that the deliverance he needs is from *"the hand of the wicked"* (v. 4). Next, he asks that God hear and act. The verb for *"save"* (v. 2) also means "deliver." As God rescues him from his foes, He will be his *"strong habitation,"* his *"rock,"* and his *"fortress."* He can go to God *"continually"* as his secure defense and protection, and as we learn later, he has done so over a lifetime. In praying for God to keep him, then, the psalmist is merely asking God to be Himself, to be true to His own revelation. He reminds the Lord: *"You have given the commandment to save me."*

Verse 4 repeats the cry for deliverance given in verse 2. Here the intensive form of the verb for *"deliver"* means "to bring into security." The psalmist has need for this security because his enemies are *"wicked,"* *"unrighteous,"* and *"cruel."* The word for *"wicked"* means "criminal, those who commit crimes." The *"unrighteous"* man is *"unjust"*; he is a lawbreaker. *"Cruel"* appears only here in the Old Testament and means "oppressor." The singular forms are probably used collectively for a group of opponents (see vv. 10, 12). The *"hand"* signifies power or possession. Thus to be taken *"out of the hand of the wicked"* is to be delivered from his power.

Verses 5 and 6 show us that this cry for deliverance is based upon the character of God and the history of His dealings with the psalmist since birth. He confesses that God is his *"hope"* and his *"trust."* He expects that God, as his *"hope,"* will act for him again and he rests secure, or "trusts," in this as he has *"from [his] youth."* The word for *"trust"* means "confidence" or "security." To *"trust"* in God is to rest upon Him, to shift our weight to Him.

The psalmist has also *"been upheld"* by God *"from [his] birth."* God was the "midwife" who delivered him from his *"mother's womb."* Knowing a lifetime of security or "trust," he declares: *"My praise shall be continually of You."*

As this first section concludes, the psalmist describes himself as *"a wonder to many."* The word for *"wonder"* means a supernatural direct display of divine power such as in the plagues of the Exodus (Exod. 11:9). It may inspire terror or worship, and is often linked to signs that reveal God's purposes. The psalmist could be a *"wonder"* because of God's gracious work in him, but it is also possible that he is a wonder because of an illness and thus a sign of judgment (cf. vv. 9–11). While others may marvel, however, God is his *"strong refuge."* Psalm 46 begins, "God is our refuge and strength, / A very present help in trouble." Secure in God, the psalmist exclaims: *"Let my mouth be filled with Your praise / And with Your glory all the day."* The word for *"glory"* here refers to the beauty of garments or jewels or the renown of a ruler.

The consequences of God's deliverance and security are praise and worship. This is always the case. As we were praying for the sick in our evening service last week a prophetic word was given that God was healing a person with an inner-ear problem, a blood disorder, and back pain. While I was preaching this man felt the power of God begin to work in his body. By the time I was through he was healed. The next week he told everyone of what the Lord had done for him. This deliverance filled his mouth with the praise and the glory of God "all the day."

Enemies' Attack

9 Do not cast me off in the time of old age;
  Do not forsake me when my strength fails.
10 For my enemies speak against me;
  And those who lie in wait for my life take counsel
    together,
11 Saying, "God has forsaken him;
  Pursue and take him, for *there is* none to deliver *him."*

Ps. 71:9–11

Now the psalmist turns to his greatest fear, that in *"old age"* God may not be there. Thus he prays not to be *"cast . . . off"* by Him.

Perhaps because of some illness he feels that God is far from him. He may also feel this due to his enemies' attack. He further asks God not to forsake him in time of failing strength, in the emotional drain caused by his enemies as they *"speak against"* him and *"lie in wait"* or "keep watch" for his *"life"* ("soul") and *"take counsel together."* Since they see his weakness (and illness?) they conclude that God has abandoned him. They see his plight as a sign of divine judgment. This is their chance, so they declare: *"Pursue and take him, for there is none to deliver him."*

A CALL FOR JUDGMENT

> 12 O God, do not be far from me;
> O my God, make haste to help me!
> 13 Let them be confounded *and* consumed
> Who are adversaries of my life;
> Let them be covered *with* reproach and dishonor
> Who seek my hurt.
>
> Ps. 71:12–13

In the crisis the psalmist prays for God not to be *"far"* away. God's distance was considered to be a sign of His judgment. In Psalm 38:21 David cries, "Do not forsake me, O Lord; / O my God, be not far from me!" Here the psalmist asks, *"O my God, make haste to help me!"* Note the personal *"my God"* and the sense of urgency in this request to *"make haste."*

The help he envisions is for the *"adversaries"* (from the word meaning "to accuse") of his *"life"* ("soul") to *"be confounded and consumed."* To *"be confounded"* is to *"be ashamed"* when their charges are refuted by God's actions. Then they will be *"consumed,"* that is, destroyed. The psalmist calls upon God to cover those *"who seek [his] hurt"* with *"reproach and dishonor."* The *"reproach"* will come as their claims are exposed as lies. Losing their credibility, they will be dishonored.

The psalmist has been adding to his earlier cry for deliverance. Stamped into each of us is a need for justice. We cry out for vindication against those who have hurt us. As our faith deepens, we have yet another longing—the desire to see God vindicated against those who have hurt Him.

A Promise for Praise

14 But I will hope continually,
   And will praise You yet more and more.
15 My mouth shall tell of Your righteousness
   And Your salvation all the day,
   For I do not know *their* limits.
16 I will go in the strength of the Lord God;
   I will make mention of Your righteousness, of Yours
      only.

Ps. 71:14–16

Even though the psalmist has not yet seen justice done, he *"will hope continually"* and will *"praise"* God *"more and more."* There is a truth to be learned here: as we worship God, our faith is built. Thus Paul says of Abraham that although humanly speaking he and Sarah could not have the son that God promised them, "He did not waver at the promise of God through unbelief, but was strengthened in faith, giving glory to God" (Rom. 4:20).

With verse 15 worship becomes witness. The psalmist will *"tell"* or "declare" God's *"righteousness"* ("righteous acts") and His *"salvation"* ("deliverance") continually, *"all the day."* He explains his torrent of praise when he says, *"I do not know their limits,"* or "numbers." God's saving deeds are more than he can recount.

The psalmist concludes that he *"will go in the strength of the Lord God."* Here is the answer when his strength fails. God's strength is His mighty power. The psalmist's commitment is clear and exclusive: *"I will make mention of Your righteousness, of Yours only."*

A Promise for Witness

17 O God, You have taught me from my youth;
   And to this *day* I declare Your wondrous works.
18 Now also when *I am* old and grayheaded,
   O God, do not forsake me,
   Until I declare Your strength to *this* generation,
   Your power to everyone *who* is to come.

Ps. 71:17–18

The psalmist's desire to tell his *"generation"* what God has done for him and them is strong, for he has experienced the trustworthiness of the Lord over an entire lifetime. From what he has been *"taught"* by God *"from [his] youth,"* he will *"declare"* God's *"wondrous works."* The word rendered *"wondrous works"* denotes God's mighty acts in creation, judgment, and redemption. Although the psalmist has been taught the redemptive history of Israel, her "creed," and will declare this, we must guard against thinking that he is just a good theological historian. The underlying reason for his witness to the "wondrous works" is the personal experience of his lifetime.

In his old age the psalmist asks God to be with him not merely so that he can experience deliverance from his enemies, but so that he can instruct this *"generation."* He wants to tell of God's *"strength"* ("arm," a symbol of might) and witness to His *"power to everyone who is to come,"* that is, to the generations which will follow. His desire is fulfilled in this psalm which carries his testimony even to us. God's gifts and His work in us are always not merely for our sakes but for the sake of others. As Jesus says, "Freely you have received, freely give" (Matt. 10:8). The church is always "one generation from extinction" (Dick Langford); we must be telling God's mighty works to others.

HOPE FOR HELP

> 19 Also Your righteousness, O God, *is* very high,
>   You who have done great things;
>   O God, who *is* like You?
> 20 *You,* who have shown me great and severe troubles,
>   Shall revive me again,
>   And bring me up again from the depths of the earth.
> 21 You shall increase my greatness,
>   And comfort me on every side.
>
> *Ps. 71:19-21*

The psalmist expresses confidence that God will *"revive"* him (v. 20). God's *"righteousness,"* or "salvation," he confesses, is *"very high,"* that is, it transcends our minds and our abilities. It is known to us, however, because God has *"done great things,"* as He does today when the church enters into a state of awakening or revival. The psalmist exclaims: *"O God, who is like You?"*

Turning to the personal again, the psalmist expresses the hope that, while God has *"shown"* him *"great and severe troubles"* (which may encompass a lifetime rather than merely his present weakness and adversity) He will *"revive"* him again. This clause literally reads, "You will turn [or, return] and keep me alive [or, make me live]." Thus he will be brought *"up again from the depths of the earth."* The *"depths"* ("deep") means the primordial sea, chaos, Sheol (cf. Ps. 88:6–12). Coming back from the edge of death, the psalmist is confident that God will *"increase"* his *"greatness"* and surround him with *"comfort."* Here his *"greatness"* is his honor which results from his trusting God.

Our God offers resurrection life. In Christ's empty tomb, risen presence, and pentecostal power the psalmist's prayer is fulfilled far beyond his own expectations. As God revives His church, the greatness of His work is also increased.

PRAISE FOR RESOLUTION

22 Also with the lute I will praise You—
    And Your faithfulness, O my God!
    To You I will sing with the harp,
    O Holy One of Israel.
23 My lips shall greatly rejoice when I sing to You,
    And my soul, which You have redeemed.
24 My tongue also shall talk of Your righteousness all
      the day long;   •
    For they are confounded,
    For they are brought to shame
    Who seek my hurt.

Ps. 71:22–24

Now the psalmist, with strong faith and confident that God will revive him and return him to a full life, vows *"praise."* He will use the *"lute"* and the *"harp"* (cf. Ps. 92:3) to accompany his song. Revival also brings the church to a new outburst of singing, as is the psalmist's experience.

Note the progression in verse 22 from praising God Himself to focusing on God's *"faithfulness"* ("truth"), His secure steadfastness, along with the expression of personal faith: *"O my God!"* Moreover, God is the *"Holy One of Israel."* Thus He is separate from His creation in His holiness; He is awesome and terrible and altogether righteous.

The psalmist's *"lips"* will manifest his joy in song before the Lord, praise that comes from his innermost being, his *"redeemed"* *"soul."* Along with his worship, there will also be witness. Thus the writer returns to the promise: *"My tongue also shall talk of Your righteousness all the day long."* Characteristically for the Psalter, God's *"righteousness"* to which the psalmist witnesses has been revealed in the confounding of his enemies. Those who seek his hurt have been *"brought to shame."* They thought God was against the psalmist but they were wrong: God acted. He was revived and his enemies were humiliated before the vindication of the Lord.

Thus we see in Psalm 71 the deliverance from crisis of an elderly man who has known God throughout his lifetime. We are included in his witness and thus encouraged to believe that as God was with him throughout the "long haul" so he will be with us in a lifelong adventure of faith.

CHAPTER SEVENTY-TWO

The Messiah's Reign

Psalm 72

The whole of the Old Testament is eschatological, moving from creation to consummation. The very beginning of history is a time of great hope—the blessing of the nations (Gen. 12:1–3). This history is redemptive and prophetic in that it promises One who will come at the end to fulfill its destiny. This is necessary because even the greatest of Israel's leaders is fallible. Moses dies outside the Promised Land and David's kingdom disintegrates within a generation. Human disappointment, however, continually points Israel beyond history to the God of history. Down through the centuries there is the cry, "When will God act and consummate His kingdom?" All of this climaxes in Jesus, the Son of God. In Him God comes to us to bring history to its appointed goal and end. Paul writes, "But when the fullness of the time had come, God sent forth His Son" (Gal. 4:4). And he tells the Ephesians that it is God's plan to "gather together in one all things in Christ, both which are in heaven and which are on earth" (Eph. 1:10).

Psalm 72 is a witness in history to the end of history. As a prophetic psalm in the full sense of the word, it describes the ideal King and

His universal reign (vv. 8–11). This reign also has more than a hint that it is eternal (v. 17). None of Israel's kings could come near the praise and expectations offered here. If this psalm were used in some coronation or enthronement liturgy, the ceremony it scripted would be dwarfed by its vision.

Commentators describe this psalm as a royal psalm and set it in the context of ceremonies surrounding the monarchy. As noted above, in this commentary it is seen as a prophetic psalm. Tradition ascribes it to Solomon, although scholars argue this point. His reign is little reflected in its language (but see v. 10). Since it is fully prophetic, the date and authorship are of little consequence. The thought here moves from a call for justice for the King (vv. 1–4) to the people's response (vv. 5–7), the King's universal reign (vv. 8–11), His care for the poor (vv. 12–13), His blessing (v. 15), His kingdom (v. 16), and His name (v. 17), ending with a blessing (vv. 18–19).

JUSTICE FOR THE KING

1 Give the king Your judgments, O God,
And Your righteousness to the king's Son.
2 He will judge Your people with righteousness,
And Your poor with justice.
3 The mountains will bring peace to the people,
And the little hills, by righteousness.
4 He will bring justice to the poor of the people;
He will save the children of the needy,
And will break in pieces the oppressor.

Ps. 72:1–4

The psalm begins with a call to God to *"give the king Your judgments."* Used in the plural, as it is here, the word for *"judgments"* means "statutes" or "ordinances." The reference is to the Torah or law which the King is to uphold and by which He rules. God's kingdom then is a rule of divine order and His law is His gift to us. The parallel clause speaks also of God's *"righteousness"* as His gift to the King. It contains the right-relationships of His covenant and is given *"to the king's Son."* The parallelism suggests that the King and the King's son are synonymous. The reason that the King is also identified as the King's Son is to assert that He is legitimate, standing in the royal line. Thus it is most important for Matthew and Luke to take Jesus' lineage back to

David in their genealogies as a necessary part of His messiahship (see Matt. 1 and Luke 3).

Having received God's *"judgments"* and His *"righteousness,"* the King's judgment will be absolutely fair, right, and just, reflecting the covenant God made with Israel. He will also judge God's *"poor"* with *"justice."* They will not be abused or destroyed. Their day will have come. As Jesus says, "Blessed are you poor, / For yours is the kingdom of God" (Luke 6:20).

The establishment of justice and righteousness will bring *"peace to the people."* This comes from the *"mountains"* while the *"little hills"* add peace *"by* [through] *righteousness."* Thus the result of the King's reign is harmony between the land and its *"people."* Peace (*šālôm*) means "wholeness," "unity," and "harmony." Here we see the full, final manifestation of the Messianic kingdom.

The theme of the poor now returns. The King *"will bring justice* [or, judgment] *to the poor"* and *"He will save the children of the needy."* Their salvation will be effected by breaking *"the oppressor"* in *"pieces."*

Thus a special work of the King is to care for *"the poor"* since no one else will. The rich exploit them and abuse them (see James 5:1–4). The Messiah, however, will lift their burdens. Isaiah prophesies of Him, "The Spirit of the Lord God is upon Me, / Because the Lord has anointed Me / To preach good tidings to the poor" (Isa. 61:1). Those who oppress them also will ultimately be destroyed. This promise is fulfilled both as Jesus defeats the devil and as He subjects the nations to His rule (see Rev. 20:10 and 19:15). It is important to remember that in His earthly ministry Jesus spent most of His energy healing and liberating the poor. He is indeed the righteous King.

THE PEOPLE'S RESPONSE

5 They shall fear You As long as the sun and moon
        endure,
    Throughout all generations.
6 He shall come down like rain upon the grass before
        mowing,
    Like showers *that* water the earth.
7 In His days the righteous shall flourish, And
        abundance of peace,
    Until the moon is no more.

                                            Ps. 72:5–7

The manifestation of God's covenant through the righteous judgments of His King brings a response of *"fear."* Psalm 33:8 commands: "Let all the earth fear the Lord; / Let all the inhabitants of the world stand in awe of Him." The response of fear is appropriate worship before the mighty King and His kingdom of peace. Such worship is to continue as long as creation lasts, *"as long as the sun and moon endure, / Throughout all generations."* Note the eschatological thrust here. No human king can receive perpetual worship. Only God's Son, the Messiah, can fulfill this promise down through all the generations of earth.

The King blesses the people and the land *"like rain upon the grass before mowing."* He is *"like showers that water the earth."* The people and the land prosper with fruitfulness before Him. *"In His days the righteous shall flourish."* This, of course, is predicated upon the King's receiving God's "righteousness" and His judging the "people with righteousness." As He is *"righteous,"* the people will reflect His character. They will be like their King, keeping covenant relationships. There will also be *"abundance of peace"* (šālôm; cf v. 3); wholeness and tranquility will rule the land. This will go on throughout all the generations, *"until the moon is no more."*

The King's Universal Reign

8 He shall have dominion also from sea to sea,
   And from the River to the ends of the earth.
9 Those who dwell in the wilderness will bow before
      Him,
   And His enemies will lick the dust.
10 The kings of Tarshish and of the isles
   Will bring presents;
   The kings of Sheba and Seba
   Will offer gifts.
11 Yes, all kings shall fall down before Him;
   All nations shall serve Him.

Ps. 72:8–11

The psalmist now announces that the blessings of the King will be for *"all nations"* as well. Thus, *"He shall have dominion also from sea to sea."* The seas mentioned here may be the Mediterranean Sea to the Persian Gulf, or the reference may mean dominion from both sides of the cosmic sea under and over the earth. Psalm 24:2 says that God founded the earth "upon the seas, / And established it upon the waters."

The King's rule will extend *"from the River* [the Euphrates; see 2 Sam. 10:16] *to the ends of the earth"* (cf. Acts 1:8). The *"wilderness"* also will submit to Him, and *"His enemies will lick the dust"*; their faces will be in the dirt before Him (cf. Isa. 49:23). Tribute will come from *"the kings of Tarshish and of the isles,"* and *"the kings of Sheba and Seba."* *"Tarshish"* (in Spain) and *"the isles"* (of the Mediterranean) represent the area far to the west of Israel. *"Sheba"* is south, in Arabia. Perhaps *"Seba"* is in Africa. The references here may intentionally reflect the glories of Solomon's reign (see 1 Kings 4:21; 10:10).

The above sampling of rulers represents the whole earth. Thus the psalmist concludes: *"Yes, all kings shall fall down before Him; / All nations shall serve Him."* Here is His universal reign.

As we have already noted, no earthly king could hope to fulfill this vision. Thus the passage is prophetic and Messianic. In the New Testament Paul tells us that every knee will bow and every tongue confess Jesus as Lord (Phil. 2:10–11). He also teaches that Christ "must reign till He has put all enemies under His feet" (1 Cor. 15:25). Therefore, in Revelation the kings of the earth bring their glory to the New Jerusalem, God's city (21:26).

CARE FOR THE POOR

12 For He will deliver the needy when he cries,
   The poor also, and *him* who has no helper.
13 He will spare the poor and needy,
   And will save the souls of the needy.
14 He will redeem their life from oppression and
     violence;
   And precious shall be their blood in His sight.

Ps. 72:12–14

The theme of the King's action on behalf of the poor now returns. *"He will deliver the needy"* and *"the poor."* The *"needy"* are those who need help, who have no options (Tom Simpson). Thus the King takes up their cause and delivers them when they call.

The King acts out of compassion: *"He will spare the poor and needy"* or, "He shall have pity upon the poor and needy." This compassion means that He will *"save"* ("deliver") their *"souls."* Salvation here is defined as redeeming them *"from oppression and violence"* (v. 14), from those who take advantage of them and grind them into the dust. The verb for *"redeem"* means "to purchase, to buy back." Thus the King purchases the poor out of bondage as God "purchased" Israel from Egypt. The price is the King's strength and energy on their behalf. The psalmist concludes that *"their blood"* is *"precious"* to the King. *"Blood"* here may be a metaphor for "life" (see Lev. 17:11).

Jesus loved the poor. He came to preach the good news to them. He delivered them from the oppression of legalistic religion and satanic domination. He healed their bodies, and He saved their souls and redeemed them at the price of His own blood. He then is the King of whom the psalmist speaks. He also calls us to live this kingdom life, ministering to the poor on His behalf.

God's Blessing

> 15 And He shall live;
> And the gold of Sheba will be given to Him;
> Prayer also will be made for Him continually,
> *And* daily He shall be praised.
>
> Ps. 72:15

The psalmist now responds to the vision of this Messiah-King: *"And He shall live."* This may well be an acclamation such as "Long live the king!" As the great King, he will receive *"the gold of Sheba,"* a proper tribute. Moreover, intercession *"will be made for Him continually."* The psalmist may envision public prayers offered in the temple for the King (cf. the prayers for the queen in Anglican churches today). Along with this intercession there will also be perpetual blessing: *"And daily He shall be praised."* The verb for *"praised"* means "to bless." The blessing of the King is the people's response in attributing goodness to Him for His gracious reign. Thus life, tribute, prayer, and blessing are all His.

God's Kingdom

> 16 There will be an abundance of grain in the earth,
> On the top of the mountains;
> Its fruit shall wave like Lebanon;
> And *those* of the city shall flourish like grass of the
> earth.
>
> Ps. 72:16

As the King is blessed the people are blessed. The psalmist describes a land of bounty. This includes *"an abundance of grain"* and *"fruit"* waving *"like Lebanon"* for Israel's farms. There is also prosperity *"like the grass of the earth"* for the cities. Even *"the top of the mountains"* where the soil is thin will produce a yield. *"Fruit . . . like Lebanon"* may mean that the fruit trees are as tall as Lebanon's proverbial cedars. This glorious kingdom reflects the glory of her King, and nature manifests the blessing of His righteous reign. Isaiah also sees a similar day, when the Messiah, "the Branch of the Lord," will be glorious, "and the fruit of the earth shall be excellent and appealing" (4:2).

His Name

17 His name shall endure forever;
His name shall continue as long as the sun.
And *men* shall be blessed in Him;
All nations shall call Him blessed.

Ps. 72:17

The *"name"* of the King represents His presence and power. To know His name is to know something of Him. To be able to call upon His name is to be able to have a relationship with Him and His regal authority. The King's *"name shall endure forever."* It will last *"as long as the sun"* lasts. People will be *"blessed in Him"* and, in turn, *"all nations shall call Him blessed."* Once again God's promise to Abraham is fulfilled by the Davidic Messiah (see Gen. 12:2–3).

A Final Blessing

18 Blessed *be* the Lord God, the God of Israel,
Who only does wondrous things!
19 And blessed *be* His glorious name forever!
And let the whole earth be filled *with* His glory.
Amen and Amen.

Ps. 72:18–19

Now it is as if a great chorus of praise must break out. The vision of the Messianic King is overwhelming. The graciousness of His rule to the poor and needy, the blessing of the whole land through Him, the submission of creation and the nations to His reign, all of this now evokes our response: *"Blessed be the Lord God, the God of Israel."* Since the Messiah rules as God's King, in seeing His kingdom and its benefits we are brought to praise the source of all things, God Himself. God is blessed because "[He] *only does wondrous things"* (from the word meaning "to be extraordinary"). These "wonders" are His mighty acts in judgment and redemption which evoke our praise.

His name, then, because it is so wonderful and *"glorious,"* is blessed forever (v. 19). The psalmist adds, *"And let the whole earth be filled with His glory."* God's *"glory"* is His "heaviness," the result of His triumph over all things, the "spoils" which He brings back from battle which give Him honor and praise. All that the psalmist can now add is "Yes, Yes," "True, True," *"Amen and Amen."* Verse 20 provides a scribal note which closes the second book of the Psalter: *"The prayers of David the son of Jesse are ended."* This was probably written before the whole Book of Psalms was collected.

Throughout Psalm 72, either we are shown a hopeless ideal which shatters in reality, or we have a truly eschatological and prophetic psalm. Certainly as far as the New Testament is concerned, it must be the latter. The major themes of this psalm reoccur in the New Testament and are consistently fulfilled in Jesus, in the fact of His first coming and in the promise of His second coming. The gospel confirms the signature of reality. Indeed, these longings, hopes, and dreams for oppression lifted, the earth restored, and the reign of righteousness are true. Look to Jesus. He fulfills this psalm and He is the center of the Psalter. In Him, the awaited Messiah, the prayers of Israel are prayed and through Him these same prayers are fullfilled. *"Amen and Amen."*

Bibliography

Allen, Leslie C. *Psalms 101–150*. Word Biblical Commentary, vol. 21. Waco, TX: Word Books, 1983.

Allen, Ronald B. *Praise: A Matter of Life and Breath*. Nashville: Thomas Nelson, Publishers, 1980.

Anders-Richards, Donald. *The Drama of the Psalms*. Valley Forge, PA: Judson Press, 1970.

Anderson, A. A. *Psalms 1–72*. The New Century Bible Commentary. Grand Rapids: Wm. B. Eerdmans Publishing Co., 1981.

———. *Psalms 73–150*. The New Century Bible Commentary. Grand Rapids: Wm. B. Eerdmans Publishing Co., 1981.

Briggs, C. A. *The Book of Psalms*. The International Critical Commentary. Vols. 1, 2. Edinburgh: T. & T. Clark, 1976.

Bright, John. *A History of Israel*. 2d ed. Philadelphia: Westminster Press, 1959.

Childs, Brevard S. *Introduction to the Old Testament as Scripture*. Philadelphia: Fortress Press, 1979.

Craigie, Peter C. *Psalms 1–50*. Word Biblical Commentary, vol. 19. Waco, TX: Word Books, 1983.

Keil, C. F., and F. Delitsch. *Commentary on the Old Testament*, vol. 5. Grand Rapids: Wm. B. Eerdmans Publishing Co. 1982.

Kidner, Derek. *Psalms 1–72*. Downers Grove, IL: Inter-Varsity Press, 1973.

Luther's Works. Vol. 10, Psalms 1–75. First Lecture on the Psalms. St. Louis: Concordia Press, 1974.

MacNutt, Francis. *The Power to Heal*. Notre Dame, IN: Ave Maria Press, 1977.

Morgan, G. Campbell. *Notes on the Psalms*. Old Tappan, NJ: Fleming H. Revell Co., 1957.

Muilenberg, James. *The Way of Israel*. New York: Harper & Row, 1961.

Routley, Eric. *Exploring the Psalms*. Philadelphia: Westminster Press, 1975.

Schaff, Philip, ed. *Saint Augustine: Exposition on the Book of Psalms*. A Select Library of the Nicene and Post-Nicene Fathers of the Christian Church, vol. 8. Grand Rapids: Wm. B. Eerdmans Publishing Co., 1979.

Spurgeon, C. H. *The Treasury of David*, vols. 1–3. McLean, VA: MacDonald Publishing Co., n.d.

Weiser, Artur. *The Psalms*. Philadelphia: Westminster Press, 1962.

Westermann, Claus. *Blessing in the Bible and the Life of the Church*. Philadelphia: Fortress Press, 1978.

———. *Praise and Lament in the Psalms*. Atlanta: John Knox Press, 1981.

Wink, Walter. *The Bible in Human Transformation*. Philadelphia: Fortress Press, 1973.